SUBURBANIZATION IN GLOBAL SOCIETY

RESEARCH IN URBAN SOCIOLOGY

Series Editor: Ray Hutchison

Recent Volumes:

RESEARCH IN URBAN SOCIOLOGY VOLUME 10

SUBURBANIZATION IN GLOBAL SOCIETY

EDITED BY

MARK CLAPSON

*Department of Social and Historical Studies,
University of Westminster, UK*

RAY HUTCHISON

*Urban and Regional Studies,
University of Wisconsin, Green Bay, WI, USA*

United Kingdom – North America – Japan
India – Malaysia – China

Emerald Group Publishing Limited
Howard House, Wagon Lane, Bingley BD16 1WA, UK

First edition 2010

Reprints and permission service
Contact: booksandseries@emeraldinsight.com

British Library Cataloguing in Publication Data
A catalogue record for this book is available from the British Library

ISBN: 978-0-85724-347-8
ISSN: 1047-0042 (Series)

Emerald Group Publishing
Limited, Howard House,
Environmental Management
System has been certified by
ISOQAR to ISO 14001:2004
standards

Awarded in recognition of
Emerald's production
department's adherence to
quality systems and processes
when preparing scholarly
journals for print

INVESTOR IN PEOPLE

CONTENTS

THE GLOBAL SOUTH

LIST OF CONTRIBUTORS

Sandra Annunziata	Department of Urban Studies, Roma Tre University, Rome, Italy
Jean Beaman	Department of Sociology and Institute for Policy Research, Northwestern University, Evanston, IL, USA
Lucia Maria Machado Bógus	Department of Sociology, Pontifícia Universidade Católica de São Paulo (PUC-SP), São Paulo, Brazil
Xiangming Chen	Center for Urban and Global Studies, Trinity College, and School of Social Development and Public Policy, Fudan University, Shanghai, China
Mara Cossu	Department of Urban Studies, Roma Tre University, Rome, Italy
Mark Clapson	Department of Social and Historical Studies, University of Westminster, London, UK
Allen Dieterich-Ward	Department of History & Philosophy, Shippensburg University, Shippensburg, PA, USA
Robert Freestone	Faculty of the Built Environment, University of New South Wales, Sydney, Australia
Richard Harris	School of Geography and Earth Sciences, McMaster University, Hamilton, Ontario, Canada
Tassilo Herrschel	Centre for Urban and Regional Governance, University of Westminster, London, UK

Ray Hutchison	Urban and Regional Studies, University of Wisconsin, Green Bay, WI, USA
William Grady Holt	Department of Sociology, Southern Connecticut State University, New Haven, CT, USA
Ratoola Kundu	School of Habitat Studies, Tata Institute of Social Sciences, Mumbai, India
Rita Padawangi	Institute of Water Policy, Lee Kuan Yew School of Public Policy, National University of Singapore, Singapore
Suzana Pasternak	Faculdade de Arquitetura e Urbanismo, Universidade de São Paulo, São Paulo, Brazil
Eric Petersen	Cambridge Systematics, Chicago, IL, USA
Simon Pinnegar	City Futures Research Centre, University of New South Wales, Sydney, Australia
Bill Randolph	City Futures Research Centre, University of New South Wales, Sydney, Australia
Xuefei Ren	Department of Sociology and Global Urban Studies, Michigan State University, East Lansing, MI, USA
Sonia Roitman	Latin American Institute, Free University, Berlin, Germany
Leticia Veloso	Department of Sociology, Universidade Federal Fluminense, Niteroi, Rio de Janeiro, Brazil
Lan Wang	Department of Urban Planning, College of Architecture and Urban Planning, Tongji University, Shanghai, China

INTRODUCTION: SUBURBANIZATION IN GLOBAL SOCIETY

Mark Clapson and Ray Hutchison

World population is expected to increase by some 2.6 billion from 6.9 billion in 2010 to more than 9.5 billion by mid-century. Most of this population increase will occur in the developing nations, and most of this increase will be absorbed in the rapidly expanding metropolitan regions of these countries – the so-called megacities of the twenty-first century (United Nations, 2009). And as urban development accelerates across the globe, most of the population increase will occur in the emerging megacities and other metropolitan areas in Africa, Asia and South America. Because the original areas of settlement in the city centre have long been established, much of the population increase in these metropolitan regions will occur in the suburban areas of cities in the Global South – areas of favelas and shanty towns alongside earlier middle-class and upper-class suburbs, newly planned gated communities and garden suburbs, and indigenous models of suburban growth that will emerge in the next century.

How far can the recent and current expansion of suburbanization across the world be understood with reference to earlier patterns of suburban expansion, in particular the 'Anglo-American' model that continues to dominate our urban disciplines, despite compelling evidence that this model is flawed even for understanding urban development in the West (Harris & Lewis, 1998)? As Richard Harris asks in Chapter 2, what can we learn about

Suburbanization in Global Society
Research in Urban Sociology, Volume 10, 1–14
Copyright © 2010 by Emerald Group Publishing Limited
ISSN: 1047-0042/doi:10.1108/S1047-0042(2010)0000010003

1

the experience of contemporary suburbanization in Africa, Asia and the Americas from studies that were largely conducted within the Anglo-American context? Should we look for a new paradigm to understand suburbanization in the early twenty-first century? Or should we look to historical continuities as well as new directions in suburban growth beyond the Anglo-American experience? This would augur for a more nuanced understanding of suburban development as a consequence of social, economic and political forces specific to place and culture, one that focuses on the *process* of suburbanization, rather than *paradigms* based on earlier models.

The reasons for this shift away from the established paradigm are clear: while influenced by locality, the social, cultural, economic and political nature and consequences of suburbanization must be understood increasingly as *global* in nature and consequences. This remains true in spite of social and cultural differences between urban regions where suburbanization has become the dominant form of urban development/growth/expansion, and it remains true while countries and continents are at different stages of economic development and governance. Unfortunately, for too long an academic focus derived from models of suburbanization based on the experiences of Anglo-American cities and suburbs prevented a more nuanced understanding of the impact of suburbanization at the local level (Clapson, 2004). This crisis has long been evident *within* countries, where the dominant paradigm has failed to account for changes that have transformed urban regions (Hutchison, 1993; Gottdiener & Hutchison, 2010), and now it is becoming evident *between* them, as the issues and problems raised by the chapters in this volume powerfully indicate. But chapters in this volume describing suburbanization in both Asia and South America point to both older and new interactions between suburban development in what has been termed the Global North and the Global South, including colonial development that echoed suburban housing (such as the English bungalow in India), created new towns based on planning principles from the garden city movement (New Delhi) and more recent community planning by architectural firms located in the United States and other countries of the Global North.

In the Global North, broadly defined as the developed world, the pattern of suburbanization that developed during the nineteenth and twentieth centuries was primarily but not exclusively middle class, and driven by a desire to escape the overcrowded and dangerous town and city centres for a private home with a garden. The 'Anglo-American' model was strongly influenced by the garden city and garden suburbs of the nineteenth and early twentieth centuries. In the United States, the romantic railroad suburbs such as Lake Forest (1856) and the streetcar suburbs such as Forest Hills Gardens (1912) privileged a comfortable private house set in a garden, a semi-bucolic vision that combined low-density suburbs with close proximity to the countryside and a commutable distance from the Central Business District and the shops and leisure facilities of the downtowns (Fishman, 2008; Stern & Massengale, 1981). Moreover, planned suburbanization also became an officially sanctioned model for urban living. In Britain, Edwardian garden cities and garden suburbs later influenced working-class housing and estate layouts following the 1919 Housing and Town Planning Act (Clapson, 2000). Across the British Empire, too, colonial versions of the suburban ideal were constructed for administrators, businesspeople, politicians and other stalwarts of imperialism.

In Britain, and in continental Europe too, the interwar suburbanization of the working classes was partly a consequence of slum clearance programmes, but also of experiments in planned working-class housing across the length and breadth of the city. The destruction due to the Second World War strengthened the rationale for official dispersal policies after 1945, increasingly involving the state provision of public housing. However, a growing tendency towards voluntary suburbanization based on home ownership, and born of affluence and consumerism, was evident among the more comfortably off sections of the working classes. The suburban aspiration was no longer a mostly middle-class phenomenon. In the United States, Canada, Australia and New Zealand, blue-collar workers often purchased their own suburban homes, with the assistance of the government subsidies to mortgage and banking interests, although in the United States the suburbanization of black households was curtailed by racist practices of the real estate industry, with the support of local and national governments.

In global society, new suburban processes are coming into being. In their diverse totality, and depending on local and national contexts, they owe something, little or nothing to established residential patterns in countries that suburbanized earlier. In many developing nations, urban populations are dislocated and resettled to make room for new commercial development (as in Mumbai) and middle-class housing (as in Manila). Large-scale migrations from the countryside into newly emerging urban centres continue in many developing countries, and account for much of the urban growth. The example of China, the Concrete Dragon, is an obvious and important one (Campanella, 2008). In Chinese urban development, Anglo-American precedents, for example, the garden city and garden suburb movements, are reborn in new cultural and spatial shapes by cultural osmosis and government diktat. The international diffusion of town planning models is at the heart of this evolving continuum: architects, planners and government officials from the Global South learn from northern exemplars of the good suburban life. This is expressed in the gated communities for the middle classes, from their naming to their emphasis on single-family private homes. Large-scale housing programmes for the poor also absorb lessons from the British garden cities and new towns, but these recent slum clearance and housing programmes are built on a spatial scale and to population densities that are not to be found in Britain. As a number of chapters in this book demonstrate, the Anglo-suburban idea of the good life has been appropriated for urban design in countries that were once British or European colonies.

As Richard Harris argues in the first and in many ways defining chapter of this volume, almost all development beyond the city centre might well be incorporated within the broad umbrella term of 'suburbanization'. Metropolitan regions have expanded as a consequence of continuing population growth, particularly in the large developing economies of Brazil, China and India, and in the emerging, if smaller, post-colonial countries in Africa and Latin America. Suburban sprawl and edge cities – an important area of research in the EU as well as the United States (Garreau, 1991; Lang, 2003; Phelps, Parsons, & Ballas, 2008) – have collided with an increasingly fragile notion of traditional urbanism, based on the high-density walking city, rich in historical architecture and cultural and economic resources, and producing, in theory at least, a high level of civic pride and engagement. However, in Chapter 6, the traditional urbanity of Italian cities is attacked as a valid mode of assessing the 'urban' qualities of new suburbs in the Italian capital city.

Urban sociology began with the study of the impact of the socio-economic changes brought about by the Industrial Revolution, and for most of the past century it has remained embedded in the city, with a focus on urban lifestyles and urban problems of the central city, even while people and employment moved to the suburbs. If the majority of persons live, and most development occurs, in areas beyond the central city, *suburban studies* might well deserve to become the new scholastic shorthand for the increasingly diverse field of academic endeavour seeking to make sense of the myriad social, cultural, economic and political processes that are inextricably intertwined with suburbanization in a global society. It is time for urban sociology to move out of the city and explore the new suburban world of the twenty-first century.

The fates of suburbs almost everywhere, whether they are recent or ageing residential areas, are underpinned by the neo-liberal policies that dominate local, national and international economies. Yet suburban development or the re-imagining of suburbia can also play an important role in repositioning both local economies and local identities. Industrial suburbs in the Global North, for example, have been transformed by the powerful forces of deindustrialization and globalization, while rural areas have experienced rapid suburbanization as new high-tech and IT industries, leisure parks and housing developments have spread across the fields. These are often provincial processes affecting particular regions, as terms such as 'silicon valley' or 'silicon fen' indicate. In Chapter 3, a study of the rapidly suburbanizing Gwinnett County outside Atlanta, Georgia, William Grady Holt demonstrates that the historical development of the global economy influences the regeneration and the place marketing of previously declining industrial regions. An emphasis on retail parks and alternative uses for a variety of industrial sites has improved the economic fortunes and the image of Gwinnett, a region that powerfully reflected the historical development of American suburbanization and structural trends in the south of the United States during the post-war years. During the 'new suburban phase' of the 1970s to the 1990s, the older rustbelt industries declined as sunbelt industries expanded. Tertiary superseded secondary, and Gwinnett emerged as a leading provincial area of sectoral and demographic change.

Metropolitan regions in the rustbelt of the American Northeast were devastated by deindustrialization beginning in the 1970s, and many communities have experienced significant loss of population and secondary employment as manufacturing firms have closed. The 'suburban strategies' discussed by Allen Dieterich-Ward in Chapter 4 were largely based on road building and retail parks, aimed at breaking down local isolation and regeneration by tempting in middle-class consumers. The image of the region was consciously addressed as well, but one legacy for a previously industrial workforce was the diminishing returns of relatively low-paid employment in the service sector jobs of the new global economy.

Many of the processes described by Holt and Dietrich-Ward in the United States have been found in the United Kingdom and EU, where research has moved from the deindustrialization of urban regions to edge city development and similar trends (Phelps, Parsons, & Ballas, 2008). Within the administrative–political contexts of city regions in Europe, the suburbs emerge as in-between places demanding renewed attention for their unique problems in urban governance. In Chapter 5, Tassilo Herrschel explores how suburbanization has created large interstitial development areas that have to be addressed as problems for governance in 'city' regions where the suburbs are more important drivers of growth than the cities themselves, and in the expanding suburban entities that raise administrative issues for national and EU regional policies. Fast-growing metropolitan regions elsewhere in the world also create demands and challenges for governments – some similar, some different – to those discussed by Herrschel (Laquian, 2005).

Urban development in Australia has followed a pattern more similar to that of the urban north than to its neighbours in Southeast Asia. First settled in the 1700s, Australian cities experienced an industrial boom in the 1800s, with urban forms similar to those of the United Kingdom. This was followed in the 1900s by a model of privatized suburbanization more similar to that of the United States, famously labelled Austerica, and lamented by more than a few critics of Australian suburbia (Boyd, 1960; Kemeny, 1977). In the new century, this means that inner suburbs, now many decades old, are under stress. In the United Kingdom there is much emphasis on the regeneration of the first suburbs, as they have been called, and in the United States as well there are new policy initiatives to rebuild the urban fringe. In Australia, a somewhat distinctive strategy for suburban renewal still strongly located within a distinctive city region is 'knockdown rebuild' (KDR). In their chapter on 'KDR' (Chapter 9), Simon Pinnegar, Robert Freestone and Bill Randolph assess advantages and disadvantages of this urban regeneration strategy in relation to a range of indicators, notably its environmental impact, gentrification, and residential mobility and choice for differing income groups. One consequence is that higher levels of residential mobility for higher income groups, and the social consequences of this along with KDR as a policy, have not always benefited poorer Australian suburbanites.

Until relatively recently most social studies of suburban living were about the white middle classes in the Anglo-American suburbs, working-class suburbs were relatively understudied, and ethnic suburban settlements were largely, if not completely, ignored, although there were a few notable exceptions (Berger, 1960; Young & Willmott, 1957). Yet the sidelined suburbs of the working classes and the peripheral ethnic enclaves once adjacent to the residential mainstream of the mid-twentieth century, both now emerge historically as pioneering developments for the suburban world that is currently unfolding so rapidly. As the chapters in this volume cumulatively demonstrate, global suburbanization is as much about lower class suburbs as wealthy bourgeois utopias, and as much about African American and Asian residential areas as white residential areas. Exclusive communities continue and many others are built from scratch but they are by no means exclusively white any longer. And across Europe, Africa, Asia and the Americas, wealthy, middling and poorer suburbs now coexist to varying degrees of stability alongside or near to each other.

While research in urban sociology and urban studies has been dominated by the model of the Anglo-American city, with the usual dichotomy between city and suburb, we know cities in many countries in the EU and elsewhere have a very different form. (They usually are considered as exceptions to the US–UK model, even though cumulatively they account to include many more metropolitan regions and larger numbers of persons!) A distinctive feature of Paris is the suburban banlieue, working-class neighbourhoods created in the 1800s with the redevelopment of Paris following the Haussman plan (Castenada, 2010). In recent decades, some of these neighbourhoods have served as a port of entry, or entrepot, for immigrant groups. And modern architects and planners created new post-war suburbs around the French capital city. In her study of the Parisian banlieu (Chapter 7), Jean Beaman provides a compelling account, based on deep interviews, of the subjectivity of French citizens of North African origin. A sense of dual nationality is strongly associated with a sense of identity with place for some, or a rejection of the banlieu by others. This is intertwined with at least two other themes, namely a segregation from mainstream French society and also a comparative dearth of suburban environmental resources when compared with the centre of the chic city.

In Rome, however, the social and spatial patterns of suburban exclusion are almost reversed. As Sandra Annunziata and Mara Cossu demonstrate in Chapter 6, one of the most commonplace accusations against very recent suburban development in Rome is a lack of social mixing in the outer residential areas. Another accusation is that the suburbs are simply residential dormitories devoid of social life and community building. But the authors show that historicist readings of the city centre and the condescension of urbanism misunderstand the germinal forms of urban living in outer areas, and ignore the opportunities for meaningful sociability from the mall to the car park to the Internet. In this, the recent suburbanization of Roma evidences some similarities with patterns of suburbanization in the Anglo-American context during the 1950s, namely the condescension of elites who wilfully ignore the community-making of 'pioneers' beyond the traditional centres.

Herbert Gans clearly understood this in his study of *Levittown*, a mass-produced suburban community outside of Philadelphia in the 1960s. Challenging myths of suburban soullessness and conformity that already had developed during the 1950s, Gans observed that people tended to bond with others of a similar occupational status, although ethnicity and religion also influenced location choices and encouraged like-with-like social interaction (1967). The consequences, however, were both integrating and segregating, as suburban communities tended towards homogenous populations of middle-class or upper-class households, and working-class and minority households were excluded. The gated community is perhaps a particular and increasingly common expression of this trend of residential segregation, where a variety of income groups and status groups corral themselves away from the threat of crime. Many of the largest gated communities are built exclusively for the wealthiest in society. This is not a peculiarly North American pattern, however. It can be identified in elite new residential areas across the world, and in particular the Global South, as a number of chapters in this volume demonstrate. It is an ongoing irruption that often exists side-by-side with many much poorer suburban settlements, raising problems over unequal access to resources, and ostensible middle-class withdrawal from the civic and financial functioning of town and city (Roitman, 2005).

Sonia Roitman's analysis of Argentinean and Mexican gated communities (Chapter 12) through the lens of local governments demonstrates that the desire for social and residential exclusivity and voluntary segregation is evidenced in most cultures. Using interviews with local government officials, Roitman highlights the role of local authorities in Latin America that tend to allow the gated community to be built despite misgivings about its impact on the financing and functioning of the wider city. She also notes the influence of planning models and architectural firms from the United States on the development of gated communities in these countries, further evidence of the globalization of suburban development.

Problems of governance and finance are powerfully overlaid by race in other suburbanizing regions of the world. The security-enhanced golf courses and gated residential compounds of white South Africa as opposed to the 'kitchens' of the poor, discussed by Eric Petersen in Chapter 8, also demonstrate newer patterns of gated community development that owe little to the American experience, and much to the continuing economic and racial inequalities of Southern Africa, both during and since the era of politically enforced apartheid. The ending of the apartheid era during the 1980s led to new patterns of racial privilege and segregation in South Africa, where new gated communities for the white population exist alongside established suburban ghettos for blacks, a pattern which is compared with the situation in Harare in Zimbabwe.

In *Cities of the South*, Dreiskens, Mermier, and Wimmen (2007) argue that the working-class experience varies greatly from country to country. Among the poorest sections of the global society, the marginalized spaces of the inner city and the inherited poverty of the nineteenth and twentieth-century urban slums have been superseded by the suburbanization of poverty and racial segregation, and the proliferation of the shanty and the favela. These are largely unplanned, just as the poorest areas of the Victorian city were the unplanned residue and residuum of urbanization and industrialization. In their discussion in Chapter 10, Suzana Pasternak and Lucia Maria Machado Bógus emphasize how economic restructuring impacts on patterns of residential segregation: the focus on both significant and more subtle differences between residential areas according to occupation and status, as the globalization of the Latin American economy drives industrial and tertiary sector employment. However, their historical perspective highlights that economic and political stability and contrasting periods of economic and political instability have long impacted development of the Brazilian city, and that this impact has been heightened by the changing demographics of the country.

The development of the Brazilian favela is also discussed by Leticia Veloso in Chapter 11. Her work reminds us that the poorest favelas are products of suburbanization, and also that they have close and complicated relationship, both socially and spatially, with other suburban working-class neighbourhoods. The spatial models presented by Pasternak and Bógus are supplemented by ethnographic fieldwork in this chapter. Veloso emphasizes the important effect that increasing crime – not just fear of crime, as is more common in the North American experience – has had on residential choice and urban life in both working-class neighbourhoods and favela communities. Her chapter also indicates the limitations of a North American approach to studying urban development that emphasizes a 'city–suburb' duality rather than the more nuanced patterns outlined in her chapter where working-class and lower class neighbourhoods share suburban space in many Brazilian cities.

The importance of the favela for understanding suburban development in South America reminds us that lower class sprawl takes different forms both within countries let alone between them. Although sprawling suburbanization is accelerating and expanding across the globe (Bruegmann, 2005), unplanned suburban development is not the only process of urban development one observes in the Global South. In Asia much recent suburbanization has been carefully conceived and operationalized from above. Just as twentieth-century Europe witnessed compulsory slum clearance and rehousing schemes, the rapidly developing economies and cultures of the Global South create displacement and rehousing pro-grammes. Many of these development programmes are based on what were originally European solutions to the chaotic and overcrowded city, to wit the garden city movement and the new town movement it gave birth to across the world during the twentieth century.

Different issues of governance, and the character of planned suburban development in Asia, are evident in a number of chapters in this volume. Significantly, planned suburbanization diverges significantly from its European garden city provenance, and produces new cultural departures. In China and Singapore, to take two examples, planned suburbanization owes much to the garden city vision mapped out in Ebenezer Howard's *Tomorrow: A Peaceful Path to Reform*, an Edwardian classic, but dear old Ebenezer ('the garden city geezer' as George Bernard Shaw dubbed him) hated suburbanization. His intention was to construct self-contained, self-governing new towns, not suburbs, at commutable distances from the older towns and cities. He and his followers were both highly critical of and wary of comparisons with suburbanization, and favoured low-rise and mostly low-density settlements. Yet consequences are nuanced, influenced by culture and the role of the state, for as in Britain and some other European countries, the government of Singapore proactively initiated and supported a large-scale policy of building new towns.

As Rita Padawangi illustrates in Chapter 13, planned new towns in Singapore are viewed explicitly as suburban settlements. In some ways the high-rise and high-density nature of many such developments often has very different social and spatial consequences to those originally hoped for by the pioneers of the garden city movement. They become 'cities within a city' unlike the satellite settlements of the United Kingdom, the greenbelt towns of New Deal, United States or the 'in-between' suburbs of city regions in Europe. But Singapore's new towns also developed self-sustaining social networks that owed as much to internal community action and informal local culture as to the role of the state, another point emphasized by Padawangi. Any understanding of neighbourhood in Singapore's new towns needs to begin with local cultures and community dynamics rather than the Anglo-American origins of the 'neighbourhood unit' as a mechanism for social planning.

In India and China the original garden city concepts of Ebenezer Howard also 're-emerged' as part of state-led projects to reduce the densities in overcrowded city centres, as Lan Wang, Ratoola Kundu and Xiangming Chen argue in Chapter 14. But in both countries – one a capitalist democracy, one ostensibly a communist–capitalist state – any intention to create socially mixed and balanced new communities has been compromised by the superior resources and housing held by higher income groups. While the authors refer to garden city and new town development, the result is very different from what Howard and others might have imagined: the high-rise housing complexes of Singapore or the gated enclaves for the Chinese and Indian middle classes are a long way in time and in terms of urban design from Howard's original vision. It is of interest that while developing very different residential communities in the rapidly growing suburban areas of the megacities of the future, urban planners in both countries have sought to connect their developments with the earlier Western models.

Large-scale planned suburban new towns have re-oriented the nature and process of urbanization in China, a point also discussed in relation to the latter country by Xuefei Ren in Chapter 15. She addresses some of these key definitional issues, some of which are flagged in Chapter 2 by Richard Harris. Emphasizing a need to discern new typologies of emergent suburban forms, Ren argues that the classic city centre or inner city versus the suburb model is inadequate to grasp the nature of much planned suburbanization in China. We should note that other studies of urban development in China have relied on the Anglo-American model when referring to urban and suburban development, even while the definition of urban–suburban boundaries in China is different from that found in the West, and do not allow for this sort of categorization. Calling for a less schematic analytical approach to different suburban forms based on process, rather than definitions taken from the Anglo-European experience and preconceived notions of how cities should function, Ren partly shares Harris's attempt to open up to scrutiny 'northern' and western typologies of suburbanization, while perhaps diverging from his category-based approach to suburbanization in global society.

While material conditions may be improving, compulsory dispersal and its consequences is a key theme underpinning some of the chapters in this volume. The poor, it seems, whilst not completely devoid of agency, and whilst sharing all the emotions and sensitivities of wealthier people, but without the economic means, migrate to and forge a living in impoverished suburbs as a consequence of political and economic forces. Again there are powerful historical precedents. Sociology emerged as an academic discipline in Europe and the United States in response to the transition from rural to urban society. Key themes for analysis included the changing nature of community as society industrialized, the increasing residential segregation of social class groups and the fate of the poor in the large rural to urban migrations. Social history as an academic discipline owes much to sociological endeavour in the urbanizing worlds of the nineteenth and twentieth centuries. Writing in the third quarter of the twentieth century, the

English social historian and communist E. P. Thompson acknowledged that both sociology and social history shared concerns with social class and living standards in industrial societies, and hoped that governments in countries entering their industrial age might learn from the British experience in the eighteenth and nineteenth centuries, and ensure that the working classes and poor might be shown greater empathy and sympathy for their changing cultural circumstances and their economic vulnerability (Thompson, 1968). Thompson's plea was optimistic as well as naïve in the call for lessons to be learned, and we know now that these lessons have been lost to the winds of capitalist restructuring and communist revisionism in the Global North and economic expansion in the Global South. The fact that Thompson was writing when British sociologists were discerning the erosion of working-class kinship and community networks in the city centres as a consequence of planned suburbanization through council housing (public sector housing) has a particular irony to it. The most famous of those social studies was MichaelYoung and Peter Willmott's *Family and Kinship in East London*, originally published in 1957 and reissued many times since in textbooks (e.g. Legates & Stout, 1996). Whether one agrees or disagrees with its prognosis for working-class community is less significant than an acknowledgement that *Family and Kinship* raised issues that go the heart of (sub)urban sociology and development studies in our current time. The impact of suburbanization (whether planned or unplanned) on the established networks of rural or urban communities is at the heart of our concerns about the poor in our global society.

'Home' remains the basis of suburban living, yet the types of places that people need and want to call 'home' are vastly different across the world, from the middle-class and working-class suburbs in Europe, to the unplanned favelas of Latin America or the shanty towns of South Africa, to the apartments in planned suburban new towns in Asia, and to the gated communities in Asia and the Americas. As one suburban century recedes and another one is growing apace, the need for urban sociology to move out of the city to the expanding suburban realm becomes more and more critical; one can almost hear Robert Park admonish his students, 'You must move beyond the ivory tower and the city, and explore the suburban mosaic of the new century!'

Urban sociology as a diverse subject area has proved invaluable to urban history and to urban studies more generally, for both the evidence it has produced and the sociological perspectives it has provided. Future scholars looking to understand the social experiences of suburbanization will continue to turn to sociological research for information and for arguments to inform their historical perspective. The work in this volume avoids one-dimensional and self-serving analyses that still permeate ill-informed and often parochial discussion about the now massive presence of suburbs and suburbanization. In contrast, the work in this volume further demonstrates a strong understanding that new subjective meanings of the suburban home as both a lived space and a liveable community are constantly being created. Hopefully, they will inform current academic debate and also prove to be of great value to future historians of global suburban society in the early twenty-first century.

REFERENCES

Berger, B. M. (1960). *Working-class suburb: A study of auto workers in suburbia.* Berkeley, CA: University of California Press.

Boyd, R. (1960). *The Australian ugliness.* Melbourne: Cheshire.

Bruegmann, R. (2005). *Sprawl: A compact history.* Chicago: University of Chicago Press.

Campanella, T. J. (2008). *The Concrete Dragon: China's urban revolution and what it means for the world.* New York: Princeton Architectural Press.

Castenada, E. (2010). Banlieu. In: R. Hutchison (Ed.), *Encyclopedia of urban studies* (pp. 52–55). Thousand Oaks, CA: SAGE Publications.

Clapson, M. (2000). The suburban aspiration in England since 1919. *Contemporary British History, 14*(1), 151–174.

Clapson, M. (2004). *Suburban century: Social change and urban growth in England and the United States.* Oxford: Berg.

Dreiskens, H., Mermier, B., & Wimmen, F. (2007). *Cities of the south: Citizenship and exclusion in the twenty first century.* London: Saqi Publishers.

Fishman, R. (2008). *Bourgeois utopias: The rise and fall of suburbia.* New York: Basic Books.

Gans, H. J. (1967). *The levittowners: Ways of life and politics in a new suburban community.* London: Allen Lane The Penguin Press.

Garreau, J. (1991). *Edge city: Life on the new frontier.* New York: Doubleday.

Gottdiener, M., & Hutchison, R. (2010). *The new urban sociology* (4th ed.). Boulder, CO: Westview Press.

Harris, R., & Lewis, R. (1998). Constructing a fault(y) zone: Misrepresentations of American cities and suburbs, 1900–1950. *Annals of the Association of American Geographers, 88*(4), 622–639.

Hutchison, R. (1993). The crisis in urban sociology. In: *Urban sociology in transition. Research in urban sociology* (Vol. 3, pp. 1–33). Bridgeport, CT: JAI Press.

Kemeny, J. (1977). A political sociology of home ownership in Australia. *Australian and New Zealand Journal of Sociology, 13*, 47–52.

Lang, R. E. (2003). *Beyond edge city: Office sprawl in south Florida.* Washington, DC: The Brookings Institution, Center on Urban and Metropolitan Policy.

Laquian, A. A. (2005). *Beyond metropolis: The planning and governance of Asia's mega-urban regions.* Baltimore: John Hopkins University Press.

Legates, F., & Stout, R. (1996). *The city reader.* London: Routledge.

Phelps, N. A., Parsons, N., & Ballas, D. (2008). *Post-suburban Europe: Planning and politics at the margins of Europe's capital cities*. London: Palgrave Macmillan.

Roitman, S. (2005). Who segregates whom? The analysis of a gated community in Mendoza, Argentina. *Housing Studies, 20*(2), 303–321.

Stern, R. A. M., & Massengale, J. M. (1981). *The Anglo-American suburb*. London: Architectural Design Press.

Thompson, E. P. (1968). *The making of the English working class*. Harmondsworth: Penguin.

United Nations. (2009). *World urbanization prospects: The 2009 revisions*. New York: United Nations.

Young, M., & Willmott, P. (1957). *Family and kinship in east London*. London: Routledge.

MEANINGFUL TYPES IN A WORLD OF SUBURBS

Richard Harris

INTRODUCTION

Consideration needs to be given to the difference [that] the diversity of cities makes to theory.
Robinson (2002, p. 549)

It is almost a decade since Jenny Robinson proposed that we look to the experience of what may be called the Global South in order to reinvigorate urban theory. She argued that, instead of focusing on a handful of high-profile metropolitan centres, with their economic, political and media elites, located mostly in the Global North, we should pay attention to ordinary cities everywhere. Echoing post-colonial writers, who have aimed to provincialize Europe, she argued that by taking a wider vision, we can expose the assumptions built in to urban theory, and develop the conceptual tools for a fuller understanding of the global urban experience. It is an inspiring vision.

Curiously, however, in her initial statement and then in a later book, Robinson (2002, 2005) said little about suburbs, those 'ordinary residential areas' (Whitehand & Carr, 2001, p. vii) that today make up the greater part of most cities. The work of Simone (2010, pp. 51–55), who makes a parallel argument about the importance of global and cultural 'peripheries', real and metaphoric, also neglects suburbs, and so, more generally, does the extensive literature on global cities, which takes up the challenge of considering cities in a worldwide context but which is parochial in its instinctive obsession with downtowns (Gans, 2009; Keil, forthcoming).

Suburbanization in Global Society
Research in Urban Sociology, Volume 10, 15–47
ISSN: 1047-0042/doi:10.1108/S1047-0042(2010)0000010004

This chapter takes up the implicit challenge, by examining the ordinary urban periphery within a worldwide frame of reference. By stepping back to look at suburbs, I argue that we gain a new perspective on their nature and meaning. This is no trivial matter. In recent years, as urbanization in many regions has accelerated, scholars have paid more attention to the urban fringe. One indicator is the number of scholarly articles in the ISI Web of Science database that contain 'suburb' in their title or abstract. The number held steady at about 100 per year in the late 1970s and 1980s, before jumping to 240 during the 1990s and 380 over the past decade.[1] Because peripheral areas loom so large, this chapter significantly extends the theoretical project that Robinson has identified.

If research on suburbs is to contribute to urban theory, scholars will need to consider how these places are developed, experienced and governed. Underlying all of these issues is the question as to what suburbs mean, not just for the culture at large but more particularly for their residents. The views of residents are vital, but have been neglected. Academic and popular coverage, including that on TV, or in movies, magazines and newspapers, has been framed by urban elites. True, especially in the early post-war decades, efforts were made to discover the views of suburban newcomers (Berger, 1960; Gans, 1967; Wilmott & Young, 1960; cf. Clapson, 1998, pp. 69–71). But such attempts have fallen off (cf. Baxandall & Ewen, 2000; Hanley, 2006), although some work is being done within different intellectual traditions, notably anthropology, in the developing world (e.g. Trefon, 2009). The paucity of insider accounts is regrettable: the views of outsiders, after all, are necessarily partial, and have often been stereotyped and critical. Starved of evidence, much recent literature on suburbs, at least in Anglo-America, has become self-referential. To develop a more complete understanding of suburbanism, we need to consider what insiders have to say. On this basis, suburban reformers – of whom there are now many – would be better equipped to frame persuasive arguments to skeptical citizens. At the same time, knowing more about what those who live and work in suburbs think, academics can develop a fuller, and clearer, conceptualization of the range of suburban experience. To that end, the purpose of this chapter is to develop a typology to organize and elucidate the diversity of suburban meanings, worldwide.

To accomplish this, it is necessary to survey the two extensive, but still disparate, literatures on areas that lie towards the urban fringe in the Global North and South. This binary distinction, once framed in terms of 'developed/developing' and then 'First World/Third World', was always inadequate and has become further blurred by the growth of 'emerging' economies. Places such as Singapore and South Korea could once be treated as exceptions, but the emergence of Brazil, China and India is underlining the need for a common conceptual framework that can make sense everywhere. Theories, and frameworks, developed in the Global North, then, must be contextualized. This can be done historically or geographically, paying attention to the diversity of experiences in each case. That said, it is important not to lose sight of the distinctive characteristics of suburban areas, before sketching how their meanings vary according to the identity and origins of those who live and work in the suburbs. I conclude by briefly suggesting some of the more important directions that future research might take.

THE PERSPECTIVES OF HISTORY AND GEOGRAPHY

Empirically, the assumptions that inform current understandings of suburbs can be probed, and if necessary challenged, through historical or geographical comparisons.[2] Past practices that differ from current norms force us to ask what it is that constitutes the norm, and how we can accommodate experiences that do not fit. In fact, historical research has served this purpose. In the field of suburban studies, it is not the European experience that most needs to be contextualized, but that of the United States. Far more has been written about U.S. suburbs than those of any other region. Evidence from the Web of Science, admittedly a source that is biased towards English language materials, indicates that, between 1975 and 2009, 67 per cent of all scholarly articles about suburbs dealt with the United States.[3] Furthermore, although some studies have focused largely on fringe development elsewhere (Phelps, Parsons, Ballas, & Dowling, 2006; Sieverts, 2003), these other experiences have commonly been compared with, or interpreted as approximations to, the American norm, sometimes as instances of the diffusion of American models (Dick & Rimmer, 1998, p. 2317; Sudjic, 1992). Zhou and Ma (2000, p. 227), for example, speak of American suburban forms as 'mature' while those of China as 'incipient'. Diffusionist thinking has been nowhere more apparent than in the literature on gated communities, often supposed to have been a U.S. invention.

Not surprisingly, then, the social science literature on U.S. suburbs has been parochial, making few references, and fewer comparisons, even with Britain or Europe (Jackson, 1985; cf. Masotti & Walton, 1976). A comparison with Britain would have underlined the fact that suburbs need not be self-governing (cf. Barker, 2009; Clapson, 2003; Harris & Larkham, 1999, pp. 8–9). A cursory glance at Europe, and especially the southern and eastern regions, would have shown that suburbs are commonly settled by workers, whether in public estates or through private owner building (Leontidou, 1990; Stanilov & Hirt, 2009). Instead, suburban self-rule has been viewed as definitive, and the notion that suburbs might contain workers or minorities was for many years hardly broached.[4] Recent historical research, however, has probed these assumptions, showing that the municipal definition of suburbs only became the norm in the twentieth century (Orum, 1995; Teaford, 1979, 1997). It has also been demonstrated that industrial and then office employment has been decentralizing for well over a century (Lewis, 2004), while fringe areas have long been settled by workers and minorities, both in the United States and in Canada (Harris, 1996, 2004; Hayden, 2003; Kruse & Sugrue, 2006; Nicolaides, 2002; Wiese, 2003).

These historical findings alone have not caused American social scientists to rediscover suburban diversity. The settlement of growing numbers of immigrants and ethnic minorities in the suburbs has also played a major role (cf. Li, 2009), as has the decline of many inner-ring suburbs (e.g. Hanlon, 2010, p. 114). But, especially during the 1980s and early 1990s, historical research had a perceptible impact. Again, this is suggested by evidence in the Web of Science database, which classifies journals by disciplinary fields. Overall, between 1975 and 2009, among the disciplines identified as publishing research on suburbs, history ranked fourth, with 661 items categorized.[5] But in the 1980s it ranked first, since when it has been overtaken by 'urban studies', 'geography' and 'environmental studies'. Without a close reading of the literature, it is impossible to say anything about the specific impact of this wave of historical research. But it is indicative that only after this wave had crested did social scientists become more alert to suburban diversity. During the 1980s, only 12 of all journal articles that dealt with suburbs made reference to workers, the working class, immigrants or minorities. In the 1990s, this number jumped to 219.[6] It appears, then, that suburban historians have informed current thinking by widening the discourse, as a recent collection illustrates (Nicolaides & Wiese, 2006).

Historical, or historically informed, research has also probed assumptions about the diffusion of American models. The growing literature on gated communities is a prime example. Researchers have recently shown that, in many world regions, such developments are a response to local conditions (e.g. Wu, 2006), and have been much influenced by local traditions (Bagaeen

& Uduku, 2010; Glasze, Webster, & Frantz, 2006, pp. 2, 7; Webster & Glasze, 2006). In Russia and China, for decades, party elites enjoyed exclusive urban and/or rural enclaves (Lentz, 2006). China also has the common precedent of enclosed *danwei* factory communities, which arguably express 'micro-level practices' that 'have always been centred on producing collective rather than individual modes of subjectivity' (Bray, 2005, p. 196; cf. Huang, 2005; Webster, Wu, & Zhao, 2006). Even a glance at the historical record, then, raises questions about the nature and meaning of the suburbs.

But for those concerned with contemporary suburban issues, historical research can appear to be of purely academic, or antiquarian, interest. The experience of other countries may seem to offer more relevant lessons. Rhetorical effect, then, is one reason to look outwards, instead of backwards. A stronger reason is that this procedure should provide examples of the widest possible range of suburban possibilities. This allows us to question additional assumptions about the suburbs, among which two stand out.

The first challenge that a worldwide perspective offers to modern Western assumptions about suburbs is to the belief that they reflect personal choice. Enforced resettlement has happened in North America and Western Europe since at least the era of Haussman in the 1850s and 1860s, and has often been associated with slum clearance. In these regions, however, because of local resistance and democratic limitations to state power, such schemes have played a minor role in suburban settlement and can often be effectively ignored. Clearance schemes have been resisted in the Global South too, as Fisher (2008) has shown for Rio de Janeiro, but resistance has often been futile, as was seen in Eastern Europe, the Soviet Union and China under communist rule. In China, for example, until recently about two thirds of all moves from the city to the suburbs were involuntary (Zhou & Logan, 2008, p. 156). From the colonial era onwards, in the developing world, forced relocation has often been unchecked, extensive and sometimes brutal (Davis, 2006, pp. 95–114). Such relocation defines a major type of experience, not least because, as Gans (1968, p. 54) has perceptively commented, the impact of the physical environment on ways of life is greatest for those who lack choice.

A second, and more important, challenge to Western assumptions is that many suburbs do not embody a rejection of the city. The classic version of this model arose when elite and then middle-class households sought seclusion, and bucolic ease, in suburban settings. Referring to these bourgeois utopias, Fishman (1987, p. 27) argues that 'suburbia ... must always be defined in relation to its rejected opposite: the metropolis'. A variation on this theme points out that cheap suburban land accommodates the ownership aspirations of workers and immigrants (e.g. Harris, 1996). In the Global South, however, as in European and American cities a century ago, many suburban settlers have come from the countryside. Urbanization has long depended on migrations, sometimes on a massive scale (McGee, 1971, p. 99; Potter & Lloyd-Evans, 1999, p. 136). These have been driven largely by the faith that cities offer better economic prospects: a job, the hope of a job or the opportunity to create a job (McGee, 1971). But city housing is often expensive, and limited in quantity. Many rural migrants end up at the fringe: in the favelas and squatter settlements of Latin America in the 1960s and 1970s (Losada et al., 1998; Mangin, 1967; Rogler, 1967, p. 515), in the peri-urban fringes of modern African cities (Simon, 2008) or in the migrant enclaves of urbanizing villages in China and Southeast Asia (Browder, Bohland, & Scarpacci, 1995; Ginsberg, Koppel, & McGee, 1991; Ma & Wu, 2005, p. 14; W. Wu, 2005, 2006; cf. Davis, 2006; Saunders, 2010). Rural–urban migration produced owner-built settlements around European and North American cities more than a century ago (Neuwirth, 2005, pp. 177–204). Historical research can establish this fact, but it is the current experience of millions of suburban poor that underlines the point most effectively that suburbs often mark a large step in the direction of the city. On this issue above all, the experience of the South forces us to rethink our assumptions about the nature and meaning of the suburbs.

CHALLENGING THEORY WITH DIVERSE REALITIES

It is no easy task to bring the experience of the Global South to bear upon our conceptualization of suburbs. It involves creating a dialogue between two literatures that have hardly communicated. The literature that has helped to constitute urban theory has dealt with suburbs, variously labelled, in the Global North. In practice, this has meant the United States and Britain, with lesser attention being given to other white settler colonies (Canada, Australia, New Zealand) and the countries of Western Europe. In the Web of Science database, between 1975 and 2009, 94 per cent of all articles that referred to suburbs pertained to one or other of these regions. The other literature concerns fringe growth in what is still often known as the developing world. Here, as Robinson (2005) has shown, urban issues have routinely been framed within a separate, 'developmental' paradigm.

Those who have written about urban fringe areas in the Global North have often misunderstood the history of suburbs, but they have been thorough in dissecting its modern forms. The literature on the United States is the richest. It has spawned well-grounded debates about the importance of edge, as opposed to edgeless, cities (Garreau, 1991; Lang, 2003; Marshall, 2000), about the impact of residential versus industrial decentralization (e.g. Stanback, 1991), about the social and cultural diversity of suburbs (e.g. Hall & Lee, 2010; Lindstrom & Barling, 2003; Webster, 2000) and about the health of inner as opposed to outer suburbs (Brookings Institution, 2010; Lucy & Phillips, 2006; Mikelbank, 2004; Hanlon, 2010, p. 114). It has even accommodated a minority who have defended suburban sprawl (Bruegmann, 2005; Kotkin, 2010), for example, by drawing parallels between household activity patterns in walking and car-based environments (Marshall, 2006; cf. Fishman, 1990). This is a literature that has left few stones, in few suburban fields, unturned.

Until recently, however, research on fringe areas in the developing world has been much more limited. At the extreme, some surveys of urban issues barely mention the fringe (Drakakis-Smith, 2000; Gugler, 1996, 1997). A recent general text, for example, devotes two chapters to cities in the 'less developed' world, but ignores peripheral growth entirely (Kaplan, Wheeler, & Holloway, 2009). More commonly, surveys mention fringe areas but concentrate on the poor, because it is supposed to be poverty that best characterizes the Global South (Davis, 2006; de Soto, 1989; Huchzermeyer, 2004; Mangin, 1967; Neuwirth, 2005; Rogler, 1967; Turner, 1969). Surveys of urbanization, then, speak of squatter settlements, but usually only in the Global South (cf. Tsenkova, Potsiou, & Badina, 2009), and they refer to middle-class suburbs only when discussing the United States or Europe (Cohen, Ruble, Tulchin, & Garland, 1996; Badcock, 2002; Macionis & Parrilla, 2007).[7] At best, as in the text by Potter and Lloyd-Evans (1999), the existence of both suburbs and squatter settlements in the Global South is acknowledged, but much more is said about the latter.

Regardless, almost all writers treat suburbs and squatter settlements separately, as if they define and inhabit worlds that are not only different but also unrelated. In the Web of Science database, between 1975 and 2009, among the 7,363 scholarly articles that referred to suburbs in their title or abstract, only 13 (0.17 per cent) also made reference to squatter settlements. These two types of area are discussed as if they bear no functional relation to one another or, in many cases, to the wider metropolitan area. In their survey of cities in the Global South, for example, Beall and Fox (2009) speak about squatter settlements in a chapter on poverty, while they reserve discussion of gated communities for a chapter on personal security. And so the broad picture is one of intellectual segregation. A telltale sign is provided by the recent, and otherwise excellent, text edited by Brunn, Hays-Mitchell, and Zeigler (2008), in which regional specialists survey *Cities of the World*. The index contains 22 entries for 'squatter settlements' and 20 for 'suburbanization', which denotes middle-class, commercial and industrial districts. There is no overlap in the page references. The implication is that one type of fringe development occurs in the South, another in the North. The further implication is that theories relevant in one context have no bearing on the other, until the South catches up.

Such schizophrenic thinking never made sense. For example, even where squatters dominated the fringe, choice areas were reserved for social elites, who thereby defined the overall pattern of suburban settlement. The point has been well established for Latin America (Amato, 1970; Ford, 1996; Morris, 1978; Lowder, 1986). But the growth of emerging economies, and recent developments everywhere, has underlined the absurdity of treating Southern and Northern cities separately. Certain types of development have become apparent everywhere. The most notable are gated communities. Although taking different forms, and drawing on local traditions, they are members of a generic type that transcends nation, or world region (Atkinson & Blandy, 2006; Bagaeen & Uduku, 2010; Glasze et al., 2006).

More significantly, many countries in what used to be the Global South have seen fringe growth that breaks established categories. Latin American cities, where squatter settlements used to be dominant but where rural–urban migration has slowed, now boast elite and middle-class suburbs, together with some edge city business developments (Caldeira, 2000; Ford, 1996; Janoschka & Borsdorf, 2006). India, whose recent suburban development has received surprisingly little scholarly attention (Sridhar, 2007), has also seen rapid suburban growth and edge city development (Benjamin, Bhuvaneswari, Rajan, & Manjanuth, 2008). In Southern Europe, informal, working-class suburbs have been joined by middle-class speculative development, and new types of sprawl (Leontidou, Afouxenides, Kourlioros, & Marmaras, 2007, p. 80). In a more racialized setting, parallel developments have occurred around South African cities (Jürgens & Landman, 2006; Murray, 2008) while, in the Middle East, Cairo especially has seen the rise of suburban middle-class 'private cities' (Dennis, 2008, p. 1102). Other parts of Africa have seen rapid urbanization, but there, as much as anywhere, peri-urban development that juxtaposes very different types of people has become common (Simon, 1992, pp. 163–167; Simon, McGregor, & Nsiah-Gyabaah, 2004; cf. McGregor, Simon, &

Thompson, 2006). Finally, after the disintegration of the Soviet bloc, Eastern Europe has come more actively into play. Once quarantined as an ambiguous Second World – a term implied, although rarely used – its experience is now acknowledged by Western scholars. In ways that parallel the Global South, its suburbs, once dominated by public housing estates, have seen diversification into private sector building, together with commercial development on an unprecedented scale (Hirt, 2007; Pichler-Milanović, Gutry-Korycka, & Rink, 2007; Stanilov & Hirt, 2009, pp. 82–89). In different ways, these recent trends mix things up, juxtaposing people and types of development. In many Islamic cities – a contentious category that extends from Indonesia to Algiers – Khan (2008, p. 1047) sees rich and poor now living in 'pockets'. Such proximity breeds fear. In Sao Paulo, Caldeira (1996, p. 318) sees 'fortified fragments', as do writers on Johannesburg (e.g. Murray, 2008). Collectively, such changes challenge distinctions between Western suburbs and the squatter settlements or public housing estates of a poorer world.

One indication of this blurring of boundaries is the growing use of 'suburb' in the Global South. During the 1980s, three quarters of all suburban references in the Web of Science database were to the United States. Since then, the number of references to suburbs in all regions has increased, but most rapidly elsewhere. Between the 1980s and the 2000s, the number of references to U.S. suburbs increased by 272 per cent.[8] This rate was outstripped by the Middle East (300 per cent), South Asia (350 per cent), Western Europe (510 per cent) and Eastern Europe (525 per cent). It was far exceeded by Latin America (850 per cent) and Southeast Asia, where the number of works categorized rose to a modest 16 from 0. Some percentage increases were based on low absolute numbers. Nonetheless, in two decades the U.S. share of suburban research had fallen to three fifths (Fig. 1).

It is Chinese development that has posed the greatest challenge for suburban theory, and that has begun to produce the most significant scholarly response. Between the 1980s and 2000s, references to suburbs in China jumped by almost 1,400 per cent, reaching 119 in the latter period. Indeed, a number of Chinese scholars have claimed that suburbanization there actually began in the 1980s: Feng and Zhou (2005, pp. 133–134) make this claim for Hangzhou, even though they present a map that shows continuous expansion since at least 1949. As the term is usually defined, suburbanization has been proceeding in China for decades, indeed centuries, but it is true that the scale of change since the early 1980s has no parallel or precedent. The forms are novel too. For three decades under communist

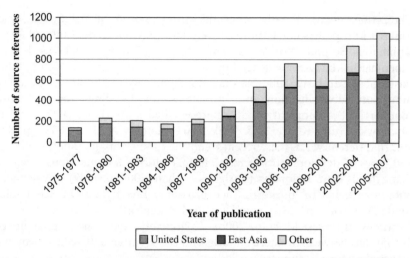

Fig. 1. Regional Trend in Suburban Research in the Web of Science Database,
1975–2007.

rule, *hokou* (residency permit) regulations inhibited rural–urban migration,
while, as in Eastern Europe, state control of land maintained a clear
boundary between city and country (Zhou & Logan, 2008, p. 140; cf.
Stanilov & Hirt, 2009). Most suburban development took the form of state
housing, or of socially mixed *danwei* work units (Bray, 2005; Wu, Xu, &
Yeh, 2007, pp. 280–282). Since the early 1990s, however, suburbanization
has gathered momentum as cities, outer urban and peri-urban areas have
industrialized (e.g. Feng & Zhou, 2005). New, market-led fringe developments have taken diverse forms (Feng, Zhou, & Wu, 2008; Huang, 2005; Li
& Wu, 2008). As W. Wu (2006, p. 224) describes, suburbs now contain a
'juxtaposition of rural villages, resettlement housing for central-city
residents, migrant communities and commodity [market] housing projects'.
Some market projects have parallels in the Global North. Others, notably
the migrant communities that cluster in once-rural villages, are similar to
suburban forms elsewhere in Southeast Asia (McGee, Lin, Marton, Wang,
& Wu, 2007; Wang, Wang, & Wu, 2009; Zhang, 2005). In some ways,
however, they are *sui generis*, in part because of the relative importance of
privately rented housing for temporary migrants (Friedman, 2005, p. 70)
and in part because of a regulatory regime that has to allow illegal
construction, extension and subdivision of rental properties, but which
strives not to admit the fact (Hudahah, Winarso, & Woltjer, 2007;

Liu, 2007; Smart & Tang, 2005; Wang et al., 2009; W. Wu, 2005, 2006). In China, too, the outcome has included fine- or medium-grained social mixing (Huang, 2005, p. 198). Because of its scale, urban fringe development in China cannot be ignored. Because of its form, it cannot be assimilated into existing models, Western or developmental. Underlining the crisis in suburban theory, it shows that we need to broaden the scope of our enquiries to encompass the world.[9]

WHY 'THE SUBURBS'?

But is 'suburb' the appropriate word? The term is problematic even in Anglo-America, where it is entrenched and widely used, in part because it is rooted in its American associations with political identity (Bourne, 1996, p. 165). Here, however, there is less and less agreement about what suburbs are, or whether, in the modern era of extended metropolitan regions, the term still has any useful meaning. Instead, researchers have proposed an array of terms. In 2003, Robert Lang listed 44, from 'anticity' through 'postmetropolis' to 'urban realm', since when others, including 'metrobur-bia', have been proposed (Knox, 2008). Bourne (1996, p. 164) has suggested that 'we jettison terms such as suburb, and the city–suburban dichotomy, as well as the intellectual baggage associated with them, once and for all'. Stubbornly, however, the older term persists, as its growing use to describe fringe areas in the Global South suggests. Most importantly, the term is still routinely used by those who live at or near the urban fringe. And so it may be unwise to abandon it just yet. We need a label of some sort and, as Hayden (2003, p. 16) has argued, neologisms that imply that 'ordinary citizens will not understand' the issues at stake may appear condescending or confusing. If we care about the views of insiders, we should pay attention to their language.

This line of argument raises a different sort of problem. 'Suburb' is freighted with meanings, which vary from place to place. When we enlarge the scope of our survey beyond Anglo-America, their variations become striking. In France, suburbs – *faubourgs* and, more especially, *les banlieues* – have mixed connotations, originally of working-class owner building, and now of state-planned, immigrant Muslim enclaves (Dikeç, 2007; Faure, 1991; Fourcaut, 2000). Further afield, the term is still used sparingly. In China, it may denote the exclusivity of new gated communities but has little purchase on the *danwei* work-unit developments that still occupy many outer districts, or on the urbanized villages that house millions of rural–urban migrants. And in some places, such as Kinshasa, 'suburb' appears to have no local resonance at all (Trefon, 2004, 2009). It could be argued that if our goal is to provincialize urban theory, it is wrong to impose a Western label where it is not relevant, or perhaps even welcome. That is why McGee (1991) proposed 'desakota' to refer to the densely settled agricultural landscapes in Southeast Asia that are being drawn into the expanding urban fringe (*desa*, village; *kota*, town). This draws attention to the specificity of the urbanization process in that region, and challenges conventional academic views, but such unique terms may discourage broader comparisons. We should acknowledge local differences in experience and meaning. To remind ourselves of, and to underline these differences, we may sometimes employ unique terms, such as *danwei, banlieu, desakota* or *gecekondu*, that have specific local meanings. But if we believe that all fringe areas share certain characteristics, then we need a single term to denote them. 'Suburb' is as good as any, and better than most.

Shared characteristics, of course, cannot be taken for granted. Those who write about suburbs have commented on the difficulties of defining their subject. One issue, at least, is easily resolved. Although some suburbs have been, and remain, residential enclaves, and although we often speak of suburbs in general as if they are essentially residential in character, urban fringe areas have always contained industries and employment of various kinds (Lewis, 2004; Scott & Soja, 1996; Soja, 2000). That may be more true now than ever, and certainly complicates any attempts at definition. But narrowing the focus to residential suburbs leaves many issues unresolved. Density and urban fringe location are obviously relevant criteria. But, how dense? How close to the fringe? In places with multiple nodes, which fringe? More importantly, why do these things matter? If the classification of a place as suburban is to be more than an academic exercise, it must be because it has some significance, whether for the social and political lives of its residents or for the wider urban economy (cf. Thorns, 1972). Unfortunately, researchers have found it difficult to link forms of settlement with distinctive ways of life, even within specific national settings. The nature of the form–culture linkage depends on social differences of class, ethnicity and gender. The challenge of identifying it across national and cultural boundaries is proportionately greater. Recognizing that our ability to establish such connections is unproven, before trying to encompass the diversity of suburbs, we need to establish a minimum definition to which suburbs everywhere conform. Only then can we hope to address what Vaughan, Griffiths, Haklay, and Jones (2009, p. 485) have recently labelled 'the type of generic problem that the suburbs represent'.

A definition of the suburbs must begin with their physical characteristics but, to be meaningful, it cannot end there (c.f. Stanilov & Scheer, 2004; Whitehand & Carr, 2001). This is acknowledged in everyday language. In my edition of *Webster's* dictionary, 'suburb' and 'suburbanization' denote physical places and trends, but 'suburban' invokes the characteristic of either 'suburbs or suburbanites'. Accordingly, the following discussion interweaves the physical and the social. For suburbs that are at least in part residential, commentators agree that two physical characteristics, low density and peripheral location, are basic. Some would add a third: that, except for the occasional school or place of worship, the quintessential suburb contains only one type of land use, so that residents must commute. This form of settlement is a common and influential suburban stereotype, but most urban fringe areas have not, and do not, conform. Instead, I would suggest that an overlooked third characteristic, the newness of the suburb, warrants attention, not least because of its social significance.

Of all criteria, peripheral location is the most fundamental of all: suburbs lie between the city and the country, or in a few cases between the city and a wilderness or desert. Difficulties arise in situations where two or more cities grow up in close proximity, so that it becomes moot whether a suburb belongs to one or the other, or indeed whether the smaller city may become an annex of the larger. A different, and even more common, challenge is posed when metropolitan areas grow, so that the distance – symbolic as well as geographical – between centre and periphery becomes very large. Hybrid, 'in-between landscapes' emerge that combine city and suburban qualities. Here, the suburb is being refashioned as the city, inviting treatment as a distinctive sort of place, with unique combinations of built forms, processes and imaginaries (Fiedler & Addie, 2008; Sieverts, 2003). Such places are readily overlooked. They lack the visual and cultural profile of the downtown, and for that reason are notably and unreasonably ignored in the literature on 'global' cities (Keil, forthcoming). At the same time, they lack the branded coherence of new subdivisions, which are strikingly marketed and readily visualized. In any rapidly-growing metropolitan area, such as Toronto, however, they constitute a common type of suburban-cum-urban landscape (Keil & Young, 2009). Here, above all, city–suburban binaries blur and may break down.

By definition, being peripheral makes suburbs less accessible to other parts of the urban area. This may not matter much for those whose everyday needs can be satisfied close by. An industrial suburb that has stores and recreational facilities is one example; modern metropolitan suburbs, where residents travel great distances by car, is another. Residents of a suburb that is peripheral to a major city, but which is not far from an edge city, may have access to a wide range of urban services (Garreau, 1991). Even so, on the average, peripherality means limited access, as a recent study of Hong Kong's new towns has effectively shown (Lau, 2010). How much this matters will vary by social class. At its starkest, it contrasts the experience of the rich and the poor. Thus, for example, Brown (1992, p. 122) argues that 'Latin American cities have not one but at least two outskirts'. One is affluent, and integrated into the city with good transportation; the other is isolated, 'poor, alienated, and', he adds, 'more populous'. It is a familiar contrast, which can accommodate a continuum.

Class is bound up with gender. A durable finding of suburban research is that geographical isolation matters most to women. Those who have either lower incomes or unequal access to household resources may not afford their own car, or perhaps even a transit fare. Since they usually bear most of the responsibility for childrearing, they are even more constrained, while children and adolescents, too, often find suburban life confining. Such patterns have been well documented in the literature on North American, Australian and many Western European cities (Clapson, 1998, p. 121; Popenoe, 1977, pp. 185–186, 1979, pp. 262–263; Strong-Boag, Dyck, England, & Johnson, 1999), and recently also for Eastern Europe (Hirt, 2008). They are surely generalizable.

Because of attenuated access to urban facilities, living on the periphery may have very specific meanings. Again, class matters, especially since it is often associated with degree of choice. Those pushed to the city's edge may be, and feel, socially marginal. The indigenous French, and then the immigrant Muslim, residents of the Parisian *banlieues* are a well-documented example in Europe, and there are many more in the Global South (Dikeç, 2007; Fourcaut, 2000). Goldstein (2004), for example, has spoken in these terms about, and for, the rural migrant residents of Villa Sebastián Pagador, on the fringe of Cochabamba, Bolivia. In contrast, those who have chosen the suburban fringe may enjoy being removed. They can enjoy certain amenities but, being able to commute and travel elsewhere, they remain connected to the city's economy, culture and politics. A key issue, then, is whether the peripheral location damages access to other important places, whether downtown or in other suburbs.

There is an interesting question, hardly addressed, as to whether being peripheral carries meanings that transcend social distinctions. Teaford (2008, p. xii) has suggested that living away from a central location entails 'a different mentality': even the most affluent suburban resident abjures claims to being in a hub of any sort, at least when she is at home. Manhattan, or even Cochabamba, can claim to be a centre of power, real and symbolic, albeit for different-sized regions, but even a prominent suburb such as Silicon Valley is in some respects placeless (Marshall, 2000, p. 83). Being peripheral, and at the extreme decentred, perhaps suburbs must mean 'ordinary'.

A second feature of suburbs is that they usually display residential densities that are intermediate between those of the city and the country. While cities have streetscapes, the suburban scene is a landscape (Whitehand & Carr, 2001, p. 1). Where land markets allocate users, the logic is compelling: suburban land is more abundant, and so cheaper than that in the city. But the urban division of labour means that suburban residents require access to workplaces, stores and other facilities in ways that encourage closer settlement than is the norm in rural areas. Sometimes the density gradient is steep, as in many urban areas under communist rule, and sometimes barely perceptible, as in many parts of the Global North and South today. Occasionally, it is reversed, as happened in with some tower block housing estates on the fringe of some Western European and many Russian and Eastern European cities, in the 1950s and 1960s. Today, for example, in Leipzig, residential densities spike near the fringe, in part because a good deal of older, war-damaged housing was never replaced (Nuissl, Rink, Couch, & Karecha, 2007, p. 148). This exception probes the rule, and indeed may not be an exception for much longer (Kabisch, Haase, & Haase, 2010). More commonly, suburban high rises have created a novel, ambiguous situation. At the scale of the building, densities are very high but, because the buildings are often spaced out, densities are moderate. That is why in China, where many suburban developments from the 1950s to the 1980s took the form of medium-rise apartments, residential densities decline quite steadily away from urban centres (Wang & Zhou, 1999). It also appears to be true in Istanbul, where modern suburbs boast the tallest residential structures but where area densities are highest in the older districts of walk-up apartments, such as Beyoglu. And it is true in many of the older, 'in-between', suburbs, where high-rises have often been erected as infill redevelopment. Density is an important and plausible criterion, but its social significance is not always clear, and in its measurement we need to pay careful attention to variations according to the scale of analysis, whether building, block, district or subdivision.

A third and equally obvious aspect of suburbs, their newness, has often been noted, but its significance remains unexplored. Suburban landscapes are often criticized for being bare and uniform. The two features often go together. Bare because trees and other vegetation have been cut down or eliminated, for even judicious plantings take years, even decades, to mature. Being bare, standardized elements in the built environment will stick out. And being new, there is likely to have been little reason, or opportunity, to alter buildings, the sorts of changes that make cities appear lived in. The changes may range from decorative, through alterations that change the massing of structures and whole blocks, to redevelopment. Some suburbs, especially those developed by small speculative builders or amateurs, never go through a uniform phase. This is especially of those suburbs that develop around, or adjacent to, pre-existing towns and rural settlements. Such places may appear permanently unfinished, while additions and extensions soon transform them. At the other extreme, there are some suburbs where even minor alterations are resisted, or prohibited by covenants, in order to maintain the character and symbolic meaning of the place (Duncan & Duncan, 2003; cf. Firey, 1947; Farley, 1964). These restrictions may be enforced collectively from the beginning, as in many modern Common Interest Developments, or developed later in the form of efforts to conserve (Clapson, 2003, pp. 71–72; Larkham, 1999). Even then, plants grow, buildings acquire a patina of age and, if only because tastes change, minor alterations change facades (Brand, 1994). It is not clear what such changes mean to local residents. Very likely, the meaning varies, not only by class, but also by culture and over time. But it is difficult to believe that the blatant novelty of the suburban scene, raw and perhaps bland, can ever be a matter of complete indifference to its residents.

The rawness of the outer suburb is social as well as physical: it is a social frontier, where networks and institutions, too, must be built. Occasionally, incomers know one another. Migrants may move en bloc, as happened with the organized land invasions around Lima in the 1950s and 1960s. Alternatively, state agencies may rehouse large numbers from a central district into a single suburb. Even in these unusual situations, considerable mixing is inevitable; new friends and social institutions must be made. More commonly, those who move into new subdivisions are strangers. This fact does not narrowly determine how they will respond. Some may feel lost; others may strive to build friendships. The result may be alienation, or frenzied networking, and both have been documented (Clark, 1966; Gans, 1967; Wilmott & Young, 1960). Gans (1968) has argued that which pattern emerges depends on social class, although ethnicity can also play a major role. Lima's land invasions, for example, were promulgated by illiterate peasants. Those that were collective depended on social organization, which declined once the suburban building phase was over (Mangin, 1967; cf.

Rogler, 1967). A comparable trajectory seems to have been common in many speculatively-built middle-class suburbs.

Clark has argued that the definitive suburban experience occupies the short period of collective adaptation to the new living environment. He (1966, p. 8) suggests that 'what suburban development essentially means is the process of transformation of the country into the city'. From his research on a variety of Toronto's post-war suburbs, he claimed that once the suburbs had been built out, and once people had settled in, made friends, established routines and in some cases moved on, 'the suburbs had clearly ceased to be suburbs'. This is a view of the suburbs as a short-lived social process: they are new, and very temporary. A weak version of this line of argument is not only reasonable but also obvious: almost every inner-city neighbourhood was once suburban; its original status had an expiry date (Miller, 2000; Whitzman, 2009). Common usage suggests that this process takes decades. In the case of Toronto's Parkdale area, for example, Whitzman (2009) argues that it took more than half a century for an 1870s suburban village to become a city neighbourhood, and two more decades before it could be referred to as a slum. But Clark assumes that, sociologically, the process is usually over in a few years. The question, then, is how quickly the transition from suburb to neighbourhood occurs, and on what basis we decide when it is complete.

How quickly an area ceases to be suburban depends in part on how rapidly it fills out. To simplify, there are two alternatives – planned and instant, or a disorganized, extended process of fringe infill – although, as always, there is scope for intermediate hybrids (Vachon, Luka, & Lacroix, 2004). Planned suburbs make for striking visuals. Whether developed by state agencies or land developers, they have received far more than their share of attention. Their very raw appearance may last for a while, but their physical development may be over in a year or two. Residents soon settle in. In general, however, disorganized and extended development has been the norm. Historically, and indeed down to the present, in the Global North, the process has typically begun with piecemeal development of individual lots in and around commuter villages, followed by the subdivision of those small, farm properties that lay closest to transportation routes, and concluded with infill, as and when enough people could afford cars to commute (Evenden, 1991; Savage & Lapping, 2003). In the South, the beginning of this pattern of suburban growth has been documented across Africa, Latin America, India and Southeast Asia, where it is now often known as peri-urban development (Brook & Dávila, 2000; Gough & Yankson, 2006; Losada et al., 1998; McGregor et al., 2006; Simon, 2008;

Wigle, 2010). With some exceptions (Fisher, 2003), in the North, these forms of outer fringe development have juxtaposed lower income rural residents with higher income, exurban commuters (Barrett, 1994; Rome, 2001; Stilgoe, 1989). The tensions are manifested in many ways, down to the preferred size and style of fence (Hirt, 2007, pp. 767, 772). In the South, too, piecemeal and infill growth has been the norm (e.g. Briggs & Mwamfupe, 2000), sometimes concentrated by transit routes into villages (Brook & Dávila, 2000), and again marked by features as fences (Trefon, 2009, p. 27). Here, however, contrasts and tensions have involved rural–urban migrants, looking for urban opportunity (Douglas, 2006). It was migrants to the Maluka fringe area of Kinshasa, for example, who nicknamed the area 'Morocco', since it opened up the 'prestige and pleasures' of the city, just as Morocco promised Africans access to opportunities in Europe (Trefon, 2009, p. 17). In time, rural villages are incorporated into the built-up area, helping to define the physical and social character of the suburban fringe (Chakraborty, 1991; Guldin, 1996; McGee, 1967, p. 148, 1991, pp. 23–24 n10; McGee et al., 2007, p. 6). How long it takes for farms and village to be assimilated into the expanding built-up area can vary greatly, depending on land-use regulations and on how rapidly the urban area is growing. The physical process of transforming city into suburb, then, can last decades.

How soon a fully built-up fringe area ceases to be suburban in the minds of its residents will in turn depend on how rapidly growth continues, and what changes to the suburban fabric are allowed. We need to know much more about what happens to suburbs after they have been developed, in other words, how they age (McManus & Ethington, 2007). It was once assumed that, because of the filtering process, as dwellings and neighbour-hoods aged they would inevitably decline. Gentrification has shown that this is not inevitable, but the growing problems in inner-ring suburbs, at least in North America, illustrate that ageing matters. So, too, does the changing relative position of each suburb with the passage of time. As new development surrounds a suburb, it becomes less peripheral. Land prices are likely to rise; the pressures for redevelopment increase, and so too may residential densities. As this happens, it becomes increasingly difficult for residents, and especially incomers, to think of the area as suburban, but we do not know when the tipping point usually comes. Sociologically, Clark (1966) is probably right in saying that the process of making a new community is largely accomplished within a few years. At that point, suburbanization as a process may be said to have run its course. But available evidence suggests that most residents continue to think of themselves as suburban for much longer. The meaning of being suburban, then, extends far beyond the period of settlement.

MEANINGFUL TYPES OF SUBURBS

In light of these observations, and within a worldwide frame of reference, what can we say about the meanings of suburban living to those who are involved? The answer depends above all on the social identities of the people in question and, to the extent that these are not already implied, on their mix of motives. The Western literature has emphasized, or indeed assumed, that the meaning of the suburbs arises from decisions of households who relocate, on a more or less permanent basis, from the city. In many cases, it has been further assumed that this option was for many decades available to a limited range of people. Stepping back to gain a larger frame of reference, it is clear that many suburban residents, defined as they have been here, have not fit one or more of these categories. It follows that the meaning of suburbanism must be systematically rethought. To that end, Fig. 2 sketches the most common types of suburban residents and, since these are typically clustered, the main types of suburban areas.

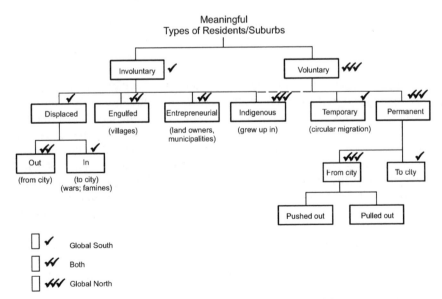

Fig. 2. A Typology of Suburbs World-Wide.

The typology presented in Fig. 2 is framed in terms of the motives and actions of those who have settled the suburbs. Most importantly, it distinguishes those who had some choice from those who did not, and those moving towards as opposed to those leaving the city. Its general purpose is to suggest not only the range of suburban experiences and types but also the logical manner of their articulation. More specifically, it shows, at a glance, broad differences in the suburban experience of the Global North and South, while pointing to areas of overlap.

Drawing, especially, on the experience of the Global South, and more generally on the extensive body of work cited earlier, it is possible to make some general and systematic observations about the more common, meaningful types of suburban residents, and of suburbs. The most fundamental difference lies between those who have chosen to live in the suburbs and those who have not. Notwithstanding the assumptions of Western theory, substantial numbers of suburban residents have not in fact chosen to live there. Perhaps the most obvious subgroups are those who have been forcibly displaced from somewhere else. In the Global North, most of these are the supposed beneficiaries, but sometimes in fact the victims, of clearance schemes. A sometimes larger, but much less easily defined, group consists of those who would have preferred to live near downtown but who were compelled to move out by land prices. Thus, Clark (1966, p. 223) claims, on limited evidence, that many fell into this category in early post-war Toronto, so that 'it was in the city rather than in the suburbs that was most likely to be found people with a strong commitment to a way of life'. He probably overstated the argument, but in general it is clear that market forces can be almost as intransigent as state agencies in directing people where to live.

In many parts of the Global South, most of those who have been forced to live in suburbs are previous residents of rural areas, who have escaped wars or famines. In post-war decades, both Singapore and Hong Kong moved hundreds of thousands of refugee squatters to resettlement estates (Smart, 2006). In these instances, many, perhaps the majority, were eventually grateful for their forced relocation. For a minority, and in many other places, resettlement has been perceived as an imposition. In varying degrees, those who are forcibly rehoused are poor, and often ill-equipped to manage in any environment. Since they are likely to be relegated to the most marginal spaces in what are already peripheral locations, these are the peoples whose lives are most narrowly constrained and determined by life at the urban fringe. This, however, does not necessarily mean that they lack optimism. What they make of suburban living is likely to vary, depending on whether they had any choice whatsoever in their relocation to the urban fringe, what they left behind and what resources they have for entering the urban mainstream.

Many others have involuntarily ended up living in the suburbs, without having to move. There are those whose farms and villages have been engulfed by the expanding tide of urban growth. In those parts of the world where agricultural settlement is dense, and where urbanization has been proceeding rapidly, these involuntary suburbanites are numerous. What they think, and make, of their situation varies enormously. In North America and Western Europe, many rural residents have resisted and resented the intrusion of urban commuters. In China in recent years, however, villagers and local governments have often embraced and encouraged the change, by establishing factories, or by extending and subdividing dwellings. Indeed, everywhere, a few involuntary suburbanites, engulfed by the expansion of a nearby city, are likely to welcome and facilitate their fate. Where land is privately owned, the most common advocate is the owner of suburban land, who is tempted to capitalize on the rise in land values that attends urban expansion, and who fights attempts to limit development, for example through zoning or the imposition of a green belt. Where they depend on property tax revenues, municipalities too may promote growth, typically in the form of those land uses that pay most in the way of taxes and that make few demands on municipal services. For those private and public agents who are entrepreneurial, then, much of the meaning of the suburb is as a field of opportunity. It is inevitable that the incorporation of rural and then peri-urban areas into the expanding suburban fringe will create tensions. But their nature and scale vary enormously.

The other type of involuntary resident is the native-born. In the North, suburbs have usually been viewed as especially suited to the raising of children. Depending, exactly, on how suburbs are defined, a majority of North Americans and Europeans, and a large minority in many other parts of the world, were willy-nilly indigenous to this environment. What they have made of this is unclear, although it has certainly varied. Faced with the difficulties of getting around in low-density settings that are poorly served by transit, some grew up rejecting the suburbs, at least until they themselves had children. A small but vocal minority have lodged some of the more vociferous objections to suburban living that have been voiced in recent decades. Many more, however, seem to have taken the suburbs – warts and all – for granted. This silent majority have simply accommodated to the way things are.

Turning to those who have chosen the suburbs, we must immediately distinguish between those who move away from the city and those who seek it. Those moving out have done so for a wide range of reasons. In general, these are quite well understood, although their local mixture is surely more diverse than we commonly realize. Among those who have moved to the suburbs, not all have actively rejected the city. Some have left the city with regret, having been pushed out by the high price of land and housing. Many have been positively attracted to suburban space and lifestyle, whether in, adjacent to or in the vicinity of the dwelling. As the suburban Chinese say: 'large house, better life' (Feng et al., 2008, p. 93; cf. Janoschka & Borsdorf, 2006). A few have sought the exclusivity of segregated suburbs, usually to enjoy their social cachet, but occasionally to preserve an ethnic identity (Li, 2009, p. 3). Many have followed decentralizing jobs, and/or welcomed the suburbs as the only affordable place in which to realize the dream of home ownership. Regardless, at least in relative terms, almost all of those who have moved out to the suburbs have done so because they found city living less attractive. Large numbers have been repelled by high crime rates, crowded streets or poor living conditions. To a lesser or greater extent, they have found the city wanting.

In contrast, those arriving in suburban or peri-urban areas from rural areas are typically seeking better economic opportunities. Sometimes these may be found in the outer fringe areas themselves, taking the form of cash farming, or employment in new factories and service industries. Alternatively, as for lower income households who have moved out of the city, suburban living provides an affordable base from which to commute to city jobs. In either case, reality may not meet expectations: in many parts of the Global South, the movement of farmers to cities has greatly exceeded the growth of urban employment. But, regardless, the motives of migrants have differed systematically from those who have fled, or been pushed out of, the centre. They want to embrace the city; the only question is whether their overtures will be successful.

For many, migration is a lottery. Unlike those who have left the city, many rural migrants do not settle permanently at the urban fringe. In the colonial era, especially in East and Southern Africa, some governments tried to regulate the movement of villagers into urban areas through some type of permit. Even today, the Chinese government does the same. Typically, migrants find ways to evade these regulations, and governments have often bent the rules to suit urban employers who want a cheap and abundant labour force. Such accommodations have most easily been justified in the name of promoting economic growth. One of the easiest ways of relaxing the rules is to allow temporary or circular migration. This might follow a seasonal rhythm, so that farm workers find city jobs for part of the year, or according to the longer and more irregular economic cycle. Either way, the availability of land and rural subsistence makes it possible to harness a migrant labour force whose low wages, poor living conditions and fringe residence embody their marginal role in the urban economy. Their suburban status is temporary; its promise, fragile and contingent.

CONCLUDING DISCUSSION

Worldwide, the range of people who live at or near the urban fringe is exceedingly diverse. The nature of those fringe areas, and the meanings they carry for their residents, is accordingly varied. This chapter has shown that amongst this variety there are a wide, but manageably finite, variety of suburbs. What it has not demonstrated, because in the present state of our knowledge it cannot, is whether it is useful to lump all of these urban fringe settlements into a common category, whatever the label. Perhaps the typology presented here will encourage the comparative research that is best suited to test that proposition.

To determine whether it is useful to consider elite and middle-class suburbs, squatter settlements, exurban villages, edgeless cities and the like, in relation to one another, researchers must address two questions. The first is whether and how these different types of suburban fringe areas are functionally related. If the squatter settlement depends on an adjacent gated community or industrial park, or vice versa, then each must be considered as part of a larger whole. This is often the case, even for large suburban areas that appear self-sufficient. As Marshall (2000, p. 66) comments about Silicon Valley: it is self-contained, in the sense that it contains workplaces, homes, stores and recreational facilities, but it relies on 'waitresses, janitors, and gardeners, and hotel managers, food service clerks, and assistant bookstore clerks, who come from over the hill'. Although several generations of scholars have argued the importance of viewing cities and suburbs as part of metropolitan wholes, researchers commonly ignore this sort of interdependence. This is especially true of those who have written about fringe areas in the Global South, where gated and squatter communities have typically been considered in isolation. Future research needs to focus on the nature and extent of interrelation between the varied types of fringe settlement.

A second important question for future research is whether such obviously diverse suburban areas have enough in common that they can plausibly be viewed as variations on a common theme, or to pose a generic type of problem for urban theory. Following other writers, I have suggested that density, newness and peripheral location are the defining qualities of suburbs. It is easy to show that the effects of each of these are contingent – on standards of living, on class, ethnicity, gender, and indeed on the hopes and fears of local residents. It remains an open question as to whether the physical environment has effects that transcend social identity and purpose. A generation ago, a small number of researchers explored this as a sociological issue and offered a tentative 'yes'. Michelson (1976, p. 73), for example, suggested that the built environment may not determine behaviour but that it does offer a 'path of least resistance' (cf. Popenoe, 1977; Tallman & Morgner, 1970). In recent years, a new generation of researchers is considering the health as well as the social effects of urban form, and reaching a similar conclusion (e.g. Leyden, 2003). We need to consolidate, extend and test such arguments, especially in the developing world.

I have argued that in order to understand the meanings of the suburbs, it is above all necessary to consider the backgrounds, purposes and experiences of their residents. That may be necessary, but it is not sufficient. Non-residents have had plenty to say about suburbs, and have generally exerted a disproportionate influence on cultural norms. They are probably overrepresented among the many authors whose work has been cited here. Local residents may resist and reject some of the more critical stereotypes, but they must have been aware of them and, at least in subtle ways, influenced by them. It would be interesting to explore in much more detail the interplay between the meanings that suburbs have had for insiders and outsiders. If nothing else, it would be of assistance to those, growing in number in recent years, who have sought to reshape existing suburbs in ways that promote human and environmental health.

In the end, the meaning of the suburbs must be understood in relation to other aspects of the suburbanization process, and most notably their political economy. As physical places, suburbs are made, and it matters by whom, under what forms of regulation and whether development is piecemeal or packaged. It matters how secure residents are, in terms of personal safety, and in the form and permanence of home tenure. Just as important is the character of the infrastructure to which they have access, ranging from schools to transportation. And meanings are invariably reflected, and reproduced, through the governance of suburbs, whether by state and quasi-state agencies, or through the markets for land and housing, which govern so much of what happens at the urban fringe. A recently funded international project, based in Canada, is exploring these issues and connections.[10] In time, it may be able to provide some answers to the questions posed here. But, in view of the trend and emphasis of recent research, its greatest challenge, which is the challenge of suburban research as a whole, will be to identify the element of unity within the obvious, and sometimes bewildering, diversity.

NOTES

1. The Web of Science online database is searchable from 1975. Reported figures are for variants of suburb, captured with use of a wildcard, thus 'suburb*'. The author acknowledges the assistance of Amy Skippen.

2. The logical analysis of possibilities offers a third approach that is not grounded in evidence.

3. The denominator for this estimate is the total number of articles ($n = 6,173$) for which a geographical identifier was given in the database. In an additional 1,190 articles, no locational reference was indicated. Based on a random test of 300 references, in 93.3 per cent of cases the regional identifier indicated that the United States was the sole or joint subject of the paper. In the remaining 6.7 per cent, the university base of the author appears to have been the point of reference. The equivalent ratio for East Asia, discussed elsewhere, was 90:10. I am not aware of an equivalent source that covers common languages other than English.

4. Or, strictly, twice forgotten. The fact was well appreciated in the 1920s (Douglass, 1925) and briefly rediscovered in the 1960s (Berger, 1960; Dobriner, 1963; Donaldson, 1969; Schnore, 1963) before being forgotten again.

5. Note that some journals, for example, the *Journal of Urban History*, are counted twice, in this case as 'urban' and 'history'.

6. Search terms were 'worker*', 'working class', 'immigrant*' and 'minorit*'. In both decades, there may be some double counting.

7. Sometimes, suburbs are discussed briefly but the subject is not perceived to be sufficiently important to warrant an index entry. For example, see Knox and McCarthy (2005, pp. 201, 204, 208, 211, 213, 220).

8. All estimates of increase in this paragraph are underestimates since they compare the decade of the 1980s with the nine-year period, 2001–2009.

9. In principle, the recent experience of urbanization in India may pose a similar challenge, but in practice not so, because it has received far less scholarly attention.

10. This project is concerned with global suburbanisms and involves researchers in many countries. Directed by Roger Keil, at York University, Canada, it is supported by a Major Collaborative Research Initiative grant from the Canadian Social Sciences and Humanities Research Council. A brief description may be found at http://www.yorku.ca/city/Projects/GlobalSuburbanism.html.

ACKNOWLEDGMENTS

The author would like to thank the Social Sciences and Humanities Research Council of Canada for financial support, and Amy Skippen for research assistance. The editors, together with Herbert Gans, Roger Keil, Robert Lewis, Terry McGee, Tony Orum and Nikhil Rao, made valuable comments on an earlier draft. Some of the seeds they planted may take time to bear fruit.

REFERENCES

Amato, P. W. (1970). Elitism and settlement patterns in the Latin American city. *Journal of the American Institute of Planners, 36,* 96–105.

Atkinson, R., & Blandy, S. (Eds). (2006). *Gated communities.* London: Routledge.

Badcock, B. (2002). *Making sense of cities.* London: Arnold.

Bagaeen, S., & Uduku, O. (Eds). (2010). *Social sustainability in contemporary and historical gated developments.* London: Earthscan.

Barker, P. (2009). *The freedom of suburbia.* London: Frances Lincoln.

Barrett, S. (1994). *Paradise. Class, commuters and ethnicity in rural Ontario.* Toronto: University of Toronto Press.

Baxandall, R., & Ewen, E. (2000). *Picture windows. How the suburbs happened.* New York: Basic Books.

Beall, J., & Fox, S. (2009). *Cities and development.* London: Routledge.

Benjamin, S., Bhuvaneswari, R., Rajan, P., & Manjunath. (2008). 'Fractured' terrain, spaces left over, or contested. A closer look at the IT-dominated territories in east and south Bangalore. In: D. Mahadevia (Ed.), *Inside the transforming urban Asia* (pp. 239–285). New Delhi: Concept Publishing.

Berger, B. (1960). *Working class suburb.* Berkeley, CA: University of California Press.

Bourne, L. S. (1996). Reinventing the suburbs. Old myths and new realities. *Progress in Planning, 46*(3), 163–184.

Brand, S. (1994). *How building learn: What happens after they are built.* Harmondsworth: Penguin.

Bray, D. (2005). *Social space and governance in urban China. The danwei system from origins to urban reform.* Stanford, CA: Stanford University Press.

Briggs, J., & Mwamfupe, D. (2000). Peri-urban development in an area of structural adjustment in Africa. The city of Dar-es-Salaam, Tanzania. *Urban Studies, 37*(4), 797–809.

Brook, R., & Dávila, J. (Eds). (2000). *The peri-urban interface. A tale of two cities.* Bangor: University of Wales.

Brookings Institution. (2010). *The state of metropolitan America.* Washington, DC: Brookings Institution.

Browder, J., Bohland, J., & Scarpacci, J. (1995). Patterns of development on the metropolitan fringe: Urban fringe expansion in Bangkok, Jakarta and Santiago. *Journal of the American Planning Association, 61*(3), 310–327.

Brown, E. (1992). War on waste and other urban ideals for Latin America. In: R. M. Morse & J. E. Hardoy (Eds), *Rethinking the Latin American city* (pp. 110–127). Washington, DC: Woodrow Wilson Center Press.

Bruegmann, R. (2005). *Sprawl. A compact history.* Chicago: University of Chicago Press.

Brunn, S., Hays-Mitchell, M., & Zeigler, D. (Eds). (2008). *Cities of the world. World regional urban development.* Lanham, MD: Rowman & Littlefield.

Caldeira, T. (1996). Fortified enclaves. The new urban segregation. *Public Culture, 8*(2), 303–328.

Caldeira, T. P. R. (2000). *City of walls. Crime, segregation and citizenship in Sao Paolo.* Berkeley, CA: University of California Press.

Chakraborty, S. C. (1991). Extended metropolitan areas. A key to understanding urban processes in India. In: N. Ginsberg, B. Koppel & T. McGee (Eds), *The extended metropolis. Settlement transition in Asia* (pp. 299–325). Honolulu: Hawaii University Press.

Clapson, M. (1998). *Invincible green suburbs, brave new towns. Social change and urban dispersal in postwar England.* Manchester: Manchester University Press.

Clapson, M. (2003). *Suburban century. Social change and urban growth in England and the U.S.A.* Oxford: Berg.

Clark, S. D. (1966). *The suburban society.* Toronto: University of Toronto Press.

Cohen, M., Ruble, B. A., Tulchin, J., & Garland, A. M. (Eds). (1996). *Preparing for the urban future. Global pressures and local forces.* Washington, DC: Woodrow Wilson Center Press.

Davis, M. (2006). *Planet of slums.* London: Verso.

de Soto, H. (1989). *The other path.* New York: Basic Books.

Dennis, E. (2008). Cairo between traces and liberal re-foundation. In: S. K. Jayyusi (Ed.), *The city in the Islamic world* (pp. 1085–1115). Leiden: Brill.

Dick, H. W., & Rimmer, P. J. (1998). Beyond the Third World city. The new urban geography of Southeast Asia. *Urban Studies, 35*(12), 2303–2321.

Dikeç, M. (2007). *Badlands of the republic. Space, politics and urban policy.* Cambridge: Blackwell.

Dobriner, W. H. (1963). *Class in suburbia.* Englewood Cliffs, NJ: Prentice Hall.

Donaldson, S. (1969). *The suburban myth.* New York: Columbia University Press.

Douglas, I. (2006). Peri-urban ecosystems and societies. Transitional zones and contrasting values. In: D. McGregor, D. Simon & D. Thompson (Eds), *The peri-urban interface. Approaches to sustainable natural and human resource use* (pp. 18–29). London: Earthscan.

Douglass, H. (1925). *The suburban trend.* New York: Century.

Drakakis-Smith, D. (2000). *Third World cities.* London: Routledge.

Duncan, J. S., & Duncan, N. G. (2003). *Landscapes of privilege. The politics of the aesthetic in an American suburb.* New York: Routledge.

Evenden, L. J. (1991). Fleetwood in Surrey. The making of a place. In: P. M. Koroscil (Ed.), *British Columbia. Geographical essays published in honour of A. MacPherson* (pp. 223–279). Burnaby, BC: Department of Geography, Simon Fraser University.

Farley, R. (1964). Suburban persistence. *American Sociological Review, 29,* 38–47.

Faure, A. (Ed.) (1991). *Les premiers banlieusards. Aux origines des banlieus de Paris (1860–1940).* Paris: Editions Créaphis.

Feng, J., & Zhou, Y. (2005). Suburbanisation and the changes of urban internal spatial structure in Hangzhou, China. *Urban Geography, 26*(2), 107–136.

Feng, J., Zhou, Y., & Wu, F. (2008). New trends of suburbanization in Beijing since 1990. From government-led to market-oriented. *Regional Studies, 42*(1), 83–99.

Fiedler, R., & Addie, J.-P. (2008). *Canadian cities on the edge. Reassessing the Canadian suburb.* Occasional Paper Series (Vol. 1, Issue 1). City Institute at York University, Downsview, Ontario, Canada.

Firey, W. (1947). *Land use in central Boston.* Cambridge, MA: Harvard University Press.

Fisher, B. (2008). *A poverty of rights. Citizenship and inequality in twentieth-century Rio de Janeiro*. Stanford, CA: Stanford University Press.

Fisher, T. (2003). Differentiation of growth processes in the peri-urban region. An Australian case study. *Urban Studies, 40*(3), 551–565.

Fishman, R. (1987). *Bourgeois utopias. The rise and fall of suburbia*. New York: Basic Books.

Fishman, R. (1990). America's new century. Megalopolis unbound. *Wilson Quarterly, 14*(1), 24–45.

Ford, L. (1996). A new and improved model of Latin American city structure. *Geographical Review, 86*(3), 437–440.

Fourcaut, A. (2000). *La banlieue en morceaux. La crise des lotissements défectueux en France dans l'entre-deux-guerres*. Paris: Créaphis.

Friedman, J. (2005). *China's urban transition*. Minneapolis, MN: University of Minnesota Press.

Gans, H. J. (1967). *The levittowners*. New York: Pantheon.

Gans, H. J. (1968). Urbanism and suburbanism as ways of life. A re-evaluation of definitions. In: H. J. Gans (Ed.), *People and plans. Essays on urban problems and solutions* (pp. 41–64). New York: Basic Books.

Gans, H. J. (2009). Some problems of and futures for urban sociology. Toward a sociology of settlements. *City and Community, 8*(3), 211–219.

Garreau, J. (1991). *Edge city. Life on the new frontier*. New York: Doubleday.

Ginsberg, N., Koppel, B., & McGee, T. (Eds). (1991). *The extended metropolis. Settlement transition in Asia*. Honolulu, HI: Hawaii University Press.

Glasze, G., Webster, C., & Frantz, K. (Eds). (2006). *Private cities. Global and local perspectives*. London: Routledge.

Goldstein, D. (2004). *The spectacular city. Violence and performance in urban Bolivia*. Durham, NC: Duke University Press.

Gough, K., & Yankson, P. (2006). Conflict and cooperation in environmental management in peri-urban Accra, Ghana. In: D. McGregor, D. Simon & D. Thompson (Eds), *The peri-urban interface. Approaches to sustainable natural and human resource use* (pp. 196–210). London: Earthscan.

Gugler, J. (Ed.) (1996). *The urban transformation in the developing world*. Oxford: Oxford University Press.

Gugler, J. (Ed.) (1997). *Cities in the developing world. Issues, theory, and policy*. Oxford: Oxford University Press.

Guldin, G. E. (1996). *Desakotas* and beyond. Urbanisation in southern China. *Ethnology, 35*(4), 265–283.

Hall, M., & Lee, B. (2010). How diverse are U.S. suburbs? *Urban Studies, 47*(1), 3–28.

Hanley, L. (2006). *Estates. An intimate history*. London: Granta.

Hanlon, B. (2010). *Once the American dream. Inner-ring suburbs of the United States*. Philadelphia: Temple University Press.

Harris, R. (1996). *Unplanned suburbs. Toronto's American tragedy, 1900–1950*. Baltimore: Johns Hopkins University Press.

Harris, R. (2004). *Creeping conformity. How Canada became suburban, 1900–1960*. Toronto: University of Toronto Press.

Harris, R., & Larkham, P. (Eds). (1999). *Changing suburbs. Foundation, form and function*. London: E & FN Spon.

Hayden, D. (2003). *Building suburbia. Green fields and urban growth, 1820–2000*. New York: Pantheon.

Hirt, S. A. (2007). Suburbanizing Sofia. Characteristics of post-socialist peri-urban change. *Urban Geography, 28*, 755–780.

Hirt, S. A. (2008). Stuck in the suburbs. Gendered perspectives on living at the edge of the post-communist city. *Cities, 25*, 340–354.

Huang, Y. (2005). From work-unit compound to gated communities. Housing inequality and residential segregation in transitional Beijing. In: L. J. C. Ma & F. Wu (Eds), *Restructuring the Chinese city. Changing society, economy and space* (pp. 192–221). London: Routledge.

Huchzermeyer, M. (2004). *Unlawful occupation. Informal settlements and urban policy in South Africa and Brazil.* Trenton, NJ: Africa World Press.

Hudahah, D., Winarso, H., & Woltjer, J. (2007). Peri-urbanisation in East Asia. *International Development and Planning Review, 29*(4), 503–519.

Jackson, K. T. (1985). *Crabgrass frontier. The suburbanisation of the United States.* New York: Oxford University Press.

Janoschka, M., & Borsdorf, A. (2006). Condominios fechados and barrios privados: The rise of private residential neighbourhoods in Latin America. In: G. Glasze, C. Webster & K. Frantz (Eds), *Private cities. Global and local perspectives* (pp. 92–108). London: Routledge.

Jürgens, U., & Landman, K. (2006). Gated communities in South Africa. In: G. Glasze, C. Webster & K. Frantz (Eds), *Private cities. Global and local perspectives* (pp. 109–126). London: Routledge.

Kabisch, N., Haase, D., & Haase, A. (2010). Evolving reurbanisation? Spatio-temporal dynamics as exemplified by the East German city of Leipzig. *Urban Studies, 47*(5), 967–990.

Kaplan, D., Wheeler, J., & Holloway, S. (2009). *Urban geography.* New York: Wiley.

Keil, R. (forthcoming). Suburbanization and global cities. In: B. Derudder, M. Hoyler, P. J. Taylor, & F. Witlox (Eds), *International handbook of globalization and world cities.* London: Edward Elgar.

Keil, R., & Young, D. (2009). Fringe explosions. Risk and vulnerability in Canada's new in-between urban landscape. *The Canadian Geographer, 53*(4), 488–499.

Khan, H.-U. (2008). Identity, globalisation, and the contemporary Islamic city. In: S. K. Jayyusi (Ed.), *The city in the Islamic world* (pp. 1036–1062). Leiden: Brill.

Knox, P. (2008). *Metroburbia, U.S.A..* Piscataway, NJ: Rutgers University Press.

Knox, P., & McCarthy, L. (2005). *Urbanization. An introduction to urban geography.* Upper Saddle River, NJ: Pearson.

Kotkin, J. (2010). *The next hundred million. America in 2050.* New York: Penguin.

Kruse, K. M., & Sugrue, T. J. (Eds). (2006). *The new suburban history.* Chicago: Chicago University Press.

Lang, R. E. (2003). *Edgeless cities. Exploring the elusive metropolis.* Washington, DC: Brookings Institution.

Larkham, P. (1999). Conservation and management in U.K. suburbs. In: R. Harris & P. Larkham (Eds), *Changing suburbs. Foundation, form and function* (pp. 239–268). London: E & FN Spon.

Lau, J. C. Y. (2010). The influence of suburbanization on the access to employment of workers in the new towns. A case study of Tin Shui Wai, Hong Kong. *Habitat International, 34*(1), 38–45.

Lentz, S. (2006). More gates, less community? Guarded housing in Russia. In: G. Glasze, C. Webster & K. Frantz (Eds), *Private cities. Global and local perspectives* (pp. 206–221). London: Routledge.

Leontidou, L. (1990). *The Mediterranean city in transition. Social change and urban development.* Cambridge: Cambridge University Press.

Leontidou, L., Afouxenides, A., Kourlioros, E., & Marmaras, E. (2007). Infrastructure related urban sprawl. Mega-events and hybrid peri-urban landscapes in southern Europe. In: C. Couch, L. Leontidou & G. Petschel-Held (Eds), *Urban sprawl in Europe. Landscapes, land-use change and policy* (pp. 71–101). Oxford: Blackwell.

Lewis, R. (2004). *Manufacturing suburbs. Building work and home on the metropolitan fringe.* Philadelphia: Temple University Press.

Leyden, K. (2003). Social capital and the built environment. The importance of walkable neighborhoods. *American Journal of Public Health, 93*(9), 1546–1551.

Li, W. (2009). *Ethnoburb. The new ethnic community in urban America.* Honolulu, HI: University of Hawaii Press.

Li, Z., & Wu, F. (2008). Tenure-based residential segregation in post-reform Chinese cities. A case study of Shanghai. *Transactions of the Institute of British Geographers, 33*, 404–419.

Lindstrom, M. J., & Bartling, H. (Eds). (2003). *Suburban sprawl. Culture, theory, politics.* Lanham, MD: Rowman & Littlefield.

Liu, G. C. S. (2007). Peri-urbanism in globalising China. A study of new urbanism in Dongguan. *Eurasian Geography and Economics, 47*(1), 28–53.

Losada, H., Martinez, J., Vieyra, J., Pealing, R., Zavala, R., & Cortés, J. (1998). Urban agriculture in the metropolitan zone of Mexico City. Changes over time in urban, suburban and peri-urban areas. *Environment and Urbanization, 10*(2), 37–54.

Lowder, S. (1986). *Inside Third World cities.* London: Croom Helm.

Lucy, W. H., & Phillips, D. L. (2006). *Tomorrow's cities, tomorrow's suburbs.* Chicago: Planners Press.

Ma, L. J. C., & Wu, F. (Eds). (2005). *Restructuring the Chinese city. Changing society, economy and space.* London: Routledge.

Macionis, J., & Parrilla, V. N. (2007). *Cities and urban life.* Upper Saddle River, NJ: Pearson.

Mangin, W. (1967). Latin American squatter settlements. A problem and a solution. *Latin American Research Review, 2*(3), 65–98.

Marshall, A. (2000). *How cities work. Suburbs, sprawl and the roads not taken.* Austin, TX: University of Texas Press.

Marshall, S. (2006). The emerging 'silicon savannah': From older urbanism to new suburbanism. *Built Environment, 32*, 267–280.

Masotti, L. H., & Walton, J. (1976). Comparative urban research. The logic of comparisons and the nature of urbanism. In: J. Walton & L. H. Masotti (Eds), *The city in comparative perspective. Cross-national research and new directions in theory* (pp. 1–16). New York: Halsted Press.

McGee, T. G. (1967). *The Southeast Asian city.* London: Bell.

McGee, T. G. (1971). *The urbanization process in the Third World. Explorations in search of a theory.* London: Bell & Hyman.

McGee, T. G. (1991). The emergence of desakota regions in Asia. Expanding a hypothesis. In: N. Ginsberg, B. Koppel & T. McGee (Eds), *The extended metropolis. Settlement transition in Asia* (pp. 3–26). Honolulu, HI: Hawaii University Press.

McGee, T. G., Lin, G. C. S., Marton, A., Wang, M. Y. L., & Wu, J. (2007). *China's urban space. Development under market socialism.* London: Routledge.

McGregor, D., Simon, D., & Thompson, D. (Eds). (2006). *The peri-urban interface. Approaches to sustainable natural and human resource use.* London: Earthscan.

McManus, R., & Ethington, P. (2007). Suburbs in transition. New approaches to suburban history. *Urban History, 34*(2), 317–337.

Michelson, W. H. (1976). *Man and his urban environment. A sociological approach.* Don Mills, Ontario: Addison-Wesley.

Mikelbank, B. A. (2004). A typology of U.S. suburban places. *Housing Policy Debate, 15*(4), 935–964.

Miller, Z. (2000). *Visions of place. The city, neighborhoods, suburbs, and Cincinnati's Clifton, 1850–2000.* Columbus, OH: Ohio State University Press.

Morris, A. S. (1978). Urban growth patterns in Latin America with illustrations from Caracas. *Urban Studies, 15,* 299–312.

Murray, M. J. (2008). *Taming the apartheid city. The spatial landscape of Johannesburg after apartheid.* Ithaca, NY: Cornell University Press.

Neuwirth, R. (2005). *Shadow cities. A billion squatters. A new world.* New York: Routledge.

Nicolaides, B. M. (2002). *My blue heaven. Life and politics in working-class suburbs of Los Angeles, 1920–1965.* Chicago: University of Chicago Press.

Nicolaides, B. M., & Wiese, A. (Eds). (2006). *The suburb reader.* New York: Routledge.

Nuissl, H., Rink, D., Couch, C., & Karecha, J. (2007). Decline and sprawl. Urban sprawl is not confined to expanding city regions. In: C. Couch, L. Leontidou & G. Petschel-Held (Eds), *Urban sprawl in Europe. Landscapes, land-use change and policy* (pp. 136–162). Oxford: Blackwell.

Orum, A. M. (1995). *City-building in America.* Boulder, CO: Westview.

Phelps, N. A., Parsons, N., Ballas, D., & Dowling, A. (2006). *Post-suburban Europe. Planning and politics at the margins of Europe's capital cities.* Basingstoke: Palgrave Macmillan.

Pichler-Milanovič, N., Gutry-Korycka, M., & Rink, D. (2007). Sprawl in the post-socialist city. The changing economic and institutional context of Central and Eastern European cities. In: C. Couch, L. Leontidou & G. Petschel-Held (Eds), *Urban sprawl in Europe. Landscapes, land-use change and policy* (pp. 103–135). Oxford: Blackwell.

Popenoe, D. (1977). *The suburban environment. Sweden and the United States.* Chicago: University of Chicago Press.

Popenoe, D. (1979). Urban sprawl. Some neglected sociological considerations. *Sociological and Social Research, 63,* 255–268.

Potter, R. B., & Lloyd, S. (1999). *The city in the developing world.* London: Longman.

Robinson, J. (2002). Global and world cities. A view from off the map. *International Journal of Urban and Regional Research, 26*(3), 531–554.

Robinson, J. (2005). *Ordinary cities. Between modernity and development.* London: Routledge.

Rogler, L. (1967). Slums neighborhoods in Latin America. *Journal of Inter-American Studies, 9,* 507–528.

Rome, A. W. (2001). *The bulldozer in the countryside. Suburban sprawl and the rise of American environmentalism.* Cambridge: Cambridge University Press.

Saunders, D. (2010). *Arrival city. The final migration and the next world.* New York: Knopf.

Savage, L., & Lapping, M. (2003). Sprawl and its discontents. The rural dimension. In: M. J. Lindstrom & H. Bartling (Eds), *Suburban sprawl. Culture, theory, politics* (pp. 5–18). Lanham, MD: Rowman & Littlefield.

Schnore, L. F. (1963). The socio-economic status of cities and suburbs. *American Sociological Review*, *28*, 76–85.

Scott, A. J., & Soja, E. (Eds). (1996). *The city: Los Angeles and urban theory at the end of the twentieth century*. Berkeley, CA: University of California Press.

Sieverts, T. (2003). *Cities without cities. An interpretation of the Zwischenstadt*. London: Routledge.

Simon, D. (1992). *Cities, capital and development. African cities in the world economy*. London: Belhaven.

Simon, D. (2008). Urban environments. Issues on the peri-urban fringe. *Annual Review of Environment and Resources*, *33*, 167–185.

Simon, D., McGregor, D., & Nsiah-Gyabaah, K. (2004). The changing rural–urban interface of African cities. Definitional issues and an application to Kumasi, Ghana. *Environment and Urbanisation*, *16*(2), 235–247.

Simone, A. M. (2010). *City life from Jakarta to Dakar. Movements at the crossroads*. London: Routledge.

Smart, A. (2006). *The Shek Kip Mei myth. Squatters, fires, and colonial rule in Hong Kong, 1950–1963*. Hong Kong: Hong Kong University Press.

Smart, A., & Tang, W.-S. (2005). Irregular trajectories. Illegal building in mainland China and Hong Kong. In: L. J. C. Ma & F. Wu (Eds), *Restructuring the Chinese city. Changing society, economy and space* (pp. 80–97). London: Routledge.

Soja, E. (2000). *Postmetropolis. Critical studies of cities and regions*. New York: Blackwell.

Sridhar, K. S. (2007). Density gradients and their determinants. Evidence from India. *Regional Science and Urban Economics*, *37*(3), 314–344.

Stanback, T. M. (1991). *The new suburbanization. Challenge to the central city*. Boulder, CO: Westview.

Stanilov, K., & Hirt, S. (2009). *Twenty years of transition. The evolution of urban planning in Eastern Europe and the former Soviet Union, 1989–2009*. Nairobi: UN Habitat.

Stanilov, K., & Scheer, B. C. (Eds). (2004). *Suburban form. An international perspective*. New York: Routledge.

Stilgoe, J. R. (1989). *Borderland. Origins of the American suburb, 1820–1939*. New Haven, CT: Yale University Press.

Strong-Boag, N., Dyck, I., England, K., & Johnson, L. (1999). What women's spaces? Women in Australian, British, Canadian, and U.S. suburbs. In: R. Harris & P. Larkham (Eds), *Changing suburbs. Foundation, form and function* (pp. 168–186). London: E & FN Spon.

Sudjic, D. (1992). *The hundred mile city*. New York: Harcourt Brace.

Tallman, I., & Morgner, R. (1970). Life-style differences among urban and suburban blue collar families. *Social Forces*, *48*, 334–348.

Teaford, J. (1979). *City and suburb. The political fragmentation of metropolitan America, 1850–1970*. Baltimore: Johns Hopkins University Press.

Teaford, J. (1997). *Post-suburbia. Government and politics in the edge cities*. Baltimore: Johns Hopkins University Press.

Teaford, J. (2008). *The American suburb. The basics*. New York: Routledge.

Thorns, D. C. (1972). *Suburbia*. St. Albans: Paladin.

Trefon, T. (2004). *Reinventing order in the Congo. How people respond to state failure in Kinshasa*. London: Zed Books.

Trefon, T. (2009). Hinges and fringes. Conceptualising the peri-urban in Central Africa. In: F. Locatelli & P. Nugent (Eds), *African cities. Competing claims on urban spaces* (pp. 15–35). Leiden: Brill.

Tsenkova, S., Potsiou, C., & Badina, A. (2009). *Self-made cities. Informal settlements in the UNECE region.* Geneva: United Nations Economic Commission for Europe.

Turner, J. F. C. (1969). Uncontrolled urban settlements. Problems and policies. In: G. Breese (Ed.), *The city in newly-developing countries* (pp. 507–534). New York: Prentice Hall.

Vachon, G., Luka, N., & Lacroix, D. (2004). Complexity and contradiction in the aging early postwar suburbs of Québec City. In: K. Stanilov & B. C. Scheer (Eds), *Suburban form. An international perspective* (pp. 38–60). New York: Routledge.

Vaughan, L., Griffiths, S., Haklay, M., & Jones, E. (2009). Do the suburbs exist? Discovering complexity and specificity in suburban built form. *Transactions of the Institute of British Geographers, 34,* 475–488.

Wang, F., & Zhou, Y. (1999). Modeling urban population densities in Beijing, 1982–1990. Suburbanisation and causes. *Urban Studies, 36,* 263–279.

Wang, Y.-P., Wang, Y., & Wu, J. (2009). Urbanisation and informal development in China. Urban villages in Shenzhen. *International Journal of Urban and Regional Research, 33*(4), 957–974.

Webster, C., & Glasze, G. (2006). Conclusion. Dynamic urban order and the rise of residential clubs. In: G. Glasze, C. Webster & K. Frantz (Eds), *Private cities. Global and local perspectives* (pp. 222–237). London: Routledge.

Webster, C., Wu, F., & Zhao, Y. (2006). China's modern gated cities. In: G. Glasze, C. Webster & K. Frantz (Eds), *Private cities. Global and local perspectives* (pp. 153–169). London: Routledge.

Webster, R. (Ed.) (2000). *Expanding suburbia. Reviewing suburban narratives.* New York: Berghahn.

Whitehand, J. W. R., & Carr, C. M. H. (2001). *Twentieth century suburbs. A morphological approach.* London: Routledge.

Whitzman, C. (2009). *Suburb, slum, urban village. Transformations in Toronto's Parkdale neighbourhood, 1875–2002.* Vancouver: UBC Press.

Wiese, A. (2003). *Places of their own. African-American suburbanization in the twentieth century.* Chicago: University of Chicago Press.

Wigle, J. (2010). Social relations, property and 'peripheral' informal settlement. The case of the Amplación San Marcos, Mexico City. *Urban Studies, 47*(2), 411–436.

Wilmott, P., & Young, M. (1960). *Family and class in a London suburb.* London: Routledge.

Wu, F. (2006). Rediscovering the 'gate' under market transition. From work-unit compounds to commodity housing enclaves. In: R. Atkinson & S. Blandy (Eds), *Gated communities* (pp. 47–66). London: Routledge.

Wu, F., Xu, J., & Yeh, A. G. O. (2007). *Urban development in post-reform China. State, market and space.* London: Routledge.

Wu, W. (2005). Migrant residential distribution and metropolitan spatial development in Shanghai. In: L. J. C. Ma & F. Wu (Eds), *Restructuring the Chinese city. Changing society, economy and space* (pp. 222–242). London: Routledge.

Wu, W. (2006). Migrant intra-urban residential mobility in urban China. *Housing Studies, 21*(5), 745–765.

Zhang, L. (2005). Migrant enclaves and impacts of redevelopment policy in Chinese cities. In: L. J. C. Ma & F. Wu (Eds), *Restructuring the Chinese city. Changing society, economy and space* (pp. 243–260). London: Routledge.

Zhou, Y., & Logan, J. R. (2008). Growth on the edge. In: J. R. Logan (Ed.), *Urban China in transition* (pp. 140–160). Oxford: Blackwell.

Zhou, Y., & Ma, J. C. (2000). Economic restructuring and suburbanisation in China. *Urban Geography, 21,* 205–236.

THE GLOBAL NORTH

GWINNETT GOES GLOBAL: THE CHANGING IMAGE OF AMERICAN SUBURBIA

William Grady Holt

INTRODUCTION

American suburbia changed drastically over the past century. Once home to wealthy white enclaves, suburbs opened to the masses after World War II through federal housing and infrastructure programs. A population shift from the American Rustbelt cities in the North and Midwest to the South and Southwest fueled the growth of new suburbs. The rise since the 1970s of global immigration from Central and South America as well as Asia helped diversify the country with the majority of this population relocating to suburbs rather than central cities. Located 20 miles outside Atlanta, GA, Gwinnett County provides an opportunity to examine how these trends have manifested. Using this county as a case study, this chapter describes how Gwinnett has evolved over three periods of growth. From its founding in the 1820s to the 1960s, the area was dominated by small towns and an agricultural-based economy separated by elites and locals. The development of infrastructure led to the New Suburban phase from the 1970s to 1990s. A national migration of rustbelters coupled with regionals from the rural South made Gwinnett an upscale, white, upper middle class Republican area. As Gwinnett became one of the country's fasted growing counties,

Suburbanization in Global Society
Research in Urban Sociology, Volume 10, 51–73
Copyright © 2010 by Emerald Group Publishing Limited
All rights of reproduction in any form reserved
ISSN: 1047-0042/doi:10.1108/S1047-0042(2010)0000010005

problems from urban sprawl appeared. In the third phase, Avoiding Slumburbia, Gwinnett wrestles with deteriorating older suburban corridors while adjusting to an influx of international migration. By 2009 Gwinnett became a majority minority county. This chapter looks at Gwinnett as a national example of a rapidly growing suburban area within a quickly expanding metropolitan area that is representative of current American suburbanization trends.

American suburbanization is characterized by a few key factors. First, these places see rapid, mostly unplanned, growth and are followed by almost immediate obsolescence as newer suburbs develop even further in the hinterlands. Second, these places create class, racial, and ethnic segregation not only between central cities and suburbs but also within suburban communities as they diversify. Finally, these places experience social and environmental problems arising from this urban sprawl (Gottdiener & Hutchinson, 2006).

While mass suburbanization began after World War II, its origins go back to the mid-19th century. Wealthy, white Protestant sylvan enclaves emerged as elites sought to escape the rapid industrialization and urbanization by waves of new immigrants to central cities. Influenced by the British Garden Town movement as well as from back to nature literature such as Thoreau's *Walden*, these new suburban enclaves offered escape from urban problems. By the 1850s places such as Cambridge and Summerville, Massachusetts, became suburbs of Boston (Warner, 1978). Outside New York City, small towns such as New Rochelle, Great Neck, and Montclair suburbanized in the late 1800s as industrial barons and the newly emerging white-collar executives class moved farther from the central city but still needed to be close enough for physical access to their offices. The establishment of commuter railroads made access easier as wealthy suburbs developed along rail lines such as Philadelphia's Main Line and Chicago's Gold Coast toward Evanston and Lake County. More professionals began to relocate to these areas as small towns became commuter suburbs. The mass production of the auto permitted people to move out to these suburbs, not reliant entirely on rail transport. By the 1920s, these tiny suburbs attracted not only residents but also upscale retailers such as downtown department stores looking to access these wealthy suburban markets (Frieden & Sagalyn, 1989). These images of suburbia set in the national psyche that the American Dream was based on social mobility that included suburban home ownership (Hayden, 1984; Jackson, 1985).

U.S. federal programs helped change the demographics of American suburbia. While started as post-Depression recovery programs under the

Hoover administration and expanded significantly by the Roosevelt administration, the federal government began a system of jumpstarting the economy by stimulating the housing sector. Prior to these reforms, home loans typically required 50% down payments with 5- to 10-year monthly payments culminating with balloon payments due at the last monthly installment. The 1930s reforms to the federal banking system created a new system of 5–10% down payments with 20- to 25-year loans amortized at the same monthly payments with no balloon payments. Post-World War II programs made suburban housing accessible to more Americans. In the 1940s the G.I. Bill provided low-interest loans, allowing honorably discharged veterans monthly home payments that were cheaper than rentals in the postwar housing crunch. Another component of the G.I. Bill offered veterans money to attend college, pushing more Americans into the upper middle class. The development of the U.S. Interstate Highway System in the 1950s permitted more people to commute from suburban homes to central cities (Jackson, 1985).

The post-World War II federal programs changed American suburbanization from wealthy WASP enclaves to mass-produced, subsidized housing for the middle classes. Levittown, New York, became the icon of this 1950s suburbanization. The opening of Long Island by rail and parkways to beaches provided easy access to these former potato fields. While Levittown became one of the first suburbs to include integration of various religious groups, it was still racially segregated (Gans, 1967). However, passage of 1960s federal civil rights legislation resulted in many African Americans and Latinos suburbanizing (Lacy, 2007).

As people moved to suburbs, retailers followed. Unlike the affluent stores and boutiques of the 1920s, the 1950s began the era of chain stores in strip shopping malls. K-Mart and later Wal-Mart began pulling shoppers from the small town main streets that now had to compete with national retailers on the fringes of their towns. As the suburbs gained in affluence, many strip malls as well as new developments used the regional indoor shopping mall format. These 1 million square feet or larger developments with their central courts and climate-controlled shopping became the new main streets of suburbia. By the 1970s the suburbs began to attract corporate headquarters relocating from central cities. IBM moved from Manhattan to suburban Westchester County, New York. Other relocations were to Sunbelt suburbs such as JCPenney's relocation from Manhattan to Plano, Texas, a suburb of Dallas–Fort Worth. These new edge cities anchored by regional shopping malls began to rival and surpass their central cities in numbers of corporate headquarters. They began to build entertainment venues as well as sports complexes to compete with the central cities (Garreau, 1991).

Another trend emerging since the 1940s is the population shift from the Frostbelt to the Sunbelt. This shift involves not only movement from central cities to suburbs but also migration from older northeastern and midwestern suburbs to suburbs in the southeast and southwest. Supported by federal programs, this trend has created major problems for rustbelt cities as well as their older inner-ring suburbs to revitalize, while at the same time, the new suburbs in the south and west are dealing with urban sprawl issues related to these migrants from environmental consequences to social issues.

Beginning with the postwar G.I. generation, Americans could move to a suburb to raise a family, seeing the house not as home but as an investment and the community as a prepackage lifestyle to consume. Federal programs enable couples to move into housing from G.I. Bill mortgages and commute to work on newly constructed highways while having services subsidized though federal and state grant programs. Thus, while they caused a suburban community to build infrastructure for their demands on schools, roads, libraries, parks, emergency services, and other municipally provided services, their tax contributions never covered the actual costs of their usage. Higher taxes and rising property values forced out locals who could not afford to keep family farms and sold for more subdivisions. Once their children have completed the town's school system, these suburbanites seek to downsize or relocate to areas with cheaper taxes (Brookings, 2000; Bullard, Johnson, & Torres, 2000). As these suburbanites retired to places such as Florida, Arizona, and the Carolinas, they placed new demands and costs on these former rural areas (Findlay, 1992).

By 1990 America was a majority suburban nation. Another demographic trend emerged, showing the growing number of international immigrants to the suburbs (Massey, 2008; Jones, 2008). Historically, immigrants arrived in "first-tier" ports of entry such as New York or San Francisco. These early immigrants from the 1840s to the 1920s came primarily from Europe. Changes to American immigration polices in the 1960s helped create a new wave of immigration primarily from Central and South America as well as Asia. While many of these new immigrants moved to traditional central city ports of entry, a new trend emerged. Once majority white suburbs such as Orange County, California, outside Los Angeles were becoming majority minority. Also, immigrants were moving into suburban areas of the American South that had never experienced the large-scale European immigrations of the 19th and early 20th centuries (Waters & Ueda, 2007). This new immigration to the American South took different forms. Some

Table 1. Total Population and Percentage Change by Decade,
1950–2009.

	Georgia		Metro Atlanta		Gwinnett County	
	Total	Change (%)	Total	Change (%)	Total	Total (%)
1950	3,444,578	10.3	726,989	64.4	32,320	11.1
1960	3,943,116	14.5	1,017,188	39.9	43,541	34.7
1970	4,589,575	16.4	1,390,164	36.7	72,349	66.2
1980	5,463,105	19.0	2,029,710	46.0	166,903	130.7
1990	6,478,216	18.6	2,833,511	39.6	352,910	111.4
2000	8,186,453	26.4	4,112,198	45.1	588,448	66.7
2009	9,829,211	20.1	5,475,213	33.1	800,080	36.0

Source: U.S. Census Bureau.

immigrants moved into older inner-ring suburbs, converting aging strip malls into centers catering to specific ethnic group's needs. Others were part of the "brain drain" in which highly educated immigrants remained in the United States after attending college. Other immigrants, typically pursuing manual labor and service employment, turned to these emerging suburbs for jobs in construction and retail (Bohon, 2006).

Gwinnett County, Georgia (located 20 miles outside Atlanta), provides a case study of the development of an American suburb dominated by private real estate interests touting growth by market forces without planning that is now dealing with the problems that emerged under this system. Table 1 shows how this region experienced significant population growth since the 1950s. Georgia's population grew from 3.4 million in 1950 to 9.8 million in 2009. Metro Atlanta's population grew from 726,898 to 5.4 million in 2009. The metropolitan Atlanta region expanded from its postwar boundaries within the City of Atlanta and adjacent Fulton and DeKalb Counties to encompass an area stretching about 150 miles square across the northern section of the state. Gwinnett County has been one of this region's centers of population growth. The county's population increased from 32,320 in 1950 to 800,080 in 2009. This region's growth is fueled by movements from central city to suburban, relocations from the Northeast and Midwest as well as international migrations.

While the American South has typically been seen in terms of a society divided by black and white populations, international migrations are changing this. Table A1 shows the racial composition of Georgia, metro Atlanta, and Gwinnett County from 1950 to 2000. In Georgia from 1950 to

1980, the state's population was primarily black or white. By the 1990s the state began to see significant growth in its other populations. Metro Atlanta and Gwinnett follow similar trends. In metro Atlanta, the population, neither black nor white, in 1950 was 235; by 2000 that number grew to 333,131, constituting 8.1% of the population. Gwinnett County was a majority white county from 1950 to 2000. In the 1990s the black as well as other populations began to outpace the growth of the white population. These population trends resulted in Gwinnett becoming a majority minority county in 2009.

Following American immigration trends, Georgia, metro Atlanta, and Gwinnett have seen significant increase in the Latino population since 1990. While Georgia's Latino population was 1% in 1980, it increased to 7.7% in 2008 from 61,000 to 729,604, with Mexicans making up about 65%. Again, similar trends occurred in metro Atlanta and Gwinnett. Although early Latino migrations to Georgia focused on rural areas such as the Hall County's poultry industry, Whitfield County's carpet mills, or Vidalia's onion fields, the majority of Latino growth is occurring in metro Atlanta with Gwinnett leading the way (Murphy, Blanchard, & Smith, 2000). According to the U.S. Census Bureau, Gwinnett's Latino population increased from 8,470 in 1990, representing 2% of the county's population, to 138,427 in 2008, accounting for 18% of the total population.

Asian immigration is increasing as well. Following a trend started in the 1980s when Asian immigrants began to relocate to Atlanta's older inner-ring, blue-collar suburbs such as Chamblee and Doraville, metro Atlanta's Asian population began to grow. This population spread northward into Gwinnett County. The location of Japanese and other Asian corporations brought in executives' families to the county. Gwinnett's Asian population increased 77% to 81,289 since 2000, making up 14% of the total population. Also, this population comes from a variety of countries including China, Vietnam, and Korea. Also, the U.S. Department of Homeland Security estimates that in 2009 Georgia's illegal immigrant population was 480,000.

This chapter's goal is to examine how Gwinnett illustrates these trends in American suburban development through three periods: small towns, new suburbia, and slumburbia. First, in the small town phase between 1940 and the 1960s, Gwinnett was dominated by rural towns. Federally sponsored development programs from the Franklin Roosevelt's New Deal in the 1930s to the Interstate Highway System and Army Corps of Engineers in the 1950s began to open up the region. During this period any growth was considered good for new job growth and community prosperity by local public and private leaders. Second, in the new suburbia phase between the 1970s and 1990s, Gwinnett became a growth magnet for corporate headquarters and relocations, placing intense strains on infrastructure from schools to roads to towns. As the majority white, middle-class migrants moved in from the declining American Midwest as well as rural South, local public and private leaders still promoted this suburban sprawl as a positive demonstration of the county's attractiveness. During the 1980s Gwinnett became one of America's fastest growing county with international corporations moving there. However, by the late 1990s, Gwinnett's population boom began to show major problems. Third, in the slumburbia phase, public and private leaders now see problems from gangs to deteriorating subdivisions to abandoned strip malls as the new growth passes beyond Gwinnett into adjoining exurban counties. As the county became a majority minority with large numbers of international immigrants – both legal and illegal – public and private leaders now question uncontrolled development patterns. The private and public leaders have returned to government to deal with these problems through Community Improvement Districts (CIDs) to reattract private investments with mixed-use developments. These projects include redevelopment of a 1980s super-regional mall with high-rise housing, building a minor league baseball stadium and hockey arena, and making old highway corridors pedestrian friendly with new urban villages. This case study serves as a broad example of American suburbanization.

SMALL TOWNS PHASE (1940s–1960s)

From the 1820s to the early 1960s, Gwinnett was a rural, agricultural-based county divided along race and class lines seen throughout the American South (Woodward, 1993). Created in 1818 as a buffer from the Cherokee and Creek nations, in 1821 civic leaders established Lawrenceville as the county's administrative seat. Like many small American towns, shops and services started springing up along the blocks immediately adjacent to the courthouse square. By the 1870s the county had rail service as these corridors linked Atlanta to other major cities. Other county towns such as Buford (1872), Duluth (1876), and Norcross (1870) as well as Lilburn (1910), Snellville (1923), and Dacula (1905) developed as railroad stops with these smaller towns growing linearly adjacent to the tracks (Flannigan, 1943).

Agriculture dominated the local economy. Since the Piedmont's red clay soil did not facilitate the large-scale cotton plantations, most of the farms were smaller, family farms (Tang, 1958). However, Gwinnett did have a few plantations that relied originally on slave labor and later on sharecroppers. Many of the farms used smaller numbers of slaves mixed with family workers. The American Civil War impacted Gwinnett that voted against succession. Although avoiding General Sherman's March to the Sea that burned Atlanta, Gwinnett's post-American Civil War economy was ruined. Reconstruction's end in the 1870s brought in Jim Crow laws, segregating blacks and whites in all public facilities (Ayers, 1992). Near the old plantations, former salves developed small communities, while African American neighborhoods emerged in the towns.

The county divided along class lines between the white elites and rural residents. The first elites emerged out of the county's early founding families. These formally educated elites established local schools and civic clubs while maintaining social and economic ties with Atlanta's elites. The rurals consisted primarily of Scot-Irish Protestant farmers who moved into the region from the Appalachian Mountains. The elites and rurals maintained separate socialization patterns as seen in their churches. Local drug store soda fountains and restaurants became the hubs of local news. By the 1940s chain five and dime stores opened shops on the Lawrenceville square. The emergence of high school sports and local company baseball teams entertained crowds. With rail and later bus service to Atlanta, elites as well as some rurals could easily get into the big city.

Just like other civic and business leaders, Gwinnett's elites became swept up in boosterism and federally subsidized development projects. Led by *Atlanta Journal* editor Henry Grady, the New South movement promoted industrial over agricultural development in the post-Civil War South (Allen, 1996; Ruthheiser, 1996; Stone, 1989, 2001). Gwinnett's elites followed Grady's ideas. Lawrenceville had cotton mills by the 1850s. However, the establishment in 1872 of the Bona Allen Tannery in Buford made this city America's largest producer of horse harnesses. Buford became a company town where rurals voted how Bona Allen Co. instructed and unionization was prevented. With the boll weevil wiping out many cotton crops in the 1920s, elites realized that the county needed to further diversify the local economy from agriculture.

By the 1930s with funding from Franklin Roosevelt's New Deal Programs, federal and state funds laid the groundwork for the county's future development. These early elites oversaw the development of U.S. Highways 29, 78, and 23, connecting Atlanta to Athens and Gainesville, respectively, through the county. For many of the rurals, Roosevelt's New Deal provided jobs through programs such as the Civilian Conservation Corps (CCC) and the infrastructure development as well as free and subsidized food products during the 1930s Depression. In the early 1940s the advent of World War II saw elites and rurals drafted into service around the world.

In the late 1940s Gwinnett remained much like it had in the previous century but that was about to change. The county experienced an economic downturn after World War II. Many returning veterans left for jobs and opportunities in Atlanta as well as other more distant places. The opening of a General Motors plant as well as other manufacturing companies in adjacent DeKalb County provided opportunities for rurals to live in Gwinnett but commute into Atlanta along the federal highways for union-scale wages. The G.I. Bill allowed both elites and rurals to attend colleges as well as provided low-interest, subsidized home mortgages. Short distances from the local towns on what were then the fringes, new homes were built following a hybridized pattern resembling something between expanded city street grids and subdivisions.

In the 1950s tensions emerged between the county and city governments. Gwinnett refused to establish public housing programs. However, Lawrenceville, through the U.S. urban renewal programs, constructed segregated housing as well as a public health center. Through a state-sponsored effort, Gwinnett voters chose to consolidate schools of the county and Lawrenceville public schools. Tensions arose when the Lawrenceville High School was to be renamed Central Gwinnett even after Dacula and Lilburn (the other two towns expected to consolidate) fought to keep their separate schools. The Lawrenceville City government spent extra municipal funds to build larger faculties than those initially planned by the county. However, it took a petition drive led by the original elites to force the name change.

Many suburbs took advantage of their central city growth coalitions. Following Atlanta's lead (Stone, 1989; Keating, 2001), Gwinnett civic and business leaders pursued new infrastructure programs to make the county more attractive for the forthcoming future development. In the 1940s state and Gwinnett elites led by then Atlanta Mayor William B. Hartsfield and the Georgia congressional delegation actively engaged the U.S. Army Corps of Engineers' plan to build a reservoir dam on the Chattahoochee River at the county's northern tip. Breaking ground in 1950 and dedicated in 1957, the $45 million Buford Dam created Lake Lanier. During the 1950s Gwinnett developed a countywide water system whose technical problems and political corruption led to a 1961 legalization of a beer tax to pay for the system. While Gwinnett had been a "dry" county, forbidding sale of any alcoholic beverages, the local growth machine led by the Chamber of Commerce pushed the change over the objections of local conservative churches.

Gwinnett government officials began to tap federal sources for the future growth they expected. These plans linked the Gwinnett Chamber of Commerce with agriculture officials at the state and county level, creating a new set of elites that would dominate county politics from the 1970s forward. By the late 1960s many of these former farm family locals would use these programs to develop their own land into subdivisions and retail developments. In 1954 the County Commission applied to the U.S. Department of Agriculture for flood-control dams. The county would win federal funds to complete six dams between 1965 and 1980. Ironically, in 1962 Gwinnett would be the only urban county to receive federal funding under the U.S. Agricultural Department's Resource Conservation and Development (RC&D) program to examine land resources and provide for future growth (Brack, 2008). Gwinnett capitalized on the development of I-85 that would connect Atlanta to the I-95 northeastern corridor by interstate highway. While the Atlanta portion of the interstate began in 1949, I-85's Gwinnett portion was not completed until 1967. A state spur interstate Georgia 316 would be built to connect Atlanta to Athens through Lawrenceville.

Like other former rural U.S. counties, Gwinnett became part of its adjacent central city metro area according to the U.S. Census Bureau in 1958. While the Georgia General Assembly established what became the Atlanta Regional Commission (ARC) in 1947 to create a regional master plan, Gwinnett was not added until 1960 but did not become an official voting member until 1971. Like other regional master plans, the ARC could be easily altered for new developments paving the way for Gwinnett's emergence as one of America's fastest growing counties in the 1970s.

NEW SUBURBIA PHASE (1970s–1990s)

American suburbs matured from bedroom communities to edge cities as seen in the Gwinnett case. From the 1970s to the 1990s, Gwinnett became a magnet for corporate, residential, and commercial growth. The county's population centers shifted from towns such as Lawrenceville and Buford to the unincorporated areas along the I-85 and U.S. 78 corridors. As the county's population exploded from 72,349 in 1970 to 352,910, this growth strained the local infrastructures. This growth created problems with roads, school, libraries, and recreation services. Also, as this rapid urban sprawl continued, environmental problems began to emerge.

Large corporate centers began to locate in Gwinnett. The 1950s and 1960s infrastructure programs for Lake Lanier, the water system, and the electric system coupled with the new I-85 made the county attractive to corporations. The southern part of I-85 closest to Atlanta initially developed as a warehouse and distribution center as the interstate opened. However, this changed in the late 1960s when Western Electric built at the I-85 Jimmy Carter Boulevard exit near Norcross. County leaders and the Chamber of Commerce lobbied Western Electric who considered locations at the next exit south in DeKalb County. However, civic and business leaders wanted this corporation in Gwinnett to help cover the tax burden of these new workers and their families.

Other office park developments emerged, attracting relocated as well as new corporations. Again, focusing on the unincorporated areas, Georgia Tech–affiliated real estate interests assembled land in the late 1960s in the far southwestern section of the county between Norcross and the DeKalb County line. Technology Park Atlanta, which grew slowly until the late 1970s, became home to the Hayes Microsystems, the country's first modem producers. These developers also added a residential component, naming this unincorporated area Peachtree Corners.

These corporate moves coupled with others to metro Atlanta meant a surge in population growth to Gwinnett. In this New Suburban era between the 1970s and 1990s, growth occurred primarily between migrations by·what can be called regionals and rustbelters. The regionals were native southerners who relocated to Gwinnett either through metro Atlanta white flight, intrastate from rural areas or interstate migrations from other nearby states. The rustbelters were part of a national trend of migration from the Rustbelt, the declining industrial areas stretching from western New York State to Chicago stretching through Pennsylvania, Ohio, Michigan, and Indiana. The rustbelters brought in the first wave of white ethnic Catholics to Gwinnett with the county's first church opening in 1970. Their large families strained the county's school and recreation services while their property taxes did not cover these expenses. Many of the rustbelters still identified with their hometown sports teams such as the National Football League's Pittsburgh Steelers or National Hockey League's Detroit Red Wings with little support to Atlanta's professional teams.

Primarily first-generation white collar, the regionals and the rustbelters saw Gwinnett as a way to social climb out of their blue-collar upbringings.

These swim and tennis club communities were seen as status symbols for this group. They moved to subdivisions in the unincorporated parts of Gwinnett such as Peachtree Corners near Norcross or the Five Forks area in the south central part of the county. They had little to no ties to the small towns. For example, the Five Forks area had a Lawrenceville zip code with a Snellville phone exchange while the new residents turned toward new schools and strip shopping centers near Lilburn to shop. These newcomers identified locally with their new high school districts. Since this growth required the Gwinnett County School to annually build new facilities, these newcomers were always looking for the next new schools egged on by real estate agents and developers.

Conflicts began to arise as the remaining older elites, tired of seeing most of the county's school taxes go into new districts, challenged these programs. Since the 1970s, real estate agents encouraged rustbelters and regionals away from the Central Gwinnett–Lawrenceville High School district, referring to its 10% black population as "urban." Since Central drew from both the elites and locals, it contained a wide class range of students from millionaires to executives to factory workers' households. During the late 1980s the subdivision sprawl along the Five Forks corridor meant a new elementary and middle school would open south of Lawrenceville, drawing city students with new subdivisions who attended the new Brookwood cluster. A subdivision civic association, horrified that children would be in school with renters and public housing residents, held private meetings with Gwinnett County Public School officials to prevent this. Instead, they proposed city students could be bused to the new school and then transferred by buses to attend yet another school further south near Snellville to avoid their children attending portable classrooms. Remnants of the old elites stopped this at formal hearings where rustbelters and regionals were embarrassed when old elites announced they were not too thrilled to have their homes relocated to a district dominated by vinyl-clad subdivisions with prefabricated fireplaces. These new white-collar rustbelters and regionals who considered themselves above the locals in Gwinnett never considered this scenario nor the fact that old elites mobilized their statewide networks including threatened legal action against the district.

For the newcomers, the subdivisions and schools were not the only ways to show their newly found upper middle class status as the American suburbs became the center of conservative politics. Like other regions of the American South, Georgia had been dominated politically by conservative Democrats since the American Civil War. Gwinnett had heavily supported

Franklin Roosevelt in part for the social and infrastructure programs directly benefiting the county. The 1960s Civil Rights era saw the southern Democrats split with the national party into the Dixiecrats who championed segregation. By the 1970s this Dixiecrat Party was forming the base of what would become the new national Republican Party (Grantham, 1994). In Gwinnett Democrats had dominated local elections until the 1980s. The influx of rustbelters, whose union blue-collar parents formed the 1980 beginnings of the Reagan Democrats, linked with the regionals, whose parents moved from Dixiecrats, along with locals who grew up under Roosevelt's New Deal subsidies but became upper middle class overnight from selling farms for developments and others from obtaining college degrees, formed this new conservative coalition. Ironically, these groups touted for less government and lower taxes while Gwinnett's entire new identity was based on government-funded infrastructure and these new-comers could not cover the costs of their demands on county services. One of the new Republican county commission's first major projects was a cross-county expressway, named the Ronald Reagan Parkway.

Gwinnett government officials who were tied directly to Chamber of Commerce representatives and developers created a house of cards that required more development to pay for existing development. So, as Gwinnett's growth moved from southwest to northeast during the 1970s to 1990s, the rustbelters and regionals fought property tax increases while pushing for school bond referendums. In 1985 a new Georgia law enabled counties to hold Special Purpose Local Option Sales Tax (SPLOST) referendums that must be for a specific purpose and not exceed five years. County officials tapped this new funding source, pushing these newcomer expenses off on sales rather than property taxes for roads, schools, libraries, and even a new county courthouse as well as a civic center.

The county's exponential growth attracted strip malls and chain stores since the 1970s; however, a regional shopping mall would not arrive until 1984. The opening of the Gwinnett Place Mall at the I-85 and Pleasant Hill Road exit marked a shift in the county. Prior to the malls' opening, Gwinnett was the largest county east of the Mississippi River that did not have a regional mall. With the new regional center came an explosion of outparcel developments from movie theaters to outlets to auto dealers in this area. By the late 1980s, Gwinnett Place drew shoppers two-hours away from Greenville and Anderson, South Carolina.

The small towns experienced changes. In Lawrenceville, the county government had leased most of the office space around the courthouse square. In 1988 when the new Gwinnett Justice and Administration Center (GJAC) opened a mile south of the square, the town's retail market collapsed. Beginning in the early 1970s with the Belk store leaving downtown for a new strip mall a mile away, Lawrenceville's downtown, the old hub of the small town shopping, began to deteriorate. As shopkeepers retired and more national discounters such as Wal-Mart and K-Mart arrived in the 1980s, the square continued to decline with pawn shops and used car dealers replacing storefronts. Fueled by the 1988 restoration of the old courthouse building into a museum and county historical society complex, Lawrenceville's civic and business leaders pursued a streetscape redevelopment of the town square. Following other main street redevelopment strategies, this first redevelopment created a Victorian downtown attractive to new shoppers but that was not historically accurate. Even the establishment of a downtown businesses authority to market the area could not starve off the fast past retail in the surrounding areas.

The new suburban era in Gwinnett saw a concentrated push away from the small towns into the I-85 corridor. Led by the Chamber of Commerce and developers, Gwinnett officials pushed this area as Gwinnett's downtown. Initially hoping to lure the new GJAC center out of Lawrenceville (state law prevented a courthouse being built outside the county seat's city limits), the development interests had used the new Gwinnett Place Mall as the catalyst for a convention center as well as county arts center located further north along I-85. They would expand the complex to include an indoor arena home to a minor league hockey as well as Arena League football teams that became a competitor with Atlanta for concert venues. Through the development of Sugarloaf Parkway, the county obtained donated land from the Eastern Airline's Pilots Pension Fund that was to be used for either government or nonprofit use. Needing more room, the Chamber of Commerce (who technically qualified as a 501(c) (6) nonprofit) was given a 20-year land lease for a new building and private club (Brack, 2008).

County planning officials who recommended tougher restrictions on development and more planning efforts were ignored or terminated. Any master planning was adjusted as needed by politicians. Gwinnett was soon to face new changes. Atlanta's hosting of the 1996 Summer Olympics that was the culmination of a century of the New South movement created the impetus for the third series of Gwinnett development that would focus on international migration and challenges from urbanization and decline.

AVOIDING SLUMBURBIA PHASE (2000 TO PRESENT)

By the 1990s American suburbs were changing as large numbers of new immigrants moved there instead of to central cities. This new growth created new challenges to American suburbs such as Gwinnett. The 1996 Atlanta Summer Olympics brought the region into the world stage, attracting large numbers of international immigrants to the county (Sjoquist, 2000). Since the late 1960s the white rustbelters and regionals had moved into Gwinnett. By the late 1990s black rustbelters and regionals began to follow them in large numbers, leaving their midwestern metros and rural southern towns. While the City of Atlanta had been seen as a Black Mecca for north to south relocations through the Atlanta University Center and the large number of black professionals, this was the first major movement of blacks to Atlanta's predominately white suburbs such as Gwinnett (Pomerantz, 1996). At the same time, many of the original 1970s white rustbelters and regionals were leaving for retirement either further into the northern part of the county and adjacent areas or to places outside the state. Some of these older subdivisions did not age well as pockets of severe developing world–level rural poverty appeared. The phenomenal growth of the past 40 years had a price including urban sprawl, rising crime levels, and international gang activities. Gwinnett was at another crossroads in which the county would have to combat the new problems that could turn this area into slumburbia.

The international migration to Gwinnett took numerous forms. The upper levels of what can be described as the globals contain two parts. First, when the Chamber of Commerce and business groups talked about internationalization, they refer typically to multinational corporations relocating headquarters and the executives that come with these companies. In 2009 Gwinnett was home to 355 of these foreign-owned firms representing 27 countries. Second, the "brain drain" of highly educated international students who come to Georgia for college and remain created another group of immigrants. These globals fit into the upper middle class images leaders projected about the county.

What Gwinnett's civic and business leaders did not expect was the another type of international migration. This group can be referred to as the laborers. As the Texas and Louisiana oil industry went bust in the 1980s, Latino, primarily Mexican but also Central American, male laborers began moving east in search of jobs. Metro Atlanta's booming housing market caught their attention (Odem, 2008). Historically, Georgia, a "right-to-work" anti-union state, had based its commercial growth on cheap labor. Gwinnett's contractors saw this primarily illegal population as a way to pay lower wages and avoid labor shortages as the county's housing boom continued into the 1990s. These laborers began to spread the word about jobs in Gwinnett. Soon the county's name was familiar to those on the Mexican border. These laborers first appeared living in older apartment complexes in Lawrenceville, Lilburn, and Norcross. These men slept six and eight in a bedroom, turning these old apartments into modern-day *Grapes of Wrath* tent cities. Living in the shadows of suburbia, this first wave saw little resentment except from displaced construction workers and contractors who refused to hire illegal labor but eventually had to either hire the illegals or fold due to their inability to compete with these lower wages.

This situation changed when the laborers, many of those who sent back money to families, began to send for these families. As their wives and children moved to the county, Gwinnett began to see pockets of severe rural developing world level poverty. While formal demographic studies from the Pew Hispanic Center and U.S. Census Bureau were showing a steady increase in Gwinnett's Latino population, Georgia State University demographers focusing on the county's pubic school populations indicated these official numbers were undercounting this highly mobile and sometimes illegal population.

Other immigrants arrived in Gwinnett due to local humanitarian relief efforts. As the centuries-old conflicts in the Balkans between Serbs and Bosnians erupted again in the 1990s, the United States agreed to take in Bosnian refugees who were fleeing ethnic cleansing under the Milosovich regime. Through local Christian-based nonprofits, Gwinnett became a center for this relocation effort. Overnight, Bosnian war refugees would be flown to Atlanta and resettled to older apartments in Gwinnett within a few days. In areas around Lawrenceville where the charity organization placed refugees that numbered about 3,000, numerous shops, cafes, and bars emerged near these apartment complexes. Interestingly, the signage usually indicated a "European" market or restaurant rather than Bosnian. This immigration brought new issues to Gwinnett. Problems with fights between Bosnians and Serbian refugees forced a local church to cancel their English language program. Also, this was the first significant Muslim migration to the county.

This religious diversity continued with the 2007 opening of the Hindu Mandir (temple) on U.S. 29 in Lilburn. As one of the largest temples in the United States, the complex, designed with lush gardens and fountains with stones from India, has attracted Indian immigrants to Lilburn, an epicenter of the 1970s–1990s rustbelt and regional relocations. Even the Protestant congregations are diversifying. At Lilburn, First Baptist Church services on

Sunday include services for Chinese, Vietnamese, Asian Indian, Hispanics, Koreans, and Arabs (Brack, 2008).

Gwinnett began to see multiple types of Asian immigration to the county. In the late 1970s along Buford Highway (U.S. 23) in DeKalb County, a corridor of Asian as well as Latino immigrants began to immerge. As the corridor grew along this area of older 1950s and 1960s strip malls and apartments, the immigrants moved into Gwinnett. Eventually, this corridor would expand along I-85 at Jimmy Carter Boulevard with a similar pattern of development as seen in DeKalb. Unlike ethnic enclaves, these corridors mixed groups even within the same strip malls where Chinese, Korean, and Vietnamese shops blended with Latino ones as well.

Gwinnett's fast-based growth brought with it environmental problems from urban sprawl. In 2009 the metro Atlanta average commute was 39.4 miles per day (Clean Air Campaign, 2010). Despite originally voting against MARTA, Atlanta's bus and subway system in the 1970s and 1980s, Gwinnett became part of the Georgia Regional Transportation System (GRTA) in the 1990s with a countywide bus service connecting to MARTA rail stations. Gwinnett's urban sprawl resulted in deforestation as well as the creation of a heat island. Between 1988 and 1998, NASA's land satellite indicated that metro Atlanta lost about 190,000 acres of tree cover. Tract subdivision replaced forests with dark roofs, impermeable road surfaces, and sod–turf lawns that reflect sunlight. This helped create a heat island in which temperatures are artificially higher, increasing carbon dioxide as well as other pollutants and accelerating the formation of smog and ozone due to increasing use of air conditioners (Creech & Brown, 2000). Presently, due to growth in places such as Gwinnett, Georgia is locked into a federal lawsuit with neighboring Alabama and Florida over Lake Lanier that is part of the Chattahoochee River system that eventually flows into Appalachicola Bay. Neighboring states argue that growth resulted in too much water outtake as well as pollution, including extra chlorination from water treatment that has hampered local fishing as well as species (Rankin, 2010).

Other quality of life problems emerged. Gwinnett's public schools had risen to be considered one of the best systems in the Southeast, drawing in many rustbelters and regionals over the past decades. This primarily white, upper middle class district became a sports powerhouse, producing numerous Olympic, professional, and NCAA Division I athletes with some programs nationally ranked by *Sports Illustrated.* Simultaneously, the Meadowcreek High School cluster along the I-85 corridor between Norcross and Lilburn showed emerging social problems from new severe international poverty. In the early 1990s the Gwinnett County Public Schools divided the district into clusters in which elementary schools combined to form middle school boundaries that then combined to form high school boundaries. These new clusters were designed to avoid the massive and often controversial annual school rezonings. While the school board initially used hard boundaries such as I-85 and U.S. highways, they began to gerrymander boundaries to keep apartments and older subdivisions that attracted lower income populations in one cluster while keeping newer subdivisions together. Meadowcreek and Parkview's clusters shared a common boundary. Looking at the Gwinnett County Public School's data from 2001, the Meadowcreek cluster was majority minority while the adjacent Parkview cluster was 72% white. By 2004 the Gwinnett County School became a majority minority district. On one hand, the district won the 2010 Broad Award for Urban Education as the county is one of the nation's largest school districts while whites move further northeast within the county. However, class more than race and ethnicity seems to a play a greater role in community stability. By 2009, this severe poverty could be seen in formal data on the schools. The U.S. Department of Education data on free lunch eligibility showed that schools with a high concentration of this laborer population had extremely large levels of students eligible for a free lunch. For example, Lilburn Middle, a feeder school for Meadowcreek, had a level of 88%, while Lawrenceville Elementary had a level of 85%. These schools are dealing with high school-age children who may be illiterate in their native language.

As Gwinnett's original rustbelters and regionals are retiring, the older subdivisions around Lilburn, Snellville, and Norcross are dealing with racial, ethnic, and class changes. Less desirable 1970s split levels and raised-ranch homes are being converted to rentals, creating absentee landlord problems. Older swim and tennis clubs are closing as new residents do not have the income or interests to maintain them. In Lawrenceville, the Western Heights section that developed in the 1950s declined significantly with the absentee landlord properties coupled with Bosnian and Mexicans who use these single-family homes illegally as multifamily dwellings, turning lawns into parking lots. Recently, City of Lawrenceville officials began to enforce restrictions on these illegal rentals. At the same time, the Cardinal Lake area of Duluth, near the Korean Community Presbyterian church, which relocated from DeKalb in 2002, continues to keep home values with the growing Asian middle class moving there.

Another problem facing Gwinnett has been the growth of serious crime. According to the FBI's Uniform Crime Statistics, the number of murders as well as the rapes and robberies has increased every year since 2000. While reports of nationally organized gangs such as the Crips and Bloods surfaced in the late 1980s, by 2010 Gwinnett was a center of international gang activity. The Mexican drug cartels blend into the growing Latino population. With the large number of rentals and apartments, they make detection problematic.

Considering larger national issues, Gwinnett has become a center of illegal immigration. Georgia is estimated to have about 500,000 illegal immigrants. While the 2008 economic slowdown slowed national growth, local service providers indicate that Gwinnett's illegal population stayed just doubling up in rentals and homes. Ironically, the initial strain on services by the rustbelters and regionals was not seen as a problem. However now that they are the county's majority, the regionals and rustbelters see the illegal immigrants who built their homes, clean their lawns, and staff their chain restaurants as a problem. In a split between civic and business leaders, the Gwinnett County Sheriff's Department received approval from the U.S. Department of Homeland Security to enforce the 287(g) program in which arrested persons found to be illegals are deported. In 2006 the State of Georgia passed sweeping immigration reform related to employment, law enforcement, emergency assistance, taxes, education, and health care (Bohon, 2006). These changes were passed over the opposition of the Gwinnett County Chamber of Commerce following its national leadership position.

As the Gwinnett's population growth shifted further northwest along the I-85 and Georgia 316 corridors, developers opened the Mall of Georgia in 1999. This super-regional indoor mall with its own lifestyle shopping center was themed with local references to the state in the new postmodern retail fashion. The following year Discover Mills, a regional-scale indoor outlet mall, opened two exits north of I-85 from Gwinnett Place, placing the older mall and its surrounding areas in severe decline.

In order to keep these older retail corridors from developing into slumburbia, county officials and developers organized three CIDs: (1) Gwinnett Place that includes the Gwinnett Place mall area, (2) Gwinnett Village encompassing I-85 along Jimmy Carter Boulevard, and (3) Evermore following the U.S. 78 corridor from the DeKalb County line toward Snellville. Created by the state legislature and needing approval of local businesses, these CIDs permit special tax districts with the funds used to pay for master redevelopment plans including streetscaping, traffic flow, and road changes, as well as marketing these new areas. The CIDs also focus on bringing in denser housing. Some of the most ambitious plans call for high-rise condominiums to be built in the Gwinnett Place Mall parking lots around a former Macy's store opening in 2010 as the country's first

Mega Mart, a Korean retailer. The Gwinnett Village CID focuses on redevelopment of the former Western Electric plant that operates with a reduced footprint for dense retail and housing.

The post-2008 credit crunch and economic downturn of the national economy impacted Gwinnett. While the county's civic and business officials pushed the I-85 corridor as Gwinnett's New Downtown since the 1980s, the opening of the Mall of Georgia prompted officials to lobby for a new minor league professional baseball stadium that brought the Atlanta Braves' AAA franchise to Gwinnett from Richmond, Virginia.

A split emerged between the development interests of the county's Republican leadership and its homeowners over rising property taxes for projects such as this stadium. Also, the county revenue shortfalls on sales taxes made officials consider cutting or closing services. Again, county officials focused on the new developments while planning to cut services in older towns. For example, in 2009 the Gwinnett County Library Board planned to close the Dacula Library Branch while opening a new branch at Hamilton Mill serving recent development subdivisions. In the 1980s Dacula residents supported the county's initial library referendum, understanding future construction would be next. They would have to wait almost 20 years as new branches were opened at Collins Hill and Five Forks to serve developers and new residents.

As Gwinnett continued to be fully developed, there was resurgence in the small towns that dominated the county until the 1960s. Numerous towns launched downtown redevelopments. However, financed by developers who made their money on sprawl, Lawrenceville's Courthouse Square became the most advanced project. Using town funds, the city brought in a professional theater company to a former church. Using this as an anchor, a private development group who had bought up most of the town's properties around the square began to seek high-end restaurants and retailers. The developers began construction of luxury condominiums in the area. In Suwanee, city leaders built entirely new city hall complex and downtown retail festival center creating a new city center. The developers cited residents' desires to have walkable places that gave them a sense of place that they saw as lacking in the county.

CONCLUSIONS

American suburbs have undergone dramatic changes since the 1940s. The post-World War II bedroom communities became major retail and commercial centers. These once white-only areas are currently some of the country's most ethnically and racially diverse areas, fueled by international migration to suburbia. By 1990 America was a majority suburban nation. The population shifts from the Rustbelt to the Sunbelt changed American politics as Democratic central cities of the Northeast and Midwest that dominated until the 1960s were replaced by conservative Republican suburban areas of the South and West. American urban sprawl strained natural resources as well. Also, America's suburbs began to deal with social problems such as crime and poverty as well as revitalization of former areas. Gwinnett County is at the forefront of these trends. This county faces many challenges that other American suburbs are addressing. As America became a majority suburban nation, these suburbs and their issues impact the entire nation.

REFERENCES

Allen, F. (1996). *Atlanta rising: The invention of an international city*. Atlanta, GA: Longstreet.

Ayers, E. L. (1992). *The promise of the New South: Life after reconstruction*. New York: Oxford.

Bohon, S. (2006). Georgia's response to new immigration. In: G. Anrig & T. A. Wang (Eds), *Immigration's new frontiers: Experiences from emerging gateway states*. New York: Century Foundation.

Brack, E. (2008). *Gwinnett: A little above Atlanta*. Norcross, GA: Gwinnett Forum.

Brookings Institution Center on Urban and Metropolitan Policy. (2000). *Moving beyond sprawl: The challenge for metropolitan Atlanta*. Washington, DC: Brookings.

Bullard, R., Johnson, G. S., & Torres, A. (Eds). (2000). *Sprawl city: Race, politics, and planning in Atlanta*. Washington, DC: Island Press.

Clean Air Campaign. (2010). Available at http://www.cleanaircampaign.com. Accessed on July 31, 2010.

Creech, D., & Brown, N. (2000). Energy use and the environment. In: R. Bullard (Ed.), *Sprawl city: Race, politics, and planning in Atlanta*. Washington, DC: Island Press.

Findlay, J. M. (1992). *Magic lands: Western cityscapes and American culture after 1940*. Berkeley, CA: University of California Press.

Flannigan, J. C. (1943). *The history of Gwinnett County, Georgia, 1818–1943*. Hapeville, GA: Taylor & Co.

Frieden, B., & Sagalyn, L. (1989). *Downtown, Inc.: How America rebuilds cities*. Cambridge, MA: MIT Press.

Gans, H. (1967). *The Levittowners: Ways of life and politics in a new suburban community*. New York: Pantheon.

Garreau, J. (1991). *Edge city: Life on the new frontier*. New York: Doubleday.

Gottdiener, M., & Hutchinson, R. (2006). *The new urban sociology* (3rd ed.). Boulder, CO: Westview.

Grantham, D. W. (1994). *The south in modern America: A region at odds*. New York: Harper Collins.

Hayden, D. (1984). *Redesigning the American dream: The future of housing, work, and family life*. New York: W.W. Norton.

Jackson, K. (1985). *Crabgrass frontier: The suburbanization of the United States*. Oxford: Oxford University Press.

Jones, R. C. (Ed.) (2008). *Immigrants outside megalopolis: Ethnic transformation in the heartland*. Lanham, MD: Lexington.

Keating, L. (2001). *Atlanta: Race, class and urban expansion*. Philadelphia: Temple University Press.

Lacy, K. (2007). *Blue chip black: Race, class, and status in the new black middle class*. Berkeley, CA: University of California Press.

Massey, D. (Ed.) (2008). *New faces in new places: The changing geography of American immigration*. New York: Russell Sage.

Murphy, A. D., Blanchard, C., & Hill, J. A. (2000). *Latino workers in the contemporary South*. Athens, GA: University of Georgia Press.

Odem, M. E. (2008). Unsettled in the suburbs: Latino immigration and ethnic diversity in metro Atlanta. In: A. Singer, S. W. Hardwick & C. Brettell (Eds), *Twenty-first century gateways: Immigration incorporation in suburban America*. Washington, DC: Brookings Institute.

Pomerantz, G. M. (1996). *Where Peachtree meets Sweet Auburn: The saga of two families and the making of Atlanta*. New York: Penguin.

Rankin, B. (2010). Georgia loses another ruling in tri-state water case. *Atlanta Journal Constitution*. Available at http://www.ajc.com. Accessed on July 21, 2010.

Ruthheiser, C. (1996). *Imagineering Atlanta: The politics of place in the city of dreams*. London: Verso.

Sjoquist, D. L. (2000). *The Atlanta paradox*. New York: Russell Sage.

Stone, C. (1989). *Regime politics: Governing Atlanta, 1946–1988*. Lawrence, KS: University of Kansas Press.

Stone, C. (2001). The Atlanta experience re-examined: The link between the urban agenda and regime change. *International Journal of Urban and Regional Research, 25*, 20–34.

Tang, A. (1958). *Economic development in the southern Piedmont, 1860–1950: Its impact on agriculture*. Chapel Hill, NC: University of North Carolina Press.

Warner, S. B. (1978). *Streetcar suburbs: The process of growth in Boston (1870–1900)* (2nd ed.). Cambridge, MA: Harvard University Press.

Waters, M., & Ueda, R. (2007). *The new Americans: A guide to immigration since 1965*. Cambridge, MA: Harvard University Press.

Woodward, C. V. (1993). *The burden of southern history* (3rd ed.). Baton Rouge, LA: Louisiana State University Press.

APPENDIX

Table A1. Total Population and Percentage by Race, 1950–2000.

		Georgia		Metro Atlanta		Gwinnett County	
		Total	Percent	Total	Percent	Total	Percent
1950	Black	1,062,762	30.85	165,115	24.60	3,044	9.42
	White	2,380,577	69.11	505,765	75.36	29,268	90.56
	Other	1,239	0.04	235	0.04	8	0.02
	Total	3,444,578	100.00	671,115	100.00	32,320	100.00
1960	Black	1,122,596	28.47	231,474	22.76	3,502	8.04
	White	2,817,223	71.45	785,019	77.18	40,035	91.95
	Other	3,297	0.08	695	0.07	4	0.01
	Total	3,943,116	100.00	1,017,188	100.00	43,541	100.00
1970	Black	1,190,779	25.95	310,632	22.34	3,896	5.39
	White	3,391,242	73.89	1,076,143	77.41	68,547	94.74
	Other	11,280	0.25	3,389	0.24	106	0.15
	Total	4,589,575	100.00	1,390,164	100.00	72,349	100.00
1980	Black	1,465,181	26.82	498,826	24.58	4,094	2.45
	White	3,947,135	72.25	1,508,640	74.33	161,903	97.00
	Other	50,789	0.93	22,244	1.10	906	0.54
	Total	5,463,105	100.00	2,029,710	100.00	166,903	100.00
1990	Black	1,746,565	26.96	736,153	25.98	18,175	5.15
	White	4,600,148	71.01	2,020,017	71.29	320,971	90.95
	Other	131,503	2.03	77,341	2.73	13,764	3.90
	Total	6,478,216	100.00	2,833,511	100.00	352,910	100.00
2000	Black	2,349,542	28.70	1,189,179	28.92	78,224	13.29
	White	5,327,281	65.07	2,589,888	62.98	427,883	72.71
	Other	509,630	6.23	333,131	8.10	82,341	13.99
	Total	8,186,453	100.00	4,112,198	100.00	588,448	100.00

FROM MILL TOWNS TO "BURBS OF THE BURGH": SUBURBAN STRATEGIES IN THE POSTINDUSTRIAL METROPOLIS

Allen Dieterich-Ward

INTRODUCTION

Governor Robert F. Casey made his first state visit to Homestead, Pennsylvania the day after his inauguration in January 1987 to announce a package of plans for restoring economic vitality to metropolitan Pittsburgh in the wake of steel's collapse. Earlier urban renewal had involved large-scale demolition of older downtowns for conversion to commercial and industrial use, but state and local officials now emphasized a two-pronged redevelopment approach largely modeled on the success of the postwar suburbs. The closure of the Monongahela River (Mon) Valley's mammoth steel mills opened large swaths of land and prompted calls for planned riverfront manufacturing and retail districts similar to those sites sprouting up at suburban interchanges. A second and related effort involved schemes to build new highways tying aging communities in the river valleys to both Pittsburgh and new suburban growth areas, such as the sprawling "edge city" of Monroeville less than 10 miles away. Indeed, Casey had a special project in mind for revitalizing the iconic Homestead – construction

Suburbanization in Global Society
Research in Urban Sociology, Volume 10, 75–105
Copyright © 2010 by Emerald Group Publishing Limited
All rights of reproduction in any form reserved
ISSN: 1047-0042/doi:10.1108/S1047-0042(2010)0000010006

of the long-delayed Mon/Fayette Expressway that would parallel the river south of Pittsburgh. "This is another big step [to] help bring businesses and jobs into the region," the governor later declared. "No longer is this valley a forgotten valley" (as cited in Basescu, 1989, p. 1).

The attempt to reinvent deindustrializing communities in metropolitan Pittsburgh as "Burbs of the Burgh" was part of a broader transition whereby working class residents of former mill towns throughout North America and Europe tried to find places for themselves within a new economic and spatial order (Dieterich-Ward & Needham, 2009; Dieterich-Ward, 2010). For Homestead, as with other communities seeking to transcend their roots as industrial satellites, the goal was not merely to build new highway links to the metropolitan core or attract potential employers to new suburban-style industrial parks, but to symbolically and materially recreate themselves in the image of their more affluent neighbors. Indeed, because of the particular pattern of growth in metropolitan Pittsburgh, the Mon Valley's declining communities along the river were often "separated only by several hundred feet of elevation and a narrow band of trees" from areas of booming growth in suburban ridge top communities such as Monroeville (Southwestern Pennsylvania Regional Planning Commission, 1968, p. 5). While "the unemployed [did] not live far from jobs," however, education levels, employment background, and employer perceptions separated manufacturing workers from jobs in expanding sectors (Bangs & Soltis, 1989, p. 12).

The postindustrial "suburbanization" of the Mon Valley serves as a window into competing visions of metropolitan space as well as conflicting interests of suburban, urban, and rural communities. In 1997, for example, a real estate developer began remaking the former site of U.S. Steel's Homestead Works into an upscale shopping center catering to the region's middle-class consumers. The project angered many former mill workers who sought more than low-wage service jobs, preservationists who sought the property for inclusion in a new national park, and local business owners who criticized developers for ignoring the existing downtown. The Mon/ Fayette Expressway also generated intense debate. Development officials declared that the "future of this Valley and of the entire area is reliant upon this vital highway," but some residents of existing suburbs as well as former mill towns in the path of the route denounced the project's negative effects on their own quality of life (Watson, 1990). "We have worked long and hard to develop our area," declared a resident from a nearby hilltop community. "Commuting in the Mon Valley is not reason enough to RUIN the lives in this borough" (Dearfield, 1988).

Homestead's trajectory since the 1970s demonstrates that communities adopting suburban strategies in order to move "beyond the ruins" of deindustrialization exhibited the type of local agency often overlooked in the standard urban declension narrative (Cowie & Heathcott, 2003). At the same time, former mill towns, mining camps, and industrial satellites faced enormous spatial inequalities that limited their ability to prosper within a postindustrial economy. In the end, the cultural, social, and material fabrication of the region by industrial capital during the early twentieth century created an integrated framework based on heavy industrial production that resisted change even as residents faced a series of economic and environmental problems rooted in the very fabric of community life. Understanding this dynamic is essential for deciphering cultural debates about the nature of suburban life, challenging oversimplified definitions of what it means to be "suburban," and uncovering the diversity of suburban populations and experiences at the turn of the twenty-first century.

MILL TOWNS, MINING CAMPS, AND SATELLITE CITIES

Even as they have critiqued urban scholars for narratives that too often stop at municipal boundaries, the new suburban history has been slow to acknowledge the complexities of metropolitan development in places like Pittsburgh, which by 1920 was the nation's most decentralized region (Kruse & Sugrue, 2006). Despite the myths of a homogenous suburban culture, the North American suburbs have always contained a smattering of population types. Further, suburbia has never been simply a demographic phenomenon, but instead resides at the intersection between space and idea. Indeed, this question of what is "suburban" has proven to be at least as contentious as the debate over the relative merits of the suburban form as various historians, geographers, and sociologists have attempted to provide a definition (Clapson, 2003, pp. 2–5).

Beginning in the early 1980s, historians began to systematically detail the physical, social, and political development of postwar suburbia, with a particular emphasis on the rise of automobile use enabled by an explosion in federal highway spending (Jackson, 1985; Fishman, 1987). Observing that the middle-class bias of the first generation of suburban historians in the 1980s blinded them to the multifaceted development of suburban space, more recent studies of the United States and Canada by Andrew

Wiese, Robert Lewis, and Becky Nicolaides point toward a more complex landscape, which also included industrial, working class, and African-American communities (Nicolaides, 2002; Wiese, 2004; Lewis, 2004). In England, American-style suburban development in communities such as Milton Keynes in North Buckinghamshire has also generated increased interest among scholars (Clapson, 2004). Comparisons can also be made between and among the postindustrial redevelopment of "brownfield" communities, such as those in metropolitan Pittsburgh, with those in other North American and European contexts (Greenstein & Sungu-Eryilmaz, 2004; Wagner, Joder, Mumphrey, Akundi, & Artibise, 2005) (Fig. 1).

As in many other cities in Europe and North America, between the 1880s and the 1920s, metropolitan Pittsburgh's urban centers, manufacturing suburbs, and mine camps experienced a massive influx of new residents drawn to the economic opportunities of the industrial metropolis. The rise

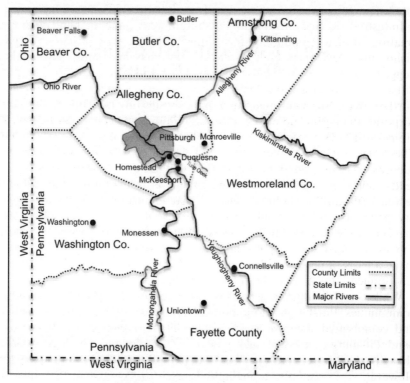

Fig. 1.   Metropolitan Pittsburgh.

of metropolitan Pittsburgh as an industrial powerhouse owed as much to the evolution of new forms of management and the conceptualization of new human–nature relationships as it did to either its location or its material resources. Entrepreneurs such as Andrew Carnegie, Ernest Weir, and Henry Frick pioneered the development of the industrial corporation, creating an interconnected system of mammoth steel mills, coking plants, and mines extending from the heavily industrialized river valleys to the mining camps of the region's mountainous interior (Muller, 2004). At the heart of this new regional culture and economy was a coal–steel–railroad nexus that linked enormous vertically integrated corporations, such as Carnegie Steel, with the region's natural resources and communities. Pittsburgh alone had 6 major trunk lines, 16 industrial and switching railroads, 15 inclines, and dozens of streetcar and feeder lines that honeycombed throughout its area (Muller & Tarr, 2003). In 1910, sociologist Paul U. Kellogg observed that these new industrial networks "bind here a district of vast natural resources into one organic whole" (as cited in Tarr, 1996, p. 172).

Industrial decentralization in Pittsburgh went hand in hand with the creation of new community forms that belie an easy urban–suburban dichotomy. Developers built dozens of enormous mills and factories that hugged the narrow flatlands up the Mon and Allegheny rivers from Pittsburgh and down the Ohio Valley through southeastern Ohio and northern West Virginia. In addition to the expansion of existing settlements, corporate managers laid out entirely new mill-oriented communities, such as Homestead (1881), Monessen (1896), and Weirton, West Virginia (1909). These sites had much in common with later automobile-oriented commuter suburbs including good transportation connections to Pittsburgh and a ready supply of cheap, flat land along the riverfronts. Greenfield sites also served a cultural and political function that sounds familiar to contemporary ears. "Cities," Weirton founder Ernest T. Weir declared, "if not breeders, were certainly magnifiers of discontent among workers. We were convinced that the principles and process on which we operated ... would make a basis of peace and harmony possible if we could establish our own environment" (as cited in Javersak, 1999, pp. 74–75).

While corresponding in general to the sequence of city building in other communities, Pittsburgh had important differences that affected the timing and complicated the process of metropolitan development. On the one hand, Pittsburgh's massive early industrialization produced a range of social changes that were embedded in the natural and built infrastructure. However, the region's topography presented a host of formidable challenges that raised costs, hindered institution building, and constrained

development. Celebrated landscape architect and planner Frederick Law
Olmsted, Jr. observed that "no city of equal size in American or perhaps the
world, is compelled to adapt its growth to such difficult conditions of high
ridges, deep valleys and precipitous slopes as Pittsburgh" (Olmsted, 1910,
p. 93). By the end of the nineteenth century, new forms of industrial
production coupled with the broken terrain of rivers and mountains created
a settlement pattern that was both heavily concentrated and spatially
dispersed as factories and communities spread out like ribbons following the
rivers and mineral deposits. Consequently, despite several annexation
campaigns, metropolitan Pittsburgh remained the most decentralized of the
nation's major metropolitan regions.

Kinship networks, bolstered by employment policies designed to splinter
class unity along ethnic lines, encouraged the formation of small tightly knit
communities. Combined with the dispersed industrial development pattern
and the region's mountainous landscape, this settlement pattern resulted in
the formation of hundreds of separate political jurisdictions extending from
tiny crossroads communities of less than a hundred residents to single-
industry mill towns such as Homestead and Weirton to the booming cities of
Pittsburgh and McKeesport (Glass, 2007). In the region's industrialized
river valleys, corporations rather than local governments provided
municipal services from water to trash collection to the hanging of
Christmas decorations. In return weak civic administrations were expected
to keep taxes low and serve the needs of industry (Fones-Wolf & Fones-
Wolf, 2003; Serrin, 1993).

The borough of Homestead, just up the Mon from Pittsburgh, provides
an important example of this process. Following the construction of the
Homestead Works in 1881, the community expanded along the flat land and
lower reaches of the river escarpment within walking distance of the steel
mill. The steel industry's dramatic expansion prompted a flood of new
immigrants to the lowland area surrounding the mill, known as "the Ward."
As select ethnic groups capitalized on increased opportunities at the
workplace, those who could afford to move abandoned the cramped, dirty,
and ethnically diverse Ward for the cleaner, roomier, and more homogenous
hilltops. At the same time, an expanding network of streetcars and later
roads opened more areas for development. In contrast to the dynamic
growth of the Ward, these newer hilltop communities in Homestead as well
as its smaller neighbors, West Homestead and Munhall, reflected more
centralized decision-making. Indeed, the original boundaries of Munhall,
incorporated in 1901, corresponded to Carnegie Land Company holdings
and U.S. Steel (formed after the purchase of Carnegie Steel by J. Pierpont

Morgan in 1901) subsequently invested heavily in public works and housing for management in the new community as well as the upper reaches of Homestead itself (Modell & Brodsky, 1998).

Despite social and physical features considered undesirable by Homestead's more affluent population, over time the Ward evolved into a thriving urban community with distinct Slovak, Hungarian, Polish, Lithuanian, and African-American neighborhoods. A dozen churches from Roman Catholic to Baptist catered to residents' spiritual needs, while numerous saloons, theaters, coffee houses, social clubs, and gymnasiums provided space for socializing and entertainment. While U.S. Steel planned for the creation of hilltop communities for management and skilled workers, the working class African-American and immigrant neighborhoods of the Ward eventually made way for a wartime expansion of the Homestead Works. Between June 1941 and June 1943, a consortium of U.S. Steel managers, local developers, and officials of the federal Defense Plant Corporation purchased and demolished the homes of more than 1,500 families, nearly half of Homestead's prewar population, as well as 12 churches, 5 schools, 2 convents and dozens of small businesses, groceries, restaurants, and saloons (Miner & Roberts, 1989). Most of those displaced were expected to find homes in new federal defense housing projects scattered throughout the region. By end of World War II, nothing remained of the Ward outside of the steel mills of the expanded Homestead Works, which was separated from the downtown business district by several active railroad lines (Wall Street Journal, 1941; Bailey, 1990).

Taken together, the cultural, social, and physical landscapes of the region created an integrated framework that resisted change even as residents faced a series of economic and environmental problems rooted in the very fabric of community life. Even by the beginning of the twentieth century metropolitan Pittsburgh's landscapes of production and consumption had created a host of environmental problems, extending from acid mine drainage and surface scarring to the concrete banked and sewage-filled rivers to the smoke-belching furnaces that kept many of the region's communities engulfed in a perpetual twilight (Muller & Tarr, 2003). Despite these environmental problems, the social and political structures of the region impeded collective action to remediate problems. Indeed, despite reaching an industrial peak in the early 1920s, as the Homestead example suggests the role of heavy industrial corporations in the region's economic and political life actually grew between the wars. However, the focus of the region's political and economic decision-makers had already begun to shift to a new type of automobile-oriented suburb on the hilltops overlooking the older industrial satellites in the crowded and polluted river valleys. As the postwar period progressed, it would be this new suburban form that increasingly supplanted the declining river valleys as the apparent key to revitalizing the region's economy and attracting new middle-class residents.

AN "EDGE CITY" IN A DECLINING REGION

Pittsburgh's suburbanization followed national trends during the postwar period, but the region's topography, political systems, and economic structures continued to shape the process of metropolitan development. Transportation improvements played an especially important role in the growth of new hilltop communities due to the mountainous topography. A progrowth public–private partnership that formed in the mid-1940s between the elite-dominated Allegheny Conference on Community Development and the local Democratic political leadership provided a means to marshal the enormous political and economic resources necessary to build highways through the region's rugged, densely populated terrain (Lubove, 1996; Mershon, 2000). As part of the city's celebrated postwar urban redevelopment program known as the "Pittsburgh Renaissance," boosters presented a vision of the region centered on an urban core functioning as a corporate headquarters, regional shopping area, and center for government and specialized services. Highways formed an integral part of this vision, knitting the region together and providing quick movement from the downtown business district, dubbed the "Golden Triangle" to a new airport under construction west of the city as well as east to the Pennsylvania Turnpike (Richards, 1945).

Unlike European cities recovering from the ravages of World War II, revitalizing residential areas was not a priority for the architects of the Pittsburgh Renaissance during the 1940s and 1950s. As a consequence, the transformation of the downtown area from mixed-use neighborhoods to a landscape dominated by high-rise offices hastened the migration of other urban functions, especially housing, to the periphery (ACTION-Housing, Inc., 1968). Indeed, civic and business leaders in southwestern Pennsylvania encouraged this demographic shift as a way to relieve postwar housing shortages, to make the region more attractive to white-collar employees, and to clear "blighted areas" for commercial and industrial uses. "It is generally recognized," conference leaders concluded, "that in Allegheny County there is enough land to furnish every family with the space needed for a decent living [and] live within easy commuting distance of the heart of the city" (Allegheny Conference on Community Development, 1944).

In contrast to metropolitan regions where suburbanization took place in a more or less concentric pattern that extended out from a central urbanized core as transportation systems improved, metropolitan Pittsburgh evolved more erratically from a series of urbanized corridors stretching along three major river systems. The mountainous landscape of the area was not generally well suited to the type of mass produced housing made famous by the contemporary development of Levittown in eastern Pennsylvania. "Although the greatest densities are to be found in the City of Pittsburgh, the broken terrain of the Region intersperses barriers to the continuities of block patterns and land development," reported the influential *Economic Study of the Pittsburgh Region* in 1963 (Lowry, 1963, p. 148). As a result, postwar commuter suburbs developed in clusters, generally on the ridge tops and in flatter areas to the north of the city, filling in the space between the earlier communities that spread along the river valleys.

Excellent access to the region's developing highway system as well as ample amounts of available and relatively flat land facilitated the postwar development of the suburban community of Monroeville, 10 miles east of Pittsburgh on a ridge overlooking the Mon Valley. Through the early part of the twentieth century, the area that became Monroeville looked much like the rest of the region's rural periphery. Primarily agricultural, the town's first real growth came from a coal boom during World War I that left much of the area scarred from surface mining. The origins of Monroeville's transformation from rural hinterland to suburban dynamo began in 1924 with the paving of the William Penn Highway (U.S. Route 22) between the community and Pittsburgh. "It was countryside in 1924," recalled local businessman W. H. 'Hook' Warner. "But the highway was paved. The automobiles began coming in. ... They started to develop farms and put in streets and dig cellars" (as cited in Foley, 1980). This prewar boom dramatically expanded during the 1950s and 1960s with the completion of the Monroeville Interchange of the Pennsylvania Turnpike (1950) and the Penn-Lincoln Parkway East (1954), which effectively refashioned the community into Pittsburgh's eastern gateway.

Regional boosters affiliated with the Allegheny Conference saw in the development of commuter suburbs such as Monroeville an opportunity to attract and retain the white-collar workers necessary to maintain Pittsburgh's status as a center for corporate headquarters. Indeed, Monroeville's population skyrocketed from 3,100 to more than 30,000 between the early 1950s and the mid-1970s. Consequently, much of the early focus within Monroeville as in other nearby communities was on planning for orderly residential expansion. In comparison to the central planning seen in English communities such as Milton Keynes, American suburbanization took place in a much more haphazard fashion with most decisions left in the hands of private companies (Clapson, 2004). In 1954, for example, home developer Sampson-Miller Associates set about creating "Garden City," a 500-acre, 1,500 home residential area on Monroeville's western edge. Allegheny Conference director Park Martin described Garden City as "the first planned and integrated unit of this size that I know of in the country. It's a big step forward and such construction as this will go far in solving our suburban problems" (as cited in Foley, 1980).

Monroeville's location and rapid population growth also enabled the community to capitalize on the postwar decentralization of urban services. Through the mid-1950s Monroeville residents along with those in nearby areas commuted to more established communities for shopping, personal services, and other consumptive activities. This changed with the purchase of a large parcel of property along U.S. Route 22 by real estate developer Don Casto, a pioneer in shopping mall construction. "This Monroeville Community will be one of America's great decentralized drive-in shopping centers," Casto predicted. On November 1, 1954, the 10 million dollar "Miracle Mile" shopping center opened with a carnival-like atmosphere featuring prizes, fireworks, and "Suicide Pete," an Evil Kneival precursor whose act included crashing through a tunnel of fire on his motorcycle (as cited in Foley, 1980).

When completed, the Miracle Mile was one of the largest suburban shopping centers between New York and Chicago and helped transform Monroeville from a commuter suburb to a regional destination. "You can't imagine what it was like then," recalled Dorothy Larson of nearby Penn Hills. "We had shopped in small towns ... [The Miracle Mile] had everything under the sun, like a bake shop, things we weren't used to having" (as cited in Foley, 1980). Monroeville's ability to provide services and levels of employment associated with urban centers rapidly grew during the 1970s and 1980s as the community added numerous hotels, restaurants, and, in 1969, an even larger regional shopping center only a short distance from the Miracle Mile. The new Monroeville Mall was so vast at 1.3 million square feet and featured such a variety of consumer goods that developers joked they could reside there in an emergency; comments that reportedly inspired movie director George Romero to use the mall as a setting for his 1978 zombie classic *Dawn of the Dead* (Dudiak, 2004).

Monroeville's expansion beyond the role of commuter suburb was due in part to the unintended consequences of the highway programs of the Pittsburgh Renaissance. The leaders of the Renaissance during the 1950s and 1960s emphasized the commercial redevelopment of the regional core, with much less attention paid to more peripheral development. During the early 1950s, Allegheny Conference executive committee member and retail czar Edgar J. Kaufmann reaffirmed his commitment to downtown shopping by undertaking a $9 million expansion while rejecting overtures from suburban developers already beginning work on the Miracle Mile. "It's logical for Pittsburgh to be a downtown center," declared I. D. Wolf, Kaufmann's Department Stores general manager in 1952. "The growth of suburban centers in other cities has been because there has been no redevelopment of the city such as we have here" (as cited in Beachler, 1952). Despite efforts to improve downtown parking, traffic, infrastructure, and the city's image, by 1961 there were six shopping areas within a two-mile radius in the North Hills and the East Hills Shopping Center on Pittsburgh's eastern end as well as the Miracle Mile and five smaller developments in nearby Penn Township (Guide-Post Research, 1961).

The development of Monroeville as a manufacturing and employment center followed a similar trajectory to its growth as a residential and retail center. Through the mid-1950s the industrial development efforts of Pittsburgh's progrowth coalition focused on creating additional space for existing industries in the river valleys. In Pittsburgh, the Urban Redevelopment Authority (URA) cleared two sites for J&L Steel, and the federal Model Cities program subsidized an expansion of Westinghouse in Turtle Creek during the late 1960s. These expansions were limited to existing large industrial employers; however, local officials grew increasingly concerned with the lack of space suitable for new manufacturing facilities. Developers wanted "a modern, attractive building all on one floor" located on a "flat parcel of land of at least ten acres on 'a main highway' with plenty of light and clean surroundings" explained one report in 1946. The author concluded, "we have almost no well-developed plant sites that would be of interest to the manufacturer of consumer goods" (Hollinshead, 1946) (Fig. 2).

In response, the Pittsburgh URA and the Allegheny Conference set out to apply the same combination of private and public resources used in downtown revitalization to stimulate new manufacturing by developing a planned industrial district with ready-made sites, physical infrastructure, utility hookups, and other incentives within the city. At first, officials focused on the neighborhood of Manchester, located on the city's North Side across from the Golden Triangle (Weber, 1988). Manchester was situated on a flat

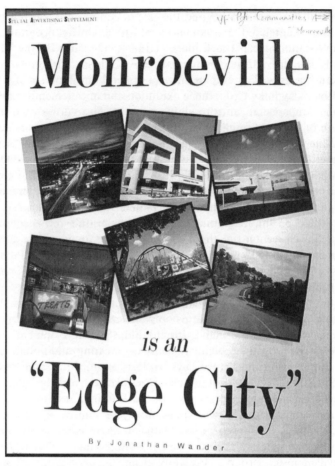

Fig. 2.   Cover of a Special Advertising Supplement in *Pittsburgh* Magazine, August 1998. Courtesy of *Pittsburgh* Magazine. Photographs Courtesy of CPS Photography. All Rights Reserved.

river plain, featured good transportation connections, already had light industries, and would meet the criteria for a "blighted" area necessary for condemnation and clearance through eminent domain. However, as in older urban areas throughout the region, redeveloping Manchester as an industrial district faced the formidable obstacles of high land costs and the need to relocate thousands of residents (Pittsburgh Regional Planning Association (PRPA), 1954). Consequently, as early as 1951 Allegheny Conference executive director Park Martin expressed doubt at the feasibility of the project and suggested that civic leaders would instead have to turn to suburban locations for planned industrial parks (Martin, 1951).

Monroeville in particular represented a choice location for light manufacturing as well as employment in research and development due to its rapid highway links to downtown administrative offices and universities, suburban atmosphere, and modern image. "The virtually unanimous preference of postwar research centers for suburban locations is striking," reported the *Economic Study of the Pittsburgh Region* in 1963. "Since they are competitors with academic institutions for professional personnel, they believe that a research center with a campus atmosphere helps their recruitment programs [and] serves as symbols of progressive management which will impress the company's customers and the general public" (Lowry, 1963, p. 98). Beginning with Westinghouse's construction of an atomic research center in the late 1930s, this focus on research and development continued with the consolidation of U.S. Steel's research facilities in Monroeville in 1953–1954. Over the next few decades, numerous corporations, such as PPG Industries, Chemical R&D, Aristech Chemical, and Cutler Hammer all established facilities in Monroeville, which also hosted more than 30 environmental companies and a supercomputing center operated by the National Science Foundation (Wander, 1998).

By the early 1990s, then, highway construction combined with a relatively flat topography had transformed the sleepy hamlet of Monroeville into one of metropolitan Pittsburgh's most important residential, retail, and employment hubs second in annual sales only to the Golden Triangle and with a convention center, the 150,000 square foot Monroeville Expo Mart that rivaled downtown Pittsburgh's David Lawrence Conference Center. Borrowing from urban scholar Joel Garreau's work on suburban development, Monroeville boosters proudly began advertising their community as an "Edge City," a suburban location that functioned much the same as a traditional urban area (Garreau, 1991). Its status as an edge city, one promotional pamphlet pointed out, "is one of a select handful in the nation ... and that makes it golden to a wide variety of businesses and to a large and very satisfied group of people who call Monroeville home" (Wander, 1998).

CONNECTING THE VALLEYS

While Monroeville and other commuter suburbs attracted new residents from both inside and outside the region, the Pittsburgh metropolitan region as a whole began to lose population during the 1960s due to decreasing employment in the area's steel mills and coal mines. In addition, intraregional demographic shifts resulted in declining core and peripheral areas separated by an expanding middle ground of suburban growth. Beginning in the 1950s federal and state-sponsored urban redevelopment programs focused on slum clearance sought to replace decaying downtowns with expanded industrial land, subsidized housing and hospital projects, and more modern business districts. However, regional employment and population loss as well as the national trend toward increasing suburban growth limited the success of these redevelopment efforts. By 1966, metropolitan Pittsburgh's older industrial satellites were "losing many of their traditional economic functions and in the process of assuming the new role of social welfare agencies catering to the needs of the Region's poor, ill-educated, unemployed, aged and generally disadvantaged" (Pennsylvania State Planning Board, 1966, p. 62).

The mill town of Monessen, 30 miles south of Pittsburgh in the Mon Valley, provides an excellent example of the limits of urban redevelopment in the region. Incorporated in 1898, the community hosted a number of major steel facilities including U.S. Steel's Monessen Works, Wheeling-Pittsburgh Steel's Rod and Wire Mills, and the American Chain and Cable Plant (Magda, 1985). The city's energetic mayor, Hugo Parentes, spear-headed a major attempt to restructure the economy and revitalize the cramped and aging downtown beginning in the early 1950s. The city's master plan adopted in 1957 called for redevelopment projects on the east and west entrances. "Eastgate," completed during the mid-1960s, resulted in the clearing of "blighted" areas and the construction of a combined community and health center, while the Westgate project, begun in the mid-1960s, was to be the most extensive urban renewal program ever planned for the Mon Valley (Redevelopment Authority of the City of Monessen, 1968).

Parentes' goal with Westgate was to eliminate one of the worst slums in the Mon Valley; more than three-fourths of the structures in the 55-acre project area were old, obsolete, or poorly maintained, while several had only dirt floors and no indoor plumbing. The project intended to rebuild the community with good housing, parks, and playgrounds, along with improving the western entrance into the city. However, while a large part of the demolition of substandard housing occurred in the area, local officials were unable to cope with the size of the area to be developed and the extra costs resulting from Monessen's rough topography. The initiative eventually bogged down in the early 1970s, leaving vacant lots along with unoccupied structures. The failure of Westgate and Monessen's redevelopment efforts in general raised the difficult question of whether the obsolete infrastructure in many of the region's aging and declining industrial towns could be modernized, and if so, who would provide the massive amount of capital required (Magda, 1985). As with similar programs in other small industrial satellites, local initiatives were simply not sufficient to overcome economic problems of a regional nature.

The continued decline of many older areas caused community leaders and residents in metropolitan Pittsburgh to rethink their approach to urban redevelopment, with an increased emphasis on building highways to connect decaying mill towns to hilltop suburban growth areas such as Monroeville. The use of highways as a structural solution to regional development problems in the Pittsburgh region dated back at least to the enactment of the Appalachian Regional Development Act in 1965 (Gauthier, 1973; Widner, 1990). Beginning in the mid-1960s, local politicians and residents put forth proposals for a system of three highways connecting the declining Allegheny, Beaver, and Monongahela River Valleys with the region's growing suburban areas. With the decline of river and rail transportation, local officials increasingly saw highways as the key to economic development in many parts of the region. "The provision of adequate transportation routes is one of the most difficult and expensive problems facing the [Mon Valley]," declared a 1961 planning report. If "communities are to remain good places to live and work during the next twenty years there must be adequate provision for the efficient and economic movement of people and goods to, from, within and through the District" (Pittsburgh Regional Planning Association, 1961, p. 17).

Regional politics, geography, and settlement patterns determined the success of various highway construction proposals in southwestern Pennsylvania. The first of the proposed routes paralleling the region's major river valleys to be completed was the Allegheny Valley Expressway, which extended northeast from Pittsburgh roughly paralleling the Allegheny River. Driven by declining population levels due to failing farms and mines, county commissioners and other local leaders in rural Armstrong County began pushing in the early 1950s for a four-lane highway to connect with the Pennsylvania Turnpike (Interstate 76) northwest of Monroeville (Claypoole, 1955). These efforts coincided with a push by the Allegheny Conference to improve the route between Pittsburgh's North Side and the turnpike (Allegheny Conference on Community Development, 1956). This political pressure as well as the route's relatively flat terrain and lower population density paid important dividends with work beginning in the mid-1960s. By the mid-1990s, completion of the expressway had resulted in the opening of "Northpointe," a 925-acre mixed-use industrial campus located at a formerly rural highway interchange. "We're in a paradigm of change," declared one official. "We're into new age manufacturing. We need to create jobs for the 24- and 25-year olds. If we had sat on our duffs and not built the [industrial] parks, then where would we be?" (as cited in Elliott, 2004) (Fig. 3).

In contrast to the Allegheny Valley Expressway, political infighting among other factors delayed any meaningful movement on highway construction in the Mon Valley through the end of the 1970s. Between 1981 and 1987 alone, the number of people employed in the steel industry in the Mon Valley declined from over 35,000 to fewer than 4,000. The growth of nonmanufacturing sectors had only a "marginal impact" in alleviating the plight of residents in the industrialized river valleys, resulting in massive out-migration that left "behind a more dependent, elderly, and difficult to employ population" (Bangs & Singh, 1988, p. 98). Local officials, state agencies, and community residents alike cast about desperately for solutions to this staggering social dislocation, but the lack of suitable commercial sites and decent highway access hampered efforts to attract new industries. Despite the "relentless ... efforts" of local leaders, the "long, hard battle to get the Mon [/Fayette] Expressway off the drawing board and into the construction stage" resulted in few results through the mid-1980s (Watson, 1990). Consequently, Governor Robert Casey's announcement in March 1987 that he would commit $40 million to resume construction on the highway was greeted with a great deal of enthusiasm. "I have made a commitment ... to revitalize the Mon Valley," the governor declared. "Rather than wait for another study ... I have decided to proceed with a portion of the long-planned expressway ... to improve this area's access to other major commercial routes." "This is excellent news," Washington commissioner Frank R. Mascara responded upon hearing the announcement. "I think the Governor recognizes that the long-term solution for developing the Mon Valley is good highways" (as cited in Kitsko, 2010).

By the 1980s the overall goal of highway construction in metropolitan Pittsburgh had changed from an essentially urban program – improve access *to* the downtown Golden Triangle – to a more suburban-oriented model of providing transportation *through* the crowded river valleys. In the eyes of proponents, this would also allow for the creation of riverfront industrial/commercial parks on the site of former steel mills patterned on the self-contained campuses that were already in evidence at many highway interchanges throughout the region. Indeed, one potential route for the Mon/Fayette Expressway took this suburban vision so far as to bypass

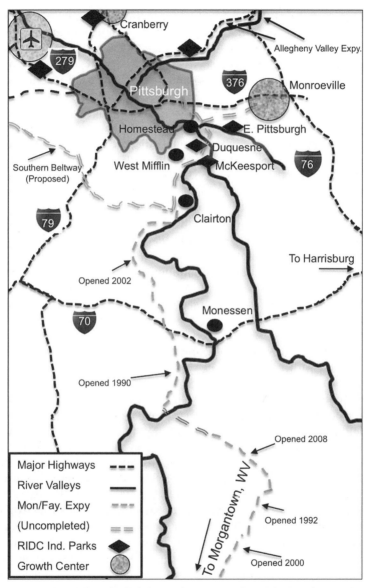

Fig. 3. Major Highways in Metropolitan Pittsburgh.

Pittsburgh entirely and instead had its northern terminus at the Pennsylvania Turnpike in Monroeville. "We stand on the threshold of economic recovery and growth," declared one group of local businessmen. We need a "highway that is a thru-way that links to other highways – highways that are easily accessible – highways that become the catalyst for transforming this area [and allow us] to finally discard the burdensome image of being a depressed and abandoned aftermath" (Greater Uniontown Area Chamber of Commerce and Greater Uniontown Industrial Fund, 1990).

With the support of the Casey Administration, the Mon/Fayette Expressway achieved some success during the early 1990s as several segments of the highway were completed between Interstate 70 and the West Virginia border. Despite the increased resources brought to bear on the project, however, the more difficult section north to Pittsburgh along the Monongahela River remained uncompleted through the end of the decade. In part this failure was due to the enormous expense and logistical difficulty of building a highway through such a densely developed and mountainous area. However, the plan itself also generated considerable opposition from suburban residents in the path of the proposed route as well as those who questioned the wisdom of more highway construction in general. "As senior citizens and thirty-five year residents of West Mifflin, we ... are too old to be uprooted and relocated in the guise of progress," complained Sarah and Norman Wiese (Weise & Weise, 1988). "This expressway will disrupt our lives, jobs and property," echoed a petition to state officials signed by more than a dozen residents. "It will not benefit anyone [and] will DIVIDE our community in half and destroy those along its path" (Dearfield, 1988) (Fig. 4).

While officials first proposed the riverfront expressways to aid the region's declining urban-industrial communities, by the early 1990s the use of highway construction as an economic development tool increasingly raised concerns among some residents about suburban sprawl, while others questioned the benefits that the Mon/Fayette Expressway would actually bring to river communities. During the late 1980s, even in the midst of industrial collapse, Pittsburgh Mayor Richard Caliguiri opposed extending the route through the city. "Over the years, the city has given up a number of neighborhoods to highway links serving suburban and regional areas. Unfortunately, these neighborhoods are never replaced or enhanced by the projects," Caliguiri explained in October 1987 (as cited in Tessitor, 1994). Similarly in 1994, environmental activist David Tessitor accused highway proponents "cloaked under 'regionalism,'" of providing an opportunity "for developers and land speculators to reap a bonanza from their land consumption while the region suffers the problems of sprawl" (Tessitor,

Fig. 4. Governor Robert P. Casey (Center Left) Opening the First Section of the Mon/Fayette Expressway. Photo Courtesy of the Pennsylvania Turnpike Commission.

1994). This debate over the suburban strategy of highway construction in deindustrialized communities carried over into other plans for redeveloping the enormous idled mill sites that dominated downtown areas, a convoluted process that holds important lessons for riverfront redevelopment efforts in similar communities throughout North America and Europe.

REINVENTING THE RIVERFRONTS

The debate over state and local plans for highway construction to support economic development in the Mon Valley revealed important and complicated fault lines resulting from postwar shifts in the economy and to hilltop suburbs. Indeed, many steelworkers and their families themselves had long since taken advantage of high industrial wages to move away from older communities to newer developments where they joined white-collar workers from the region's burgeoning health care and technology sectors (Tarr & Di Pasquale, 1982). This movement of middle-class residents away from Pittsburgh's industrial satellites created a long-term and fundamental social crisis that was only exacerbated by the collapse of steel. "The communities that are supposed to benefit from the Expressway through some mystical process of capital attraction," wrote one commentator, "are already little more than retirement communities and open air museums" (Siuta, 1987). Some residents argued for a community-focused redevelopment program emphasizing industrial heritage and reuse of existing building stock. However, in communities such as Homestead, this essentially urban outlook was often overshadowed by a more suburban strategy of flattening "brownfield" sites in an attempt to reinvent them as greenfields.

As with the Pittsburgh Renaissance, redevelopment efforts during the 1980s and 1990s were spearheaded in large part by the Allegheny Conference and its affiliated organizations in partnership, albeit sometimes strained, with the region's political leadership. Top-down programs to extend the economic growth of Pittsburgh's universities and middle-class suburbs to former mill towns largely focused on converting abandoned riverfront mill sites to planned industrial districts overseen by the nonprofit Regional Industrial Development Corporation (RIDC), which was initiated by the conference in the mid-1950s. Between 1955 and 1980, the RIDC used a combination of public and private funds to develop three industrial parks in suburban locations outside of Pittsburgh encompassing more than 1,670 acres of developed land with 130 different companies employing more than 11,000 people (Grata, 1980; Spatter, 1982a, 1982b). However, the organization came under increasing fire during the late 1980s for using public funds to further develop hilltop suburbs at the expense of the region's deindustrializing river valleys (Barnes, 1991). "We don't know how they rationalize how they can create low-cost parks in the suburbs when so much needs to be done in the Mon Valley and the city," complained one local official. "We're [distressed areas] competing for scarce state resources" (Perlmutter, 1991).

As a result, the RIDC began shifting emphasis from its three major suburban industrial parks to managing facilities at a number of urban sites, including three University Development Centers in the Oakland section of Pittsburgh, Carnegie Mellon University's Software Engineering Institute, and the Pittsburgh Technology Center (Barnes, 1991). Following the collapse of the steel industry, the RIDC also agreed to oversee the conversion of a number of former mills into riverfront industrial parks suitable for small- and medium-sized businesses. The sites, which included the 92-acre Westinghouse Plant in East Pittsburgh, U.S. Steel's 135-acre National Tube Works in McKeesport, and U.S. Steel's 240-acre Duquesne

Works (rechristened the Keystone Commons, Industrial Center of McKee-sport, and City Center of Duquesne, respectively), then became the centerpieces of state and local redevelopment strategies for the Mon Valley (Stouffer, 1988; McKay, 1989).

Despite the differences with urban brownfield sites, the RIDC explicitly continued to develop its properties based on the same planning principles as in its existing suburban industrial parks. By 1992, development officials could point to a number of successes at old plant sites, such as Keystone Commons, which had attracted about 40 companies with a work force of more than 400 (Spatter, 1992). Two year later, the facility had grown to 48 tenants and 650 employees, approaching the 800 employed at the Westing-house Plant in its last years. Mixed-use development in the three RIDC parks included a marina with room for 210 boats in McKeesport as well as a wide variety of firms from cookie makers to machine shops. "It's not like when we had 10,000 to 15,000 employees, naturally, but it's a start," Turtle Creek clothier Ben Forman declared. "It upgrades the whole area – rather than the deterioration you see in [other Mon Valley] communities" (as cited in Chute, 1994). "Duquesne is a very pleasant place to work," agreed Eric Hoffman, president of K2T, a robotics firm founded by three CMU faculty members, which leased space in the RIDC's City Center facility. "This is centrally located to where our employees live. There is free parking, a 150-acre playground and wildlife" (as cited in Fuoco, 1997) (Fig. 5).

The transformation of hulking mill sites into attractive, modern work-places was a time-consuming and expensive process that involved completely transforming an urban-industrial landscape that had formed over the course of a century and negotiating a wide variety of variables from environmental hazards to highway access. The most important obstacle to brownfield redevelopment during the 1990s was the presence of contamina-tion from decades of industrial production. In Duquesne and McKeesport, RIDC removed 2,200 barrels of oil chemicals and other toxic liquids, disposed of asbestos lined pipes and tanks, eliminated old PCB-laden electrical transformers, and even dug up an old railroad car. The cost of meeting environmental regulations created a rift between local developers and state environmental officials, whom RIDC president Frank Robinson accused of believing "that industry is evil and [that] everybody is dragging their feet on the cleanup – which we all want" (as cited in Fitzpatrick, 2001). Cleanup costs and the uncertainty of achieving environmental standards also limited private investment, with many local banks and potential tenants opting instead for hilltop suburban sites despite significant tax breaks and other incentives designed to lure employers to the riverfronts (Select

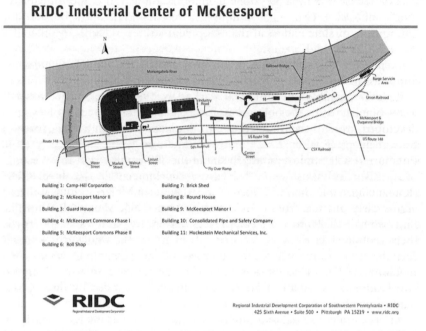

RIDC Industrial Center of McKeesport

Building 1: Camp-Hill Corporation   Building 7: Brick Shed

Building 2: McKeesport Manor II   Building 8: Round House

Building 3: Guard House   Building 9: McKeesport Manor I

Building 4: McKeesport Commons Phase I   Building 10: Consolidated Pipe and Safety Company

Building 5: McKeesport Commons Phase II   Building 11: Huckestein Mechanical Services, Inc.

Building 6: Roll Shop

RIDC

Regional Industrial Development Corporation of Southwestern Pennsylvania • RIDC
425 Sixth Avenue • Suite 500 • Pittsburgh PA 15219 • www.ridc.org

Fig. 5. RIDC Industrial Center of McKeesport (Former Site of National Tube). Courtesy of the Regional Industrial Development Corporation.

Committee on Pennsylvania's Industrial Development Corporations, 1992). "I would love to have a private interest come down here, buy five acres and build a building," RIDC president Brooks Robinson explained in 1999 as he surveyed the rubble strewn field that still constituted much of the Duquesne City Center. "It would be great. It's upsetting me, because ... there's still a lot of butt-ugly around here" (as cited in Fitzpatrick, 1999).

The problems with developing suburban-style industrial campuses in the Mon Valley also affected parallel efforts to remake the riverfronts as sites for consumption. In 1988, the same year that U.S. Steel transferred its former mill sites in McKeesport and Duquesne to public development officials, it sold the Homestead Works to a Cleveland-based manufacturer, the Park Corporation, for more than $2.75 million (Stouffer, 1988). The Homestead site subsequently became a hotly contested battleground between the Park Corporation and the nonprofit Steel Industry Heritage Corporation (SIHC), which wanted to preserve part of the site as a museum and visitor's center for the proposed Rivers of Steel National Heritage Area (National Park Service, 1989; Lubove, 1996). While the Park Corporation did agree to preserve some artifacts and allowed the removal of others for storage, it opposed a more comprehensive proposal and by 1995 had demolished nearly all of the plant's structures including a number of important heritage sites (Crumb, 1990; Lubove, 1996; Vorce, 1990).

Redevelopment efforts in Homestead as well as other sites in the region were complicated by the political and social structures of the region that had developed during the industrial era. Unlike more centrally organized brownfield projects, such as those in Germany's Ruhr Valley, or even in Pittsburgh itself, redevelopment in the Mon Valley took place across dozens of jurisdictions that often lacked even rudimentary planning departments (Kunzmann, 2002; Perkins, 2007). The Homestead Works alone sprawled across three municipalities – Homestead, West Homestead, and Munhall – that had trouble providing basic services as they reeled from the collapse of their economic base let alone paying for the costs associated with the revitalization of riverfront brownfields. As a result, site cleanup and redevelopment took place almost solely at the discretion of a private corporation, with only modest input from local groups and little attention paid to potential effects on the community.

After demolition and cleanup was complete Park eventually sold the site to Continental Real Estate Corporation, an Ohio developer which specialized in suburban shopping malls. Rather than making the area's industrial heritage the centerpiece of its redevelopment strategy, Continental unveiled plans for "The Waterfront," a suburban-style "super regional" shopping mall laid out in a typical low-rise suburban design with compartmentalized "big box" style retailers separated by massive parking lots. After prodding by historical preservationists, Continental did incorporate a few elements of Homestead's industrial past into site design; these artifacts remained relatively scattered and largely decontextualized. Despite the name, The Waterfront also made little use of the Mon itself with only a small riverfront park and bicycle trail running along part of the length of the site. Despite strong support for the project by local politicians, active rail lines also continued to wall the area off from older business districts with only one access point that would bring visitors through downtown Homestead.

As with the RIDC industrial parks, The Waterfront's developers chose to treat the site mainly as a tabula rasa, with characteristics that could be found at any suburban interchange. "Pittsburgh doesn't have a good reputation as a retail market," explained Continental Chairman Frank

Kass. "Many (retailers) question the demographics in the surrounding areas (from the Waterfront). But, when they see the flatness of the Waterfront site and see the accessibility, then they're sold" (as cited in Elliott, 2000). Brownfield redevelopment in the Mon Valley was a costly, complicated process and there is no doubt that local communities are better off with these projects than they would have been without. Nevertheless, a number of important questions remain about the long-term viability of using suburban strategies for revitalizing deindustrialized mill towns such as those in the Mon Valley. Neither highway construction nor planned industrial and commercial districts have had much success in alleviating the problems of urban decline still plaguing communities throughout metropolitan Pittsburgh. As a result, newer redevelopment efforts on Pittsburgh's South Side and in Hazelwood just across the river from Homestead have explicitly turned away from the suburban approach to a more explicitly urban community-oriented model (Perkins, 2007; Hollander, 2009).

CONCLUSION – SUBURBAN STRATEGIES FOR THE TWENTY-FIRST CENTURY?

The decision to adopt suburban strategies for economic development in postindustrial Pittsburgh emerged out of a particular set of issues facing the region in the 1950s and 1960s. The urban redevelopment programs of the Pittsburgh Renaissance failed to provide the type of flat, open, highway-oriented green space locations attractive to expanding industrial sectors, prompting the region's corporate and political elite to create organizations such as the RIDC to oversee the construction of suitable sites. As the region's river valleys lost population and grew more isolated from new growth centers in the hilltop suburbs, communities such as Homestead, Duquesne, and McKeesport became, in effect, *more* rural even as former peripheral areas such as Monroeville grew into "edge cities." Consequently, the mill towns did not share in the economic transformation that remade other parts of the region into "postindustrial" centers of high-tech manufacturing and service provision. The creeping decline of the steel industry subsequently prompted the call for new highways to connect these older industrial satellites to the region's growth centers. When Mon Valley residents did begin to reimagine their communities in the 1980s and 1990s, like most other rural areas they did so as junior partners promoting a low-cost/low-wage alternative to more traditional suburban locations.

Adopting a suburban strategy of highway construction implicitly acknowledged the failure of earlier urban redevelopment campaigns to substantially change decaying central business districts and urban neighborhoods. Proponents tried to put a good face on the issue, but the construction of highways such as the Mon/Fayette Expressway, even when completed, had only an indirect impact on alleviating poverty in downtown areas. While the portion of the Mon/Fayette Expressway linking Interstate 70 with Jefferson Hills, a hilltop suburb five miles west of the Mon was finally opened in 2002, the remainder of the route continues to be on hold due to a lack of funding. Even within the Mon, a growing number of local officials have questioned the utility of completing the route amid worries that the highway would simply contribute to the draining of resources and population from existing communities (Santoni, 2010) (Fig. 6).

During the first decade of the twenty-first century, the results of suburban-style commercial and industrial development in postindustrial Pittsburgh were similarly mixed. Both The Waterfront in Homestead and

Fig. 6. Open hearth stacks from the Former U.S. Steel Homestead Works Grace a Parking Lot at the Waterfront Shopping Complex. Photo Courtesy of Amanda Dieterich-Ward.

the RIDC industrial parks in McKeesport and Duquesne have continued to attract new employers, but the spillover effects on existing communities are often complicated to assess. The symbolic transformation of urban brownfields into suburban greenfields could take place only by largely ignoring surrounding neighborhoods, with the result that too often the new developments had little direct impact on downtown areas that still feature boarded-up storefronts, high rates of poverty, and continued out-migration (Cloonan, 2010). Monroeville itself, once the envy of its neighbors in the Mon Valley, has begun to show signs of problems once considered the domain of older industrial satellites. "In the 1950s, '60s and '70s, we grew up as part of the exit out of the city and into the suburbs," explained the city's mayor. "But now we have traffic issues and aesthetic issues" that increasingly require revitalization programs of their own (as cited in Schooley, 2002). Unlike centrally administered "edge cities" in the United Kingdom, however, political fragmentation continues to make comprehensive planning difficult in metropolitan Pittsburgh. As a result, since 2000 Monroeville's population has declined by five percent as regional growth has shifted to other outlying areas to the north and west.

These concerns about the viability of suburban strategies for providing economic and urban revitalization in deindustrialized communities suggest the need to rethink such approaches for the context of the twenty-first century. Undoubtedly, Mon Valley communities are much better off with these suburban-style developments than if the sites remained rusting abandoned hulks. Nevertheless, alternative planning models seen in places such as the Ruhr Valley in Germany and the Flemish region in Belgium can provide good comparative frameworks by which to judge the successes and failures of these projects (Kunzmann, 2002; Vanheusden, 2007). Of course, more comprehensive approaches to revitalizing America's older industrial satellites, and those in metropolitan Pittsburgh in particular, face important social and political obstacles that make the types of redevelopment seen in other postindustrial nations much more difficult to achieve.

That said, a handful of relatively recent initiatives have sought to move beyond the traditional suburban strategies that have guided development since the mid-1980s. Rather than continuing to focus on building the last leg of the Mon/Fayette Expressway, for example, a number of local groups have called for a more urban-oriented approach to highway planning that would develop the Mon Valley's existing transportation infrastructure with a focus on preserving and linking older downtown areas (PennFuture, 2002). Similarly, a number of recent mill site redevelopment projects such as Pittsburgh's SouthSide Works, five miles downriver from The Waterfront in Homestead, have explicitly tried to fit new facilities into existing neighborhoods rather than using the existing brownfield-to-greenfield model (Perkins, 2007). While the future of the deindustrialized "Burbs of the Burgh" remains unclear, these alternative models for revitalization offer a compelling new framework through which to interpret the legacy of Pittsburgh's industrial past, as former mill towns and industrial satellites seek to find places for themselves within the postindustrial future.

REFERENCES

ACTION-Housing, Inc. (1968). *Population trends and housing requirements in Allegheny county to 1980: The urban renewal impact study*. Pittsburgh, PA: ACTION-Housing.

Allegheny Conference on Community Development. (1944). Report of working committees of the Allegheny Conference on Community Development. *Allegheny Conference on Community Development Records* (MSS 285, Box 377, Folder 2). Library and Archives, Heinz History Center, Pittsburgh, PA.

Allegheny Conference on Community Development. (1956). *Allegheny Conference on Community Development ... Presents*. Pittsburgh, PA: The Conference.

Bailey, K. (1990). Defense housing in greater Pittsburgh, 1941–1945. *Pittsburgh History, 73*(Spring), 17–28.

Bangs, R., & Singh, J. (Eds). (1988). *The state of the region: Economic, demographic and social trends in Southwestern Pennsylvania*. Pittsburgh, PA: University of Pittsburgh Center for Social and Urban Research.

Bangs, R., & Soltis, T. (1989). *The job growth centers of Allegheny county*. Pittsburgh, PA: University of Pittsburgh Center for Social and Urban Research.

Barnes, T. (1991). RIDC chief answers critics. *Pittsburgh Post-Gazette*, February 22, p. 7.

Basescu, R. (1989). Casey breaks ground for expressway. *Uniontown Herald-Standard*, January 21.

Beachler, E. (1952). *The story of Pittsburgh's No. 1 headache*. Pittsburgh, PA: Pittsburgh Press.

Chute, E. (1994). Keystone commons at five years. *Pittsburgh Post-Gazette*, April 7, p. E1.

Clapson, M. (2003). *Suburban century: Social change and urban growth in England and the USA*. New York, NY: Berg.

Clapson, M. (2004). *A social history of Milton Keynes: Middle England/Edge City*. Portland, OR: Frank Kass Publishers.

Claypoole, W. (1955). Untitled [Letter to R. A. House, Jr.]. William H. Claypoole Papers (AIS.1982.16, Box 2, Folder 40). Archives Service Center, University of Pittsburgh, Pittsburgh, PA, April 4.

Cloonan, P. (2010). Empty buildings part 4: McKeesport's many vacant structures are on the market. *McKeesport Daily News*, April 28. Retrieved from http://www.pittsburghlive.-com/x/dailynewsmckeesport/s_678501.html.

Cowie, J., & Heathcott, J. (Eds). (2003). *Beyond the ruins: The meanings of deindustrialization*. Ithaca, NY: ILR/Cornell University Press.

Crumb, J. (1990). Residents favorable to plans for mill site. *The Pittsburgh Press*, July 5.

Dearfield, N. (1988). Untitled [Letter to Governor Robert Casey]. Robert P. Casey Papers (RG 10, Box 172, Folder 11). Pennsylvania State Archives, Harrisburg, PA, May 26.

Dieterich-Ward, A. (2010). From Satellite City to 'Burb of the Burgh': Deindustrialization and community identity in Steubenville, Ohio. In: J. Connolly (Ed.), *After the factory: Reinventing America's industrial small cities* (pp. 49–85). Lanham, MD: Lexington Books.

Dieterich-Ward, A., & Needham, A. (2009). Beyond the metropolis: Metropolitan growth and regional transformation in Postwar America. *Journal of Urban History, 35*(7), 943–969.

Dudiak, Z. (2004). Harper's mine birthplace of Monroeville mall. *Times Express*, April 28. Retrieved from http://www.yourmonroeville.com/timesexpress/article/harpers-mine-birthplace-monroeville-mall

Elliott, S. (2000). On the waterfront: Frank Kass' approach to development makes $300 million project a contender. *Pittsburgh Business Times*, June 16. Retrieved from http://pittsburgh.bizjournals.com/pittsburgh/stories/2000/06/19/focus1.html

Elliott, S. (2004). Armstrong gains, loses trying to strengthen economy. *Pittsburgh Business Times*, April 23. Retrieved from http://pittsburgh.bizjournals.com/pittsburgh/stories/2004/04/26/story7.html

Fishman, R. (1987). *Bourgeois utopias: The rise and fall of suburbia*. New York: Basic Books.

Fitzpatrick, D. (1999). The ReDevelopment of RIDC. *Pittsburgh Post-Gazette*, August 22.

Fitzpatrick, D. (2001). The Mon Valley – Haves and have nots with a mix of envy and frustration. *Pittsburgh Post-Gazette*, October 14, p. C1.

Foley, E. (1980). For Monroeville the bloom is not off the 30-year boom. *Pittsburgh Post-Gazette* (Pgh. East Ed.), March 20, pp. 1, 3.

Fones-Wolf, K., & Fones-Wolf, E. (2003). Cold war Americanism: Business, pageantry, and antiunionism in Weirton, West Virginia. *Business History Review, 77*(1), 61–91.

Fuoco, L. (1997). Ghost of past, future vision seen in tour of steel valley. *Pittsburgh Post-Gazette*, July 2, p. S1.

Garreau, J. (1991). *Edge city: Life on the new frontier*. New York: Doubleday.

Gauthier, H. (1973). The Appalachian development highway system: Development for whom? *Economic Geography, 49*, 103–108.

Glass, M. (2007). *Changing spaces – Communities, governance and the politics of growth*. Doctoral dissertation. Pennsylvania State University, University Park, PA.

Grata, J. (1980). RIDC doing a job by helping many keep theirs. *The Pittsburgh Press*, January 22.

Greater Uniontown Area Chamber of Commerce and Greater Uniontown Industrial Fund. (1990). The Mon Valley/Fayette expressway must be built without delay [statement to the Pennsylvania Turnpike Commission]. Robert P. Casey Papers (RG 10, Box 172, Folder 11). Pennsylvania State Archives, Harrisburg, PA, July 31.

Greenstein, R., & Sungu-Eryilmaz, Y. (2004). Introduction: Recycling urban vacant land. In: R. Greenstein & Y. Sungu-Eryilmaz (Eds), *Recycling the city: The use and reuse of urban land* (pp. 1–12). Cambridge, MA: Lincoln Institute of Land Policy.

Guide-Post Research. (1961). *Neighborhood shopping vs. downtown shopping*. Pittsburgh, PA: Pittsburgh Press, Inc.

Hollander, J. (2009). *Polluted and dangerous: America's worst abandoned properties and what can be done about them*. Lebanon, NH: University Press of New England.

Hollinshead, F. (1946). Locating industry in the Pittsburgh area, an address to the members of the Pittsburgh Junior chamber of commerce, June 14. Reprinted in *Allegheny Conference Digest*, 1(4) (September 1946), 9–10.

Jackson, K. (1985). *Crabgrass Frontier: The suburbanization of America.* New York: Oxford University Press.

Javersak, D. (1999). *History of Weirton, West Virginia.* Virginia Beach, VA: The Donning Company.

Kitsko, J. (2010). PA Turnpike 43: Mon/Fayette expressway, March 14. Retrieved from http://www.pahighways.com/toll/PATurnpike43.html

Kruse, K., & Sugrue, T. (Eds). (2006). *The new suburban history.* Chicago, IL: University of Chicago Press.

Kunzmann, K. (2002). Creative Brownfield redevelopment: The experience of the IBA Emscher park initiative in the Ruhr in Germany. In: R. Greenstein & Y. Sungu-Eryilmaz (Eds), *Recycling the city: The use and reuse of urban land* (pp. 201–218). Cambridge, MA: Lincoln Institute of Land Policy.

Lewis, R. (Ed.) (2004). *Manufacturing suburbs: Building work and home on the metropolitan fringe.* Philadelphia, PA: Temple University Press.

Lowry, I. (1963). *Economic study of the Pittsburgh region, Vol. II: Portrait of a region.* Pittsburgh, PA: University of Pittsburgh Press.

Lubove, R. (1996). *Twentieth century Pittsburgh, Volume Two: The post steel era.* Pittsburgh, PA: University of Pittsburgh Press.

Magda, M. (1985). *Monessen: Industrial boomtown and steel community, 1898–1980.* Harrisburg, PA: Pennsylvania Historical and Museum Commission.

Martin, P. (1951). Does Pittsburgh need an industrial development district? An address to Western Pennsylvania chapter, society of industrial realtors. *Allegheny Conference on Community Development Records* (MSS 285, Vertical File "Speeches"). Library and Archives, Heinz History Center, Pittsburgh, PA, January 9.

McKay, J. (1989). RIDC will spend $20 million to revamp Westinghouse plant. *Pittsburgh Post-Gazette,* January 19, p. 14.

Mershon, S. (2000). *Corporate social responsibility and urban revitalization: The Allegheny Conference on Community Development, 1943–1968.* Doctoral dissertation. Carnegie Mellon University, Pittsburgh, PA.

Miner, C., & Roberts, P. (1989). Engineering an industrial Diaspora: Homestead, 1941. *Pittsburgh History, 72*(Winter), 4–25.

Modell, J., & Brodsky, C. (1998). *A town without steel: Envisioning Homestead.* Pittsburgh, PA: University of Pittsburgh Press.

Muller, E. (2004). Industrial suburbs and the growth of metropolitan Pittsburgh, 1870–1920. In: R. Lewis (Ed.), *Manufacturing suburbs: Building work and home on the metropolitan fringe.* Philadelphia, PA: Temple University Press.

Muller, E., & Tarr, J. (2003). The interaction of natural and built environments in the Pittsburgh landscape. In: J. Tarr (Ed.), *Devastation and renewal: An environmental history of Pittsburgh and its region* (pp. 11–40). Pittsburgh, PA: University of Pittsburgh Press.

National Park Service. (1989). *America's industrial heritage project: Southwestern Pennsylvania.* Washington, DC: U.S. Department of the Interior, National Park Service.

Nicolaides, B. (2002). *My blue heaven: Life and politics in the working-class suburbs of Los Angeles, 1920–1965.* Chicago, IL: University of Chicago Press.

Olmsted, F. (1910). *Pittsburgh main thoroughfares and the downtown district: Improvements necessary to meet the city's present and future needs, a report.* Pittsburgh, PA: Pittsburgh Civic Commission.

PennFuture. (2002). *The citizens' plan: An alternative to the Pennsylvania Turnpike Commission's plan to complete the Mon–Fayette Toll Road* (September. Retrieved from http://www.pennfuture.org/UserFiles/citizensplan_82702.pdf). Harrisburg, PA: PennFuture.

Pennsylvania State Planning Board. (1966). *Regional development reconnaissance: Region 12. A Staff Working Paper*. The Board, Harrisburg, PA.

Perkins, N. (2007). A tale of two Brownfield sites: Making the best of times from the worst of times in Western Pennsylvania's steel valley. *Environmental Affairs Law Review, 34*(3), 503–532.

Perlmutter, E. (1991). Officials critical of RIDC practices: Question use of public funds. *The Pittsburgh Press*, February 7.

Pittsburgh Regional Planning Association (PRPA). (1954). *North side study*. Pittsburgh, PA: The Association.

Pittsburgh Regional Planning Association. (1961). *Steel valley district: A long range development plan for the boroughs of Homestead, West Homestead, West Mifflin and Whitaker*. Pittsburgh, PA: The Association.

Redevelopment Authority of the City of Monessen. (1968). *Annual report, 1968*. Monessen, PA: The Authority.

Richards, W. (1945). A fifty-seven-million-dollar program. *Allegheny Conference Digest, 1(2)*, 6–10. Allegheny Conference on Community Development Records (MSS 285, Box 129, Folder 5). Library and Archives, Heinz History Center, Pittsburgh, PA, December.

Santoni, M. (2010). Grass grows as Mon–Fayette expressway project idles. *Pittsburgh Tribune-Review*, May 16.

Schooley, T. (2002). For all its commercial success, Monroeville still has image issues. *Pittsburgh Business Times*, October 4. Retrieved from http://pittsburgh.bizjournals.com/pittsburgh/stories/2002/10/07/focus3.html

Select Committee on Pennsylvania's Industrial Development Corporations. (1992). *Sharing the wealth: A report on Pennsylvania's industrial development corporations*. Harrisburg, PA: Pennsylvania House of Representatives.

Serrin, W. (1993). *Homestead: The glory and tragedy of an American steel town*. New York, NY: Vintage Books.

Siuta, C. (1987). Untitled [Letter to Governor Robert Casey]. Robert P. Casey Papers (RG 10, Box 172, Folder 11). Pennsylvania State Archives, Harrisburg, PA, August 12.

Southwestern Pennsylvania Regional Planning Commission. (1968). *Issues in a region of contrasts*. Pittsburgh: The Commission.

Spatter, S. (1982a). RIDC good economic tonic for district. *The Pittsburgh Press*, January 18.

Spatter, S. (1982b). Hi-tech sites give realtors a boost in industrial sales. *The Pittsburgh Press*, November 28.

Spatter, S. (1992). Creating jobs: Old plant sites attract new manufacturers. *The Pittsburgh Press*, March 15, p. F7.

Stouffer, R. (1988). Big mills sites go public. *New York Times*, September 18, p. R25.

Tarr, J. (1996). The Pittsburgh survey as an environmental statement. In: M. Greenwald & M. Anderson (Eds), *Pittsburgh surveyed: Social science and social reform in the early twentieth century* (pp. 170–189). Pittsburgh, PA: University of Pittsburgh Press.

Tarr, J., & Di Pasquale, D. (1982). The mill town in the industrial city: Pittsburgh's Hazelwood. *Urbanism Past and Present, 7*(1), 1–14.

Tessitor, D. (1994). Don't follow the yellow brick road [Letter to the Editor]. *Pittsburgh Post-Gazette*, June 12, p. F1.

Vanheusden, B. (2007). Brownfield redevelopment in the European Union. *Environmental Affairs Law Review, 34*(3), 559–576.

Vorce, C. (1990). It's history now, Homestead roll shop comes down despite museum plans. *The Pittsburgh Press*, June 30.

Wagner, F., Joder, T., Mumphrey, A., Jr., Akundi, K., & Artibise, A. (Eds). (2005). *Revitalizing the city: Strategies to contain sprawl and revive the core.* Armonk, NY: M.E. Sharpe.

Wall Street Journal. (1941). Steel towns: Two in Pittsburgh will be made over by plant expansions. *Wall Street Journal*, July 19, pp. 1, 3.

Wander, J. (1998, August). Monroeville is an "Edge City". *Pittsburgh* (Special Advertising Supplement), 118–119.

Watson, R. (1990). Untitled [Letter to Governor Robert Casey]. Robert P. Casey Papers (RG 10, Box 172, Folder 11). Pennsylvania State Archives, Harrisburg, PA, July 12.

Weber, M. (1988). *Don't call me boss: David L. Lawrence, Pittsburgh's renaissance mayor.* Pittsburgh, PA: University of Pittsburgh Press.

Weise, S., & Weise, N. (1988). Untitled [Letter to Governor Robert Casey]. Robert P. Casey Papers (RG 10, Box 172, Folder 11). Pennsylvania State Archives, Harrisburg, PA.

Widner, R. (1990). Appalachian development after 25 years: An assessment. *Economic Development Quarterly, 4*, 291–312.

Wiese, A. (2004). *Places of their own: African American suburbanization in the twentieth century.* Chicago, IL: University of Chicago Press.

CITIES, SUBURBS AND METROPOLITAN AREAS – GOVERNING THE REGIONALISED CITY

Tassilo Herrschel

Cities, especially of the metropolitan scale, have increasingly gained in importance as foci and drivers of economic development and competitiveness at national and international levels. Using a somewhat broad and generalised understanding of 'city', such an urban focus is propagated as the most effective approach to economic development policies (Porter, 2000; Cox, 1997; Raco, 1999; Swyngedouw, 2004; MacLeod, 2002; Peck, 2000). Implicitly, from their external perspective, such arguments concetrate on the central cities as visible foci of their respective urban areas, with their town halls and other cultural and institutional places of policy making. The suburban areas, by contrast, and, certainly, those spaces between the cities, fade into the background. They are merely included as 'natural' extensions of the core cities, rather than actors in their own right, and as such are deemed to benefit from their belonging to, functional integration with or merely geographic proximity to an urban region. From that perspective, the spaces outside the urban cores fade into the background, and their policy makers with them. Yet, their interests, agendas and priorities may differ from those of the central city, including the benefits of involvement in a regional agenda. Their perspectives may differ not just from those of other

Suburbanization in Global Society
Research in Urban Sociology, Volume 10, 107–130
Copyright © 2010 by Emerald Group Publishing Limited
All rights of reproduction in any form reserved
ISSN: 1047-0042/doi:10.1108/S1047-0042(2010)0000010007

suburban areas within a metropolitan area, but also, and in particular, from those of the core city (in monocentric city regions) or several core cities in the case of polycentric city regions. They may also differ from those areas on the edges of, or in between, such urban regions.

In addition, for some interests, there may be more common ground with local areas beyond any one metropolitan area. Suburbs may look beyond 'their' central cities to other suburban localities elsewhere, with which they share common problems, ambitions and agendas. The picture thus, as discussed here, is more complex than the term 'metropolitan area' may suggest at first: it goes beyond a mere geographic understanding and includes a range of varying, topic-specific, policy-driven linkages within and across the spatial scales of sub-local to regional. Territory clearly matters (Healey, 2000), even if the boundaries of such regionally 'scaled-up' (Herrschel, 2005) urban areas remain somewhat fuzzy. They vary with the internal dynamics of a city region and its changing position (role) in the wider economic landscape. Rather than hierarchical governmental arrangements, debates on city regions revolve around their dynamic aspects, that is functional relationships and policy networks between actors at local and city-regional level. Such networks, as discussed below, create a different spatiality than that of the conventional notion of space as a contiguous territory defined by a surrounding boundary: linear, spatially selective and policy defined. This translates into clear distinctions between those that are part of the system and those that are not – be they localities, organisations or individual personalities. The result is a sharp and varying distinction between 'core' and 'periphery' through the lens of specific policy agendas. This follows the distribution of social and communicative connections. As agendas are achieved, or change, so do once established policy networks and thus the inclusion or exclusion of actors. Some suburban areas may play a more visible and influential role in a metropolitan area than others for some policy issue, while others move to the foreground of policy making for other agendas. The picture is thus one of flux in the role and engagement of different elements of urban regions – city, suburb and semi-rural periphery.

This chapter contains three main sections: the first discusses suburbanisation as the underlying process of city regionalisation in Europe, and the shifting balances between urban core and suburban areas in terms of 'weight' in a city region. The second looks at the concept of city regions as spatial and functional construct, as well as policy-making entity (governance). The third section examines the implications of new forms and mechanisms of city-regional governance, especially the shift from a territorially to an agenda-driven, network-based rationale of 'city region', using illustrative examples. This includes a shifting inclusion and exclusion of actors and localities, with varying degrees of marginalisation and the creation of 'in-between' spaces.

SUBURBS AND THE EXTENSION OF THE CITY INTO THE CITY REGION

Since the 1950s, and the steadily growing mobility of people and production (economic activity) as a result of the shift to road traffic, especially in North America, suburban areas have grown rapidly as residential areas and places of (post-industrial) economic activity (Hoffmann-Axthelm, 1998). People moved from 'the country' and, especially, the established central cities to the more spacious and cheap to develop peripheral locations. In Europe, differences have emerged on the basis of established planning law and thus availability of land for development, and of historic legacies in the relationship between 'city' and 'country'. Thus, for instance, while in Germany cities were distinctly separate from their surrounding areas in legal terms and land ownership, in Italy, cities have been viewed as 'owning' or controlling the surrounding areas to the extent that these are subservient to the cities' developmental needs (Heitkamp, 1998).

Conditions are different again in post-communist Eastern Europe. There, the legacy of state authoritarianism and developmentalist communist party-controlled planned economies created an environment that provided very specific conditions for market-led Western-style urban development. Especially, under the initial uncertainties and vacuum in legislation, the only gradually emerging formulation of new paradigms and political agendas and priorities in the early years of post-communist transition, a weak development control system provided more 'North American' than Western European conditions for neo-liberal, speculatively driven development. This resulted in extensive out-of-town developments for retail and distribution, especially along the main arterial roads between urban areas. Western developers and retail chains knew how to exploit the absence of clear planning rules and the initial, perhaps somewhat naive, euphoria about any form of influx of expressions of Western ways of life. At the same time, the legacy of run-down, dilapidated old city cores with unclear property ownership, and a concentration of large sections of the urban population in massive high-rise, prefabricated concrete housing estates built under communism in the peripheries of cities, surrounded by sections of 'in-between open land', attracted rapid and expansive, architecturally unimaginative developments among and between the existing socialist era suburban fabric of high-rise estates (Christ, 1998).

The result has been North American-style strip development on the edges of existing cities and towns, geared to the car-based customer. This diverts such central functions from the gradually regenerated, often rather Disneyfied, historic built environment in the city centres. This, then, limits the scope for the established cities and towns to re-establish a sufficient functional relevance to act as a sustainable economic base for their competitive standing, let alone expansion. In addition, a growing number of residents living on the housing estates move to the sprawling new developments of detached dwellings on the edges of villages in the urban peripheries. This adds to a further dispersion of urban life and function, leading to a clear shift in the power balance between city core and suburbanising periphery. This creates a growing mismatch between a traditional perception, certainly in Europe, of the city centres being the hubs of an urban area's functionality and centrality, and the surrounding hinterland being the 'supplement', providing auxiliary roles. This shift, exacerbated by fiscal regimes that reward *local* 'success' in attracting business activity and/or dwellers, such as in the Berlin metropolis (Hauswirth, Herrschel, & Newman, 2003), raises questions about the internal dynamics in city regions (metropolitan areas). What is the role of policy making when considering the balance between local agendas and those of the functional urban region as a whole?

Such shifting balances in fiscal capacity, and thus the scope to define and, most importantly, implement local policies, have become widespread in Western cities, being particularly stark in North America. Deindustrialising, economically declining and socially selectively depopulating older city centres with ageing infrastructure face increasingly stiff competition from younger, more affluent and economically growing suburbs. Not surprisingly, these are increasingly reluctant to play 'second fiddle' to the established old city cores in urban regions, even though those cities provide the name and, important for an external audience (Herrschel, 2005), recognition factor for the whole region. This may provide cause for resentment and envy, and undermine scope for developing a more comprehensive, less localist perspective as precondition for more concerted efforts in adopting a city-regional perspective with associated tailor-made, supportive policies. Localism is never far away, and the aspiring suburbs want their newly gained economic power and status recognised and translated into political influence within 'their' wider city region. Effectively, they ask for a new hand of cards in the allocated local roles, and positions within a metropolitan are challenging the historic pre-eminence of the old urban core. In some instances, especially in North America, such as in the greater Vancouver region in Western Canada, the former suburbs, such as Surrey, have overtaken the city Vancouver's population of around half a million, with steadily growing numbers and an equally growing economy. There is thus fierce competition for political influence within the city region, with the 'new kid on the block' referring to its population size and underlying growth rates as justification for challenging established power relationships in the region.

Inevitably, and unsurprisingly, these dynamics and shifts in economic relevance and perceived democratic legitimacy through a broadened voter base shape the framework for, and dynamics of, city-region-wide govern-ance. Such shifts include the roles of actors and the 'reach' of their influence within the city region, and here especially the role, visibility and assertiveness of the suburban 'hinterland'. New alliances may be drawn up, established ones terminated and actors gain or lose in influence. The result is a shifting balance between being included in, excluded from or simply ignored by policy networks and their actors, creating new peripheralities and exclusions, or abandoning established ones. This leads to the creation of 'in-between spaces and actors' – such as manifested in the concept of 'in-between cities' ('Zwischenstadt', see Sieverts, 1998), 'edge cities' (see Garreau, 1991) or exopolis (after Soja, 1992). These new, emerging spaces gain in relevance within city regions and seek to join the main actor networks – at least for day-to-day business. This corresponds to the shifting balance in social, economic and functional terms between the different elements of a city region, and subsequently shapes their inter-relationships and policy agendas. These follow specific, distinctly local interests and objectives, and may, as part of that, lead to the bypassing or exclusion of municipalities with which there are fewer common interests, irrespective of a shared spatial proximity. Separateness and divisions can also be found at the sub-local level, such as illustrated by gated communities that seek to build fortress-like housing blocks as protected enclaves of higher social status within areas of rather less well-to-do residents established in the wider neighbourhood.

Suburbs may thus no longer be presumed – from an outside perspective – to be almost automatically subsumed under the spatial and functional umbrella of the central city. Thus, while those advocating new (city-) regionalism (Cox, 1997; Whitehead, 2003) to provide part of the answer to globalisation-induced pressures for greater competitiveness, more recent comments have challenged the salience of linking cooperation with competitiveness in such a normative way (Kantor, 2008). In fact, spatially defined city regions may not want to be viewed as one entity, nor would they seek to become one, but rather maintain distinct differences and separateness.

GOVERNANCE, CITY REGIONS AND SUBURBS: PART OF TERRITORY OR POLICY NETWORKS

The beginnings of a more urban-focused perspective can be seen in the late 1980s when the EU undertook a series of studies of European cities. This work not only located cities in regional contexts but also sought to analyse specifically urban factors that made some cities more successful than others (Boddy & Parkinson, 2004). Urban analysis drew on different academic traditions to regional studies and in particular sought explanation of relationships between government and other actors as part of 'urban governance' and the attempt, for example, to build 'growth coalitions' to maximise local development potential and opportunities, including 'boosterist' urban policy (Short, Bentona, Lucea, & Waltona, 1993). Understanding changing European space and governance includes both an urban and a regional dimension. Cities are now seen as the motors of regional economies (Hall, 1998) driven by new forms of governance that seek to respond to the competitive pressures generated by globalisation.

An important part of this argument is the proposition that cities and regions have increasingly become economic spaces and actors in their own right, with some commentators seeing their disconnection from their national contexts (Scott, 2001; Barnes & Ledebur, 1998). This has sharpened the focus on cities not merely as localities, but also as locations that reach out into the region in a symbiotic, yet also contested and competitive relationship. The significant impact of global economic change is therefore at the regional scale with core cities as economic drivers situated in functionally related regional clusters that, again, are part of national and international economic and political networks. The notion is thus not so much one of fixed, bounded and clearly defined territories surrounding a core city as 'hinterland', but rather a fuzzy, variable and network-defined spatial backcloth that merely locates agenda-driven collaborative relationship between actors.

Keating and Loughlin (1997) emphasises the importance of under-standing relations between actors at varying scales, including city regions in all their scalar vagueness. A weakness in the network approach is a tendency to identify and map network connections between governmental levels or between public and private sectors, while paying less attention to the varying 'weight' of different interests and their abilities to gain influence, or resist the danger of losing influence and becoming marginalised and peripheralised. Some networks and some network members will be more powerful than others, and this can change over time and with shifting policy agendas. Institutional hierarchies are being supplanted by network forms of governance and negotiations between interests of different actors – be these localities, organisations or social groups and personalities. It is this broadening out of actors that marks out the concept of governance. While the concept of government concentrates on governing hierarchies and formal decision making, governance points to horizontal networks of influence, intergovernmental negotiation and cooperation, and the blurring of public and private boundaries in negotiating and defining policies. Governance can be seen not as a means of control but as an 'attempt to manage and regulate difference' (Kearns & Paddison, 2000, p. 847). There is thus a distinct managerial undertone. The concept is applied at both city and regional levels, and the focus is on the challenges of identifying and negotiating shared interests as the basis of – temporary – cooperation. And governance covering a territory is the sum of such negotiated collaboration and the underlying linkages between actors.

Governance with such an inherently cooperative arrangement allows a combination of both maintaining existing governmental structures with their associated clearly defined portfolios of power, responsibility and, crucially for effective policy making, finances and simultaneously engaging in varying, goal-driven, informal arrangements that define a region through the territories represented by the participating actors. They may join or leave without having to surrender powers or being tied in institutionally with high exit barriers. Instead, networks and linkages between actors, whether institutions, organisations or individual persons, define hierarchies of relevance and influence in terms of defining and setting a policy agenda. Kantor (2008) refers to such more open and, importantly, not permanently binding arrangements as 'coordination'. Their main feature is an absence of 'formalized alliances and programs' (p. 114), and the underlying driver is, essentially, a local self-interest, the pursuit of which makes collaborative policy coordination seem opportune at the time. The regional dimension such collaboration takes is then more an incidental 'side effect' than specific policy objective. Kantor (2008) distinguishes between three types of political coordination at the regional level in a liberal market democracy, based on the range of actor interests and the macro-political (primarily national) context. The degree to which shared and agreed policy agendas can bundle otherwise diverse actor interests and to which macro-political (i.e. primarily national) contexts allow policy responses to be formulated, coordinated and collaboratively implemented are affirmed as key factors in regionalisation at the metropolitan scale.

These new spatialities, fragmented by a multitude of linear spaces – that is 'corridors of communication' – reflect a growing trend towards *'regionalised localisation'* and increasingly virtual and non-contiguous policy-making spaces (Herrschel, 2009; Allen, Massey, & Cochrane, 1998; Heeg, Klagge, & Ossenbrügge, 2003). Such constructs operate at the regional scale and function as a dynamic, continuously re-adjusting framework for the location and connection of these locally rooted nodes of political interaction and communication. The underlying (actual or perceived) pressure to seek maximum competitiveness may thus essentially reinforce 'atomised' vari-abilities and inequalities in opportunities. These can be found in a multitude of intersecting and overlaying networks, nodes and linkages between actors and decision makers – be they localities, agencies or individuals. Yet this fragmentation undermines the coherence and contiguity of regional spaces. And this may well contradict (see Kantor, 2008) the perception of 'new regionalism' (Keating, 1998; MacLeod, 2002) as a mechanism to connect individual spaces to a larger, and thus more powerful and convincing, spatial economic and policy-making entity, such as a city region.

The concept of city-region-wide policy making across municipal bound-aries and associated governance arrangements arose vis-à-vis a perceived growing pressure for increased (but offensive and defensive) globalisation-driven competitiveness. It was becoming increasingly evident that these challenges could no longer be appropriately addressed in a compartmenta-lised, locality-based approach to policy making within metropolitan areas. Yet nature and scale of city regions are not at all clearly defined, sitting somewhere between the local and regional levels. The concern with city regions reflects the realisation that the local scale is too limited in its extent, needing to reach 'up' the scalar ladder to the regional scale. This raises wider questions of the relationship between scales in a vertical, yet also horizontal, direction, with the latter referring to inter-municipal collaboration. Castells (1989) argues that city regions have become the main points of reference in a globalisation and knowledge-driven 'new spatial logic'. This involves dynamic, continuous change, lesser importance of administrative spatial entities, variable collaborative arrangements as drivers of economic and political (and social) spatialities and a growing reliance on communicative social–political networks and connections.

Increasingly, governance is moving away from territorially based relationships between places to less formalised, more topically selective and temporal arrangements, based on networks between actors and 'their' localities (Provan & Kenis, 2007). Variations in such connectivity of, and between, places and actors circumscribe the scope for participating in a network of competitors, as they shape and reflect variations in comparative attractiveness. Different degrees of connectivity also shape the scope for having access to, and participating in, policy-making networks and their impact on formulating policy agendas. This difference creates new, and manifests old, hierarchies of connectivity and access to, and relevance in, decision-making processes. The outcome is the emergence of networks constructed of variably dense and relevant connections and thus differing reach and political weight.

Networks and their characteristics and functioning have attracted attention from both sociologists and economists, although both approach the topic from quite different ends. While economists have focused on networks from a strategic, managerial business perspective, driven by an economic rationality, sociologists have focused more on the personality factor and the circumstance within which actors are situated and, subsequently, make their decisions (see, e.g. Burger & Buskens, 2009). Communication links – physical, informational and social – emerge historically, and, if leading to a successful network, they may develop their own dynamics, shaping actors and agencies in their objectives and behaviours. The result may mean greater cooperation and a sense of shared purpose, or the opposite, abandoning existing links because they served their purpose, and interests 'have moved on'. A network thus shows two dimensions: it depends on the power, influence and effectiveness of the participants and, in return, shapes (i.e. strengthens or inhibits) an actor's scope for effective policy making. The main drivers of such linkages are. on the one hand, integrated, systemic conditions and, on the other, more ad hoc and personality-based social characteristics as an inter-personal network (Law, 1999). The question then is: how responsive to changing conditions and circumstance a network is, and what scope there is for actors to join and leave as objectives and conditions change? Will those shaping the network allow newcomers to join and, potentially, 'upset' the established balance of power and ways of doing things within it? With attention directed to the virtues of informal (network-based) relationships in metropolitanised governance (Kantor, 2008), it is the societal–political dimension of accepting and reinforcing 'core' and 'margin' that needs to be considered as well, not merely geographic distance and accessibility. Agenda-based proximity (propinquity) between actors and localities matters, not merely geographic distance. These emerging and changing 'geographies of centrality and marginality' (Paasi, 2006, p. 194) will inevitably create new boundaries and borders, inclusions and exclusions between those who are 'inside' and those who are 'outside' the relevant networks – be they whole localities or individual neighbourhoods, organisations or personalities. Network communication-defined spaces thus go beyond physical connectivities (infrastructure) and include linkages between and within institutions and other actors.

For some commentators, networked forms of governance open up new progressive possibilities for urban and regional governance. Amin and Graham (1999), for example, see progressive aspects of 'reflexive' networks, that is those that consciously adapt to external challenges. Rather than following hierarchically imposed rules and policies, new strategic directions for cities and regions could emerge from within. Such new political capacities may compensate for the widespread disaffection from traditional politics (see Clark & Hoffman-Martinot, 1998). Citizens may become more attached to governing regimes that can deliver, especially the 'non-material' public goods sought by the new middle class. New networked forms of urban and regional governance may be better at competing with other cities and regions and at delivering some types of local services. This kind of normative claims has much in common with the ideas of the 'new regionalism'.

These new spatialities, fragmented by a multitude of linear spaces – that is 'corridors of communication' – reflect a growing trend towards 'regionalised localisation' and increasingly virtual and non-contiguous policy-making spaces (Herrschel, 2009; Allen et al., 1998; Heeg et al., 2003). The underlying (actual or perceived) pressure to seek maximum competitiveness thus essentially reinforces 'atomised' variabilities and inequalities in opportunities. These can be found in a multitude of intersecting and overlaying networks, nodes and linkages between actors and decision makers – be they localities, agencies or individuals. Yet this fragmentation undermines the coherence and contiguity of urban spaces in their broader sense.

SUBURBS IN POLYCENTRIC CITY REGIONS

The main interest in urban governance focuses on the urban 'cores' as the presumed representatives of metropolitan (urban) areas, without much further analysis of the internal variations of such areas – especially the shifting roles and relevance between core cities and 'their' suburban (urbanising) areas. Conventionally, higher tier governments tended to establish 'regions' as part of their own managerial (top-down) agendas, not necessarily listening to the regions affected, especially when part of hierarchical planning regimes. All localities situated within a region's boundaries were part of it and subject to related policies. From such an external, generalising perspective, cities, their suburbs and surrounding wider hinterland may, from an external perspective, all be viewed as part of the bigger territorial 'package' of regions as contiguous spaces. From an internal (inside) perspective, however, there may be other, stronger linkages to like-minded actors and localities within and also between spatially and functionally defined city regions when it comes to campaigning for specific policy issues.

Two main scalar perspectives of city regions may be distinguished:

(1) the *external*, region-wide perspective, focusing on the city-region's outside visibility as one entity in a competitive national and international setting;
(2) the *internal*, intra-regional perspective and its concern with uneven developments, divisions and differences in role and influence within an urban (metropolitan) area.

This scalar duality reflects the somewhat vague nature and conceptualisation of 'metropolis' and 'urban', respectively, appearing, and being projected for competitive reasons to the outside world, as one entity. At the same time, it offers a much more differentiated, possibly even divided and localist-competitive picture 'inside'. Acknowledgement of the possible internal variations is offered by the concept of polycentric urban regions (PURs; see Bailey & Turok, 2001), addressing the internal variations within metropolitan areas as 'core' and 'non-core', that is suburban in-between spaces. PURs may be understood as regions with at least two urban centres with good connections through which they share into providing key urban functions, whereby the quality and characteristic of 'urban' is not so clear. Is it based on physiognomy, functional diversity and quality, or the sheer size of population?

Relationships – functional, political and spatial – vary between urban and suburban areas, shaped by their respective agendas and occurring commonalities among them. This may include specific *suburban* agendas that underpin alliances and collaborative governance arrangements between suburban areas, just as the same may work for the core urban areas for specific *urban* (central city) concerns. But then there are also linkages across

	Poly-centric (2+ core cities) City Region		Suburb 1	Suburb 2
	Mono-centric CR			
	Core City 1	Core City 2		

Core City 1	Alliances between core cities in a poly-centric city region to:
	    a) control and counteract suburbanisation (esp. retail) to protect city centres,
	    b) portray urban qualities and aggregate centrality (functional standing) for the whole city region to outside investors in a competitive setting. Suburbs are subsumed as 'complementary' to core cities.
			City 1: Urban area projected as one functionally complementary space in competitive city marketing	

Core City 2			*City 2*: Urban area projected as one functionally complementary space in competitive city marketing	
Suburb 1	As scenario *City 1*	As scenario City 2	*Inter-suburban* alliances to pursue a joint 'front' against the core city in policy agendas across a city region	
Suburb 2				

Fig. 1.   Intersection of Policy Agendas and Alliances Between Types of Actors in Monocentric and Polycentric City Regions.

categories, that is between urban and suburban actors and interests where interests collide and complement each other, as illustrated in Fig. 1. Several layers of governance relationships, arrangements and practices may overlap and intersect, reaching from sub-local, neighbourhood-based concerns and policy objectives, such as new retail developments versus residential interests within a suburb, to inter-locality competition (or alliances), such as between suburbs or between individual suburbs and the central city. Or, there may be city-region-wide collaborations, involving all suburbs and the core city in the pursuit of increased competitiveness and its marketing to a wider national or international audience. In PURs, there may even be more layers, involving two or more old established urban centres and 'their' respective policy networks, and inclusions and exclusions of parts of a city region.

Connectivity – physically and socially – matters, because the weaker these links, the more disconnected and thus invisible as distinct, separate entities these suburban spaces will be within their urban (city-regional) context. The city-focused network perspective finds one example in the concept of C2C, that is city-to-city, cooperation, an acronym introduced by Nigel Ringrose (UNDP, 2000 in Tjandradewi & Marcotullio, 2009). This refers to political linkages and relationships between cities at different spatial scales, transnational to sub-national, 'based on mutuality and equity' for 'mutual benefit'. This reflects the view that even at this global scale, only cities – and that implies first and foremost the core cities as visible beacons of their respective city regions – really matter. All else is presumed largely invisible and irrelevant, because it is 'networking between cities [that] is generally seen as the most effective way to strengthen the capacity of cities to solve major environmental and social problems, deliver urban services to their residents and develop effective urban governance and management structures' (Tjandradewi & Marcotullio, 2009, p. 166). Consequently, it is not surprising to find urban networks increasingly dominating the policy agenda and debate, such as the United Kingdom's core cities network and the Europe-wide urban network.

This of course is inevitably a rather generalised perspective, reducing distinctions largely to the two categories of 'urban' and 'non-urban' or, slightly more selectively in terms of size, 'metropolitan' and 'non-metropolitan' characteristics interests. There is thus an implicit dual categorisation, quite simplistically based on an urban–rural dichotomy. The picture, however, is much more complex, especially in metropolitan areas, with varying degrees of urbanisation affecting surrounding hinterlands, underpinned by ongoing changes and, unless strictly imposed, rather fuzzy boundaries between localities of different degrees of urban influence. And suburbs sit somewhere within these fuzzy spaces of varying degrees of urbanisation – or metropolitanisation – their interests, needs and agendas in danger of being overlooked because of their lower public profile and recognition factor. There are important implications of such a selectively localising, core urban, suburban or city-regionally focused approach to policy measures and governance arrangements.

In an idealised world, urban–rural connectivities would be based on complimentary interests – and the recognition of those – but in reality, such may not necessarily be the case. In those instances where areas and places are outside the primary network between the urban centres, they will find themselves with a weaker bargaining position, potentially being ignored, 'shut out' or marginalised. And this can well happen even within metropolitan regions – if actors and their agendas are deemed of little interest or benefit to the goals and agendas of the key policy makers who are part of, and shape, the dominant policy-making network. Not all actors – be they places, organisations or individuals – will therefore possess the same opportunities of access to political networks and decision making. Still, the polycentric model, given its usually larger number of 'cores', is seen by policy makers as less likely to be exclusive, because of its lesser imbalance between dominant cities 'and the rest'.

SUBURBS AS EMERGING 'IN-BETWEEN SPACES' AND ASPIRING PERIPHERIES

The current emphasis on cities – in a generalisation comprising both central city and suburbs – as economic nodes reinforces an understanding of space as defined by a sum of networks, with all else being 'in between' and little more than 'background'. There is little concern, it seems, about the actual roles and relevance of those 'in-between spaces'. Suburban areas represent such 'in-between spaces' also in their functional–physiognomic characteristics. They sit on the edge of – or between – established urban centres, with much lesser distinctiveness and thus recognisability, and a primarily function-driven role. Yet, increasingly, they are growing in importance, even overshadowing their respective metropolitan cores as the identifier of the whole metropolitan region. Especially in North America, but also in the only recently developed market-driven functional landscapes of post-communist Eastern Europe, it is the 'edges', the in-between suburban spaces that become the main foci of economic activity and connectivity. Yet the old cores possess the name, the recognition factor for 'their' metropolitan areas, irrespective of de facto functional economic relevance. There is thus a mismatch between functional importance and political recognition and visibility as place.

Instead, they are presumed to benefit from secondary 'trickle down' effects purely by being implicitly inside urban (metropolitan) spaces – however defined. This manifests and perpetuates the status quo of who is 'in' and who is 'out' of the competition for achieving better economic opportunity and development. And this again sets the parameters for the nature of local agendas, the composition and relevance of actors, the quality, reach and effectiveness of alliances, and the types and creativity of networks. Given such unevenness in likely scope and opportunity, even within the same socio-political and economic system, questions arise about potential response strategies of those finding themselves less visible and effectively marginalised in the new focus on the urban variety of regions (areas). The signs are, as Faludi (2003) observes, that primary attention is being given to the building of city regions as champions of national economic competitiveness, and to the role of associational responses by individual neighbouring municipalities in aiding that process (Herrschel & Newman, 2002; Salet, Thornley, & Kreukels, 2003). Much less interest, however, is shown in the effects these concentrations of interest and political resources and ambitions are having on the wider spatial development and the scope for maintaining a more balanced and thus ultimately more sustainable development of contiguous territories. And this includes nodes, networks as well as 'in-between' areas and, in particular, the suburban spaces with their growing functional economic relevance (new balance of importance?).

Cities expand into the region no longer in a concentric, but, increasingly, polycentric way, with new functional centres emerging within and between suburban areas of varying quality and socio-economic composition. This questions the notion of suburbanisation as some indistinguishable, essentially homogenous sprawl from the monocentric (old urban) core into the periphery. The (growing) internal functional, physiognomic and social and economic differentiation (see gated communities, edge cities, exurbs, etc.) reflects, but also generates, variations in ambitions and agendas, with some suburban areas sharing more commonality, at least for a set of policy topics and for a particular time period, than others. But they all feel (and are perceived and conceived) as being 'outside' the old established urban centre. The result is competing, overlapping and intersecting commonalities that translate into corresponding relationships and alliances in the policy-making field between and across suburban communities within functional city regions. When it comes to larger scale agendas, such as economic competition at the national or international scale, however, the suburbs and 'their' respective urban centres may discover common interests in a sense of region-based, rather than locally based, allegiance and sense of shared purpose.

Each of these alliances and policy networks revolves around a single or set of distinct policy agendas that provide the raisons d'etre for these very alliances. These are thus time limited and may well end with the achievement of the set agendas. The whole system of city-regional governance may thus be imagined as three dimensional, with networks developing within and across the spatial scales of policy agendas. The key ingredient for the formation of these alliances and policy networks is the sense of shared purpose and interest, however temporary it may be. These may be complimentary, or contradicting, with some actors participating in different networks that may embrace varying spatial scales and objectives. There is thus a fragmented political landscape in metropolitan areas (city regions) with varying and continuous reconfigurations that cannot be neatly distinguished into local and supralocal, that is city-region-wide matters. The answer thus is not simply installing different levels of government to 'manage' urban–suburban competition and variation, as these two are inflexible and lack sufficient variability and responsiveness to changing agendas. Responding governance arrangements need to be more imaginative and variable. This points in the direction of the concept of 'new regionalism' as a much less formalised, and instead more ad hoc and 'bottom-up', agenda-driven form of supralocal (but not necessarily region-wide) collaborative form of policy making. And this includes a wide range of actors both inside and outside of government as part of city-regional governance 'regimes' (Mossberger & Stoker, 2001), with business leaders being particularly important within the group of policy-making actors. This applies in particular to economic policies that have, as part of the suburbanisation process, increasingly also taken a regional perspective (see Cox, 1997).

These debates about city-regional cooperation revive long-standing concerns about the interdependence of cities and suburbs. Proponents of the new regionalism seek to prove the mutual economic benefits of cooperation on infrastructure investment, environmental planning and service management. Swanstrom (2001) argues for a regional approach, emphasising cooperation on economic, equity and other grounds. Arguments for city–suburban cooperation stress the economic costs of separation between city and suburb and the mutual benefits of cooperation. Cooperation is essential for the containment of sprawl and promotion of 'smart growth' (Ross & Levine, 2001, p. 319). The economic argument that emphasises effective relations between businesses and between business and communities at regional scale is thus joined to arguments about equity and environmental performance across regional economies.

In Britain, the Core Cities Initiative suggests an ongoing belief in rather more elitist urban structures with few but highly competitive, internationally connected urban nodes. Being widely *connected*, and being seen to be so, has become an expression of 'success' and relevance in shaping the path for future development. And this includes EU policy agendas that seem to accept localised inequalities in development potentials as a price worth paying for improved overall economic prospects. This seems to abandon conventional regional development goals with their inherent notion of contiguous territories and a concern with improving their economic development as a whole in the pursuit of 'balanced' development prospects and opportunities. For instance, the EU's URBACT II urban network tries to negotiate between urban and non-urban spaces by pursuing both 'old' and 'new' objectives. While on the one hand there is a continued concern with working towards greater cohesion, on the other, the strategy seeks to enhance urban competitiveness. This approach is illustrated by the cover to the brochure *Regions for Economic Change – Networking for Results* (EC, Brussels, 16–17 February 2009). As part of that, C2C networking is actively encouraged as the best way forward to achieve greater economic competitiveness in a global setting and for specified competitive industries. Not directly involved spaces are expected to benefit for some 'trickle down', and this seems to include suburbs, which are not mentioned explicitly as separate entities – either as an integral part of an urban municipality or as a separate locality on the edge (outside of) or between identified urban municipalities.

The new informal policy-oriented responses by territorially 'virtual' organisations challenge well-established, strongly formalised and techno-cratically implemented regionalism as a form of inter-municipal coordina-tion of development strategies. The recent statutory acknowledgement and manifestation of the Association of Greater Manchester Authorities (AGMA) is one example of such bottom-up, locality-based regionalisation that tries to capture suburban 'in-between spaces' in a polycentric functional urban region. The AGMA is the 'light' version of the former Greater Manchester Metropolitan County (GMMC), abolished in 1986, with a mere coordinating, rather than governmental role in its own right.

The Manchester metropolitan area has developed an increasingly energetic city-regional agenda, supported and facilitated by Manchester's developed 'trendy' and 'creative' reputation, especially when set in its Northern English context. Its origin as birthplace of the Industrial Revolution underpins its claim to being at the forefront of change and new developments and innovation. These characteristics have been promoted and used as a way to identify and frame response strategies to the challenges of economic competitiveness away from the UK economic hub of London and the South East. Using initiatives and policy projects to promote the city as 'world class' clearly sought to challenge London's pre-eminence, and this strategy was supported by national policies of supporting the competitive position of the main metropolitan areas outside London as part of its new, city-focused regional strategy (see also the Northern Way project as 'virtual' region underpinning a group of cities across Northern England; Liddle, 2009).

Perhaps not surprisingly, given its regional pre-eminence, in the late 1990s, Manchester suggested an extension to its administrative boundaries to achieve a better match with its functional economic and social area. It was a rather conventional approach to 'regionalise' through expansive administrative re-territorialisation. Such a move would have taken Manchester officially, in statistical terms, beyond the 1 million threshold as a single local authority, and thus allowed it to move up the hierarchy in the league of European cities, providing more recognition and a louder voice. The proposal set off alarm bells among the other, smaller municipalities adjacent to Manchester, fearing a 'take over' by the 'big fish in the pond'. Historically entrenched localism and related rivalries rebelled against such a 'threat'. In addition, very much illustrating a suburban perspective, there was anxiety about having to subsidise Manchester's large bill for social services and benefits, a reflection of deep-seated views of socio-economic divisions between old core city and suburbs. There were also memories of the former Manchester-centric GMMC of 1974, abolished in 1986, which consisted of 10 metropolitan boroughs. However, such Manchester-dominated 'Super City' proposal caused a suburban and 'hinterland' backlash and reinvigorated a somewhat dormant, lose umbrella organisation, the AGMA that had succeeded the GMMC to provide a platform for coordinating some services for the city region. Its members agreed in the summer of 1998 to review their operation and strengthen their cooperation in the interest of a more integrated city-regional approach to some aspects of governance, driven by concern about competitiveness vis-à-vis other metropolitan regions in the United Kingdom and beyond. An agreement was signed at the end of 2009 with the then government about a new statutory status for the Manchester City Region. Yet it works through the existing municipalities that also provide democratic legitimacy.

This change in the concept of 'regions' and 'regionalisation' towards a more collaborative, 'loose' arrangement with no high hurdles to changing membership is also illustrated by the changing appreciation of the role of the 'regional extension' to the core city in Leeds over the last decade. While its economic development strategy of the late 1990s (Leeds City Council, c. 1997) made no reference to the surrounding region of Yorkshire, because, so one officer in the economic development unit pronounced at the time, 'there is nothing in it for us engaging with them', there is now an explicit reference to other participants in a Leeds urban region. The Leeds City Region Partnership is a collaborative arrangement comprising the city of Leeds as leading actors, and the surrounding municipalities. And this is, as part of city-regional marketing, advocated in form or the new slogan 'intelligence driving growth'. This is a bottom-up arrangement, similar to that established last year for the Greater Manchester City Region, and represents a much more inclusive view of the city region than the conventional 'core–periphery' perspective. How this translates into power relationships and networks between and across the different 'types' of localities within the city region is, however, another question. With such 'spaces' defined by networks and connections between actors, rather than boundaries drawn around territories as complete, integral entities, the existence and quality of connectivities will define the degree to which individual actors (places, organisations, individuals) are able to 'attach themselves' to such a 'virtual region' (Herrschel, 2009), and participate in its policies. This is inherently unpredictable in scope and outcome and makes planning and policy objectives much more difficult to put into practice, especially at a geographically broader, less clearly localised level.

The current plans for the Madrid city regions use such a network-based nature of a city region, based on communication links, and are intended not as a top-down model of imposed city regionalisation, but rather a bottom-up defined model that involves a wide range of governmental and non-governmental actors with city-regional interests (Heitkamp, 1998). This is a response to the rapid, property development–driven suburbanisation and thus expansion of Madrid, with some of the affected towns and villages around Madrid city experiencing a three-fold increase in their population within a few years (Heitkamp, 1998). This development occurred in individual localities, based on perceived speculative opportunities, without functional integration and connection to the city region. The question, as in other expanding (suburbanising) city regions, is thus one about how to address the growing regional scale of urban development: through a new, formal layer of regional governance or through collaborative inter-local policy making when addressing agendas that possess a supralocal (regional) dime (Heitkamp, 1998). The transport strategy for the Madrid region (Guerra, 2000) is one step in the direction of a wider regional perspective, but it is rather more following speculation-driven suburbanisation and provides a connective framework, than setting the agenda.

Just as fundamental for meaningful city regionalism as connectivity are fiscal arrangements. Do they support regional perspectives and agendas by individual municipalities? The example of the metropolitan region of Berlin–Brandenburg in eastern Germany illustrates time lag in the adjustment of city-regional governance to changing functional imperatives in an ever more metropolis-focused developmental competitiveness. Overcoming long-established and deep-seated city–suburb antagonisms and mistrust, especially under the conditions of a stark asymmetry between the function-rich inner metropolitan area and the much less developed, fundamentally rural, outer area with small municipalities, has proved challenging. Engaging in cooperation can be a long-term political process and has proved more likely to develop where controversial issues are avoided and 'win–win' opportunities are perceived. Flexible, 'open' cooperation with varying partners and low entry and exit thresholds thus seems to be the format most favoured. In a federal system with strong local traditions and quite autonomous municipalities, adopting a regional perspective needs to yield local advantages. It is local, where electoral approval needs to be achieved, and there may well be considerable differences in views and expectations between the urban centre and the suburban and semi-rural periphery.

The fiscal system of population-based and business tax-generated local revenues sets the parameters for inter-local competition rather than collaboration. The Joint Planning Authority of Berlin–Brandenburg as 'bridge' between the two federal states sees itself as a source of new regional visions. The planners claim some success in promoting regional conscious-ness and argue that, in the face of proposed regional development frameworks in which not all communes win, initially strong localist opposition is lessening. Throughout the 1990s, incentives to greater intergovernmental cooperation were not strong enough to encourage *Land* and local governments to break out of self-interested and localist habits.

The detail of the Berlin–Brandenburg case points to the uneven nature 'variety of new regionalisms' in response to different circumstances (Jonas & Ward, 2002, p. 397). Choices between local and regional perspectives are structured by the institutional frameworks of regional and local government and by the economic circumstances surrounding a city region. Depending on relative economic prospects, this shapes a sense of shared grief or shared success, whereby the former is likely to be a stronger 'glue' for city-regionalist thinking than the latter.

CONCLUSIONS: GOVERNANCE, ASPIRING SUBURBS AND POLICY NETWORKS IN CITY REGIONS

Concern about global competitiveness drives an increasingly localised city-focused policy agenda at national and EU levels. This projects urban areas in a rather general light as cohesive entities attached to a leading core city as the centre of an urban region. This follows an underlying notion of the conventional, territorial image of a core city surrounded by an expanse of complimentary, functionally dependent and increasingly peripheral sub-urban areas. Reality, however, is much more complex, with a patchwork of different types of 'suburbs' surrounding one or more urban cores. They are connected in varying constellations by a network of differing collaborative relationships. These stretch between different suburbs and their actors, as well as between the core cities and a varying number and range of suburbs. There is thus no longer an underlying, clearly defined urban territory that *contains* the various suburban places and actors, but rather a clustering of different – and changing – collaborative relationships and networks. This reflects a growing status of suburbs as actors in their own right next to, or even vis-à-vis, the main core city. They seek to formulate their own policy objectives and priorities, and subsequently set out to build their own alliances, or join or leave existing ones in line with their set agendas. Ultimately, this may reduce the urban core to just one player among several. Urban regions are thus much more dynamic and variable than conventional dichotomy between urban and suburban models.

The nature of networks places emphasis on narrow, inherently linear operating linkages between nodes (actors), rather than encompassing two-dimensional territories. The scope to belong to a *network* as a strategic objective is quite different from the so far much more spatially driven territorially based approach, where the location of an individual actor in an area also means automatically belonging to it. In contrast, by their very nature, networks cannot cover a space contiguously. Instead, they subdivide a space into separate 'corridors of connectivity', separated by 'left out' areas in between. These in-between spaces, their size and number depending on the density of actor nodes' (organisations, localities) network connections, reflect new, or reinforced old, divisions between the 'included' and 'excluded'. And this, again, creates new marginalities on the basis of uneven access to power structures, policy-making processes and agenda-setting possibilities. While physical infrastructure in its varying presence immediately translates into a public perception of difference in accessibility – usually expressed as distance costs (Copus, 2001) – social–political connectivities are much less obvious. They are thus more difficult to gauge and predict in their likely impact. They are also much less easy to alter or, indeed, utilise.

While 'territory', 'boundary' and 'structure' continue to be the key elements of governance, globalisation demands a broader perspective with a greater variety of forms of governance across city regions, embracing urban, suburban and 'in-between' places. Some authors refer to 'soft institutionalism' (MacLeod, 2001, 2004) to denote the inherent variability, even 'fluffiness', of 'new' city regionalism. With its emphasis on informal alliances and policy-defining arrangements, processes and their rationales are more difficult to follow, the role of different actors more difficult to identify and follow, and legitimacy more difficult to secure. While physical infrastructure can be modified through investment, thus altering perceptions of distance and thus marginality, connectivities between political and economic actors are much more difficult to influence and observe. Other actors – places, organisations and individuals – may thus find it difficult to join, so as not to upset the existing relationships and balances of power negotiated between those actors who are already part of the network and functioning as nodes.

REFERENCES

Allen, J., Massey, D., & Cochrane, A. (1998). *Rethinking the region*. London: Routledge.
Amin, A., & Graham, S. (1999). Cities of connection and disconnection. In: J. Allen, D. Massey & M. Pryke (Eds), *Unsettling cities*. London: Routledge.
Bailey, N., & Turok, I. (2001). Central Scotland as a polycentric urban region: Useful planning concept of chimera? *Urban Studies*, *38*(4), 697–715.
Barnes, W., & Ledebur, L. (1998). *The new regional economies: The US common market and the global economy*. London: Sage.
Boddy, M., & Parkinson, M. (2004). *City matters: Competitiveness, cohesion and urban governance*. Bristol: Policy Press.
Burger, M., & Buskens, V. (2009). Social context and network formation: An experimental study. *Social Networks*, *31*(1), 63–75.
Castells, M. (1989). *The informational city*. Oxford: Blackwell.
Christ, W. (1998). Von Innen nach Außen-Weimar als Exerzierfeld der Moderne. In: W. Prigge (Ed.), *Peripherie ist Überall* (pp. 174–193). Frankfurt: Campus.
Clark, T., & Hoffman-Martinot, V. (Eds). (1998). *The new public culture*. Oxford: Westview Press.
Copus, A. (2001). From core–periphery to polycentric development: Concepts of spatial and aspatial peripherality. *European Planning Studies*, *9*(4), 539–552.
Cox, K. (1997). *Spaces of globalization: Reasserting the power of the local*. New York: Guilford Press.
Faludi, A. (2003). Unfinished business: European spatial planning in the 2000s. *Town Planning Review*, *74*(11), 121–140.
Garreau, J. (1991). *Edge city: Life on the new frontier*. Garden City, NY: Anchor Books.
Guerra, L. (2000). Towards a sustainable mobility in the Madrid region. In: *Informationen zur Raumentwicklung*. Theme issue 'Europäische Metropolregionen' (pp. 665–670). Bonn, Germany: BBR (Bundesamt für Bauwesen und Raumordnung).
Hall, P. (1998). *Cities in civilization*. London: Weidenfeld & Nicolson.
Hauswirth, I., Herrschel, T., & Newman, P. (2003). Incentives and disincentives to city-regional cooperation in the Berlin–Brandenburg conurbation. *European Urban and Regional Studies*, *10*(2), 119–134.
Healey, P. (2000). New partnerships in planning and implementing future-oriented development in European metropolitan regions. In: *Informationen zur Raumentwicklung*. Theme issue 'Europäische Metropolregionen' (pp. 745–750). Bonn, Germany: BBR (Bundesamt für Bauwesen und Raumordnung).

Heeg, S., Klagge, B., & Ossenbrügge, J. (2003). Metropolitan cooperation in Europe: Theoretical issues and perspectives for urban networking. *European Planning Studies*, *11*(2), 139–153.

Heitkamp, Th. (1998). Madrid, Eine Region im Wandel. In: W. Prigge (Ed.), *Peripherie ist Überall* (pp. 208–231). Frankfurt: Campus.

Herrschel, T. (2005). Creative regionalisation. Making regions for upscale and downscale consumption – Experiences from post-socialist eastern Germany. *Geojournal*, *62*(1), 63–69.

Herrschel, T. (2009). Regionalisation, 'virtual' spaces and 'real' territories. A view from Europe and North America. *International Journal of Public Sector Management*, *22*(3), 261–272.

Herrschel, T., & Newman, P. (2002). *Governance of Europe's city regions*. London: Routledge.

Hoffmann-Axthelm, D. (1998). Peripherien. In: W. Prigge (Ed.), *Peripherie ist Überall* (pp. 113–121). Frankfurt: Campus.

Jonas, A., & Ward, K. (2002). A world of regionalisms? Towards a US–UK urban and regional policy framework comparison. *Journal of Urban Affairs*, *24*(4), 377–401.

Kantor, P. (2008). Varieties of city regionalism and the quest for political cooperation: A comparative perspective. *Urban Research & Practice*, *1*(2), 111–129.

Kearns, A., & Paddison, R. (2000). New challenges for urban governance: Introduction to the review issue. *Urban Studies*, *37*(Pt. 5/6), 845–850.

Keating, M. (1998). *The New Regionalism in Western Europe*. Cheltenham: Edward Elgar.

Keating, M., & Loughlin, J. (Eds). (1997). *The political economy of regionalism (Cass series in regional and federal studies)*. London: Frank Cass (Routledge).

Law, J. (1999). After ANT: Complexity, naming and typology. In: J. Law & J. Hassard (Eds), *Actor network theory and after* (pp. 1–14). Oxford: Blackwell.

Liddle, J. (2009). The northern way: A pan-regional associational network. *International Journal of Public Sector Management*, *22*(3), 192–202.

MacLeod, G. (2001). Beyond soft institutionalism: Accumulation, regulation, and their geographical fixes. *Environment and Planning A*, *33*(7), 1145–1167.

MacLeod, G. (2002). New regionalism reconsidered: Globalization and the remaking of political economic space. *International Journal of Urban and Regional Research*, *25*(4), 804–882.

MacLeod, G. (2004). Beyond soft institutionalism: Accumulation, regulation, and their geographical fixes. In: A. Wood & D. Valler (Eds), *Governing local and regional economies: Institutions, politics and economic development* (pp. 57–89). London: Ashgate.

Mossberger, K., & Stoker, G. (2001). The evolution of urban regime theory the challenge of conceptualization. *Urban Affairs Review*, *36*(6), 810–835.

Paasi, A. (2006). *Cities in a world economy* (3rd ed.). London. Pine Forge Press.

Peck, J. (2000). Doing regulation. In: G. Clark, M. Feldman & M. Gertler (Eds), *The Oxford handbook of economic geography*. Oxford: Oxford University Press(chap. 4).

Porter, M. (2000). Location, competition, and economic development: Local clusters in a global economy. *Economic Development Quarterly*, *14*(1), 15–34.

Provan, K., & Kenis, P. (2007). Modes of network governance: Structure, management, and effectiveness. *Journal of Public Administration Research and Theory*, *18*(2), 229–252.

Raco, M. (1999). Competition, collaboration and the new industrial districts: Examining the institutional turn in local economic development. *Urban Studies*, *36*(5–6), 951–968.

Ross, B., & Levine, M. (2001). *Urban politics: Power in metropolitan America* (6th ed.). Itasca, IL: Peacock.

Salet, W., Thornley, A., & Kreukels, A. (Eds). (2003). *Metropolitan governance and spatial planning*. London: Spon.

Scott, A. (2001). *Global city-regions*. Oxford: Oxford University Press.

Short, J. R., Bentona, L. M., Lucea, W. B., & Waltona, J. (1993). Reconstructing the image of an industrial city. *Annals of the Association of American Geographers, 83*(2), 207–224.

Sieverts, Th. (1998). Eine Deutung der Zwischenstadt (Interpretation of the 'in-between city'). In: W. Prigge (Ed.), *Peripherie ist Überall* (pp. 98–111). Frankfurt: Campus.

Soja, E. (1992). Inside exopolis: Scenes from Orange County. In: M. Sorkin (Ed.), *Variations on a theme park: The New American city and the end of public space* (pp. 94–122). New York: Noonday Press.

Swanstrom, T. (2001). What we argue about when we argue about regionalism. *Journal of Urban Affairs, 23*(5), 479–496.

Swyngedouw, E. (2004). Globalisation or 'glocalisation'? Networks, territories and rescaling. *Cambridge Review of International Affairs, 17*(1), 25–48.

Tjandradewi, B., & Marcotullio, P. (2009). City-to-city networks: Asian perspectives on key elements and areas of success. *Habitat International, 33*, 165–172.

UNDP. (2000). *The challenges of linking*. New York: Unites Nations Development Programme.

Whitehead, M. (2003). In the shadow of hierarchy: Meta-governance, policy reform and urban regeneration in the West Midlands. *Area, 35*(1), 6–14.

URBANITY BEYOND NOSTALGIA: DISCOVERING PUBLIC LIFE AT THE EDGE OF THE CITY OF ROME

Sandra Annunziata and Mara Cossu

INTRODUCTION

The contemporary city of Rome is being built differently from the expanding post-war peripheries. New, mainly private residential developments are changing our perception of the cityscape. According to the General Plan, these projects are designed to encourage a polycentric metropolitanization, with mixed uses and facilities. But they have been critiqued for producing urbanscapes that 'discourage urbanity' because the relevant organizational and functional dimensions of public life have been almost totally neglected: foremost among these are the provision of public goods, services to citizens, high-quality standards of construction and an infrastructure allowing for spatial mobility. The main argument for urbanity emphasizes 'the way of using the space of the city' in combination with spontaneous forms of interaction within that urban space. This argument contests the production of the contemporary suburban areas of the city and is based upon a sort of nostalgia for the urbanism inherited in the romantic conceptualization of the modern European city, made visible in the celebrations of historical city places. It gives rise to dissatisfaction with the recently built environment which has been critiqued for its 'absence of urbanity'.

Suburbanization in Global Society
Research in Urban Sociology, Volume 10, 131–152
ISSN: 1047-0042/doi:10.1108/S1047-0042(2010)0000010008

Despite – or perhaps because of – this criticism, little attention has been given to deepen the quality of life in those places from an agents-based perspective. Our fieldwork observation challenges this absence of understanding. It was conducted in two settlements, New Ponte di Nona and Romanina. In-depth interviews with local residents suggest that these communities represent 'reserves of urbanity' in which new forms of interaction may be interpreted as the 'learning process of living together', a precondition of both tolerance and civil respect that works as preliminary step in the achievement of public life in the urban periphery.

URBANITY IN ROME

Rome is well known for its historical heritage. The imperial city and the magnificent baroque urban spaces created by the 'city of the Pope' are often epitomized as essential for civic life, a 'place where strangers meet and, consequently, the public sphere can be formed' (Sennett, 1974, 1992). But this characterization does not fit with the configuration that Rome assumes today, a large metropolitan area surrounded the historical centre that grew without constraints, where almost two-thirds of the urbanized land of the capital city had been developed in the last 50 years (INU, 2008). New growth is occurring, apparently without being inscribed in a proper strategy of urban development. Such growth is on the surface inimical to the spatial pattern of the European cities, and in particular, the Mediterranean city that is oriented towards compactness (Secchi, 2005). In spite of that, suburbanization is expanding in contemporary Rome along the main consular roads that spread from the core of the city towards northern, southern and eastern regions. In this particular case, suburbanization is also combined with diffuse sprawl in the so-called Roman Agro, the agricultural land that until recently was a fundamental part of the economy of the city (Indovina, 1970, 2000).

Earlier phases of suburbanization in Rome occurred within the peripheries that Pasolini described as 'the crown of thorns that surrounded the city of god'. With this phrase he caught the condition of urban poor in new developments occurring at the fringe of the city during the 1950s.[1] The term 'periphery' incorporates two main characteristics, one geographical, namely 'farness from the city centre' and the other social, to wit 'mainly working class' (Insolera, 1993). This produced something akin to with a 'diffuse social malaise' and urban blight. Moreover, peripheries have been studied and described by Ferrarotti (1974) as places where the 'solidaristic block' of the middle class was forming. This term has also been used to describe former public housing planned as a self-independent unit to guarantee public facilities for the uses of the 'planned community' (Quaroni, 1956 quoted in Di Biagi, 2001). These units were located beyond informal settlements, which have historically been driven by all sorts of speculation (Insolera, 1993).

After 20 years of relative silence in Italian academia, Roman peripheries are back on the urban research agenda (Ferrarotti & Macioti, 2009). In this chapter we will emphasize historical interpretative categories that describe the suburbs that have emerged in recent decades. In doing so, we seek also the notion of urbanity in order to describe something new happening in contemporary urban spaces.

The usual description of the periphery of Rome, contrasted with the thriving city centre, is out of date. It fails to explain the complexity of the city. As De Jong argues, the central city has always been considered to be dense, diverse, heterogeneous and the locus of high culture and employment opportunities. On the contrary the suburbs were 'stereo-typed as residential enclaves of cultural vacuity, homogeneity, dispersion, a polarization that has proven stubbornly resistant to revision' (2010). Areas that once were beyond the peripheries of 'Pasolinian memory' are today a substantial part of Roman city life; they are places for an intense and vibrant urban life even as they experience gentrification. Simultaneously, a new generation of suburbanization, happening at the fringe of the metropolitan area, is giving rise to many issues.

In recent decades the city of Rome has registered a new wave of building development. Large, mainly private residential settlements have been constructed in a different way to the earlier post-war era of expansion. They are boosted by the General Plan which aims to achieve a more diffuse and polycentric system, and which represented a new opening towards specula-tion because it was not able to counter the oversized previous plan designed in 1962. Rather than being inhabited by the working classes or the urban poor, the new settlements are designed to host the housing demand of a new middle class, choosing a particular introverted housing typology to reflect status and exclusivity, for instance at New Ponte di Nona. Even when these new settlements have been combined with some sort of hybrid social housing (for instance cooperative and affordable housing blocks at Romanina) the notion of high-quality urban places as a site for social mixing is not the high priority associated with the traditional urban core of Italian cities.

A familiar critique accuses suburban settlements of diminishing a sense of belonging, producing alienation and anonymity and the all-too-familiar characteristics of dormitories. In other words, 'suburbs are commonly perceived as essentially non-urban and as non-places without a spatial logic of their own' (Vaughan, Griffiths, Haklay, & Jones, 2009, 2010). By contrast, this chapter offers a possible interpretation of an alternative version of suburban settlement, in the wake of Webster (2009). In contemporary Rome the recently built environment is not simply 'far from the center' or 'homogeneous' and 'lacking in urbanity' but also a place where new forms of urbanity need to be discovered.

The new settlements give rise to several issues about public life in contemporary city: individuals who choose to live there want to be 'far' from the congested city centre, but still 'in' close proximity to the main attractions that are nowadays represented by the 'temple of consumerism'. A double desire, being 'far' but also 'in' is well expressed by the tendency of the flattening between inner city and suburban areas as described by De Jong: 'exemplified in the emergence of hybrid (sub)urban conditions such as inner city big-box retail, densification of suburban villages near transit, and parking practices' (2010). This is particularly true for the city of Rome where private residential settlements represent the catchment areas for huge commercial box stores and shopping malls that are located just beyond them. The growth of shopping malls, in a vibrant city such as Rome, angers those who privilege traditional urbanism, yet at the same time they provide a fresh basis for public life in new settlements. This can be seen as originally an 'American' phenomenon that occurred some 20 years later around the capital city of Italy.

Within this framework, the case studies offer the opportunity to go beyond suburban stereotypes. Instead of the anonymous, impersonal and stereotypical notion of suburbs, the chapter suggests that those areas represent 'reserves of urbanity' where it is possible to discover the germinal forms of public life, and to begin a re-definition of the relationship between contemporary urban settlement and public life. The first part of the chapter presents the political rationale for recent suburban development as evidence in the General Plan. The second part of the chapter analyses three main positions found in literature concerning the contemporary city conceptualized under the labels of nostalgia of urbanity, absence of urbanity and a call for new visions of urbanity. The last part of the chapter describes how and to which extent the fieldwork observation demonstrates that public life occurs also at the fringe of the city, assuming new forms within unpredictable spaces. The chapter aims to challenge the idea that urbanity can only happen in a dense, heterogeneous and diverse compact urban fabric. By looking at suburban settlements in Rome, we argue that it is possible to find the social evidence for a newer definition of contemporary urbanity, a fresh under-standing of the 'art of living together' in urban spaces.

PRESENTING THE CASE: THE NEW GENERATION OF SUBURBAN SETTLEMENTS IN ROME

The new generation of suburban settlements has mostly been planned along the administrative boundaries of the city and located beyond the so-called 'centralities' or urban hub areas. According to the General Plan, Comune di Roma (2007), such developments are aimed to decentralize the main employment locations traditionally situated in the city centre across a more diffuse and polycentric system (Marcelloni, 2003). They are expected to be multimodal nodes, located in close proximity to rail stations (Fig. 1).

Even though they have been designed to encourage mixed uses in a suburban environment, the new suburban settlements have been accused of producing landscapes that do not encourage urbanity in the sense of the 'art of using the space of the city' as argued by the French sociologist Raymond (1998). The result seems to satisfy individual and private interests and reinforces real estate market speculation (Berdini, 2008b). Moreover, suburban development superficially appears to undermine the common ground for urban living: a system of shared resources such as public space, public facilities and common goods. Other relevant organizational and functional dimensions of urbanity have been neglected: public goods supply, services to citizens, quality standards, mobility infrastructures. The general 'iron-cure' for urban mobility was to strengthen railway connections. In spite of that, metropolitan region of Rome is still characterized by a large private car-dependent mobility (Tocci, 2008; Insolera, Morandi, & Tocci, 2008), partly due to Rome's favourable location in the local and national road system. New Ponte di Nona and Romanina provide interesting contrast to examine some key infrastructural issues (Fig. 2).

New Ponte di Nona is located at the eastern edge of the city, along the highway that connects Rome with the Abruzzo region. It has been planned to include a new railway station (with 2,000 parking spaces); a shopping mall considered as one of the main commercial attractions in the metropolitan area with more than 200 shops; public and private services (such as the municipal building and hospital services); a new covered market, and a hotel and conference centre. The open space is supposed to become a theme park with a sports centre. Notwithstanding the General

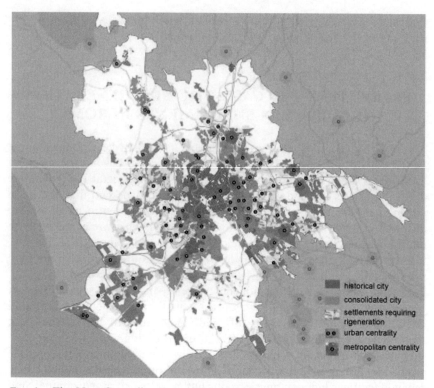

Fig. 1. The New Centrality Foreseen by the General Plan. *Source:* The General
Plan of Rome.

Plan, most of the public infrastructure has yet to be completed: the houses
and the huge shopping mall still enjoy only minimal services (accessibility,
transportation, public services).

The private developer that drove the building activity, according to a
private–public agreement, was in charge of (sub)urbanizing the whole area,
providing streets and utilities together with dwellings. In 1995 the agreement
between the city and the consortium was set and, after 10 years, the public
authority should have got back the area completely urbanized. Currently,
about 4,600 housing units have been completed, sold and inhabited by
about 18,000 citizens. In 2007 a new motorway junction, planned by the
municipality, was opened to guarantee, at least, connection by car. Adjacent
to the junction, a huge shopping mall opened and became the main centre of
neighbourhood life. Now, the junction is the main entrance both for the

Fig. 2. The Case Studies Location. *Source:* The General Plan of Rome, Manipulated by Sandra Annunziata.

neighbourhood and for the mall, consolidating an unsustainable car dependency for which the development has been criticized. Currently, New Ponte di Nona, numbers 6,000 housing units, is located beyond pre-existing housing settlements (Fig. 3).

Romanina is located at the south-eastern edge of the city, over the highway ring and closed to Tor Vergata University campus. It is notably different from New Ponte di Nona in terms of a more diverse history of social and spatial developments. It started to be informally settled immediately after the Second World War, hosting most workers immigrating to Rome in that period. During the 1960s and the 1970s, informal housing increased. This was accompanied by the first warehouses and storefronts allowed by the General Plan from 1962. During the 1980s and the 1990s the construction of wholesale centres among the existing storefronts increased the commercial character and image of the area, saturating the north-western quadrant with edge-city style developments. However, many vacant lots towards the south of the area remained by the end of the last century. In the last 15 years, real estate and public housing activities were concentrated on the remaining underdeveloped parts of the

informal settlement 1950
public housing 1960-70
new settlements
new Ponte di Nona
centrality with shopping mall

Fig. 3. New Ponte di Nona Plan and the Surrounding Neighbourhood.

area (Fig. 4). New neighbourhoods and malls of almost any size (including Ikea, Decathlon, Mediaworld, etc.) spread in juxtaposition to existing development. Roads are still under construction to support the large volume of traffic, a situation exacerbated by inadequate public transport.

The master plan for the Romanina area was designed by Manuel Salgado, the winner of an international competition (Gruppo Scarpellini, 2008). Yet commercial interests have influenced the rollout of the plan. Much land is owned by an important real estate company in Rome, responsible for the whole planning and building activity, even though no clarifications were provided about the urban functions and services to be required. The company engaged in a sort of struggle with the municipality, claiming for a greater area of admitted building surfaces in return for the extension of the existing underground line and the construction of the centrality station foreseen by the General Plan. Currently, building activity has yet not started, and no compromises seem to be under discussion at local government level.

Recent transformations influenced by real estate dynamics are common to several edge areas of the city. In 2008 a well-known national report showed

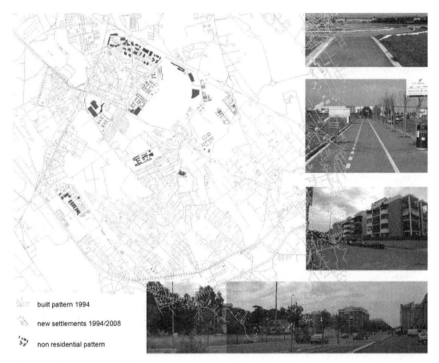

built pattern 1994

new settlements 1994/2008

non residential pattern

Fig. 4. Chronological Development of Patterns and Building Typologies at Romanina.

these settlements as a scandal and placed blame on the public authority collusion with private speculators. This episode, called 'The Kings of Rome' (Mondani, 2008), resulted in a debate among political actors and technicians responsible for the plan. The politicians and planners argued that the good intention of the General Plan was to re-balance private and collective interests in suburban development. On the other side, the main criticism was carried out by radical left scholars, who sustained that 'common interests were completely left behind by private speculation' (Berdini, 2008a, 2008c; De Lucia, 2005). They also blamed privatization for the absence of vitality in new suburbs.

THE NOSTALGIA OF URBANITY

As noted in the introduction, urbanity refers to the city; it lacks an empirical reference to the suburbs. To expand the notion of urbanity, we address first the nostalgic position towards historical thriving places, and the common critique that new planned suburbs demonstrate an absence of urbanity.

We conclude with reassessment of urbanity in relation to recent suburban development based upon our fieldwork.

Based simply on their physical design, New Ponte di Nona and Romanina could be considered perfect targets for critics of suburbanization, places where the conditions for urban living and the traditional organizational and functional dimensions of civic life have been almost totally neglected. Both settlements seem to promote a simplified urbanity, mainly rooted in the spatial proximity between dwelling and consumption. This reduces drastically the public realm defined by Lofland (1998) as those areas where genuine interaction among strangers can, to certain extent, produce tolerance and civil respect (Sennett, 1974). Public intellectuals and scholars accused the City Board for giving priority to private interests and consequently a neo-liberal version of the city driven by privatization and land consumption (Berdini, 2008b; De Lucia, 2005). This criticism reflects the nostalgia for the urbanity of the modern European city, an historicism made visible in the celebrations of historical city places.

Many key theories in urban sociology have focused upon the impact of urbanism (the structural characters of cities, consisting of size, hetero-geneity, and density and affecting the spatial distribution of activities) and urbanity (the resulting residents' psyche, cognitive modes, value and behavioural patterns). Urbanity can be experienced differently according to the spatial order of different places. In this view, urbanity is the social psychological adaptation to the immediate macrolevel structural feature of urban places (Tiettle & Gramsmick, 2001). As noted, it is characterized by traits such as tolerance of strangers.

In the field of planning, the term 'urbanity' has been translated into technical principles in order to produce higher densities, and to encourage diversity and mixed use (Jacobs, 1961). Issues about the distinctive qualities of urban spaces, and how to enhance them, have been the cause of continuing concern for urban designers. In particular, within the field of urban design, the place-making approach uses the term 'urbanity' as a label to express a sort of nostalgia of urbanity, ignoring certain aspects of the traditional historical city space and attempting to reintroduce the virtue of the compact city without renouncing post-modern lifestyles and reverting to a monolithic city culture. This phenomenon is apparent in gentrified neighbourhoods or central places. According with the success of certain localities, urban designers are fostering urbanity in order to design good-looking places (Montgomery, 1995) and to make the city more attractive when competing in a global arena. By contrast, recent suburbs, where such notions of urbanity were not included in the design, have been consequently accused of a 'normative absence of urbanity' (Haussermänn & Siebel, 1987).

THE ABSENCE OF URBANITY

In the last 15 years the field of planning has developed increasingly innovative urban policies to foster growth and development worldwide (Fainstein, 2008; Secchi, 2005). Almost every metropolitan region of Europe and North America is characterized by the growth of new regional hubs connected by new or improved transport systems (Bertolini, 2006). These regional hubs are the most evident spatial outcome of globalization, suggesting spatial mobility instead of proximity as a valuable aspect of urban contemporary life.

Many efforts have been made to evaluate the planning process and the form of multilevel governance necessary to complete these projects. They have often been studied from the point of view of their financial viability: as high-risk financial projects, they have been primarily geared towards profitability and have been later accused of producing landscapes inimical to or indifferent towards urbanity (Fainstein, 2008; Gualini & Majoor, 2007), despite the fact that their strategic framework was intended to achieve new forms of urbanity (Salet, 2008).

REDISCOVERING URBANITY IN NEWLY BUILT DEVELOPMENT

Recent positions in urban research have opened up the meaning of urbanity beyond the perspectives offered by Raymond, Sennett and others. It is possible to better understand urbanity as the 'practice of living together in a system of shared resources' (Annunziata & Cossu, 2010) and to a certain extent as a learning process that encompasses innumerable types of urbanity, including forms of intersection between different practices that actually produce something new in urban space. The issue of urbanity has been compared with living conditions in a highly mobile society. A high level of mobility could be considered more important to achieve urbanity than the traditional concept of proximity (Bertolini, 2006).

Additionally, other areas of research expose practices that combine resistance to urban change, bottom-up local projects and the formation of bonds of co-existence strongly situated among the Italians (Cremaschi, 2008a, 2008b; Bianchetti, 2008a, 2008b; Chase, Crawford, & Kaliski, 1999). Vaughan et al. (2009, 2010) try to underline the centrality of suburbs to everyday life, showing that they have an independent public life that is real, measurable and diverse as in the urban city centre. Cremaschi (2008b) argues that urbanity can be seen as the 'art of living together' producing, to certain extent, a way of behaving that can be considered the precondition of both tolerance and civil respect that work as preliminary steps in the exercise of citizenship. So it is possible to argue that the nostalgic notion of urbanity is inadequate to explain the different kinds of urban life people are experiencing today. The city of Rome suggests that the contemporary city includes a complex range of new settlements, activities, forms of interactions, populations that frame a highly differentiated and plural city. A more complex phenomenon of urbanity is coming into being. Hence, recently built urban settlements can be considered as laboratories where urbanity can be investigated as a 'learning process' more than an ideological position. As Lofland suggests 'we have to seek to understand urban settlement rather than condemn them, [...] to look upon the city as human habitat rather than to shun it as alien territory' (1998). Our empirical work has focused on understanding what forms of action, interaction, sociability and political participation can be identified in new suburbs at the edge of Rome. We conducted a neighbourhood study whose methodology included fieldwork observation and active participation. The fieldwork included active participation in meetings of neighbourhood groups and political organizations as well as spontaneous groups that advocate for their living environment. The fieldwork also utilized in-depth interview with key persons in the groups.

PUBLIC LIFE IN SUBURBAN AREAS: CLAIMS, STRUGGLES AND SOCIAL PRACTICES

Reinterpreting the perspective of urbanity allows general questions to be asked about the shape of the city produced throughout recent decades in Rome. It implies not only a focus on the types of produced spaces (private or public) and on their location (urban or suburban) but also an in-depth examination of social practices. Nonetheless the empirical cases challenge the dichotomy upon which most of the debates about suburbanization were centred. The allegedly anonymous suburb, in fact, becomes the stage for a number of bottom-up initiatives and forms of interaction. They could be considered, in all respects, as a context for new urbanity as well as a preliminary exercise for the production of public life in suburban areas. They represent forms of action that bring together ideas and visions of how the surrounding built environment should be. What possible forms of interaction do suburban areas generate? What are their implications for the production of public life? Our fieldwork recognizes three main spaces for the re-localization of public life: the space of local action and resistance, the space of the web, the space (outside or inside) of the shopping mall.

LOCAL ACTION

The inhabitants of New Ponte di Nona are agitating for what they consider to be their rights: public services and infrastructure that guarantee the exercise of basic activities such as mobility and accessibility. When the first inhabitants arrived in 2002, the housing at New Ponte di Nona was relatively affordable, compared to the real estate market in the city. They are convinced they made a very 'good investment' and in some cases 'a very good deal'. Besides, the expectations according with their investment are very high: 'we have not bought a deteriorating house, not even one decaying periphery but a new apartment in a neighbourhood that will develop in the future'. Hence, according with the rhetoric used by the real estate agent who sold them their house, the settlement is expected to flourish and to become a vital and multifunctional site.

However, all the necessary components of social and civic life are far from being available at present. For this reason the inhabitants called themselves 'pioneers' because when they arrived 'nothing was there yet'. After their arrival they realized that the neighbourhood, which was described by the real estate agents as a 'new well connected centrality in a green belt with themed park and sports facilities', was in reality a 'distant periphery, not well connected, lacking in basic public services'. For that reason, the inhabitants decided to organize themselves as a 'neighbourhood committee' in order to confront several issues and to make claims for public services. With the aim of building a dialogue with local officials they started to meet weekly and discuss their possible ways of action. In order to strengthen their claims, they chose to follow different frames of action. First of all they wrote a specific request for attention regarding their living conditions, addressed to the Mayor (Walter Velroni). In particular, they were asking for more infrastructure and facilities. Moreover, the inhabitants started to orientate their efforts towards specific requests using different kinds of media. In order to share their opinions and to communicate with other groups in the city they opened an online *forum* (www.viapontedinona.it) that is used to discuss issues, update documents and provide a calendar of activities. The forum became a reference point for those who chose to buy a new house in the surrounding area: 'When we chose our home we looked at the forum. We knew that there were many things missing, but we have been encouraged to involve ourselves in the struggle'. In the meantime some volunteers started to publish a local journal, *Viapontedinona*, in order to reach all the neighbours who share similar problems but are not familiar with internet (Fig. 5). The magazine was designed to publicize the neighbourhood committee activities, to inform about the achieved improvements and to

Fig. 5. The Local Magazine at New Ponte di Nona.

provide general advertisements related to neighbourhood life. It also offers general information, as for instance the weather forecast '*from a local amateur*'. The shopping mall is the major sponsor for the local journal which distributes more than 5,000 copies. After a while, the forum, the magazine and the 'neighbourhood committee' were contributing to enhance the sociability in the neighbourhood.

Even though the committee made formal requests to the Mayor, no institutional replies were provided. For that reason the president and the members of the neighbourhood committee decided to organize official demonstrations. They were arranged to take place in the neighbourhood streets and, according to local magazines and interviews, they were a success in terms of participations. By means of its actions, the committee generated a collective demand that represented a real request of urbanity.

Currently, the neighbourhood committee receives formal attention from local officials and it is directly interacting with the formal political sphere. The president of the committee has been elected, with a relatively high majority, as counsellor at the local municipality. This sort of political involvement is well known in the social history of the city of Rome: historically, peripheries have been forging places for political participations and therefore they represent an important locale for political engagement and significant vote-catchment areas for politicians. Even if public space within the suburbs is not *the public sphere par excellence*, we consider that it could be a place where a political community can be formed and, thus, a form of interaction can evolve into a structured and developed public sphere.

How the inhabitants build their neighbourhood socially depends on different aspects: their involvement in political struggles and claims, their sharing of commonalities, their agreement of how to act and what do to. In fact in both cases not all the inhabitants were involved in the committee activities. Other groups were less involved in political claims and more orientated towards cultural activities. One group of inhabitants founded a cultural association to promote initiatives and opportunities to meet: 'Of course the political claims are important, however what inhabitants really need is an occasion to meet others, so we decided not only to protest but also organize some events' (http://assopontedinona.it). They promoted a football tournament, a photography concourse and they also established a website for their advertising.

At Romanina, almost every neighbourhood has owned its 'neighbourhood committee' since the 1990s, mainly dealing with traffic (parking, traffic lights, crosses, etc.) and green space issues. The most recent settlements still are not represented within the existing committees. In 2002, when the

planning process for the New General Plan was ongoing, the local committees decided to join together for facing with a single voice the dialogue
with the municipality within the participation process for the plan. Hence,
they gave birth to the 'Territorial Community of the 10th Municipio',
gathering not only local committees but also local environmental and
cultural associations. It aims at 'enhancing the work of the existing
committees and associations rather than resetting the diverse realities
co-existing on our territory' (Comunità Territoriale X Municipio, 2009).

In 2009, the Territorial Community presented a document titled
'Contribution to the urban development of south-eastern quadrant' in a
public conference. It represents a further step in the aggregation of local
interests and actions as it was signed by two neighbouring territorial
communities. It deals with centralities' issues to directly dialogue with the
municipality in changing building provisions and has a more skilful
approach when compared to the standard proposals and documents
produced by the local communities. It asks for a rebalancing of quantities
of building units under construction within centralities foreseen by the
General Plan, proposing in some cases the cancellation of the private
centralities, Romanina among the others:

> We think that this danger (the exploitation of the demand of social housing for
> aggravating the spread of the city) can be avoided. Moreover, we think that the
> oversizing of the General Plan recently approved is scarred by an excessive number of
> centralities where [even] real estate companies find it difficult to locate proper functions,
> underpinning their inconsistency. We think that the General Plan has been bent by a
> renewed thrust towards building expansion and that it can be reviewed and corrected
> inverting the tendency to create new peripheries [lacking] functions and qualities.

THE INTERNET

In both study areas, the internet played a key role in structuring, supporting
and spreading local civic actions and became part of the public arena of
New Ponte di Nona and Romanina. It is used not only by neighbourhood
committees and cultural associations: many individual bloggers have started
to write their own opinions concerning the neighbourhood as well as
providing to enhance their urban environment. In New Ponte di Nona,
inhabitants have started to recognize themselves as *pontenonini*, a label that
promotes identity even though they have just arrived in the neighbourhood.
Furthermore, the label represents the desire of involvement into neighbourhood's life. For instance in social networks, that are non-spatial by

definition, members meet in a group called 'New Ponte di Nona inhabitants', as a label under which people share space-based commonalities. They discuss their needs and opinions about future neighbourhood improvements. As a result, interactions are happening even though no public spaces are supplied for these interactions. As an alternative, the public realm is developing and forming on the web: You Tube, Facebook, individual Bloggers, web pages and online forums are becoming important interface for building up local affiliation, but also for sharing local identities and 'getting to know the neighbours'.

The website is the main vehicle for aggregating the diverse neighbourhood committees within the Territorial Community at Romanina. It has been recently restyled to emphasize private citizens' interests around planned public events (demonstrations, etc.). But not all communication is socially orientated. Social networks in this case are not simply used to build local identities or to share commonalities linked to place. They also articulate critical issues raised by individuals, and express individual interests as well as group enthusiasms. In this sense, they provide a representation of lively, intermittent and unpredictable practices taking place within the area, particularly in empty and underused places, offering a perfect stage for skaters, rallies, tracers and so on (Fig. 6).

SEE YOU AT THE MALL

The shopping malls at New Ponte di Nona and Romanina play an important role in the daily life of the people living there. In the last decades Rome has been surrounded by huge shopping malls, localized just behind new residential settlements, providing the catchment area to sustain their activities 24 hours a day, 7 days a week. Strong critical arguments are arising against shopping mall in urban areas, basically arguing that 'while the shopping mall are lighting themselves the city and its neighbourhoods are turning off their vitality' (Berdini, 2008b). This position is coupled with the discourse concerning the erosion of 'traditional' public space by privatization. These arguments are strengthened by an enormous literature concerning shopping malls as manifestations of non-place (Augè, 1992), representing the decline of a genuine and free public sphere inherited in 'pure' public space. However, many interdependences between the malls and the inhabitants of the suburbs have been developed and the simplistic dichotomy between residential and consumption areas is not useful.

Fig. 6. Web Pages and Blog of New Ponte di Nona.

At New Ponte di Nona, when in 2007 the Roma East Shopping Mall opened, the inhabitants were enthusiastic: 'Honestly I was in the first line to enter when it opened'. In this case the mall represents metaphorically and physically the centre of the neighbourhood and it is the place where interactions occur. In this respect there are some conditions that may allow a non-place to turn into a place (or vice-versa). Precisely these conditions rely on the interdependence between the neighbourhood and the mall. In the case of New Ponte di Nona the mall represents 'the centre' and the 'meeting point', and much of the interaction among inhabitants is produced inside it: 'if we want to do something, spend time with friends, we go there'. The mall provides open meeting spaces, an air-conditioned environment, more than

200 shops, restaurants, a playground for children, a cinema and other entertainment facilities, including its own events. Unexpected or spontaneous opportunities for meetings also occur at the mall. For instance the municipality required the Roma East Shopping Mall human resource to employ certain numbers from within the municipal area. The job application process has been strongly publicized by local magazine and neighbourhoods' web pages with the effort of the neighbourhood committee and inhabitants. Additionally, according with a regional act, the group that is managing the mall is required to assume for a year a percentage rate of disadvantaged workers. Thus the shopping mall, instead of being non-place, is a physical space where spontaneous socialization occurs not only among shoppers but also it can be assumed among workers, and where there is no one-class tier of interaction.

The built environment at Romanina is very heterogeneous: it includes informal settlements, old commercial and industrial areas, new public and private housing developments, and urban parks. Yet there are still 'in-between' spaces which seem to have become forgotten and underused borders between self-referential areas. These spaces represent a form of parochial realm (Lofland, 1998), where there is little chance to meet strangers or the non-inhabitant. But how much does that matter? The malls at Romanina offer several opportunities for meeting all sorts of people: the emptiness of the occasional plaza, and the lack of business in suburban streets and parks is counterbalanced by the aggregation of the population outside and within the malls. While the configuration of the surrounding neighbourhoods appears to represent the denial of casual public interactions associated with the public realm, malls and even parking lots have become spaces for interaction with the others. Even demonstrations and strikes find their place outside and within the mall instead of in front of the Ministry of Welfare. At the same time, leisure and entertainment activities seem delocalized in the mall that is symbolically and physically the centre of the neighbourhood. This phenomenon of re-localization can be interpreted as a form of adaptation to the surrounding built environment and as a signifier of new forms of urbanity.

CONCLUSION: PUBLIC LIFE IN CONTEMPORARY SUBURBS

The field research revealed how New Ponte di Nona and Romanina seem designed to satisfy the needs of private interests and speculation, with open spaces marked by consumer box stores and large streets dominated by cars. As a consequence, New Ponte di Nona and Romanina should in traditional narratives be candidates for the grim label of hostile and alienated spaces, due to the absence or underuse of traditional public spaces creating dense and diverse environment, the traditional measurements for the achievement of public life.

But this is not really true. Despite the criticism of privatization and lack of urbanity, suburban realities challenge the dichotomous terms upon which much of the debate about suburbanization has been structured. In particular, they show how the contemporary city continues to facilitate the exercise of advocacy and the voicing of local activism. Since the arrival of the inhabitants, forms of interaction and exchange have been spontaneously produced. The neighbourhoods have started to be subject to a multiplicity of struggles and confrontation at the local and municipal level. Inhabitants were involved in claims concerning visions and ideas about how their neighbourhood should improve and in some cases shared them with their neighbouring contexts to create wider and active visions encompassing more than one urban quadrant.

New forms of interaction such as the internet declare the rise of reflexive forms of urbanity that do not require traditional public spaces for their articulation (Apostol, Antoniadis, & Banerjee, 2009), but also represent forms of adaptation to the surrounding built environment. While the physical design of the neighbourhoods would seem to deny casual public interactions traditionally identified with the public realm, the web, the malls and other liminal spaces between public and private become privileged places for interaction. Local activism, the use of web pages and networking, and the shopping mall are real and virtual spaces where public and civic life is intensively occurring in new suburbs, with empirically evidenced levels of political involvement and participation. Both virtual and real physical places contextualize social interaction. Romanina and New Ponte di Nona did indeed function as 'reserves of urbanity' in which the opportunity for something new happening in urban spaces can be shown to exist. In this respect, new forms of urbanity can be anticipated as a possible outcome of an ongoing learning process of living together. They represent types of behaviour that can be considered as the precondition of both tolerance and civil respect. After all, they work as preliminary steps in the compulsory obligation of living together in a system of shared spaces and resources.

NOTE

1. The work of Pierpaolo Pasolini is fundamental for understanding the social history of the periphery of Rome. He wrote *Ragazzi di vita* (1951), *Una vita violenta* (1959), and *Storie della città di Dio. Racconti e cronache romane* (1950–1956). He also directed several movies that were located in the periphery of Rome, for instance, *accattone* (1961) and *Mamma Roma* (1962).

REFERENCES

Annunziata, S., & Cossu, M. (2010). Roma oltre il Piano: forme di urbanità per la città contemporanea, with Mara Cossu. Paper presented at the XXIII SIU Conference, Roma (pp. 25–27) Febbraio.

Apostol, I., Antoniadis, P., & Banerjee, T. (2009). Places on the net. Available at www.nethood.org

Augè, M. (1992). Non-Lieux. Introduction à une anthropologie de la surmodernité; trad. Dominique Rolland, Nonluoghi. Introduzione a una antropologia della surmodernità. Milano: Elèuthera, 1996.

Berdini, P. (2008a). Roma tra pianificazione e contrattazione. Dupt, Universita di Firenze n. 2.

Berdini, P. (2008b). Una città a misura della grande distribuzione. il Manifesto del 5 luglio 2008.

Berdini, P. (2008c). La città in vendita [The city on sale]. Donzelli, Roma.

Bertolini, L. (2006). Fostering urbanity in a mobile society. Linking concepts and practices. *Journal of Urban Design, 11*(3), 319–334.

Bianchetti, C. (2008a). Urbanistica e sfera pubblica [Urbanistic and public sphere]. Donzelli, Roma.

Bianchetti, C. (2008b). Quantità e quiete: il discorso ideologico sull'abitare [Quantity and Quiet: the ideological arguments about urban living]. In Archivio di Studi Urbani e Regionali n. 94.

Chase, J., Crawford, M., & Kaliski, J. (1999). *Everyday urbanism.* New York: Monacelli Press.

Comune di Roma. (2007). Le nuove centralità urbane e metropolitane. Relazione generale del nuovo piano regolatore di Roma.

Comunità Territoriale X Municipio. (2009). Contributo sullo sviluppo urbanistico del quadrante Sud-Est alla conferenza cittadina, 26 Febbraio 2009.

Cremaschi, M. (2008a). Tracce di quartiere. Il legame sociale nella città che cambia [Traces of neighborhoods, explorations into city change]. Angeli, Milano.

Cremaschi, M. (2008b). Urbanità e resistenza [Urbanity and Resistence]. In Archivio di Studi Urbani e Regionali, n. 94, 2008.

De Jong, J. K. (2010). (Sub)urban public space and public life in the flattening city, Conference proceeding, PLIC: Public life in the in-between city, Haifa, Israel, 6–10 June.

De Lucia, V. (2005). Il nuovo Prg di Roma e la dissipazione della campagna romana [The new master plan of the city of Rome, the erosion of roman rural land]. Meridiana, 4.

Di Biagi, P. (2001). Il piano INA CASA e l'Italia degli anni 50'. Donzelli, Roma.

Fainstein, S. (2008). Mega project in New York, London and Amsterdam. *International Journal of Urban and Regional Research, 32*(4), 768–785.

Ferrarotti, F. (1974). *Roma da capitale a periferia.* Roma-Bari: Laterza.

Ferrarotti, F., & Macioti, M. I. (2009). Periferie. Da problema a risorsa, Sandro Teti Editore.

Gruppo Scarpellini, Immobilfim. (2008). Progetto urbano Romanina. Proposta di schema di assetto preliminare. Available at www.farecentroaromanina.com

Gualini, E., & Majoor, S. (2007). Innovative practices in large urban development project: Conflicting frame in the quest for 'new urbanity'. *Planning Theory and Practice, 8*(3), 297–318.

Haussermänn, H., & Siebel, W. (1987). Neue Urbanität, Suhrkamp, Frankfurt.

Indovina, F. (1970). *La città diffusa.* Marsilio: Venezia.

Indovina, F. (2000). *1950–2000: L'Italia è cambiata.* Milano Franco Angeli.

Insolera, I. (1993). Roma moderna: Un secolo di storia urbanistica: 1870–1970. Torino: Einaudi.

Insolera, I., Morandi, D., & Tocci, W. (2008). Avanti c'è posto, Storie e progetti del Trasporto Pubblico a Roma, Donzelli, Roma.

INU. (2008). Rapporto dal territorio 2007. Inu Edizioni, Roma.

Jacobs, J. (1961). *The death and life of great American cities.* New York: Random House.

Lofland, L. H. (1998). *The public realm. Exploring the city's quintessential social territory.* New York: Aldine de Gruyter.

Marcelloni, M. (2003). Ripensare la città contemporanea, Il nuovo piano regolatore di Roma [Rethinking the contemporary city. The Masterplan of Rome]. Laterza, Roma.

Mondani. (2008). I re di Roma, Episode of Report, Rai Tre. Available at http://www.rai.tv

Montgomery, J. (1995). Urban vitality and the culture of cities. *Planning Practice and Research, 10*(2), 101–109.

Raymond, H. (1998). Urbain, convivialité, culture. In Les Annales de la recherché urbaine, n. 37.

Salet, W. (2008). Rethinking urban projects: Experiences in Europe. *Urban Studies, 45*(11), 2343–2362.

Secchi, B. (2005). La città del ventesimo secolo. Laterza: Roma-Bari (XXth century city).

Sennett, R. (1974). *The uses of disorder: Personal identity and city life.* New York: Norton.

Sennett, R. (1992). *The fall of public man.* New York: Norton.

Tiettle, C. R., & Gramsmick, H. G. (2001). Urbanity: Influences of urbanness, structure, and culture. *Social Science Research, 30*(2), 313–335.

Tocci, W. (2008). La lezione di Roma [The lesson of Rome]. l'Unità, 18 maggio 2008.

Vaughan, L. S., Griffiths, S., Haklay, M. E., & Jones, C. E. (2009). Do the suburbs exist? Discovering complexity and specificity in suburban built form. *Transactions of the Institute of British Geographers, 34*(4), 475–488.

Vaughan, L. S., Griffiths, S., Haklay, M. E., & Jones, C. E. (2010). The shape of belonging in the outer London suburbs: Beyond a discourse of alienation. In: *Conference proceeding, PLIC: Public life in the in-between city*, Haifa, Israel, 6–10 June.

Webster, R. (2009). *Expanding suburbia: Reviewing suburban narratives.* New York: Bergahn Books.

IDENTITY, MARGINALIZATION, AND PARISIAN BANLIEUES

Jean Beaman

[The 2005 uprisings] were around the time that I got married, and I kept hoping that they did not burn my wedding hall because that was where the riots were, near my wedding hall, so I just kept saying to myself that I hope they do not burn my wedding hall. Actually, I got many cancellations because of this, people who did not come because they were scared that their car would be burned. The photographer quit three days before the wedding because he was afraid of being attacked, robbed. Otherwise, we kept trying to analyze these events ... why they burst out, and it was more a social problem than death. The death of the two adolescents triggered the release of a social discomfort, that right now we are fed up with having to claim who we are ... We have big problems, I don't know if you know, we have problems finding a job, we have problems finding housing. It took my husband and I six months to find housing, and still it was the friend of a friend who rented us his apartment, who was the landlord. But our application file was never taken seriously [by other landlords], even though my husband works in finance and I work also. We make enough money. I remember they were asking for [someone with a salary of] three times the rent, and even with only my salary we had enough money. So we had a lot, and they [other landlords] didn't want us. They kept telling us, "We just rented to another couple, it happened quickly," it was always this, or "we changed our mind, we have to do some repairs, so we are not going to rent it," it was always something. And once, an older woman told me very clearly when we checked out an apartment, she said to us, "Yes, why not?" And when we called her again to schedule another viewing of the apartment, she said, "No, you understand, there was a French couple who came, so we rented it to them, it's just easier." And me, I vividly remember feeling disgusted, and I said to her, "But Madame, we are French also." But they were white French, you see what I'm saying? And my husband, it was at that moment, when he began, he told me "you see, we have to leave France. We'll never be recognized as

Suburbanization in Global Society
Research in Urban Sociology, Volume 10, 153–175
Copyright © 2010 by Emerald Group Publishing Limited
All rights of reproduction in any form reserved
ISSN: 1047-0042/doi:10.1108/S1047-0042(2010)0000010009

'normal people,' because we both have jobs and we could only find an apartment
through a friend."

Safia,[1] a 32-year-old journalist with dual Tunisian and French nationality, is
discussing how the 2005 uprisings in the banlieues of Paris affected her. The
narrative illustrates her frustrations related to being a second-generation
Maghrébin immigrant in France. (The Maghrèbins are from the Maghreb,
the countries of Tunisia, Morocco, and Algeria that France colonized. I use
this term and "North African" interchangeably.) Married with two young
children, she currently rents an apartment in Cergy-Pontoise, a western
banlieue. She and her husband, who is of Algerian origin, want to buy a
house but are already worried that it will be difficult. Growing up, Safia
witnessed her parents being shamed and humiliated because of their
immigrant status and lack of educational attainment (they are both
illiterate). She always hoped to escape her social background in order to
avoid such experiences. Safia grew up in a middle-class Parisian neighborhood near the Louvre, and her husband grew up in a *cité* (public housing
complex) near Paris. Yet the similarity of their experiences – both to each
other and to their parents – illustrates the difficulties still faced by those of
immigrant origin in France. Despite their professional and material success,
Safia and her husband are not able to live anywhere they can afford, which
they attribute to their social location. While Safia is different in some ways
from those who participated in the uprisings as portrayed by the national
and international media, she nonetheless feels similarly excluded from full
participation in mainstream French society.

Despite being born and raised in France, second-generation Maghrébin
immigrants are often made to feel different: not French. Having French
nationality does not mean that one is still not perceived as an immigrant.
For example, the term "estranger," or foreigner, is often used to refer to
second-generation immigrants in official discourse, even though they were
born in France (Silverman, 1992; Stolcke, 1995; Tin, 2008). Due to France's
Republican ideology that does not recognize identity-based group categor-
izations, the census, conducted by the Institut National de la Statistique et
des Etudes Economiques (INSEE), does not ask about the racial or ethnic
origin of those born in France. The social location of many second-
generation Maghrébin immigrants makes them marginalized in multiple
ways, including religion and socioeconomic status (Noiriel, 1996). They are
often thought of as having "unsettled identities," as they are often between
their parents' culture and the French culture they are socialized into at
school (Body-Gendrot, 1993). Second-generation Maghrébin immigrants

are therefore an appropriate site to examine the complexities of cultural identity, ethnicity, difference, and marginalization in French society.

In this chapter, I discuss how second-generation Maghrébin immigrants in France relate to place (namely, living in the banlieues) and how this relationship informs how they self-identify. Based on interviews and participant observation in a banlieue community organization, I argue that second-generation North African immigrants agentically respond to place-related marginalization in ways that allow them to assert being a French citizen and claim a legitimate place within French society. As ethnic origin cannot be legitimately discussed in French public discourse, place becomes a more legitimate way to acknowledge social difference. This was evident when considering the coverage of the 2005 uprisings and the banlieues in which they took place (see Koff & Duprez, 2009; Sedel, 2009). Identification based on where one lives is often a euphemistic way to invoke other identifications that are not as legitimate, such as ethnic origin (Bentouhami, 2009; Silverstein, 2008; Tissot, 2008). As Safia's narrative illustrates, second-generation North African immigrants can be marginalized through the difficulties they experience finding housing and in moving in particular spaces. How individuals such as Safia invoke place therefore becomes implicated in how they self-identify. Yet, what emerges here is that second-generation Maghrébin immigrants do not relate to place in a way that negates their attachment to French society.

BACKGROUND AND RELEVANT LITERATURE

While I do not intend to provide an exhaustive survey of North African emigration to France and the history of banlieue and urban formation in France (see Stovall, 2003), I nonetheless provide a brief background related to place and immigrants in order to contextualize how place is invoked, or is not, in second-generation North African immigrant identities. France's relationship with the Maghreb began with the colonization of Algeria in 1830, of Tunisia in 1831, and of Morocco in 1931. Algeria remained in French control until 1962, and Tunisia and Morocco remained in French control until 1956.

World War I brought immigrants from these former French colonies en masse to France for work, and many of them settled outside of cities, such as Paris, in the banlieues, due to the presence of cheaper housing (Stovall, 2003). With World War II, the Algerian War of 1962, and the fall of the Fourth Republic, the immigrant population only increased. This growth in the number of North African immigrants saw more of them living in *habitations à loyer modéré* (subsidized housing complexes, or HLMs) in the banlieues, albeit in the more dilapidated complexes, as opposed to the *bidonvilles*, or shanty towns, where they were previously (Dikeç, 2007; Hargreaves, 1996; Silverstein, 2008; Weir, 1993). As more and more *français de souche* moved out of HLMs to private housing due to low-interest loans from the French government in the early 1970s, HLMs and banlieues became even more associated with those of immigrant origin (Simon, 1998; Tissot, 2008). Due to an economic recession and declining employment opportunities, France temporarily suspended immigration of non-European workers in 1974 (Stovall, 2003). However, this led to migrant workers settling permanently with their families in France as opposed to returning to their country of origin (Body-Gendrot, 1993; Kaya, 2009).

Government policies have targeted various aspects of the living conditions of those of immigrant origin. Because of France's Republican ideology, governmental policies often target particular geographical spaces over communities based on particular identities, as in the United States (creating, e.g., a territorial affirmative action instead of an ethnic-based affirmative action) (Dikeç, 2007). A 1989 law created *les zones d'éducation prioritaire* (educational priority zones, or ZEPs) to provide increased educational attention to students from disadvantaged regions (Calves, 2004; Dikeç, 2007; Simon, 1998). A 1991 law was passed to prevent residential concentration based on ethnic origin (though the term ethnic origin was not used due to Republican principles) (Dikeç, 2007). Yet today, those of Maghrébin immigrant origin tend to reside in the banlieues of major cities, fueling concerns of *la communitarianisme* (communalism) (Dikeç, 2007; Simon, 1998). Banlieue has also often been employed as a "catch-all" term for *les quartiers sensibles* (at-risk or vulnerable neighborhoods), *les quartiers difficiles* (problem or underprivileged neighborhoods), ZEPs, *les zones urbaines sensible* (sensitive urban zones, or ZUS), *les zones à urbaniser en priorité* (priority urban zones), and *les quartiers populaires* (working-class neighborhoods) (Dikeç, 2007; Hargreaves, 1996; Tissot, 2008).

Even though France is not characterized by the same degrees of residential segregation as is the United States (Wacquant, 2007), place is nonetheless often used to mark difference, particularly for those of immigrant origin such as Safia (Oberti, 2007; Preteceille, 2008; Silverstein, 2008; Simon, 1998). Many banlieues continue to have large concentrations of those of immigrant origin. As of 1990, the Seine-Saint-Denis département consisted of 45 percent of youth of foreign origin. Also, Paris and the départements of Hauts-de-Seine and Val-de-Marne each had more than

30 percent youth of foreign origin. As such, populations of foreign origin have been historically relegated to disadvantaged spaces, including banlieues (Tribalat, 2004). Marginalization vis-à-vis place is often heightened in particular spaces, such as banlieues, which have connotations that are attached to particular populations, such as second-generation North African immigrants (Bouamama, 2009). Therefore, even those second-generation Maghrébin immigrants who do not live in banlieues are nonetheless connected to them because of how this population is positioned in French society (Amara, 2006; Hargreaves, 2007; Stovall, 2003). Second-generation Maghrébin immigrants, who are often subsumed within the banlieue imagery, must reconcile the meanings of these places with their processes of identity construction.

Moreover, considering the case of banlieues further illustrates how identification based on place often euphemistically stands in for ethnic origin. Banlieue residents "were never described in terms of the racism and discrimination they faced, excluding them from participation in the economy; instead they were considered in terms of problems they supposedly posed to the entire society because of their insurmountable difference" (Tissot, 2008, p. 368). As such, France's color-blind ideology veils the realities facing those marginalized due to their immigrant background. French scholars are more likely to emphasize the socio-economic segregation facing banlieues (Oberti, 2007; Simon, 1998; Wacquant, 2007), over the ethno-racial segregation facing the banlieues (Lapeyronnie, 2008; Tissot, 2008). Those banlieues with a high concentration of those of immigrant origin rarely represent only one ethnic origin, meaning, for example, that neighborhoods with those of Algerian origin often also have residents of Tunisian or Moroccan origin (Simon, 1998). The amount of research on conditions facing banlieues has especially exploded since the 2005 uprisings. Banlieues are often characterized by mass unemployment, predominance of *les cités*, absence of two-parent family structure, deskilled workforce, high percentage of residents on public assistance, low levels of educational attainment, and physical compactness (Avenel, 2007; Kokoreff, 2003; Lapeyronnie, 2008; LePoutre, 1997; Maurin, 2004; Rey, 1996; Stebe, 2007; Wacquant, 2007).

Second-generation Maghrébin immigrants often face marginalizations other than those that are place-related, including ethnic origin and religion. In positing that second-generation North African immigrants can face multiple marginalizations, I apply Berger's (2004) notion of "intersectional stigma," in which the negative effects of multiple marginalized social locations are compounded by their associated stigmatized identities.

Place-related stigma is one such type of marginalization. For example, living in the banlieues often carries an associated stigma (Dikeç, 2007; Silverstein, 2008; Wacquant, 2007), though scholars debate the degree to which this stigma intersects with other marginalized statuses. For example, according to Wacquant (2007):

> The French banlieue is a territorial entity containing a mixed, multiethnic population; it suffices for the residents of the Quatre Mille or any other defamed *cité* of the French urban periphery to hide their address to make this status disappear and 'pass' in the broader society – unless they get spotted by their 'degaine' (physical demeanor and dress) and speech patterns. (p. 181)

He therefore acknowledges the stigma that banlieue residents may face, yet I argue he underestimates how such stigmas intersect with other marginalized statuses. The divergent ways that second-generation North African immigrants relate to place reflect their experiences of margin-alization, particularly in ways that transcend a place-related stigma. For example, Safia's experiences that opened this chapter are reflective not just of place-related marginalization – where she can and cannot live and perceptions of where she does and does not belong – but also of marginalization based on the simple fact of being of Maghrébin origin.

In considering how this population relates to place and how that informs how they locate themselves in French society, I follow Gieryn's (2000) definition of place as having three features – geographic location, material form and physicality, and meaning and value. Put simply, "place is space filled up by people, practices, objects, and representations" (Gieryn, 2000, p. 465). Extant social scientific research has shown how the symbolic meanings individuals attach to place are implicated in processes of identity formation (see Cuba & Hummon, 1993; Gieryn, 2000). As individuals define what a place is and is not, they are also asserting an aspect of who they are and who they are not. According to Gieryn, "place sustains difference and hierarchy both by routinizing daily rounds in ways that exclude and segregate categories of people, and by embodying in visible and tangible ways the cultural meanings variously ascribed to them" (2000, p. 474). I apply the Gotham and Brumley's (2002) framework of "using space" that refers to "the range of activities individuals engage in to create, present, and sustain a personal identity tied to place and to contest alternative meanings, degradations, and stigma of residential life and space" (Gotham & Brumley, 2002, p. 269). Individuals do not therefore passively respond to their spatial environments. I extend their framework to consider how the relationships individuals have with place serve as tools for making sense of and responding to their social location and present and past experiences of marginalization. Rather than focusing on the particular identities second-generation Maghrébin immigrants ascribe to place, I address how this population invokes place in constructing a French identity.

METHODOLOGY

My data were collected through two means: (1) semi-structured interviews with 49 second-generation North African immigrants living in the Parisian metropolitan region (or Ile-de-France); (2) six months of participant observation at the Nanterre Association, a community organization in Nanterre, a banlieue west of Paris. Research was conducted during the 2008–2009 academic year. For the purposes of this research, and following the conventions of previous research (Simon, 2003), the term "second-generation North African immigrant" refers to someone who was born in France and has one or two parents who immigrated to France from the Maghreb. My sample of 49 interview respondents included 22 women and 27 men. Interview respondents range in age from 21 to 48 years old (the average age being 32 years old). In terms of parents' country of origin, 29 of them are of Algerian origin, 12 are of Moroccan origin, and 8 are of Tunisian origin. Three respondents are products of mixed-race relationships, meaning one parent is white and the other parent is Maghrébin. All respondents are *Franciliens*, or Ile-de-France residents. Thirty-five percent of respondents live in Paris, and 65 percent live in the banlieues, mostly in the inner ring départements of Seine-Saint-Denis, Val-de-Marne, and Hauts-de-Seine. All respondents have French nationality, and about one-third of them have dual nationality (with the country of their Maghrébin origin). All respondents except for one are employed at least part-time. Partially due to how I recruited my sample, which I discuss below, the majority of respondents have professional, middle-class types of employment and have an education level of a college degree or higher. All names and identifying information have been changed as per Human Subjects guidelines.

Respondents' parents are first-generation immigrants who emigrated from the Maghreb between 1950 and 1970, primarily for economic reasons. Often fathers came to France first for work, and mothers later followed them. They often have low levels of educational attainment, often not greater than elementary school; some respondents' parents are in fact illiterate in French. All respondents' parents speak Arabic. Usually fathers worked in low-skilled jobs, such as construction, while mothers were homemakers or did domestic labor. For example, Loubna, a 27-year-old of Moroccan origin, who volunteers at the Nanterre Association, explains that her parents emigrated from Morocco for "the construction of France." Her father, who has a high school education, came first in 1970 and married her mother, who never attended school and only learned to read and write about five years ago, in Morocco in 1973. She followed him to France in 1976.

I recruited respondents through contacting various organizations and associations (in person and via mail, telephone, and email) in both Paris and its banlieues, as well as placing calls for participants on Internet forums and websites that cater to this population. In order to participate, individuals had to be born in France, be over 18 years of age, live in the Paris metropolitan area, and have at least one parent from the Maghreb. I included three respondents in my sample even though they were not born in France because they immigrated when they were two years of age or younger. These individuals themselves identified as second-generation immigrants, and other scholars define second generation by their place of initial socialization and primary schooling (see Noiriel, 1996). Due to the difficulties with recruitment and obtaining access to a large respondent sample, I employed snowball sampling (Small, 2009). Because of this, my sample is relatively homogeneous in terms of educational attainment and employment status. Many of my respondents were involved in the same professional and social networks. Because of my outsider status (i.e., not being a Maghrébin second-generation immigrant), snowball sampling was crucial for getting me "inside" this group. Once I was able to build rapport with respondents, they introduced me to potential respondents. Interview questions addressed a variety of topics related to second-generation North African immigrant experiences including ethnic, cultural, and national identity, social networks, employment, family history and parental background, relationship to parents' country of origin, educational experiences, perceptions of racism, discrimination and marginalization, and religion. I conducted the interviews in French and digitally recorded them, unless respondents requested otherwise. A native French-speaking transcriber later transcribed the interviews. When analyzing my data, I kept the interviews in French and translated them myself during the writing process.

In the process of contacting various organizations and associations for respondents, I made contact with the Nanterre Association,[2] a community organization in the western banlieue of Nanterre (about 90 minutes from Paris by commuter train), and was able to supplement my interviews with six months of participant observation there. The association directors offered to help me make connections for potential interviewees in exchange for volunteer work (eight of my respondents were in some way affiliated with the Nanterre Association). The Nanterre Association was founded in 1994 by five residents who grew up in the neighborhood of Petit Nanterre, a complex of public housing projects.[3] My ethnographic experiences at the Nanterre Association were invaluable for shedding light on how social difference is marked and how individuals respond to it. I was able to participate in the everyday lives of the population in which I was interested. I was able to build rapport in this setting mostly due to my French language skills and my awareness of French society due to previously living in Paris. I became very attached to those I encountered at my field site. In addition to conversations with staff, volunteers, and neighborhood residents and involvement in panel discussions and social events, my main involvement with the Nanterre Association was teaching English classes to elementary school, high school and college students, and adults.

My position as an outsider, not only as a researcher, but also as an American and black woman, undoubtedly shaped how my respondents perceived me. Several scholars have reflected on the advantages and disadvantages of being an outsider while conducting qualitative research. Interactions between researcher and respondents can be thought of as "construction sites," where the identities of both parties are negotiated based on similarities and differences in background and social location (Horowitz, 1986; Lacy, 2008; Venkatesh, 2002). Similar to what other American researchers have experienced conducting research overseas (see Killian, 2002; Lamont, 1992; Pickering, 2007), being American was often an advantage in my interactions with respondents. They assumed that I was unfamiliar with Maghrébin and French culture, so they explained in detail things that they might otherwise have not. Conducting my research during the Barack Obama's presidential campaign often led to conversations with respondents about race and racism, upward mobility, and multiculturalism that might not have otherwise occurred without my prompting. While I was conscious of not imposing an American-style understanding of race and ethnicity to the French context, some respondents invoked such a conception, particularly in explaining their experiences and the differences they saw between being a minority in the United States and that in France. The perceptions of my personal biography, particularly my racial identity, were often invoked in my interviews and other interactions with respondents, most often to draw symbolic boundaries with or against their own identity. Being a member of an "othered" group in the United States also undoubtedly informed my findings, as I entered my research with my own assumptions due to my social location. Though researchers are never "ideologically free" (Keaton, 2006), I remained cognizant throughout the research process of not imposing my own understandings over those of my respondents. Finally, it is important to note the limitations of my methodology. My findings may be affected by my focus on the Parisian metropolitan region, as second-generation immigrant experiences that influence identity may significantly differ in other regions in France. Also due to my use of snowball sampling, it is difficult to generalize to the entire population of second-generation North African immigrants.

THE NANTERRE ASSOCIATION
AND PETIT NANTERRE

"We have to expose ourselves to the world outside of our own, outside of the banlieues," exclaims Lamence Madzou, a former gang leader from Essonne, a southwestern banlieue of Paris. He is speaking to a group of students, parents, and community members at one of the Nanterre Association's regular panel discussions, or *debats*, events that bring in outside speakers to discuss issues affecting this community. Even though this was a cold December evening, this *debat*, titled "Une plongee dans les bandes et gangs de banlieue" or "A dive into the world of suburban gangs," was particularly packed with people. As is often the case with panel discussions at the Nanterre Association, there were not enough chairs for all the attendees. Madzou is presenting on this panel with various academics because of a recent book he co-wrote, *J'etais un Chef de Gang* (or *I was a Gang Leader*) (Madzou, 2009). He speaks passionately about growing up amid difficult circumstances in Essonne. His immigrant parents had difficulty finding work despite their qualifications and were often unemployed. As more and more residents of immigrant origin moved into his neighborhood, he adopted what he describes as a "black identity." In 1987, he and four friends started a gang, which would grow to include over 100 members. He recounts how his gang fought other gangs over control over territory in Paris and how he later spent four years in prison. Years after leaving the gang, he still sees his attachment to Essonne as a crucial element of his identity (this is in addition to his ethnic origin). He wrote his memoirs in order to expose life in banlieues to those outside of it. He feels that in the future, identity groups in France will be based on neighborhood and geography, as more and more people express their attachment to where they live or where they are from.

This is a message that clearly resonates with the Nanterre Association community. The community organization is located in the neighborhood of Petit Nanterre, a *cité* that Mamadou, a second-generation Algerian immigrant and one of the organization's directors, describes as "enclosed." Petit Nanterre is an impoverished neighborhood; it is considered a priority urban zone (*un zone à urbaniser en priorité*, or ZUP) by the state government. According to the INSEE, about 86 percent of neighborhood housing is public housing. Neighborhood schools are failing, and consequently many students are not equipped to pass the Baccalauréat (BAC) exam, the exam all French students must pass on finishing high school in order to pursue further studies. There is not really a large diversity of people – across socioeconomic status and ethnic origin – living in this neighborhood.[4] For these reasons, Mamadou sees the Nanterre Association – and other community organizations like it – as playing an important role in establishing and reinforcing a social fabric in the neighborhood and in challenging problems that neighborhoods like his typically face. Silverstein and Tetreault (2006) note the crucial role that organizations such as the Nanterre Association play in *cités* such as Petit Nanterre: "Through after-school tutoring programs, cultural and religious associations in the cités constitute a parallel, if severely underfunded, education system that attempts to compensate for the depressed conditions in French schools, including poor facilities, over-crowded classrooms, teachers unknowledgeable of or inflexible to the students' multicultural needs, and the tracking of many children to vocational diplomas from an early age. The same associations also provide day-care for working mothers and legal advice for local residents, particularly regarding the regularization of their immigration documentation. Indeed, such a parallel structure operates with the tacit knowledge and minimal funding of the French state, which has largely devolved the provision of many such social, educational, and legal services to local assns" (2006, pp. 10–11).

The Nanterre Association serves the local neighborhood through educational, cultural, and social activities, including field trips to Paris monuments, panel discussions, and after-school tutoring. The majority of those served by the association are of immigrant origin. The organization serves students starting at age six, their families, as well as adults in need of assistance in areas such as literacy and finding employment. For Mamadou and the other employees at the Nanterre Association, it is important not just to ensure the educational achievement of students in the community but also to expose them to life and culture outside of their neighborhood. *Debats* such as this one on gangs, which included Madzou and also various university professors, serve this purpose. Students also often go on field trips to landmarks in Paris and the countryside. Ultimately, the Nanterre Association wants Petit Nanterre youth to, as the other director Hafid explains, "take control of their future and convince them[selves] that they are not victims."

Petit Nanterre is both physically and socially separated from Paris, and in many ways exhibits a distinct culture often cultivated by the Nanterre Association. Yet difference here is used to acknowledge sameness, as the Nanterre Association community affirms their Frenchness and place in French society. Nanterre Association therefore has place in the Petit Nanterre neighborhood as well as in French society at large. As banlieues are increasingly portrayed as "spaces of hostility to the French state" (Silverstein, 2004), that the Petit Nanterre community challenges these prevailing meanings, and contests the stigmas associated with it, is an example of how marginalized individuals in French society nonetheless claim a place within French society.

When asked what defines the Petit Nanterre neighborhood, Mamadou stresses the idea of solidarity:

> Everyone knows each other, regardless of their age. We have a genuine affection for each other here. Everyone who lives here has lived here for a long time ... Even when people leave, they always come back. People keep ties, even after they leave. Everyone is always in the street, for weddings, parties, etc ... There is a strong Maghrébin community here, even if we are not the only people here. People are really involved in each others' lives, sometimes too much. But still it is different from Paris, where everyone basically keeps to themselves ... This neighborhood is first of all defined by its people, not its social problems. It is really important to us in this neighborhood to keep that solidarity, not to lose that.

Others besides Mamadou reinforce the distinct, close-knit culture that is prevalent in Petit Nanterre. For example, the organization co-sponsors a "Banlieue, je t'aime" (Banlieue, I love you) week. As part of this week, the Petit Nanterre community has a carnival-like parade leading from the Nanterre Association to the commuter train station that connects Nanterre to Paris. I marched with the group of students, parents, staff, and volunteers, many of them dressed in costumes, wearing masks, and carrying decorated umbrellas, while neighbors threw confetti from the windows of their HLMs and drivers honked their horns as we drove by. It was immediately clear how activities such as these put forth by the organization cultivate a sense of community in the Petit Nanterre neighborhood, one which is greatly needed to counteract its prevailing problems.

Mamadou acknowledges that not everyone in Petit Nanterre feels the same way he does. According to him, many people are uneducated and unemployed and do not see an end to their situation. "When you have so many obstacles stacked on each other, it is hard to know where to begin." Growing up in Petit Nanterre, he remembers encountering people like this – people who dealt drugs hoping for economic success, etc. "Today, they are either in prison or dead," he explains. While Mamadou sees living and working in Petit Nanterre as constitutive of his individual identity, one which allows him to contest the significance of this stigmatized space and emphasize its positive aspects, others relate to living in Petit Nanterre by disidentifying with it.

One winter Sunday afternoon, I went to visit Harmellia, a 21-year-old business student of Moroccan origin with long blonde hair and blue eyes, at her HLM complex, which is located about five minutes away from the Nanterre Association. (Because of Harmellia's physical appearance, I did not immediately recognize her as being of North African origin. A few other respondents who do not appear phenotypically of Maghrébin origin note how this fact mitigates their experiences of discrimination, compared to those of their peers.) I went to help her with an English essay on Dante's *The Divine Comedy*. Petit Nanterre is commercially dead on Sundays; the supermarkets and other stores are closed, as most are in France on Sundays. Yet the neighborhood is alive with kids playing outside and mothers pushing strollers. Harmella's HLM building reminds me of an old college dormitory – not terribly clean, but not disastrous either – with a very narrow elevator. The walls and floors are a blandish white color, such as one would expect to find in a large high school or industrial building.

In contrast, Harmella's two-bedroom apartment that she shares with her mother is quite nice and reasonably well sized and features décor and furniture from IKEA. She has lived in Petit Nanterre her entire life, and I ask how she feels about it:

> I don't like this neighborhood at all ... There are many people here who are in difficult situations. The same people are concentrated into this tiny neighborhood. And most of them are unemployed, immigrants, who did not have the chance to go to school ... who have lots of children, who take advantage of the social services we have in France and who do not integrate because they are all grouped together in the same space. So, the children are often disrespectful, they curse a lot, their parents do not really discipline them, so ... they are little delinquents ... I know it is not good to generalize, but in this neighborhood the people are like that ... People who succeed do not stay in this neighborhood. There are other neighborhoods in Nanterre where the people who are also Arabs, blacks or whatever, and it is not the same as here.

Harmellia often volunteers at the Nanterre Association, and credits it with her educational achievement. She first encountered the Nanterre Association after failing the BAC exam twice and had heard of it through friends and family in her neighborhood. Harmellia was able to get the tutoring she needed in order to pass it and eventually enter business school. Despite her connection to the Nanterre Association, Harmella's vision for her future does not include her present neighborhood. Once she finishes school, she plans to move to Paris and live in a more "mixed" neighborhood. In constructing her identity as French of Maghrébin origin and a practicing Muslim, Harmellia distances herself from the much maligned place where she has spent her entire life. Her construction of a typical banlieue resident or Nanterre resident does not include her. In contrast to Mamadou, how she relates to place is through distancing herself from it. Petit Nanterre is implicated in her individual identity insofar as it denotes who she is not, rather than who she is. Harmellia claims her Frenchness through asserting her difference from her banlieue neighbors.

Moreover, Hafid argues that he and other Petit Nanterre residents are just as French as Sarkozy. Regardless of the differences in how Mamadou and Hafid versus Harmellia relate to place – here, living in Petit Nanterre – they nonetheless all see themselves as having a legitimate place in French society. Their relationship to place is one way they affirm their Frenchness.

RELATIONSHIPS TO RESIDENCE

Focusing on respondents' relationships to place provides another way to think about how second-generation North African immigrants are marginalized and they respond to such marginalization. Abdelkrim, a 32-year-old with dual French and Algerian nationality, grew up in an immigrant-rich neighborhood in a small town in central France. When he was younger, he lived in an HLM complex (see Fig. 1) with those of North African origin. Because of this, he does not remember feeling different growing up until he attended a middle school outside his neighborhood (where there were fewer people of immigrant origin). "That is when everything changed," he recalls, "you discovered others and they discovered you. And we didn't have the same life." Sometimes he became friends with these people, oftentimes he did not. Because of experiences such as these, Abdelkrim struggled to come to terms with his French identity as he grew up. In this case, place becomes a way to think about how difference is marked. Once Abdelkrim left his neighborhood, his difference from others was made visible to him, which in

Fig. 1. HLM Complex in Nanterre. Photo by Author.

turn caused him to think about his French identity in different ways. Previous research has shown how individual ethnic identity is most influenced by that individual's interactions outside of ethnic enclaves, where their exposure to discrimination and prejudice is heightened (Eid, 2008). As such, one's relationship to place has deeper implications for marginalized populations.

Hicham is a 29-year-old of Moroccan origin who identifies as both French and Maghrébin. He has spent most of his life in a *cité* in Poissy, a western banlieue about 15 miles from the center of Paris. His family settled there because his father was a factory worker for Peugeot, a French car company that is headquartered there. He describes his neighborhood as a bit "special," as it is part of an urban renewal program. On one of the few evenings Hicham was in Paris, he explained to me how he and other residents fought against project demolition and provided insight into his attachment to this *cité*:

> We had a mayor who wanted to destroy the neighborhood, because in this neighborhood you have a lot of people of foreign, Maghrébin, African origin, and he wanted to eradicate the population ... that's what he [the mayor] said, I no longer want any of you in this neighborhood or in this town. You see, this is a racist person ... Oh yes, and we had a meeting where he came to present the plans for renewal and at the end he said, "If I had known, I would have brought a translator with me to explain this to you" ... but

we understand French very well. And then he said, "I am going to ask you to leave the room because we are going to have to ask the cleaning staff to disinfect." He believes that we are germs. He kept saying such violent things.

AUTHOR: And what did everyone say?

HICHAM: They revolted, we revolted, and we formed a collective. And that was 4 years ago, we have fought against him for four years ... So the apartments, the exterior of the apartments, everything is degraded, you come see ... Everything is degraded, the living conditions, there are rats. Oh we had everything, everything. We had the odors from the sewer, we had the odors of the trash that is stacked together, coming up almost to the first floor of a building ... Oh yeah, the trashcans, they wouldn't come to empty them ... we didn't have any hot water during winter, no heat in winter, oh yes.

AUTHOR: But this isn't illegal?

HICHAM: Yes it's illegal, and we complained ... but the government was slow to do anything ... They had posted a sign [at the *cité*] stating that it was going to be demolished. We hired a lawyer and we fought to delay the demolition up to the mayoral election ... Now there is a new mayor. He launched a new plan, the residents are involved in it, we are staying in the neighborhood.

Hicham beams when he mentions their success at reclaiming their neighborhood. Similar to Mamadou, Hicham emphasizes the social cohesion characterizing his neighborhood. "It's like a family here ... there is a solidarity. Everyone knows each other here. Sure the living conditions are a bit difficult, but now they are improving, it's getting better." He sees living in his Poissy *cité* as constitutive of his identity, something which has implications for each facet of his life. Being educated in French schools and growing up in an immigrant-rich *cité* have led Hicham to see himself as having a double culture; he is defined by being both Maghrébin and French.

This combination allows Hicham to feel deeply connected to his neighborhood, and value being a French citizen, despite the marginalization he sees connected to where he lives:

It's difficult for people in neighborhoods like this ... because society put them in difficult situations ... and as soon as we make an effort, we find a wall in front of us ... As for me, I had a lot of trouble finding my first job after I finished school. It took 1 1/2 years for me to find my first job, but my classmates who were named François, Edouard, Frédéric, it took them 6 months or 4 months to find a job, but for me it took 1 1/2 years.

This experience in part made him understand why other neighborhood youths would be similarly frustrated with living in France and therefore not see the point of studying and doing well in school and why events like the 2005 uprisings can occur. Contrary to what Wacquant (2007) would argue, Hicham could not "pass" in larger French society. To him, his name connotes not only his Maghrébin ethnic origin, but also that he lives in one of Paris' beleaguered banlieues. Despite the problems he sees in his neighborhood, he has no plans to move because of his feelings of attachment to the area. Hicham also wants to be a role model for others in his neighborhood.

While also a banlieue resident, Hinda, a 33-year-old youth worker of Tunisian origin and divorced mother of a 7-year-old daughter, identifies vis-à-vis ethnic origin and relates to where she lives differently. She has lived in the northeastern banlieue of Drancy for the past seven years. She dislikes living in Drancy, and describes her neighborhood as "sad." Hinda explains that she "did not choose this neighborhood" and would rather live in Paris but it is too expensive. "It is not particularly pretty ... the buildings are sad, there isn't much life here, we are a little too far outside [of Paris] here," she laments. She feels similarly unconnected to where she lives as does Harmellia, and hopes to move soon, either to Paris or another banlieue closer to Paris. Hinda identifies as French of Maghrébin origin, as she feels every French person has origins, not just her. She does not deny her ethnic origin; rather she does not consider herself less French than someone who is white. Here, Hinda relates that by living in Drancy she sees herself as a French citizen. That she is surrounded by those who look like her in Drancy is irrelevant; she dislikes living in Drancy for the same reasons any *Francilien* would.

Nadir, a 36-year-old television reporter of Algerian origin, is similarly passionate about the banlieue where he lives as Hicham. However, Nadir eschews invoking his Algerian origin in how he self-identifies. Instead, he emphasizes his strong attachment to the Saint Denis *cité* near the Stade de France (soccer stadium) where he grew up and continues to live, save for eight years when he lived in Australia. He describes his neighborhood as the typical French *cité*, with lots of families of immigrant origin with modest backgrounds. Nadir is well aware of the perceptions and problems associated with living in banlieues. For him, it is important to counteract these stigmas and be a good example for others in the neighborhood. He distinguishes himself from others who have no real attachment to the *cité* and move away as soon as they can. "If everyone who succeeded left the neighborhood," he explains, "only those who could not leave would live there and that it what creates problems, then you have a real ghetto." Nadir uses his connection to Saint Denis to understand the marginalization he faces as a second-generation North African immigrant:

> I feel more and more the fact that I live in Seine-Saint-Denis, because it is the poorest département in France, it is the département of the excluded, it is really the département

that no one cares about, we are really just left there ... so, that's why I feel a solidarity, a solidarity with the blacks who suffer in our country, a solidarity with those at Gaza. I feel a solidarity with all who suffer, I feel a solidarity with them because I lived the same suffering myself when I was a kid. We didn't have money to buy things, we were constantly stopped by the police for no reason, and because we didn't have a lot of opportunities we had the same [kinds of] jobs.

Living in Seine-Saint-Denis defines Nadir. It defines who he is and is not and provides a way for him to identify with those he sees in similarly marginalized positions. Just as he does not always feel attached to his Algerian origins depending on the particular situation in which he finds himself, he also vacillates between being and not being French.

The connection between how one relates to the place where one lives and how one sees himself or herself as a minority within French society also extends to those who do not live in banlieues. Djamila, a 49-year-old divorcee who has always lived in the 20th arrondissement of Paris, claims a singular identity as exclusively French, rather than referencing her Algerian origin. For Djamila, "France belongs to everyone who lives here." She fully identifies as French because she was born and raised in France. She characterizes her neighborhood as a *quartier populaire*, and acknowledges that people who live in *quartiers populaires* are often stigmatized in larger French society. She thinks that more neighborhoods should be as diverse as hers. However, living in a *quartier populaire* or being of Algerian origin is not relevant for Djamila in how she self-identifies. She does not feel any strong connection or attachment to her neighborhood, even though it is the only neighborhood she has ever lived in. Though she feels indifferent to where she lives, Djamila will most likely stay in her neighborhood but only because she feels it is the only thing she knows, not because she feels attached to it.

In contrast, Mohamed, a 30-year-old of Algerian origin, sees himself as embodying a double culture and recognizes both his Algerian origin and French nationality as constitutive of himself. After growing up in Avignon, a small town in southern France, and moving to Paris for work about six years ago, he currently lives in a *quartier populaire* in Paris' 13th arrondissement, near the Porte de Italie. His neighborhood is full of people who look like him. "There are many blacks and Arabs. And I like that ... because I feel like I am in a familiar element," he explains. It is important for Mohamed to live in a neighborhood like this, rather than a more bourgeois neighborhood. As he is one of the few non-whites at the insurance office where he works, Mohamed appreciates residing in a place where that is not the case. He sees having a double culture as a richness, as he has learned two different codes of behavior or ways of being – Maghrébin and French. How he relates to where he lives reflects this understanding. Mohamed operates within a French code while at work, while also operating within a Maghrébin code while at home. Reda, a 32-year-old Human Resources consultant of Algerian origin who lives in Paris' ninth arrondissement, similarly sees himself as embodying both French and Maghrébin cultures. While he currently lives in a "nice, bourgeois neighborhood," he grew up in a *quartier populaire* in Meaux, a banlieue in the Seine-et-Marne département near Disneyland Paris. Due to this, Reda did not recall feeling different growing up; it was only when he moved to Paris a few years ago that he felt "othered" because he grew up in the banlieues (or ghettos, as he refers to them). He still sees himself as being "socially marked" because he once lived there. Therefore, he grew up in Maghrébin-centered environment in Meaux and currently lives in a French-centered environment in his bourgeois Parisian neighborhood. Because of these different residential experiences, Reda sees himself as having lived in two different worlds – French versus Maghrébin.

Similar to Hicham and Nadir, Nasser also foregrounds place in how he self-identifies. Yet, he does so to an even greater extent, as even though he no longer lives in Marseilles but in Paris, he still identifies as being from Marseille before he mentions being a practicing Muslim or being of Algerian origin. When I ask Nasser about the degree to which his ethnic origin factors into his identity, he responds that he is Marseillais before anything else. He reveals in how his co-workers identify him as "the one from Marseilles." Growing up in Marseilles, a populous town in southern France where most of the residents are of Maghrébin immigrant origin, Nasser does not recall ever feeling different. Similar to Reda, Nasser only started to feel like an outsider, particularly in relation to his religion and ethnic origin, when he moved to Paris about nine years ago. He feels that his Maghrébin friends who grew up in other cities such as Paris, Lille, or Strasbourg did not have the same childhood experiences as he did. In Marseilles, it seems to Nasser, one was more likely to draw attention for being *français du souche* than for being an immigrant.

Growing up in a predominately immigrant community buffered him from the childhood stigma that other second-generation North African immigrants often experienced. Nasser stresses how different Marseilles is from other cities due to the profound presence of North African culture there:

I remember the newspaper *Le Monde* did a study related to the children of immigrants, and when people were asked 'what are you?', etc., 98 percent of them said Marseillais, whether they were children of immigrants or not, they said Marseillais. I should say that Marseilles they are many emigrants, it is the first French port, it was the point of entry from the [former] colonies. So people here claim being Marseillais first of all, so it is for this reason that I see these differences [between Marseilles and other cities]. So I don't care if people see me as French or not, as long as I am Marseillais, I'm fine.

That Nasser uses place to supersede any other identification serves as a strategic tool in navigating issues of ethnic and cultural identity. His attachment to being from Marseilles was further cemented during the 2005 uprisings, where Marseilles was the one large city that was not affected:

You are going to say that I talk too much about Marseille, but I remember when reporters asked the [Marseille] youth, they said "Why didn't anything happen here?" and one guy said, "I am not so stupid to burn my neighbor's car, I am not so stupid to burn down the gymnasium where I play, where I hang out." People think these actions bring about something, but they do not bring about anything.

By stressing the connections among Marseille residents, Nasser is also asserting the implications of place for how he constructs his identity. He is also actively contesting stigmas associated with immigrant-rich places in order to assert himself with French society.

What the representative narratives of Abdelkrim, Hicham, Hinda, Nadir, Djamila, Mohamed, Reda, and Nasser illustrate is the varying degree to which second-generation North African immigrants perceive that place marks them as different and how they relate to place reflects how they see themselves in French society. How they relate to place and the degree to which where they live is implicated in their identity often mediates these feelings of difference and serves to challenge the stigmatization with which second-generation North African immigrants are often associated. These narratives suggest that regardless of whether or not second-generation North African immigrants live in banlieues or in Paris, place is one lens through which to understand this population's both perceptions of and responses to marginalization related to their Maghrébin origins.

NOTES

1. All names and identifying information have been changed as per Human Subjects guidelines.
2. The real name of this organization has been changed as per Human Subjects guidelines. However, I chose to identify the banlieue, as I have with all the banlieues and neighborhoods in this chapter.
3. About 25 percent of all public housing is located in the Ile-de-France region (Laurence & Vaisse, 2006).
4. Not all of Nanterre exhibits the same demographic characteristics as does Petit Nanterre. According to INSEE, as of 2006, Nanterre has an unemployment rate of

13.4 percent, in comparison with 8.8 percent for France as a whole, and a population of 88,316 persons.

REFERENCES

Amara, F. (2006). *Breaking the silence: French women's voices from the ghetto*. Berkeley, CA: University of California Press.
Avenel, C. (2007). *Sociologie des "Quartiers Sensibles"*. Paris: Armand Colin.
Bentouhami, H. (2009). Violence and non-violence in the French political discourse: The case of hate speech against the banlieue. Paper presented at Constructing Black France: A Transatlantic Dialogue, New York.
Berger, M. T. (2004). *Workable sisterhood: The political journey of stigmatized women with HIV/AIDS*. Princeton, NJ: Princeton University Press.
Body-Gendrot, S. (1993). Migration and racialization of the postmodern city in France. In: M. Cross & M. Keith (Eds), *Racism, the city, and the state* (pp. 77–92). London: Routledge.
Bouamama, S. (2009). *Les classes et quartiers populaires. Paupérisation, ethnicisation et discrimination*. Paris: Editions du Cygne.
Calves, G. (2004). Color-blindness at a crossroads in contemporary France. In: H. Chapman & L. L. Frader (Eds), *Race in France: Interdisciplinary perspectives on the politics of difference* (pp. 219–226). New York: Berghahn Books.
Cuba, L., & Hummon, D. M. (1993). A place to call home: Identification with dwelling, community, and region. *The Sociological Quarterly, 34*, 111–131.
Dikeç, M. (2007). *Badlands of the republic: Space, politics, and urban policy*. Malden, MA: Blackwell Publishing Ltd.
Eid, P. (2008). *Being Arab: Ethnic and religious identity building among second generation youth in Montreal*. Montreal, Quebec: McGill-Queen's University Press.
Gieryn, T. F. (2000). A space for place in sociology. *Annual Review of Sociology, 26*, 463–496.
Gotham, K. F., & Brumley, K. (2002). Using space: Agency and identity in a public-housing development. *City & Community, 1*, 267–289.
Hargreaves, A. G. (1996). A deviant construction: The French media and the 'banlieues'. *New Community, 22*, 607–618.
Hargreaves, A. G. (2007). *Multiethnic France: Immigration, politics, culture, and society*. London: Routledge.
Horowitz, R. (1986). Remaining an outsider: Membership as a threat to research rapport. *Urban Life, 14*, 409–430.
Kaya, A. (2009). *Islam, migration, and integration: The age of securitization*. London: Palgrave Macmillan.
Keaton, T. D. (2006). *Muslim girls and the other France: Race, identity politics, and social exclusion*. Bloomington, IN: Indiana University Press.
Killian, C. (2002). Culture on the weekend: Maghrébin women's adaptation in France. *International Journal of Sociology and Social Policy, 22*, 75–105.
Koff, H., & Duprez, D. (2009). The 2005 riots in France: The international impact of domestic violence. *Journal of Ethnic and Migration Studies, 35*, 713–730.
Kokoreff, M. (2003). *La force des quartiers: De la Delinquence a L'Engagement Politique*. Paris: Payot.

Lacy, K. (2008). *When ethnographers fail: Lessons from cross-race fieldwork in middle-class suburbia*. Ann Arbor, MI: University of Michigan.

Lamont, M. (1992). *Money, morals, and manners: The culture of the French and American upper-middle class*. Chicago: University of Chicago Press.

Lapeyronnie, D. (2008). *Ghetto urbain: Segregation, violence, pauvrete en France aujourd'hui*. Paris: Robert Laffont.

Laurence, J., & Vaisse, J. (2006). *Integrating Islam: Political and religious challenges in contemporary France*. Washington, DC: Brookings Institution Press.

LePoutre, D. (1997). *Coeur de banlieue: Codes, rites, et langage*. Paris: O. Jacob.

Madzou, L. (2009). *J'etais un Chef de Gang*. Paris: La Découverte.

Maurin, E. (2004). *Le ghetto francais: Enquéte sur le séparatisme social*. Paris: Seuil.

Noiriel, G. (1996). *The French melting pot*. Minneapolis, MN: University of Minnesota Press.

Oberti, M. (2007). *The French Republican model of integration: The theory and cohesion and the practice of exclusion. Some sociological reflections after the riots in France*. Paris: Observatoire sociologique du changement.

Pickering, P. M. (2007). *Peacebuilding in the Balkans: The view from the ground floor*. Ithaca, NY: Cornell University Press.

Preteceille, E. (2008). *La segregation ethno-raciale a-t-elle augemente dans la metropole parisienne?* Paris: Observatoire sociologique du changement.

Rey, H. (1996). *La peur des banlieues*. Paris: Presses de la Fondation nationale des sciences politiques.

Sedel, J. (2009). *Les medias et la banlieue*. Paris: Editions Le Bord de l'eau.

Silverman, M. (1992). *Deconstructing the nation: Immigration, racism, and citizenship in France*. London: Routledge.

Silverstein, P. (2004). *Algeria in France: Transpolitics, race, and nation*. Bloomington, IN: Indiana University Press.

Silverstein, P. (2008). Thin lines on the pavement: The racialization and spatialization of violence in postcolonial (sub)urban France. In: K. Ali & M. Rieker (Eds), *Gendering urban space in the Middle East, South Asia, and Africa* (pp. 169–206). New York: Palgrave Macmillan.

Silverstein, P. A., & Tetreault, C. (2006). Postcolonial urban apartheid. *SSRC Quarterly: Items and Issues, 5*, 8–15.

Simon, P. (1998). Ghettos, immigrants, and integration: The French dilemma. *The Netherlands Journal of Housing and the Built Environment, 13*, 41–61.

Simon, P. (2003). France and the unknown second generation. *International Migration Review, 37*, 1091–1119.

Small, L. M. (2009). 'How many cases do I need?': On science and the logic of case selection in field-based research. *Ethnography, 10*(1), 5–38.

Stebe, J.-M. (2007). *La Crise des Banlieues: Sociologie des quartiers sensibles*. Paris: Presses Universitaires de France.

Stolcke, V. (1995). Talking culture: New boundaries, new rhetorics of exclusion in Europe. *Current Anthropology, 36*, 1–24.

Stovall, T. (2003). From red belt to black belt: Race, class, and urban marginality in 20th century Paris. In: S. Peabody & T. Stovall (Eds), *The color of liberty: Histories of race in France* (pp. 351–369). Durham, NC: Duke University Press.

Tin, L.-G. (2008). Who is afraid of blacks in France?: The black question: The name taboo, the number taboo. *French Politics, Culture and Society, 26*, 32–44.

Tissot, S. (2008). *'French suburbs': A new problem or a new approach to social exclusion?* (pp. 1–10). Pittsburgh: Center for European Studies, University of Pittsburgh.

Tribalat, M. (2004). The French 'melting pot': Outdated – Or in need of reinvention? In: S. Milner & N. Parsons (Eds), *Reinventing France: State and society in the 21st century* (pp. 127–142). New York: Palgrave Macmillan.

Venkatesh, S. (2002). 'Doing the hustle': Constructing the ethnographer in the American ghetto. *Ethnography, 3,* 91–111.

Wacquant, L. J. D. (2007). *Urban outcasts: A comparative sociology of advanced marginality.* Cambridge, UK: Polity Press.

Weir, M. (1993). Race and urban poverty: Comparing Europe and America. *Brookings Review, 11*(3), 22–27.

THE GLOBAL SOUTH

THE LIFE CYCLE OF JOHANNESBURG SUBURBS

Eric Petersen

INTRODUCTION

South Africa has long been an intriguing subject of study, particularly for scholars from the United States. The intensification and dismantling of the apartheid state offers a wealth of material to political scientists and social movement theorists. As the African country with the highest White population, race relations are always in the foreground, as they are in most studies of U.S. urban (and suburban) policy, while they are only just beginning to be taken as a serious 'issue' in European social science. U.S. scholars may occasionally look at South Africa as if it were a distorted mirror.[1] Depending on one's perspective, as well as the focus of the study, South Africa can be taken as a hopeful symbol of reconciliation or as a warning of the great difficulty in overcoming decades of oppression and systemic inequality. This chapter focuses on the generally overlooked aspect of suburbanization in South Africa, which, surprisingly enough, in certain respects looks very much like U.S. suburbanization.

This chapter will begin with a general examination of African suburban development, arguing that many settlements fall somewhere between suburb and slum. It will briefly examine contemporary suburban development in the context of different patterns of colonial development in different regions of Africa before turning to the suburbs of Johannesburg as a special case.

Suburbanization in Global Society
Research in Urban Sociology, Volume 10, 179–204
ISSN: 1047-0042/doi:10.1108/S1047-0042(2010)0000010010

179

This chapter will then examine suburban development in metropolitan Johannesburg from 1902 to 2002 through a historic account focusing on race and class. This history can be broken into approximately four phases: (1) pre-war establishment and gradual growth of suburbs, (2) post-war expansion and the aggressive use of racial land use planning, (3) suburban withdrawal coming at the closing of apartheid era in the early 1990s and (4) metropolitan agglomeration that dissolved the suburban boundaries and created a multi-level metropolitan government for Greater Johannesburg.

The level of government involvement in residential choice, both urban and suburban, has been very high in Johannesburg, inscribing into law practices that are prevalent but not state-sanctioned in many other societies. Any examination of Johannesburg suburbanization that ignored the impact of apartheid would be fatally compromised; this chapter insists that the history of the suburbs must be viewed through the perspective of race but argues that class politics played nearly as significant a role in determining the region's geography. To that end the upper-class suburbs of Sandton and Randburg will be juxtaposed against lower-class Sophiatown/Triomf. Particular attention will be paid to the post-apartheid era where the northern suburbs attempted to distance themselves from urban problems. This chapter will end with a review of the economic and political pressures that led to the 'swallowing' of Johannesburg's suburbs through agglomeration.

AFRICAN SUBURBANIZATION: OVERVIEW

A preliminary scan of the literature on African suburban development suggests certain definitional problems. Settlements that appear to be outside the city boundaries may be recaptured at a later date, surrendering their suburban pretensions, as was amply demonstrated in Johannesburg.[2] Clearly there is considerable growth outside formal urban boundaries, simply because the explosive growth of African cities has overwhelmed the local authorities – especially in the provision of housing (Rakodi, 1997). These informal settlements are more typically considered slums, and certainly slum-like conditions exist in the vast majority of, if not in fact all, African metropolitan regions (Davis, 2006).

Few authors describe these rapid growth settlements as suburbs at all, yet the separation between suburb and slum may in fact be fairly narrow, particularly in rapidly developing countries. The research question for any particular settlement in Africa revolves around its suburb-like qualities and its slum-like qualities. While beyond the scope of this chapter, one would generally contend that slums are marked by informality in most aspects of social life and lack legitimacy granted by the state. Without legitimacy, there are also no transferable property rights. African suburbs, as opposed to slums, are further along on the formality spectrum, although it is certainly likely informal practices are present in the suburbs.

Taking a narrow definition of suburb, the only African suburbs appearing in the literature are case studies based in Egypt, South Africa, Zimbabwe, Zambia, Nigeria and Kenya. As with most African issues, the existence of suburbs appears to be rooted in each country's colonial experience. To be absurdly reductive, the more extensive the colonization – particularly if settlement was made by the British – the more likely each country is to have suburbs. However, this holds only for sub-Saharan countries where the colonial power largely supplanted the existing political situation – often but not always tribal and village based (O'Connor, 1983). Northern Africa was a different situation where colonial-era laws did not interpenetrate the native political and legal system, based on Islamic law, as thoroughly.[3]

Further complicating the situation is that the British and French legal systems had different foci, particularly when it came to town planning (Njoh, 2007).[4] French political thought has generally privileged the metropole, and the suburbs have been host to marginalized groups (Fishman, 2003). Thus, the British approach was more likely (relative to the French, Portuguese or Belgians) to leave institutions in place that would be generally supportive of suburban planning (Njoh, 2007). Smout (1980) argues that British colonial towns in sub-Saharan Africa established on the basis of building large settlements for Europeans grew with natives settling in the remaining territory (this is certainly the case in Johannesburg), whereas others settlements started from an existing village and expanded in a more ad hoc fashion. Consequently, the primate cities not under British control were more territorially constrained from the 1970s onward when African urbanization accelerated. As a further consequence, these cities would be more likely to sprout slums rather than suburbs. Along the same lines, British colonies put capital in for road development that was not solely trade-related, giving these regions a boost in terms of suburban development (Herbst, 2000).[5]

Of all African cities outside South Africa, Harare (Zimbabwe) has the clearest parallels to the suburban development pattern of Johannesburg with the key differences stemming from the smaller scale of the city and that the political transfer of power occurred in 1980.[6] Harare was founded by European settlers in 1890 under the name Salisbury. Suburbanization came early to Salisbury, just as with Johannesburg. As early as 1903, farmland to the north of the city was converted to suburban lots (Chikowore, 1993). Low-density suburbans developed primarily to the north and northeast through the 1940s and 1950s (Davies, 1986; Zinyama, 1993). As White settlers migrated in greater numbers to Zimbabwe (then part of the Central African Federation) in the 1950s, additional medium-density suburbs were established to the southeast and southwest (Zinyama, 1993).[7]

Full independence from White minority rule came to Zimbabwe in 1980. Racial restrictions were set aside, and Blacks began moving into formerly White suburbs (Cumming, 1993). Over time, a Black elite developed and developed a taste for large suburban lots (Rakodi, 1995). Lower income Blacks, particularly migrants looking for work, moved to the south and southwest (Cumming, 1993; Potts, 2000).

CONTEMPORARY AFRICAN SUBURBAN DEVELOPMENT

There are two trends that have emerged in African suburban development. Since the 1970s, major increases in urbanization rates have occurred in nearly every African country. Combined with explosive population growth at the national level, the growth in the urban population between 1970 and 2000 is incredible, often 300–500% increases at the national level.

The inability (or unwillingness) of the state to provide housing has led to massive informal settlements, many of these outside the city boundaries where the local government has even less incentive to provide housing or infrastructure. While provision of water and electricity is generally compromised in African megacities, the situation is considerably worse in these slum-like settlements. The megacity most known for having a large extra-urban population in slum-like conditions is Lagos (Aina, 1989; Gandy, 2006). Nairobi appears to be suffering from large informal settlements and a general lack of key infrastructure (Lee-Smith, 1989; Obudho, 1997). This is certainly the popular view of African metropolitan development.

A recently emerging countervailing trend in Africa is the rise of the security regime, well-illustrated by the gated communities that have arisen in the northern suburbs of Johannesburg. The pressures of the growing informal settlements on the local state have led elites around the world to withdraw into enclaves, many of which would be considered suburban (Caldeira, 1999). Fishman (2003) elaborates this argument: 'As even the most authoritarian states are overwhelmed by the task of maintaining services and security at the core of the megacity, the bourgeoisie opts out for privatized settlements at the periphery ... [that] reproduce in the megacity the relations of economic and cultural domination that characterize the global economy as a whole' (pp. 6–7). The main distinction between this withdrawal and the European suburban enclaves established at the height of colonialism is that class has replaced race as the basis for segregation. There are suggestions this is occurring in Johannesburg. Despite Africa's general marginality to the global economy, globalization has not left the continent untouched, and neoliberal practices are on the rise in many metropolitan regions (Ferguson, 2006), particularly Johannesburg (Murray, 2008), to which this chapter turns next.[8]

PRE-WAR SUBURBAN DEVELOPMENT IN JOHANNESBURG

European colonization of South Africa began in 1652 when the Dutch East India Company established an outpost at what became Cape Town. Dutch settlement continued until the early nineteenth century when the British annexed the Cape of Good Hope and began sending their own emigrants, ultimately leading to the Boer Wars. In the late nineteenth century, diamonds and gold were discovered in the interior of South Africa, an area known as the Transvaal, and the British drive to exploit these resources led directly to the second Boer War. Although these claims have been contested, South African historians claim that the mine sites were unpopulated and the Transvaal was practically a *tabula rasa* prior to the gold rush (Carr, 1987). This landscape was soon to be carved into racial enclaves, with the most productive land (in terms of both mineral rights and agriculture) reserved for Whites (Robinson, 1999; Beavon, 2004). (See Fig. 1 for a map of Johannesburg and its main suburban regions, c. 1991.)

Founded in 1886 as a mining camp, Johannesburg is a relative newcomer as a city, although its suburban development ran only somewhat behind comparable development in the United States – and indeed it had largely caught up with U.S. trends in suburbanization in the post-war era. The demands of a mining economy completely upended South African society, although it was not until the end of the second Boer War (with the British defeating the Dutch settlers in 1902) that political stability was reached and extensive exploitation of natural resources and native labour began

Fig. 1.   Metropolitan Johannesburg. *Source*: Stats SA, adapted by author.

(Lemon, 1982). Even in the early years of Johannesburg's settlement, there was an internal tension between the demands of employers seeking cheap labour and the desire to push natives far from European living quarters (Rogerson, 1982). Native mine workers, along with imported Indian labour, lived very close to central Johannesburg in slums simply called 'Kaffir Location' and 'Coolie Location' (Beavon, 2004).

The first of many forced relocations of non-Whites occurred in 1904 when the residents of these 'locations' were relocated to Klipspruit, approximately 15 miles southwest of the city at the eastern edge of what became Soweto (Beavon, 2004). The transportation from Klipspruit to the mines was extremely poor. The inter-urban train only ran twice a day, taking nearly an hour in each direction; employers found that the unreliable service was causing unsustainable labour shortages (Beavon, 2004). Industrialists then lobbied successfully for residence permits for their African workers, allowing them to stay in Johannesburg rather than being forced to return nightly to Klipspruit.

This policy change – the precursor to the pass laws so hated during the apartheid era – returned African males to Johannesburg in such numbers that by 1911, only 7 years after the first ethnic-based removal, nearly 50% of the population of Johannesburg was African (Beavon, 2004).[9] Unsurprisingly, many Johannesburg neighbourhoods again became slums, particularly as rooms were let illegally and informal living arrangements grew more prevalent (Parnell, 2003).

This general disorder and crime became a push factor, inducing many business owners to retreat across the Parktown Ridge into an area initially set aside for White farmers (Carruthers, 1993). Other suburban areas were available, particularly to the east of the city, but the geological break of the ridge provided physical as well as psychological separation from the city, which was heartily embraced by the elites (Beavon, 2004). The imprint of this pattern of suburban settlement remains in place to this day.

Transportation to these suburbs was quite limited until the Johannesburg Town Council began to plan for electric tramways to the suburbs in 1903. Unlike the situation in the United Kingdom and the United States where transit development was almost entirely financed by private transit operators (in return for franchise rights), Johannesburg partially subsided the construction of tramlines, and transfer of the tramways to the Johannesburg Municipal Tramways occurred within 10 years for the majority of the lines (Spit & Patton, 1976). After a rocky start-up period with equipment problems and power failures on a daily basis, the tramways were well established by 1911 with two northern branches to Parktown and

Norwood, two western spurs, four eastern lines and two lines south to Turffontein and Forest Hill (Spit & Patton, 1976; Beavon, 2004).

Even more critically for the future of suburban development, a road-building programme was begun around 1910, leading to upgraded east–west connections in the region and three major roads north of the city into Sandton (Beavon, 2004). Johannesburg town planners were closely monitoring the car-oriented transport planning in the United States (Foster, 1981), and this is one reason suburban development in Johannesburg is more closely aligned with U.S. rather than U.K. patterns. This emulation grew even more pronounced after the end of World War II.

The tramways were extended and consolidated between 1911 and 1920, and the large residential compounds in the north of Johannesburg were split, leading to gradual increases in population density (Beavon, 2004). The northern suburbs remained quite exclusive, however, and middle-class Whites moved to the east of the city, with English-speaking working-class Whites moving to the south of Johannesburg. Lower-class Afrikaans-speaking Whites settled to the west, interspersed with Black, Coloured and Indian settlements. It is worth noting that the inter-urban railway only ran one east–west line at this time. When the tramway was extended west to Brixton in 1917 and to Sophiatown and Newlands by 1919, it became possible for White commuters to abandon the railway.[10]

In *Cry, the Beloved Country*, written in 1948 while the events were still in living memory, Alan Paton describes the outcome of the White man breaking up the tribes via the Native Areas Act of 1913 without replacing them with a workable system, since they were interested solely in native labour (Paton, 1948; Davenport, 1991). Paton details the vices that the rootless natives fall prey to when they come to the big city, and the plot of the novel involves a Black pastor travelling to Johannesburg and attempting to bring his family back to symbolically rebuild his tribe. Paton clearly felt, correctly, that the process could not be reversed. Many Africans became urbanized, living in wretched slums and having only tenuous legal rights to remain in the city, generally tied to their continued employment. The White response is telling. After importing tens of thousands of Africans to work in the mines and forcing them to live in the most appalling conditions, the Whites began to fear for their safety. They required native labour and yet they did not want natives to live near them, one of the many unsustainable internal contradictions that lay behind state policy towards natives.

Racial fears were always near the surface in South Africa, leading to explicitly racial policy-making at the national level (Hilton, 2008). The Natives (Urban Areas) Act of 1923 increased restrictions on natives living in urban centres, although one loophole left women unregistered and essentially unregulated (Davenport, 1991). The Urban Areas Act reinforced white privilege at the regional level, reserving nearly all unsettled territory for Whites and largely forbidding Blacks from owning property. In metropolitan Johannesburg, there were two important exceptions grand-fathered in when the Urban Areas Act was passed: Alexandra and Sophiatown were freehold regions where it was possible for Africans to lay claim to the land. Both of these regions had been unwanted by White settlers because they were next to municipal dumps and open sewer systems (Beall, Crankshaw, & Parnell, 2002). Furthermore, Alexandra had been subdivided into lots too small, relative to neighbouring Sandton.

One important feature of the Urban Areas Act was that accommodation had to be provided elsewhere in the region for the African and Coloured populations removed from Whites (Beavon, 2004). This left the local government responsible for providing housing, and thus it became deeply entrenched in what evolved into the apartheid system. In Johannesburg, relatively small townships were set aside for natives to the east and west of the city (the Western Native Township in fact bordered Sophiatown to the south). A considerable larger settlement called Orlando Township was constructed to the southwest of the city at the eastern edge of the future Soweto (Beavon, 2004).[11] Despite this construction, housing shortages were always pressing, particularly in Black areas. By 1937, the single-unit houses in Orlando were all occupied, yet the migration of Africans to the city for work was accelerating, with their numbers increasing by nearly 100,000 by 1946 (Davenport, 1991).

POST-WAR SUBURBAN EXPANSION

Unlike much of the developed world, Johannesburg and particularly its suburbs grew throughout the late 1930s. After 1945, suburban development accelerated in Johannesburg (back in line with global trends in the developed world). The housing gap grew to dangerous levels, particularly for African labourers lured to the metropolis. In Johannesburg and the Black townships, illegal shacks were thrown up in backyards, houses were subdivided and squatter settlements were established, particularly near Orlando (Beall et al., 2002).

The reaction on the part of Whites was predictable and perhaps inevitable, given their sense of being a besieged community surrounded by hostile natives. On the one hand, wealthy Whites withdrew from

Johannesburg to the extent practical, while at the national level, the National Party played on racial fears and racial animosities, coming to power in 1948 on a platform of keeping natives in their place. *Cry, the Beloved Country* by Paton (1948) is a key text exploring the racial fears emanating from the suburbs that drove politicians to increasingly punitive measures.[12]

The National Party delivered. The Group Areas Act of 1950 went beyond existing segregation-based policy in that it enshrined four racial groups in the law and explicitly allocated territory along racial lines (McCarthy, 1992). As would be expected, African settlements were the least desirable and most crowded, while Coloured and Asian settlements offered a slight improvement. In metropolitan Johannesburg, a large Coloured settlement was established in Eldorado Park, somewhat to the south of Soweto, while Lenasia, a large Asian colony, was established to the southwest of Soweto near a military base in 1963 (Lupton, 1993; Christopher, 1994).

The labour demands of the mining industry were so pressing that exemptions had always been carved out that undermined native resettlement to some extent, but national politics overrode local concerns after 1950 (Davenport, 1991).[13] In fact, the national government felt that the Johannesburg City Council was moving too slowly in removing Blacks from the western territories, and the Natives Resettlement Act was passed in 1951 to authorize resettlement, even over the objections of the relevant local authorities (Posel, 1991). The most notorious example in metropolitan Johannesburg of forced resettlement is the case of Sophiatown/Triomf. The chapter will briefly consider the case of Sophiatown before examining life in the northern suburbs.

SOPHIATOWN

Sophiatown was one of the few places in metropolitan Johannesburg where Africans could legally own property. This special legal status evolved from the fact that as the township was settled in 1910s, it was next to a large sewage system and garbage dump – and thus was essentially unwanted by White South Africans, although White suburbs encircled Sophiatown and Newclare (Beavon, 2004). Despite the middle-class strivings of some of its residents, most Sophiatown housing was crowded and only marginally better than the shanty towns that sprung up on the edges of Johannesburg. Crime was high, and many residents drank heavily in unlicensed bars called shebeens (Themba, 2006).

Despite these drawbacks, Blacks with upwardly mobile ambitions did tend to settle in Sophiatown due to the lack of options for self-autonomy elsewhere in the region (Goodhew, 2004). In the 1950s, there was a very brief cultural and literary Renaissance based in Sophiatown associated with the literary magazine *The Drum* (Stein & Jacobson, 1986). By the mid-1950s, it was intolerable that an island of Blackness could exist surrounded by White suburbs (Posel, 1991). Using the authority granted by the Natives Resettlement Act, the national government relocated Black residents of Sophiatown and Newclare in several waves between 1955 and 1959 (Beavon, 2004; Goodhew, 2004).

The earliest removals were less fraught with conflict in the sense that Sophiatown residents took this as an opportunity to upgrade their housing situation. At this time Soweto was densely crowded but still had detached homes. Furthermore, many Sophiatown residents were renting from landlords and were not the legal freeholders at all by the 1950s. Later waves of removal were far more contested. The remaining residents were forcibly removed in 1959 and forced to load their belongings onto waiting trucks (see Fig. 2).[14] Many of the structures were bulldozed, and the area was rebuilt and renamed Triomf (Goodhew, 2004). Sophiatown was rezoned for Whites only. It was essentially designated a residential area for lower-class, largely Afrikaans-speaking Whites who were the natural supporters of the National Party.

Apartheid never fully 'succeeded' in the central cities, but was remarkably effective in the lower-class and middle-income suburbs of Johannesburg. The situation was more complicated in the northern suburbs as will be discussed below. The effectiveness of apartheid laws even after three decades can be seen in the rigid demographic segregation persisting in 1980 (see Table 1). Sophiatown was 98% White, Eldorado Park was 98% Coloured, Lenasia was 95% Asian, Alexandra was 95% Black and 5% Coloured, and Soweto was 100% Black.

Income data from the South African Census suggest that the Asians in Lenasia were better off than the Coloured residents of Eldorado Park, but the working-class Whites were generally better off than either of these groups. Tellingly, no high-income Whites were to be found in Sophiatown; they were all in Sandton or Randburg. Further parsing of the Census data would be required to tease out whether particularly high concentrations of no-income individuals (Asians in Lenasia in 1970; Blacks in Soweto in 1980) are primarily due to large numbers of children, 'traditional' households where women are not expected to work or high unemployment among men.[15] Fortunately, the reverse situation is clearer. When the

Fig. 2. Forced Removal in Sophiatown. *Source:* Bob Gosani/Drum Social
Histories/Africa Media Online.

no-income/economically inactive rate is particularly low (under 10%), this
indicates only working adults are present, as when Blacks were working as
servants in the northern suburbs.

These relatively stark disparities pose a number of questions: would
working-class Whites in the western suburbs compare their situation
favourably to Coloured or Asian suburban residents or would their
reference group be to other White residents? Furthermore, was the National
Party's attempt to gain political advantage and suppress class-based
tensions (within the White minority) by exploiting race-based divisions
still working?

Table 1. Population Groups, 1970–2001, Selected Suburbs.

	Population by Race – 1970 (%)				Population by Race – 1980 (%)				Population by Race – 1991 (%)				Population by Race – 2001 (%)			
	White	Coloured	Asian	Black	White	Coloured	Asian	Black	White	Coloured	Asian	Black	White	Coloured	Asian	Black
Sophiatown	97	2	1	0	91	1	0	2	82	9	0	9	67	15	4	14
Brixton	92	0	0	8	82	2	0	9	81	3	1	15	30	8	6	57
Turffontein	90	0	1	8	87	0	1	8	84	3	1	12	34	8	4	55
Eldorado Park	0	99	0	0	0	96	1	1	0	94	3	3	0	92	1	7
Newclare	0	94	4	1	0	94	4	1	1	93	3	3	1	88	3	8
Lenasia	0	3	96	2	0	0	95	3	0	1	93	6	0	3	83	14
Soweto	0	0	0	100	0	0	0	100	0	0	0	100	0	1	0	99
Alexandra	0	5	0	95	0	0	0	95	0	0	0	100	0	1	0	99
Parktown	74	0	0	26	73	1	1	16	70	3	3	24	29	3	8	61
Sandton	66	1	2	31	71	0	1	26	70	2	1	27	61	1	6	33
Randburg	81	0	0	18	80	0	0	16	78	2	0	20	67	2	4	27

Source: South Africa Censuses 1970, 1980, 1991 and 2001.

The answer to these questions seems to be that these generalized fears of violent racial strife seem to have been ultimately sufficient for Whites, particularly White suburbanites, to throw their lot in with the National Party government. While better educated Whites in the northern suburbs are often portrayed as being more liberal and thus more conflicted over supporting the government, fears of apocalyptic racial uprising seemed at the back of many Whites' minds.

NORTHERN SUBURBS: SANDTON AND RANDBURG

In fact, nothing better illustrates the contradictions of the apartheid state as played out in the suburbs than the servant issue. Paton (1948) reveals that suburban households relied heavily upon native labour. Nearly every well-to-do household had a cook, and many households had gardeners and drivers as well. The housewives insisted that these servants be able to live on the grounds, and this was grudgingly allowed prior to 1950, although there was clearly anxiety regarding the lack of White control over this Black suburban presence. Cooks often brought other family members to live with them and might shelter friends without valid work passes, depending on the willingness of their employers to turn a blind eye to this practice.

In native parlance, Africans called the suburbs the kitchens, suggesting that the name of the actual suburb was irrelevant to them, which is strangely appropriate given how anonymous – and replaceable – servants were to their employers. The critical mass of Africans living in these elite suburbs was another source for the apartheid-era laws. Certainly the intent of these laws was to force servants out of the suburbs to face long commutes (Posel, 1991). However, it seems suburban housewives ultimately proved better at subverting the apartheid government than the industrialists of Johannesburg. The northern suburbs never were completely deracinated. In 1970, Randburg was 18% Black and Sandton was still 31% Black, essentially all due to servants living with White families (see Table 1).

The servant issue aside, the northern suburbs underwent important transformations after World War II. Following the lead of U.S. planners (McShane, 1994), tramways were eliminated in 1948, in favour of buses and of course car-oriented development (Spit & Patton, 1976; Beavon, 2004).[16] Car ownership in metropolitan Johannesburg increased dramatically throughout the 1950s. While planning for superhighways began in the 1940s (roughly equivalent to the U.S. experience), South Africa was not able to construct its highway network as quickly. The M1, an important trunk line, connected Johannesburg and Pretoria by the mid-1950s, also linking Johannesburg and Sandton (and to a lesser extent Alexandra). The ring road that bypasses central Johannesburg was planned at roughly the same time, but was only constructed in phases from the 1960s until the Southern Bypass was finally completed in 1986 (Mitchell, Luyckx, & Stanway, 1990). The Eastern Bypass portion of this ring road, serving the northern suburbs and enabling sprawling suburban development (see N1 in Fig. 1), was constructed first.

The political transformation may have been even more important. Sandton and Randburg were not autonomous municipalities or even autonomous suburban zones in 1950. Instead, they were districts under the authority of the Peri-Urban Areas Health Board, which was viewed as unresponsive to the new settlers' concerns as the region grew more suburban (Carruthers, 1993). In 1957, Randburg gained a measure of political autonomy, although at the cost of its boundaries being redrawn so that it would be more likely to return a National Party candidate rather than one from the competing United Party (Carruthers, 1993). Gaining independence for Sandton was considerably more contentious, but this was achieved in 1969 when boundaries north of Johannesburg were adjusted yet again (Carruthers, 1993). These boundary skirmishes were nothing compared to those that took place in 1993–1994, as will be outlined below.

Suburban growth was steady. The population of Sandton grew by 40% between 1970 and 1980 and by 48% between 1980 and 1991. The equivalent population growth figures for Randburg were 45% and 36%. Life was pleasant in these communities, and visiting Americans often compared the northern suburbs to South California, based on the prevalence of swimming pools, tennis courts and golf courses (Grubbs, 2008). By the late 1980s, as South Africa neared the end of the apartheid regime, the suburban mosaic in Johannesburg included many different types of suburbs, not merely elite suburbs to the north (in the process of becoming self-enclosed enclaves). Middle- and low-income White suburbs, and lower middle- and low-income suburbs for Coloured and Asian residents, as well as low-income regions for Blacks, were also present, although Alexandra and Soweto are the least like western suburbs and are often categorized as slums. The low-income territories and elite enclaves are found in many other African countries. What is particular to South Africa (and pre-1980 Zimbabwe) is the wider income range of White suburbs and the suburbs that developed for Coloured and Asian residents of Johannesburg.

SUBURBAN WITHDRAWAL AT THE END OF APARTHEID ERA

Ultimately, the stark disparities of the apartheid era were not sustainable. Facing intense internal and external pressure, political leaders began to consider the unthinkable: granting political power to the non-White masses. Change was in the air starting around 1990; White flight from the city to the northern suburbs accelerated, and gated suburban communities became common (Jürgens & Gnad, 2002). Even prior to the official dismantling of apartheid in 1994, racial restrictions were less rigorously enforced in the western suburbs, as can be seen in the 1991 Census (see Table 1). Blacks comprised 9% of Sophiatown's population in 1991, rising to 14% in 2001. After 1994, reintegration was fairly slow and fraught with difficulties, but it did occur in lower- to middle-income suburbs (Prinsloo & Cloete, 2002).

The northern suburbs such as Sandton and Randburg remained exclusive, although eventually Blacks and Coloured elites (largely from the new governing class) began moving to Sandton, particularly the less exclusive districts within Sandton (Rule, 2002). Less than a decade after the end of official apartheid, the Black population has spread out, with nearly every district comprised of at least 25% share of Black Africans. The historically Black townships remain 75–100% Black, and the new peri-urban fringe (Midrand and Kempton Park) is 50–75% Black. In clear contrast, the White population has concentrated further into Sandton, Randburg and Roode-poort, which are approximately 60% White. An interim population report for 1996 recorded that 70% of the region's entire White population had withdrawn into enclaves in the northern and eastern suburbs (Tomlinson & Larsen, 2003). Brixton and Turffontein, for example, went from 80% White to 30% White between 1991 and 2001 (Table 1). This White withdrawal to 'safer' suburbs seemingly parallels Detroit's fraught relationship with its suburbs. Racial divisions, on the ground at least, appear to be just as strong as they were during apartheid.

One development not seen in the apartheid era was business investment actively avoiding the central city, and the relative decline of retail opportunities in central Johannesburg. Shopping centres were built almost exclusively in the suburbs, although some of these centres had been developed earlier, in the mid-1980s (Tomlinson & Larsen, 2003). Strategic withdrawal to the suburbs was enabled by extensive suburban office development and the creation of a counter-CBD in Sandton (Beavon, 2004). Business rentals in the

Sandton CBD increased nearly 300% between 1990 and 2002; more critically, between 1994 and 2000, the Johannesburg CBD had lost two-thirds of the listed companies it headquartered (including the Johannesburg Stock Exchange), while Sandton doubled the number of listed company head-quarters during the same period (Beavon, 2004).

During the negotiations over the form of governance to follow the multi-racial elections to be held in 1994, considerable attention was paid to governmental boundaries. ANC officials were confident they would control the Johannesburg government, and they had a multitude of promises to meet, most involving improved service delivery and amelioration of the housing shortage (Bond, Dor, & Ruiters, 2000; Beall et al., 2002; Murray, 2008).

The temptation to cross-subsidize services for the urban poor with suburban tax receipts was irresistible. White suburban interests pushed for Alternative A – an option that left the suburbs largely intact, radiating out from the CBD, which would be its own district. ANC officials prevailed with Alternative B where the number of Metropolitan Substructures (MSS) was limited to 4 (Mabin, 1999; Tomlinson, 1999). In the Eastern MSS, Sandton would lift Alexandra. A portion of Soweto was reassigned to the Northern MSS, although the majority of Soweto remained in the Southern MSS. Finally, most of Meadowlands was assigned to the Western MSS to be cross-subsided by Roodepoort. A key advantage of this scheme (and hardly unnoticed by either the White politicians or the ANC negotiators) was that Blacks would comprise a majority in every district and thus lock in an electoral advantage at the local level (Mabin, 1999).

This 'power grab' was probably not the primary reason for White withdrawal to the suburbs and the rise of gated communities, but it appears to be a contributing factor, along with rising crime levels and a general sense that Johannesburg was on a downward spiral (Beall et al., 2002; Jürgens & Gnad, 2002; Harrison & Mabin, 2006).[17] The sheer number and scale of these gated communities was considerable by 2005. Street closings that severely restrict movement have closed entire subdivisions, making them off-limits to non-residents, in effect privatizing this territory. The vast majority of these closings are in Sandton and Randburg with some closings to the east of Johannesburg and in the peri-urban northern reaches of the region; it is worth noting that many of these street closings are not done with proper authorization and are technically illegal (Harrison & Mabin, 2006). (Fig. 3 shows the gateway to Dainfern – a fairly typical 'security village' in the northern suburbs.)

Fig. 3. Gateway to Dainfern, a 'Security Village' in the Northern Suburbs. *Source:*
Harrison and Mabin (2006, p. 8).

METROPOLITAN AGGLOMERATION IN GREATER JOHANNESBURG

The new Johannesburg council found itself still facing considerable
budgetary shortfalls, as well as potential civil unrest over unmet expectations on the housing and service delivery front (Mayekiso, 2003).[18] It
certainly did not help matters for hundreds of thousands of additional
migrants from neighbouring countries, particularly Zimbabwe, to come to
Johannesburg looking for work (Kihato, 2008). By 1999, the Council was
facing a severe budgetary crisis and the proposed strategy was laid out in
iGoli2002 (Murray, 2008). First, the government would be restructured on a
metropolitan basis with all four MSS merged into the Greater Johannesburg
Metropolitan Council by 2002 (Mabin, 2007). The victories in the hard-
fought struggle for the political independence of the northern suburbs were
swept away. Second, through this agglomeration, Johannesburg would start
marketing itself as a global city (Mabin, 2007).[19] Third, the government

would consciously market itself as business-friendly and open to privatiza-tion of services, which was not well received in all corners. The iGoli2002 report was considered fairly weak on this third point, but iGoli2030 had a strong focus on turning Johannesburg into a 'world-class business location' and was viewed more positively by business elites (Murray, 2008, p. 88).

Regardless of the iGoli2030 plan's ultimate success, the metropolitan agglomeration that went forward in 2002 has brought to an end the era of the autonomous suburb in Johannesburg. While the rapid growth and low densities of these suburbs seem more fitting for a U.S. metropolitan region than an African megacity, the consolidation and agglomeration that swallowed these suburbs has few parallels in the United States, though sharing many similarities with the metropolitan agglomeration of Toronto.

CONCLUSIONS

While Johannesburg's suburban development at first seems strangely out of place in an African metropolis, the growth of the suburbs seems less anomalous when considered in the larger context of colonialism. The European settlers, primarily British, imported their own values and pro-suburban biases. Just as critically, they imported British planning practices and enough of the British legal systems to allow for the private transfer of land (critical to this early phase of suburbanization). While the distinction between suburb and slum is often blurred in Africa, the evidence suggests that former British colonies with the highest levels of European settlement will have the most extensive and well-defined suburbs.

Johannesburg's suburbs reflected both racial and class differences, with elite residents of Sandton and Randburg the most able to defend their way of life against the African Other. These racial fears were at the heart of the apartheid-era laws governing land use and employment, and led to a number of forced relocations of Blacks away from White suburbs. The paradox was that White South Africans were heavily dependent on Black labour in the industrial and domestic spheres, setting up a tension between strict segregation and accommodation of labour that played itself out throughout the metropolis. Somewhat ironically, the northern suburbs were actually less segregated (when including the servant class) than the working-class suburbs, particularly Sophiatown.

As the apartheid era was unwinding, Whites withdrew to the suburbs and began to employ defensive architecture and enclose their enclaves in the name of security. As in other African countries, the elites privatizing their territory in this fashion are no longer exclusively White. At the metropolitan level, business interests began a strategic withdrawal to the Sandton CBD, causing considerable hardship to the Johannesburg central city. While the White withdrawal from Zimbabwe was more extensive, there was not a critical mass of Whites in the suburbs to justify the establishment of a counter-CBD; otherwise, the pattern is largely the same.

The main departure from Fishman's (2003) script is that the central city politicians were sufficiently aligned with the National Party – and they had a monopoly on political power – that they were able to push through a metropolitan agglomeration that enabled them to tap into suburban resources. The elites may still be living separate lives in their 'fortress suburbs', but in the larger regional picture, they do help to provide services throughout the region. In Johannesburg, the partial cross-subsidation built into the four MSS scheme of 1995 gave way to full metropolitan agglomeration in 2002. This resource grab is always a potential hazard for a metropolitan suburban elite living in a region with massive unmet needs and severe inequality; there are at least some limits to how far one can go and still remain within the region for work considerations. However, the situation is not entirely favourable for those who favour redistributive policies. The suburban elite may have the last word, for the iGoli2030 plan, while not precisely an austerity budget, is designed to make Johannesburg business-friendly and calls for the privatization of most urban services. If fully enacted, it will push Johannesburg well along the path of the neoliberal practices, perhaps making the city safe once again for its suburban elites.

NOTES

1. For their part, South Africans normally do not turn to the United States but look to Zimbabwe as a counterfactual if native Africans had won political independence 20 years earlier. Certainly at present, most South African political scientists wish to avoid following Zimbabwe's trajectory (see, e.g. Dewar, 1991; Davies, 1992).

2. The formal political independence of suburbs makes it harder (though obviously not impossible) to 'swallow' them through boundary changes and agglomeration. I would argue that British colonists were more interested in the distinction between urban settlement and formal suburb than other European colonists; thus, the legal systems they left behind had an extensive treatment of suburban property rights.

3. There do appear to be defining characteristics of the Islamic city in Africa that can be distinguished from the colonial cities in sub-Saharan Africa (Abu-Lughod,

1987). The existence of an Islamic legal framework does not seem to hinder informal settlements being built in Cairo, although many of these settlements were ultimately regularized (Ismail, 2006).

4. However, the French did follow the lead of the British in one respect: expropriation of all territory which would then be allocated for the benefit of the colonial power with limited land grants returned back to the natives (Njoh, 1999).

5. Herbst (2000) postulates that after the colonial period ended, countries colonized by France and Belgium should have been able to redirect resources towards their own citizens' needs by building more roads. However, he finds that the early advantage in road infrastructure in former British colonies is 'locked in'. This is particularly true in South Africa and Zimbabwe.

6. Zimbabwe and South Africa are unique in being colonial powers (or at least under minority white rule) through the first wave of explosive urbanization in 1960–1980, allowing for the possibility of protecting the suburban districts from the encroachment of informal settlements.

7. Prior to 1971, the suburbs were almost completely autonomous, but Greater Salisbury was established in 1971 that put them under some level of municipal administration (Davies, 1986). It is unclear if this entailed revenue sharing or if the suburbs retained semi-independence under a multi-level governmental structure such as Johannesburg suburbs between 1994 and 2002.

8. Some researchers argue that neoliberalism has actually made further strides in Cape Town, South Africa, than Johannesburg (Lemanski, 2007; McDonald, 2008).

9. Incidentally, the African presence in Johannesburg hovered at 50% until the mid-1950s when apartheid housing laws were instituted and segregation was enforced more thoroughly, particularly with respect to the checking of employment and residency passes (Posel, 1991).

10. It should not be a surprise that racial segregation was imposed on the tramway system from its inception with Africans being forced to ride 'natives-only' cars with restricted service (Spit & Patton, 1976; Pirie, 1992).

11. Those leading the slum clearance were proud of their work and argued native lives would be much improved in the newly built two- and three-room brick houses available in Orlando (Carr, 1987). While Orlando, much less Soweto more generally, is rarely described as a suburb, the settlement pattern of detached single-unit homes with small fenced lots – restricted to nuclear families – is consistent with working-class suburban development (Parnell, 2003).

12. Stories of imperiled white suburban women preyed upon by blacks took on a life of their own during the 1940s. Attacks – real or imagined – on women struck at the heart of white South Africa and resulted in ferocious reprisals and of course further state repression. African women, on the other hand, were a threat. Not only did they engage in prostitution and the selling of unlicensed alcohol, but also in the poorer neighbourhoods they had been found cohabitating with white men (Beavon & Rogerson, 1986; Parnell, 2003).

13. In a partial concession to the industrialists, the local state administered the pass laws and became unofficial 'labour bureaux' (McCarthy, 1992, p. 27). In addition, as non-whites were pushed further from the employment zones and generally lived too far for inter-urban train travel, the Johannesburg City Council was required to subsidize bus service, leading to conflicts when this service proved to

be less than satisfactory, including a significant bus boycott in Alexandra in 1957 (McCarthy & Swilling, 1985; Khosa, 1995).

14. The residents who underwent this humiliating experience might actually be considered fortunate, for others away from home when removal was attempted might well end up with their possessions left out on the porch or on the street (Themba, 2006).

15. Until 2001, South Africa Census income was reported on an individual, not household, basis.

16. Johannesburg's dismantling of its rail transit (aside from the inter-urban train) took place well before most U.S. cities completed the task.

17. 'Fortress suburb' architecture is increasingly common in the United States and parts of Western Europe (Low, 2001; Vesselinov, Cazessus, & Falk, 2007). Most commentators argue that gated suburbs go hand in hand with urban (and metropolitan) austerity measures and a neoliberal political agenda valuing property rights over social justice, which in turn leads to the privatization of security for the wealthy. The situation is more complicated than that in Johannesburg, but the view from the suburbs appears to be a neoliberal one.

18. It is clear that government spending on non-whites has increased dramatically since 1994 (van der Berg, 2006); however, the needs (and expectations) are so great that the government has got little credit.

19. Given how world cities are ranked in the social science literature, it is entirely plausible that tripling the reported population by including the northern suburbs and Soweto would cause Johannesburg to advance up in the standings.

ACKNOWLEDGMENTS

I would like to acknowledge Stats SA for granting use of the 2001 South African Census data and the GIS boundary layers for Johannesburg. I would like to thank Philip Harrison and Pion, publisher of *Environment and Planning B*, for allowing me to reproduce the photograph of Dainfern, as well as Robyn Keet at Africa Media Online for her assistance. Finally, I would like to thank the librarians at the Melville J. Herskovits Library of African Studies at Northwestern University for their assistance in locating key materials, and Dr. James Petersen and the editors for their comments.

REFERENCES

Abu-Lughod, J. L. (1987). The Islamic city – Historic myth, Islamic essence, and contemporary relevance. *International Journal of Middle East Studies, 19*(2), 155–176.
Aina, T. (1989). Popular settlements in Metropolitan Lagos, Nigeria: A socio-economic and structural survey of the habitat of the urban poor. *Third World Planning Review, 11*(4), 393–415.

Beall, J., Crankshaw, O., & Parnell, S. (2002). *Uniting a divided city: Governance and social exclusion in Johannesburg*. Sterling, VA: Earthscan Publications.

Beavon, K. (2004). *Johannesburg: The making and shaping of the city*. Pretoria, South Africa: University of South Africa Press.

Beavon, K., & Rogerson, C. M. (1986). The changing role of women in the urban informal sector of Johannesburg. In: D. Drakakis-Smith (Ed.), *Urbanisation in the developing world* (pp. 205–220). London: Croom Helm.

Bond, P., Dor, G., & Ruiters, G. (2000). Transformation in infrastructure policy from apartheid to democracy: Mandates for change, continuities in ideology, frictions in delivery. In: M. Khosa (Ed.), *Infrastructure mandate for change: 1994–1999* (pp. 25–46). Cape Town, South Africa: HSRC Press.

Caldeira, T. (1999). Fortified enclaves: The new urban segregation. In: S. Low (Ed.), *Theorizing the city: The new urban anthropology reader* (pp. 83–107). New Brunswick, NJ: Rutgers University Press.

Carr, W. J. P. (1987). The story of black settlement on the Witwatersrand. In: R. Musiker (Ed.), *Aspects of Johannesburg history*. Johannesburg: University of the Witwatersrand Library.

Carruthers, J. (1993). *Sandton: The making of a town*. Rivonia, South Africa: Celt Books.

Chikowore, E. (1993). Harare: Past, present and future. In: L. Zinyama, D. Tevera & S. Cumming (Eds), *Harare: The growth and problems of the city* (pp. 3–6). Harare, Zimbabwe: University of Zimbabwe Publications.

Christopher, A. J. (1994). *The atlas of apartheid*. New York: Routledge.

Cumming, S. (1993). Post-colonial urban residential change in Harare: A case study 1890 to 1990. In: L. Zinyama, D. Tevera & S. Cumming (Eds), *Harare: The growth and problems of the city* (pp. 153–175). Harare, Zimbabwe: University of Zimbabwe Publications.

Davenport, R. (1991). Historical background of the apartheid city to 1948. In: M. Swilling, R. Humphries & K. Shubane (Eds), *Apartheid city in transition* (pp. 1–18). Oxford, UK: Oxford University Press.

Davies, D. H. (1986). Harare, Zimbabwe: Origins, development and post-colonial change. *African Urban Quarterly, 1*(2), 131–138.

Davies, R. J. (1992). Lessons from the Harare, Zimbabwe, experience. In: D. M. Smith (Ed.), *The apartheid city and beyond: Urbanization and social change in South Africa* (pp. 303–313). New York: Routledge.

Davis, M. (2006). *Planet of slums*. New York: Verso.

Dewar, N. (1991). Harare: A window on the future for the South African city? In: A. Lemon (Ed.), *Homes apart: South Africa's segregated cities* (pp. 191–204). Bloomington, IN: Indiana University Press.

Ferguson, J. (2006). *Global shadows: Africa in the neoliberal world order*. Durham, NC: Duke University Press.

Fishman, R. (2003). *Global suburbs*. Research Paper. University of Michigan Urban and Regional Research Collective. Retrieved from http://sitemaker.umich.edu/urrcworking papers/all_urrc_working_papers/da.data/308464/Paper/urrc_2003-01.pdf

Foster, M. S. (1981). *From streetcar to superhighway: American city planners and urban transportation, 1900–1940*. Philadelphia, PA: Temple University Press.

Gandy, M. (2006). Planning, anti-planning and the infrastructure crisis facing Metropolitan Lagos. *Urban Studies, 43*(2), 371–396.

Goodhew, D. (2004). *Respectability and resistance: A history of Sophiatown.* Westport, CT: Praeger.

Grubbs, L. (2008). "Workshop of a continent": American representations of whiteness and modernity in 1960s South Africa. *Diplomatic History, 32*(3), 405–439.

Harrison, P., & Mabin, A. (2006). Security and space: Managing the contradictions of access restriction in Johannesburg. *Environment and Planning B, 33,* 3–20.

Herbst, J. (2000). *States and power in Africa: Comparative lessons in authority and control.* Princeton, NJ: Princeton University Press.

Hilton, J. (2008). Unsettling Johannesburg: The country in the city. In: A. Huyssen (Ed.), *Other cities, other worlds: Urban imaginaries in a globalizing age* (pp. 121–146). Durham, NC: Duke University Press.

Ismail, S. (2006). *Political life in Cairo's new quarters: Encountering the everyday state.* Minneapolis, MN: University of Minnesota Press.

Jürgens, U., & Gnad, M. (2002). Gated communities in South Africa: Experiences from Johannesburg. *Environment and Planning B, 29,* 337–353.

Khosa, M. (1995). Transport and popular struggles in South Africa. *Antipode, 27*(2), 167–188.

Kihato, C. (2008). Governing the city? South Africa's struggle to deal with urban immigrants after apartheid. In: F. Demissie (Ed.), *Postcolonial African cities: Imperial legacies and postcolonial predicaments* (pp. 261–278). New York: Routledge.

Lee-Smith, D. (1989). Urban management in Nairobi: A case study of the Matatu mode of public transport. In: R. E. Stren & R. R. White (Eds), *African cities in crisis: Managing rapid urban growth* (pp. 276–304). Boulder, CO: Westview Press.

Lemanski, C. (2007). Global cities in the south: Deepening social and spatial polarization in Cape Town. *Cities, 24*(6), 448–461.

Lemon, A. (1982). Migrant labour and frontier commuters: Reorganizing South Africa's Black labour supply. In: D. M. Smith (Ed.), *Living under apartheid: Aspects of urbanization and social change in South Africa.* Boston: Allen & Unwin.

Low, S. M. (2001). The edge and the center: Gated communities and the discourse of urban fear. *American Anthropologist NS, 103*(1), 45–58.

Lupton, M. (1993). Collective consumption and urban segregation in South Africa: The case of two colored suburbs in the Johannesburg Region. *Antipode, 25*(1), 32–50.

Mabin, A. (1999). From hard top to soft serve: Demarcation of metropolitan government in Johannesburg. In: R. Cameron (Ed.), *The democratisation of South African local government: A tale of three cities* (pp. 159–200). Pretoria, South Africa: J.L. van Schaik.

Mabin, A. (2007). Johannesburg: (South) Africa's aspirant global city. In: K. Segbers, S. Raiser & K. Volkmann (Eds), *The making of global city regions: Johannesburg, Mumbai/ Bombay, São Paulo, and Shanghai* (pp. 32–63). Baltimore: Johns Hopkins University Press.

Mayekiso, M. (2003). South Africa's enduring urban crisis: The local state and the urban social movement with particular reference to Johannesburg. In: P. Harrison, M. Huchzermeyer & M. Mayekiso (Eds), *Confronting fragmentation: Housing and urban development in a democratising society* (pp. 57–75). Cape Town, South Africa: University of Cape Town Press.

McCarthy, J. J. (1992). Local and regional government: From rigidity to crisis to flux. In: D. M. Smith (Ed.), *The apartheid city and beyond: Urbanization and social change in South Africa* (pp. 25–36). New York: Routledge.

McCarthy, J. J., & Swilling, M. (1985). South Africa's emerging politics of bus transportation. *Political Geography Quarterly, 4*, 235–249.

McDonald, D. A. (2008). *World city syndrome: Neoliberalism and inequality in Cape Town.* New York: Routledge.

McShane, C. (1994). *Down the asphalt path: The automobile and the American city.* New York: Columbia University Press.

Mitchell, M., Luyckx, L., & Stanway, R. (1990). The Johannesburg National Ring Road. In: D. Bayliss (Ed.), *Orbital motorways: Proceedings of the conference organized by the institution of civil engineers*, Stratford-upon-Avon, 24–26 April (pp. 122–141), Thomas Telford, London.

Murray, M. J. (2008). *Taming the disorderly city: The spatial landscape of Johannesburg after apartheid.* Ithaca, NY: Cornell University Press.

Njoh, A. (1999). *Urban planning, housing and spatial structures in sub-Saharan Africa: Nature, impact and development implications of exogenous forces.* Brookfield, VT: Ashgate.

Njoh, A. (2007). *Planning power: Town planning and social control in colonial Africa.* London: UCL Press.

O'Connor, A. (1983). *The African city.* London: Hutchinson & Co.

Obudho, R. A. (1997). Nairobi: National capital and regional hub. In: C. Rakodi (Ed.), *The urban challenge in Africa: Growth and management of its large cities* (pp. 292–334). Tokyo: United Nations University Press.

Parnell, S. (2003). Race, power and urban control: Johannesburg's inner city slum-yards, 1910–1923. *Journal of Southern African Studies, 29*(3), 615–637.

Paton, A. (1948). *Cry, the beloved country.* New York: Scribners.

Pirie, G. H. (1992). Travelling under apartheid. In: D. M. Smith (Ed.), *The apartheid city and beyond: Urbanization and social change in South Africa* (pp. 172–181). New York: Routledge.

Posel, D. (1991). Curbing African urbanization in the 1950s and 1960s. In: M. Swilling, R. Humphries & K. Shubane (Eds), *Apartheid city in transition.* Oxford, UK: Oxford University Press.

Potts, D. (2000). Urban unemployment and migrants in Africa: Evidence from Harare 1985–1994. *Development and Change, 31*, 879–910.

Prinsloo, D. A., & Cloete, C. E. (2002). Post-apartheid residential mobility patterns in two South African cities. *Property Management, 20*(4), 264–277.

Rakodi, C. (1995). *Harare, inheriting a settler-colonial city: Change or continuity?* New York: Wiley.

Rakodi, C. (1997). Residential property markets in African cities. In: C. Rakodi (Ed.), *The urban challenge in Africa: Growth and management of its large cities* (pp. 371–410). Tokyo: United Nations University Press.

Robinson, J. (1999). Spaces of democracy: Remapping the apartheid city. *Environment and Planning D, 16*, 533–548.

Rogerson, C. (1982). Apartheid, decentralization and spatial industrial change. In: D. M. Smith (Ed.), *Living under apartheid: Aspects of urbanization and social change in South Africa.* Boston: Allen & Unwin.

Rule, S. (2002). Post-apartheid Parkhurst: Gentrification and deracialisation. In: R. Donaldson & L. Marais (Eds), *Transforming rural and urban spaces in South Africa during the 1990s: Reform, restitution, restructuring* (pp. 225–248). Pretoria, South Africa: Africa Institute of South Africa.

Smout, M. (1980). The village component of African cities. *Proceedings of the Geographical Association of Zimbabwe, XIII*, 9–19.

Spit, T., & Patton, B. (1976). *Johannesburg tramways: A history of the tramways of the city of Johannesburg*. London: Light Railway Transport League.

Stein, P., & Jacobson, R. (1986). *Sophiatown speaks*. Johannesburg: Junction Avenue Press.

Themba, C. (2006). *Requiem for Sophiatown*. New York: Penguin Books.

Tomlinson, R. (1999). Ten years in the making: A history of the evolution of metropolitan government in Johannesburg. *Urban Forum, 10*(1), 1–40.

Tomlinson, R., & Larsen, P. (2003). The race, class, and space of shopping. In: R. Tomlinson, R. Beauregard, L. Bremner & X. Mangcu (Eds), *Emerging Johannesburg: Perspectives on the postapartheid city* (pp. 43–55). New York: Routledge.

Van der Berg, S. (2006). Public spending and the poor since the transition to democracy. In: H. Bhorat & R. Kanbur (Eds), *Poverty and policy in post-apartheid South Africa* (pp. 201–231). Cape Town, South Africa: HSRC Press.

Vesselinov, E., Cazessus, M., & Falk, M. (2007). Gated communities and spatial inequality. *Journal of Urban Affairs, 29*(2), 109–127.

Zinyama, L. (1993). The evolution of the spatial structure of greater Harare: 1890 to 1990. In: L. Zinyama, D. Tevera & S. Cumming (Eds), *Harare: The growth and problems of the city* (pp. 7–31). Harare, Zimbabwe: University of Zimbabwe Publications.

SUBURBAN REINVESTMENT THROUGH 'KNOCKDOWN REBUILD' IN SYDNEY

Simon Pinnegar, Robert Freestone and Bill Randolph

INTRODUCTION

Cities are continually built and unbuilt (Hommels, 2005), reflecting cycles of investment and disinvestment across space, the machinations of housing and urban policy interventions, and shifting patterns of household need, demand, choice and constraint. The drivers of change are fluid and reflect shifting political, institutional, technological, environmental and socio-economic contexts. Urban landscapes evolve in concert with these changes, but the built environment tends to be defined more in terms of spatial fixity and the path-dependency of physical fabric. Suburban neighbourhoods register this dynamism in different ways as they have flourished, declined and subsequently revalorised over time. Changes initiated through redevelopment, from large-scale public renewal to alterations and renovations by individual owner-occupiers, are long-standing signifiers of reinvestment (Montgomery, 1992; Munro & Leather, 2000; Whitehand & Carr, 2001). Our concern here relates to a particular form of incremental suburban renewal: the increasing significance of private 'knockdown rebuild' (KDR) activity. KDR refers to the wholesale demolition and replacement of single homes on individual lots. We are interested in the scale

Suburbanization in Global Society
Research in Urban Sociology, Volume 10, 205–229
Copyright © 2010 by Emerald Group Publishing Limited
All rights of reproduction in any form reserved
ISSN: 1047-0042/doi:10.1108/S1047-0042(2010)0000010011

and manifestations of this under-researched process and, in particular, the new insights offered to debates regarding gentrification, residential mobility and choice, and in turn, potential implications for metropolitan housing and planning policy. Our focus is Sydney, Australia.

Characteristics of Australia's suburban fabric – its low densities, the separation of house and land value markets, and ageing stock – arguably foster lot-based, individual-led renewal activity. The process appears to be more prevalent in higher income areas (as a proportion of total housing stock), driven by prestige, over-consumption and capitalisation of high property values. More intriguingly, KDR is reshaping the city's lower value suburbs, where the homebuyer conveyor belt, traditionally channelling 'step-up' purchasers from established settings to the greenfield fringe, has weakened. Evolving neighbourhood socio-economic and cultural character-istics are transforming the demand drivers within those localities, with KDR arguably indicative of owners affirming their spatial fix in situ, rather than mobilising their capital and re-fixing it elsewhere. Staying put has become more attractive at the same time as the appeal of relocating to distant, poorly serviced outer suburbs has declined.

We start with a brief overview of the extent and nature of KDR across the Sydney metropolitan area, introducing the zones of principal interest in this chapter, namely the post-war middle and outer ring suburbs stretching westward from the city centre. We then engage with a series of conceptual issues raised by the emerging influence of KDR activity in these relatively lower value, ageing suburbs. First, what does KDR contribute, if anything, to gentrification debates? Does it reflect different negotiations in the spatial fixing of individual households' capital, both financial and social? Second, how does insight into the causes and outcomes of KDR impact on our understanding of residential mobility, location choice and the implications of investment in situ for local market dynamics and neighbourhood change? Third, we argue that KDR has increasing policy relevance not only in terms of reevaluating the demand drivers shaping cities, but also options for urban consolidation (or intensification) as part of metropolitan-wide planning strategies.

SYDNEY'S KDR GEOGRAPHIES

It is difficult to ascertain precise figures regarding the extent of KDR activity, although industry published data, anecdotal evidence and media interest would indicate that KDR is making a significant contribution not just to piecemeal suburban renewal but also to new dwelling provision in

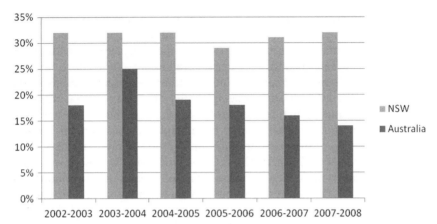

Fig. 1. Knockdown Rebuild Activity As a Percent of New Housing Starts, NSW and Australia. *Source:* HIA (2008).

Australian cities. The Housing Industry Association (HIA) provides an annual tracking of KDR as a percentage of total new housing starts by Australia's largest 100 home builders in each State and Territory (HIA, 2008). As Fig. 1 illustrates, in the 6 years to 2007–2008, KDR has represented around 15–20 per cent of the total starts nationally, and significantly more in NSW, where it has accounted for upwards of 30 per cent. With total new construction figures fluctuating between 30,000 and 45,000 annually across NSW during this time, this would suggest around 10,000 KDR properties in NSW per year alone.

The majority of this activity will have been in Sydney. In order to drill down into the metropolitan geography of KDR we draw upon local authority planning records. While the terms and codes used in Development Application (DA) records vary between Local Government Areas (LGAs), most enable identification of one-for-one demolition and consent for new development on an individual site. Initial analysis has involved the collation and geocoding of KDR activity from LGA and DA records. Of a total of 43 LGAs in the metropolitan area, 30 were able to supply data for the 2005–2009 period, and across these authorities, around 6,500 incidences of (or at least submitted proposals for) KDR can be identified. Based upon HIA's data, and even accounting for absent LGAs and our Sydney rather than NSW-wide focus, this would appear to undercount total activity.[1] These data do, however, provide a useful initial overview of where KDR activity is taking place across the metropolitan area.

Although some areas have experienced higher rates of KDR than others over this period, activity can be seen across all submarkets. It manifests itself in the turnover of $1 million properties and their replacement with multi-million dollar architect-designed homes in the high value Eastern Suburbs and the North Shore; in inner city fringe areas where older dwellings sitting on consolidating land values are being turned over and replaced with new infill housing; and then further westward, where post-war suburbs with modest weatherboard cottages are being replaced with project homes. Interspersed within these geographies is a more diffuse articulation of KDR across suburbs carried out spontaneously by largely middle class households. Sydney's property-obsessed media have noticed the significance of KDR within suburban property markets, as evidenced in one recent report:

> Starting all over again: More than 60 years after the post-war building boom, Sydney suburbs are getting a facelift
>
> A desperate shortage of available land is prompting homeowners to call in the bulldozers to tear down their existing house and start again ... Fibro cottages and double-brick homes are being cleared and replaced with contemporary style housing. In some suburbs ... house after house is being pulled down and replaced, with some streets now unrecognisable to an older generation. (*Sunday Telegraph*, 4 April 2010)

Although we do not yet know the expressed motivations and behaviours of individual households undertaking KDR at this stage in our research, Census and housing market data can help tease out the socio-economic and market characteristics of the localities where KDR activity is more prevalent. As noted, KDR is taking place across a spectrum of suburban submarkets. But within the contexts of each of these submarkets, KDR appears to take place in localities that have relatively higher market values, older population profiles and higher incomes. KDR locations are also home to larger households, families and a more stable population, with significantly less turnover in terms of households moving. There is a higher propensity for a non-English language to be spoken at home, particularly in the highly diverse communities of the western suburbs. Such characteristics are arguably as expected, and to a large degree pick up a number of necessary preconditions for KDR activity to take place. First, the one-for-one nature of the suburban renewal activity points towards majority homeownership localities, with single dwellings and good sized lots. Second, the process involves significant capital outlay, including the effective discounting of the to-be-demolished property on the site. This inevitably trends activity towards households with above-average incomes, and older households who have, through the passage of time, built up equity. An initial hypothesis suggests that some common factors tied to broader economic, financial and market restructuring are at play, but overlain with a range of more locally defined social, cultural and institutional settings. For the remainder of this chapter, we concentrate on KDR activity taking place in the middle and established outer ring suburbs.

FIXITY AND FLUIDITY OF CAPITAL IN AUSTRALIA'S SUBURBAN LANDSCAPE

Although continual change to urban form and function is a citywide phenomenon, the ordinary suburban areas which Gleeson (2006) terms the 'Australian heartlands' are usually overlooked in favour of discussion of higher density renewal in the inner city. The sprawling post-war suburban landscape of middle ring Sydney exemplifies the 'Australian Settlement' (Kelly, 1992) in spatial form. The low-density plot and street layouts provided a geographical fixing of residential development to balance the interests of capital and labour, providing a decent quality of life for both low- and middle-income groups during the stable years of the post-war 'long boom'. Suburbs were 'fair' and 'functional' and offered security, a good standard of living and avoided the class antagonisms (at least perceptibly) seen in other advanced economies (Gleeson & Low, 2000). As Davison (1997, p. 16) notes, 'the great Australian sprawl is not just an unfortunate planning aberration, it is us'. While there was a degree of monotony in the landscape introduced by the prevalent role of public housing 'pattern books' in the 1950s and 1960s, most development was the variegated outcome of 'a multiplicity of individual investment decisions' (Vandermark & Harrison, 1972, p. 1) reflecting in turn a high prevalence of owner-builder activity.

The post-war period was a time of high demand and severe housing shortage compounded by labour and material constraints. In response, self-build – either through incremental construction as funds allowed, or erection of kit or project homes – became central to home provision. The proportion of owner-builders nationally peaked in 1954 at 40 per cent, and accounted for about a third of all new house building throughout the 1950s (Besley, 2002; Dingle, 2000). It was not uncommon for nascent suburbs, with minimal services and lacking sewerage, to be home to households living in glorified garages while the family home was constructed as resources

permitted over many years. This period was also defined by the use of
fibrous cement panels ('fibro'), filling a void in the availability of more
traditional building materials as well as constituting a malleable and
affordable sheeting conducive to the skills and incremental nature of the
individual builder process. Between 1947 and 1961, as Australia moved
towards a predominant homeownership society, 116,740 fibro homes were
added to Sydney's housing stock (Spearritt & DeMarco, 1988). Its
manifestation throughout what are now the middle ring suburbs has been
engrained by recognition of the 'fibro belt', which defines large swathes of
the suburban landscape from Bankstown to Blacktown and down through
Holroyd and Fairfield (Pickett, 1997) (Fig. 2).

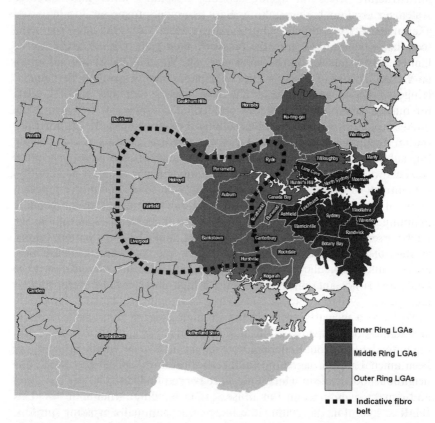

Fig. 2.   Sydney's Inner, Middle and Outer Ring Geographies and Indicative 'Fibro
Belt'. *Source:* A. Tice, City Futures Research Centre, 2010.

The hallmark of the contemporary global suburb is diversity manifested in social, economic, political and environmental terms (Nicolaides & Wiese, 2006). The middle ring suburbs developed mainly in the immediate post-war era exemplify these new suburban realities, which collectively question the usual suburban stereotype of 'homogeneous bastions of untroubled prosperity' (Orfield, 2003). They face new challenges of revitalisation and densification (Clapson, 2003). Sydney's in-between suburbs are typical in terms of beginning to show their age. Gleeson (2006, p. 46) has described a decline in the 'netherworlds of the private rental market, studded with decrepit housing stock and generally wearing the mantle of public neglect'. Stilwell (2005) characterises the same suburbs as being 'in limbo', with infrastructure stress on ageing schools, hospitals, water and sewerage systems, a local tax base shrinking relative to more prosperous localities and a failure to attract more affluent residents. At face value, these predicaments seem broadly comparable to the pressures facing the 'First suburbs' in the United States (Lee & Leigh, 2007; Puentes & Warren, 2006; Short, Hanlon, & Vicino, 2007), or those faced by post-industrial cities in the United Kingdom and Europe affected by low housing demand and the need for market restructuring (Audit Commission, 2009; Cole & Nevin, 2004; IGA-Buro, 2005; Pinnegar, 2009). However, despite sharing issues of social-spatial disadvantage and an ageing stock profile, Sydney's post-war middle ring suburbs continue to efficiently function as relatively affordable housing markets within the wider metropolitan context.

Contrary to associations with sprawling suburban monotony, a patch-work of fibro and weatherboard properties can be seen (some proudly maintained, some festooned with alterations, others somewhat dilapidated), interspersed with three storey walk-up blocks, dual occupancy subdivisions, clusters of townhouses in gun barrel blocks and more recent high density apartments, particularly around town centres and rail stations. The landscape is not anarchic, yet presents a high degree of visual disorder. It has, perhaps, not outgrown the 'Australian ugliness' exposed by Robin Boyd back in the early 1960s, but more prosaically demonstrates flexibility and adaptation over time. While all built form is by its nature spatially fixed, the individual lots that underline housing markets in suburban Sydney have been amenable to a degree of fluidity. Both houses, and more broadly the neighbourhoods within which they sit, have responded to shifting pressures and drivers over time. In this sense, the incremental renewal signified by KDR sits comfortably within the logic of a continually evolving 'restless' urban landscape (Knox, 1993). However, does it signify more substantive structural changes to the forces shaping these neighbourhoods?

SIMPLY A NEW ARTICULATION OF GENTRIFICATION, OR A DIFFERENT BEAST?

Sydney is no stranger to gentrification, and the transformation of its inner suburbs has in many ways echoed and informed understanding of the phenomenon internationally (Bounds & Morris, 2006; Bridge, 2001; Engels, 1994, 1999; Kendig, 1984; Rofe, 2009). Through the 1950s and 1960s, rounds of disinvestment and devalorisation of inner residential areas accompanied reductions in overcrowding, and the movement of industry and population to the suburbs. For example, the population of inner city LGAs Leichhardt, Marrickville, Randwick, Sydney, Waverley and Wool-lahra collectively declined by over 100,000 (18 per cent) between 1954 and 1981, despite an increase in the number of dwellings (Spearritt & DeMarco, 1988). It has only been in the past 20–30 years that those trends have reversed.

During the early 1970s, state government and developer stakeholders in major inner city renewal rubbed against the housing needs in disadvantaged communities such as Woolloomooloo and Glebe which adjoin the Central Business District. The involvement of the Whitlam Labor Government, through the activities of a short-lived national Department for Urban and Regional Development, alongside a strengthening emphasis on preservation of heritage and valued existing urban fabric through the Green Bans movement, prompted a renegotiation of appropriate policy responses for tackling social and housing problems in these localities (Jakubowicz, 1984; Roddewig, 1978; Sandercock, 1975; Troy, 1978). Although a number of freeways spliced the city, much of Sydney's inner suburban fabric remained intact. It has been progressively gentrified since by processes seen elsewhere: typically focused on neighbourhoods with attractive heritage stock, a cultural shift from working to middle class values and shifts in tenure from private rental to owner occupation.

A current gentrification 'frontier' (Hackworth, 2007; Smith, 1996) marking the interstices between reinvestment and *relative* disinvestment can be seen, weaving through the outer reaches of Sydney's inner west. Much of this activity can be considered to follow the conventional pattern, with gentrifiers priced out of more favoured suburbs to the east coming in search of value provided by the next-most-attractive property on good blocks of land with good infrastructure. Reinvestment is likely to manifest itself through adding value by upgrading existing dwellings, although deteriorated property may present opportunities to start again through KDR activity.

However, a continued pulse westward appears to fall off about 12–15 km from the CBD. At this point, the appeal for middle class pioneers seeking value appears to quickly dissipate. Yet a visual audit beyond this point in the traditionally lower value, lower income suburbs of the middle ring highlights a significant level of reinvestment. Much of this inevitably reflects more universal renovation activities, but significant levels of recapitalisation through KDR activity can also be seen. In such environments, streetscapes are changing incrementally, with the outcome of new construction often signifying a dramatic change in the type, quality, floor space and character of new dwellings (Fig. 3). Original 3-bedroom, 1-bathroom owner-built weatherboard cottages showing their age sit alongside replacement project homes, primarily on a relatively modest scale (3–4 bedrooms, 1–2 bathrooms) with a smattering of new suburban palaces of 5–6 bedrooms with a similar number of bathrooms and multiple garages. The size of lot and limited planning restrictions – provided height, set back and floor space regulations are met and no heritage conservation restrictions apply – facilitate this reinvestment and spatial fix of capital, seemingly out of synch with wider housing market values in these neighbourhoods.

Scanning current property values across a representative fibro belt suburb provides insight into local price points within the market. An unmodernised weatherboard cottage on a 600 m^2 block with reasonable proximity to the local town centre is on the market for \$400,000 (Sydney's median housing price is approaching \$600,000). These older properties with values little above the vacant lots are being marketed as such, as 'land value' and an 'opportunity to build new'. A well-maintained property of a similar size and equivalent lot might achieve a sale in the mid-\$400,000s. Skip to the more expensive property pages and a new KDR family home might command a price in the low \$500,000s; at the top end a typical 'McMansion' awaits offers over \$750,000.

This KDR activity represents a significant investment focused on the individual home but also tied to the neighbourhood. Is this good old fashioned gentrification? To an extent, the process can be seen as a continuation of established rounds of disinvestment and reinvestment identifiable in earlier phases of urban development (Harvey, 1974; Kendig, 1979; Seek, 1983; Smith, 1979). If we follow the view that it is the broader processes driving urban change – whether defined through structural economic change, neoliberal policy, changing socio-demographic profiles and preferences, and/or creation of new institutions and partnerships – rather than the material forms of gentrification that are of primary interest, then KDR sits comfortably within the broader context of this

Fig. 3.   KDR Activity in Sydney's West. *Source:* The authors.

transformation (Badcock, 2001; Hackworth, 2007; Hammel, 1999; Smith & Williams, 1986). KDR shares many drivers aligning it to production-side interests: a response to disinvestment, a transformation of the built environment through the fixing of capital and a significant rise in market value post-redevelopment. Furthermore, as the values between vacant land and unmodernised older properties and more well-kept dwellings demonstrate, values are primarily made up of the land component rather than value represented by the actual property, a trend that has intensified in lower value suburban areas in recent years (Newton, 2010). This makes the renewal of such sites a more economically viable prospect. Indeed, the very separation of land and property value explicit within KDR considerations arguably provides a clean demonstration of the conceptual components of Smith's rent-gap original hypothesis (1979). However, other factors raise at least four issues for further consideration.

First, while some KDR activity will be instigated by incomers to a neighbourhood – who may move in because underlying land values, plot size and planning conditions are conducive to rebuilding – a significant proportion of KDR activity represents reinvestment by existing households. Indeed, much of the marketing by builders specialising in KDR emphasise the benefit of, to quote a typical advertisement, 'new home, same neighbourhood'. Inner-city gentrification has been largely associated with a process of 'upward' filtering (Hamnett, 1984) tied to the emergence of an up-skilled higher income labour market, whereas many of the localities experiencing significant KDR activity in the western suburbs are less directly tied to the well-paid employment opportunities of 'global' Sydney (Dodson & Berry, 2004; Fagan & Dowling, 2005). In these locations, the process appears to be driven by local and subregional factors, with upwardly mobile households choosing to redevelop houses within their suburb or stay on their own land and rebuild. As such, KDR activity can be seen more as in situ social and asset consolidation rather than invasion by 'incomers'. Although this disrupts assumptions regarding displacement pressures on existing communities in the initial instance, over time such activity parallels the loss of affordable stock for future households and the changing function and role of local housing markets – with outcomes akin to more traditional gentrification processes.

Second, space – and the spatial manifestation of cycles of investment and disinvestment – has been seen as integral in tying explanations of gentrification to the broader processes of urban social, economic, political restructuring. Although the rent-gap thesis provides a counterweight to neoclassical economics and 'a production side corrective to traditional filtering theory' (Lees, Slater, & Wyly, 2008, p. 63), geography and the spatial relocation of capital retain a significant role in explanation, whether in terms of links drawn between gentrification and the suburbs as spatial fix (Harvey, 1978), the 'locational' switching of capital or identification of a gentrification 'frontier' (Hackworth, 2007). Circuits of capital have typically found it more cost effective to relocate to new spaces (e.g. through suburbanisation) until a time when disinvestment makes it viable to return, rather than stay put. The in situ reinvestment signified by KDR might appear contrary to such flows and movement of capital elsewhere.

Third, while studies have moved on from overdrawn dichotomies between production and consumption side explanations (Clark, 1992, 2005; Hamnett, 1991; Lees, 2000; Lees et al., 2008; Slater, 2006; Smith, 1996; Williams, 1986), it is still interesting to consider whether the distinctive nature of KDR outcomes provides any useful insight into understanding consumption related factors. The architectural merits of the low-density fibro belt do not demonstrate immediate parallels with the Victorian terraces of Paddington and Surry Hills in Sydney (and likewise Clapham in London or the solid brownstones of New York). Indeed, its appeal is its apparent lack of anything worth saving in terms of urban design and heritage. Here, capital reinvestment is not pursuing a particular form of housing stock conducive to more consumption-oriented theses (Jager, 1986). Nor are these suburbs on the cusp of a 'latte'-led transformation (Slater, 2006). Rather, there appears to be investment in locality through reworking existing lots in familiar streets. It is the *expendability* of the existing built form, with homes coming towards the end of their expected lives, which enables local households to re-fix capital in their locality without the need to trade up or trade down through relocation.

Fourth, it is difficult to ascribe this fragmented, individual, incremental process to broader shifts in large-scale financial, institutional and policy interests, whether in terms of disinvesting or reinvesting in these neighbourhoods (Hackworth, 2007). Lot-based renewal has not been accompanied by the emergence of concerted, coordinated interest from the major developers, although a number of mid-sized companies have identified KDR as an important business niche. The fibro belt looks like an individuated quilt without the imprint of big institutional interests because – with the exception of Housing Commission estates built between the 1950s and 1970s – that is essentially what it historically has been and continues to be. The process of KDR in these areas can thus be seen to follow a long-term trajectory of locally shaped and defined investment.

Nevertheless, underlying factors that rework the demand characteristics behind these individual decisions pull us back towards more structural explanations. As discussed in the following section, broader dynamics shaping the middle and established outer ring suburbs' housing demand over recent decades are shifting. Devalorisation of parts of the city is predicated in large part on assumptions that capital will be tempted to cheaper, more efficient locations outward towards the fringe. Where the fringe no longer offers a relatively advantageous spatial fix, further light is shone on potential factors shaping the growth in KDR.

RESIDENTIAL CHOICE, MOBILITY AND HOUSING MARKET DYNAMICS

The fibro belt's pivotal role in providing a lower value entry point to housing markets in Sydney continues today. However the dynamics of those markets appear to have changed. While its broad function remains, the continually evolving drivers and constituent elements of those markets reflect wider economic and market changes that shape the city. Much of western Sydney has been built out by waves of in-migrants and immigrants: in the post-war decades by returning servicemen and migrants from southern Europe, and subsequently by a wealth of nations including significant populations from Vietnam and Lebanon. Local authorities such as Fairfield and Liverpool – 30–40 km from the city – now constitute the heart of Sydney's multicultural population. As new households have formed, and new in-migrants arrive in middle and established outer ring suburbs, a 'conveyor' has traditionally carried out a net number of movers to the ever more distant fringe and new housing opportunities. Although this net flow outward continues, its scale and characteristics appear to have shifted over the past decade. An analysis of Census data indicates that these numbers have fallen in some locations, and the characteristic of households moving out along the conveyor appears to be changing (City Futures Research Centre, 2008; NSW Department of Planning, 2010a; Randolph, Pinnegar, Easthope, & Tice, 2010).

Despite continued housing growth and predictions that a further 770,000 homes will be needed in metropolitan Sydney by 2036 (NSW Department of Planning, 2010b), the demand for new housing on the urban fringe of Sydney in recent years has tracked below historical trends (NSW Department of Planning, 2010a). Developers argue that it is a question of supply, with insufficient land release, inefficient planning processes and the high cost of infrastructure levies imposed. However, the changing nature of flows towards the fringe also arguably reflects a change in levels of demand for new lots. A range of factors can be posited for these shifts. First, urban consolidation policies over the past 30 years (Bunker, Holloway, & Randolph, 2005; Lewis, 1999; NSW Department of Planning, 2005; Searle, 2007; Spearritt, 2000) will have contributed to this slowdown as other housing options become available in existing suburbs. However, this is unlikely to be the primary factor. As Newton (2010) notes in the context of Melbourne, most densification has focused in and around the city centre rather than the 'greyfield' suburbs 5–25 km out, with the latter accounting for less than 20 per cent of total new stock.

Second, the market function played by the middle ring as a gateway for overseas migrants ensures that the nature of flows into these areas will impact upon the future trajectory of household mobility from these localities. If in-flows were to increase then one might expect, as housing pathways unfold over time, for this to provide a continued pool of prospective out-movers moving along the conveyor to the fringe, with options determined by consumer preferences and income profiles of those households. Conversely, if in-flows decreased, then this would be expected to have a knock-on effect on the size and characteristics of the potential 'out migrants' pool over time. While levels of overseas migration have remained strong in many middle ring suburbs, for example Auburn and Parramatta, two traditional hubs – Fairfield and Canterbury – actually saw modest falls in their non-Australian born populations between the 2001 and 2006 Census (City Futures Research Centre, 2008). Fairfield has tradition-ally been a core feeder market for neighbouring Liverpool and the release areas to its west, and it is interesting to reflect that the slowing down of demand for new homes in this submarket would appear to parallel these structural changes (NSW Department of Planning, 2010a).

These shifts in household trajectories are significant, but do not automatically point towards an explanation for KDR activity within the middle ring. Our third factor returns to the rent-gap hypothesis and the question of relative house prices. Fig. 4 demonstrates the fall off in median single dwelling (Torrens) and apartment/townhouse (strata) prices between Sydney's CBD and the urban fringe. House prices for all 2009 sales in a 10 km band from the centre westward to Fairfield–Liverpool have been extracted from the NSW Valuer General's dataset and aggregated to provide median values in 3 km bands. The graph highlights a steeper drop commencing 12–15 km from the CBD (where the middle ring suburbs

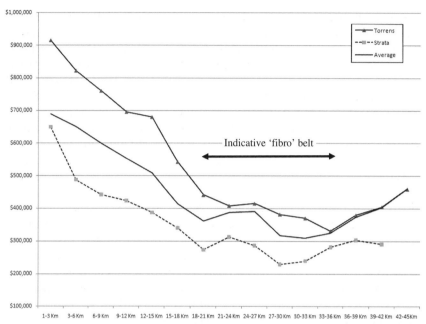

Fig. 4. Median Values for Total, Single Dwelling and Strata Sales by Distance from CBD in 2009. *Source:* NSW Valuer General data, mapped by A. Tice, City Futures Research Centre, 2010.

commence) and then a continued gradual decline with lowest median values seen 25–35 km distant. Values then pick up fairly significantly towards the metropolitan fringe. In large part this reflects the changing role of the fringe in recent decades from an affordable entry point for first home purchasers to larger and higher value properties increasingly geared towards 'step-up' and aspirant markets (Gwyther, 2004; Allon, 2008).

Rather than focusing on the gulf between inner city values and our lower value areas, it can be argued that it is the 'rent-gap' with recently constructed properties out on the fringe that underpins key drivers of change being seen in the fibro belt. If a new home costs \$550,000 on a 450 m^2 block of land in a poorly serviced new release area, and you are sitting on a 600 m^2 block in an established neighbourhood, closer to the CBD with a market value of \$400,000 on which a similar project home can be constructed for \$200,000, then upgrading through KDR without spatially relocating starts to look economically viable. Add to this the removal of stamp duty, legal, real estate agent fees and moving costs, and the equation becomes all the more competitive. Compared to traditional models of gentrification that have focused on flows of in-movers and the displaced, KDR represents an opportunity for existing households to benefit from the rent-gap by re-fixing capital without having to exercise housing pathways through relocation.

Although it would be incorrect to ascribe the significant shift seen in household flows to KDR activity – not least because many households are still moving out to the fringe and KDR numbers remain a small percentage of total new build activity – the presence of KDR does raise some interesting questions regarding traditional models of residential choice and mobility. Classical filtering models suggest that as households progress up the housing ladder and levels of equity build, equity is extracted and re-fixed in a different spatial location. Equally, choosing to reinvest rather than move seems, at first glance, to be against the residential trends of Australian and US metropolitan areas in the 1980s and 1990s. In some US suburbs, mobility rates are such that on average 50 per cent of a suburb's population move in a five-year period depending on level of homeownership (Lucy & Phillips, 2000). In Australia, 43 per cent of all households are likely to move within a period of five years, indicating that relocation is the predominant means by which households improve their housing situation (Maher, 1994). Australian research also suggests that housing quality, size and type, rather than location, has long been the predominant factor influencing households to move (Wulff, 1993). This may explain why most relocations, with the exception of younger households, are short distance (Maher, 1994) and essentially define local or subregional housing market geographies (Brown & Hincks, 2008; DTZ Pieda, 2004; Jones, Leishman, & Watkins, 2004; Maclennan & Bannister, 1995; Pinnegar, 2007).

Residential location and preference studies typically focus on push and pull factors that help shape households decisions to move. However, place attachment acts as an important counterweight (Brown, Perkins, & Brown, 2003; Gieryn, 2000; Massey, 1995). The ways in which people experience their neighbourhoods affect their identities and experiences as well as their actions, which in turn influence the social and political economy of a place. Acknowledging that households make decisions based not only on purely rational factors but also on their emotive attachments to place and neighbourhood, for example through familial or cultural ties, is likely to underpin much of the appeal of KDR. And unless neighbourhoods are experiencing signs of severe disinvestment (rare even in Australia's more disadvantaged localities), then the familiarity provided by staying close to local amenities and services, family and friends, children's schools and

Table 1.   Selling 'Knock Down and Rebuild' in Sydney.

Masterton Homes	Wincrest Homes	Rawson Homes
Out with the old ... and in with the new!	Out with the old ... and in with the new	Knock Down Rebuild is our speciality
'If you've lived in it for a number of years, you probably own it or at least have plenty of equity ... You could move into a new home, but it would mean leaving an area you enjoy living in. It would mean moving away from your neighbours and friend, local shops and schools'	'Renovating can be expensive, selling and buying a harrowing experience, and you may have to move further than you would like. Knock Down Rebuild Experience is: affordable excellence at its best!'	'You love your area, you really like your street, you even like your neighbours, but your house has seen better days ... So what are your options? ... You can pack up and relocate to a different neighbourhood, or you can work around your home's current problems and renovate or you can knock down and rebuild! Just think you can have the house of your dreams right where you are!'

Source: www.masterton.com.au; www.wincrest.com.au; www.rawson.com.au

places of worship presents a strong case in favour of in situ reinvestment. Recognising this attachment to place is not lost on the building companies spruiking their KDR services in Sydney (Table 1).

Phrases extracted from company websites combine to make a compelling case for the convenience, financial common sense and family stability of upgrading in place:

- 'Continue living in your suburb/street with existing neighbours'
- 'Children don't have to change schools'
- 'Carry on using your local amenities/services'
- 'Erase hassle of selling/buying a new home'
- 'Add value to your land'
- 'Have your say on building specifications'
- 'Renovating costs twice as much per square metre as building a new home'
- 'No real estate or stamp duty fees'.

The emerging popularity of KDR therefore seems to reaffirm preferences to stay in place, and suggests that established neighbourhoods are retaining aspirant households. It also offers an option for older households wanting to remain in the neighbourhood but who would prefer to replace their current home with a new property which has fewer maintenance concerns, perhaps built on a single level or to universal design principles. The ability to exercise choice – to re-fix residential capital but to do so by staying in situ – clearly raises interesting questions regarding household mobility patterns, changing functional roles of neighbourhoods within the city and the nature of broader housing market dynamics.

KDR AND IMPLICATIONS FOR METROPOLITAN PLANNING POLICY

Finally, we consider the implications of the KDR phenomenon for metropolitan planning policy. Three issues are canvassed. First, all metropolitan strategies for Australian cities share significant urban con-solidation targets and there is now considerable expectation for Australia's middle suburbs to take a significant quantum of the new dwellings required (Forster, 2006; Newton, 2010; Randolph, 2006; Randolph & Freestone, 2008; Searle, 2007). Sydney's West Central subregion, where the focus of our interest falls, is expected to accommodate around 95,000 or 15 per cent of the new dwellings needed to accommodate projected population increases (NSW Department of Planning, 2005). Much of this is to be concentrated around major activity centres, although the breakdown of figures indicates that up to 70 per cent of new stock in existing neighbourhoods is expected to focus on smaller town centres, 'villages' and indeed outside those centres altogether. This suggests that a fairly robust level of modest densification is required outside those foci, for example through subdivision, small-site amalgama-tions and medium density renewal. However KDR confounds this to a certain extent, transforming older stock but doing so by replacing one-for-one, therefore not increasing overall numbers and precluding the renewal of those lots which hitherto might have been considered ripe for redevelopment at higher densities. As a result, KDR continues a tradition of development outcomes which are based upon economic viability and demand – in this case from the individual lot owners to remain and rebuild – rather than subscribing to the hypothetical numbers game of urban capacity studies (Bramley, 1993; Pinnegar, 2007; Randolph et al., 2010).

Second, by potentially scuppering intentions to amalgamate sites to enable higher density redevelopment, KDR activity has ramifications not only in terms of meeting dwelling targets but also for broader environmental intentions tied to renewal activity. Paralleling similar policies in other states, the NSW Government has enacted standards for new building through BASIX (the Building Sustainability Index), requiring all significant residential construction (new homes and renovations over $50,000) to meet new energy and water efficiency guidelines (NSW Department of Planning, 2006a, 2006b). The task of reworking and retrofitting ageing neighbourhoods to these new environmental standards is seen as one of the most significant challenges facing our cities as we move towards more carbon constrained futures (Batty, 2007; Newton, 2008, 2010; Pinnegar, Marceau, & Randolph, 2008). In his investigation of suburban renewal potential in Melbourne, Newton (2010) argues that site amalgamation is required to enable redevelopment opportunities where energy and water efficient design can be provided at a cost-effective scale. This approach is seemingly hindered through the lot-based fragmented nature of KDR. Equally, however, it may be that an incremental, individual-led approach to retrofitting the suburbs is more feasible – both economically and politically – even if not leading to the kind of step change envisaged by Newton (2010).[2] Furthermore, debates regarding asset and infrastructure under-utilisation that add weight to urban consolidation arguments, powerful in the depopulated tracts of the US First Suburbs (Hudnut, 2003), are perhaps less convincing in an Australian suburban landscape that started out creaking and continues under strain.

Third, and returning to the question of broader structural change, by dampening household flows, in situ reinvestment by existing households reduces the availability of stock for incomers. If these localities have traditionally played a vital role as an entry point for first home buyers, then the loss of this function, as the vacancy chain process begins to break down, raises some concern. It is an interesting social policy dilemma: is the 'uplift' and stabilisation of these old fibro suburbs acceptable if the gentrification pressures are coming from within? While KDR potentially offers good social sustainability outcomes for certain neighbourhoods, it reflects broader restructuring dynamics taking place within Sydney that the city's current metropolitan planning strategy is ill-prepared to respond to. The viability of Sydney's greenfield areas – now located 40–50 km from the city centre – is determined by demand from nearby established areas and, as previously mentioned, there is evidence emerging of a slowdown in some submarkets. Developers argue that releasing more land and reducing levies on new construction can turn this trend around. This may be so; however, the prospective market for their product appears to be shifting in terms of both its nature and scale. While KDR is not the cause of this, we would argue that it is symbolic of the broader restructuring taking place in household mobility, residential preferences and circuits of residential capital.

CONCLUSION

This chapter has considered a particular form of suburban renewal: the increasing significance of incremental 'knockdown rebuild' activity. It has sought to unpack a series of conceptual issues raised by the emerging influence of KDR activity in Australia's post-war suburbs, drawing on preliminary analyses of the recent Sydney experience. It has sketched the scale and manifestations of this under-researched process and, in particular, considered whether KDR offers new insights into residential choice, suburban mobility and gentrification debates.

In many respects, the presence of KDR activity can be seen as a positive as much as a concerning trend within Sydney's metropolitan dynamics. Although not conforming to more traditional manifestations of gentrification, KDR can in large part be understood in terms of broader spatial and market restructuring processes. Its distinctiveness is reflected in owners reaffirming investment in situ rather than mobilising their capital and re-fixing it elsewhere. Staying put, and the options for staying put, have never looked so good. A rent-gap can be seen, but it appears that it is the emerging gap with new development on the urban fringe, rather than filtering and displacement pressures from the inner suburban areas, that contributes to the appeal of KDR in these suburbs. In this regard, debate is prompted as to whether this internal reinvestment and transition reflect a positive outcome in terms of community, neighbourhood and housing market trajectories. At the same time, reinvestment in place raises issues for meeting urban consolidation targets in metropolitan strategies, the retrofitting of environmentally sustainable design standards and the disruption to the conventional 'conveyor' dynamics of lower value suburban housing markets.

NOTES

1. A potential reason for this discrepancy could be that we excluded demolitions that led to redevelopment through dual occupancy or multi-unit provision.

2. While these new homes will be BASIX compliant and therefore meet particular benchmarks, it is likely that the KDR process will have seen a modest home replaced with a significantly larger property where any potential gains will be somewhat obviated.

REFERENCES

Allon, F. (2008). *Renovation nation*. Sydney: UNSW Press.

Audit Commission. (2009). *Housing market renewal: Programme review 2008/2009*. London: Audit Commission.

Badcock, B. (2001). Thirty years on: Gentrification and class changeover in Adelaide's inner suburbs, 1966–1996. *Urban Studies, 38*(9), 1559–1572.

Batty, M. (2007). The creative destruction of cities. *Environment and Planning B: Planning and Design, 34*, 2–5.

Besley, J. (2002). Home improvement: Suburban works-in-progress. Suburbia, National Trust of Australia (NSW), 23–25 February 2002. Available at http://www.nsw.nationaltrust. org.au/conservation/files/suburbia%20Besley.pdf

Bounds, M., & Morris, A. (2006). Second wave gentrification in inner-city Sydney. *Cities, 23*(2), 99–108. doi: 10.1016/j.cities.2005.09.001.

Boyd, R. (1960). *The Australian ugliness*. Melbourne: Cheshire.

Bramley, G. (1993). Land use planning and housing market in Britain. *Environment and Planning A, 25*, 1021–1051.

Bridge, G. (2001). Estate agents as interpreters of economic and cultural capital: The gentrification premium in the Sydney housing market. *International Journal of Urban and Regional Research, 25*, 87–101.

Brown, P., & Hincks, S. (2008). A framework for housing market area delineation: Principles and application. *Urban Studies, 45*(11), 2225–2247.

Brown, B., Perkins, D., & Brown, G. (2003). Place attachment in a revitalising neighbourhood: Individual and block levels of analysis. *Journal of Environmental Psychology, 23*(3), 259–271.

Bunker, R., Holloway, D., & Randolph, B. (2005). The expansion of urban consolidation in Sydney: Social impacts and implications. *Australian Planner, 42*(3), 23–30.

City Futures Research Centre. (2008). *Our changing city. Sydney: A census overview 2001–2006*. Sydney: City Futures Research Centre UNSW.

Clapson, M. (2003). *Suburban century: Social change and urban growth in England and the USA*. Oxford: Berg.

Clark, E. (1992). On blindness, centrepieces and complementarity in gentrification theory. *Transactions of the Institute of British Geographers, 17*, 358–362.

Clark, E. (2005). The order and simplicity of gentrification: A political challenge. In: R. Atkinson & G. Bridge (Eds), *Gentrification in a global context: The new urban colonialism* (pp. 256–264). London: Routledge.

Cole, I., & Nevin, B. (2004). *Road to renewal: Early implementation of the housing market renewal pathfinder programme in England*. York: Joseph Rowntree Foundation.

Davison, G. (1997). The great Australian sprawl. *Historic Environment, 1*(13), 10–17.

Dingle, T. (2000). Necessity is the mother of invention, or do-it-yourself. In: P. Troy (Ed.), *A history of European housing in Australia* (pp. 57–76). Cambridge: Cambridge University Press.

Dodson, J., & Berry, M. (2004). The economic 'Revolution' in Melbourne's west. *Urban Policy and Research*, *22*(2), 137–155.

DTZ Pieda. (2004). *Housing market assessment manual*. London: Office of the Deputy Prime Minister.

Engels, B. (1994). Capital flows, redlining and gentrification: The pattern of mortgage lending and social change in glebe, Sydney, 1960–1984. *International Journal of Urban and Regional Research*, *18*(4), 628–657.

Engels, B. (1999). Property ownership, tenure and displacement: In search of the process of gentrification. *Environment and Planning A*, *31*, 1473–1495.

Fagan, R., & Dowling, R. (2005). Neoliberalism and suburban employment: Western Sydney in the 1990s. *Geographical Research*, *43*, 71–81.

Forster, C. (2006). The challenge of change: Australian cities and urban planning in the new millennium. *Geographical Research*, *44*(2), 173–182.

Gieryn, T. (2000). A space for place in sociology. *Annual Review of Sociology*, *26*, 463–496.

Gleeson, B. (2006). *Australian heartlands: Making space for hope in the suburbs*. Sydney: Allen & Unwin.

Gleeson, B., & Low, N. (2000). *Australian urban planning: New challenges, new agendas*. Sydney: Allen & Unwin.

Gwyther, G. (2004). Paradise planned: Community formation and the master planned estate. *Urban Policy and Research*, *23*(1), 57–72.

Hackworth, J. (2007). *The neoliberal city: Governance, ideology and development in American urbanism*. New York: Cornell University Press.

Hammel, D. (1999). Re-establishing the rent gap: An alternative view of capitalized land rent. *Urban Studies*, *36*(8), 1283–1293.

Hamnett, C. (1984). Gentrification and residential location theory: A review and assessment. In: D. Herbert & R. Johnston (Eds), *Geography and the urban environment, progress and applications* (pp. 252–261). Chichester: Wiley.

Hamnett, C. (1991). The blind man and the elephant: The explanation of gentrification. *Transactions of the Institute of British Geographers*, *16*(2), 173–189.

Harvey, D. (1974). *Social justice and the city*. London: Edward Arnold.

Harvey, D. (1978). The urban process under capitalism: A framework for analysis. *International Journal of Urban and Regional Research*, *2*(1), 100–131.

Hommels, A. (2005). *Unbuilding cities: Obduracy in urban socio-technical change*. Cambridge, MA: MIT Press.

Housing Industry Association (HIA). (2008). Outlook for the residential sector. Available at http://www.bulkygoodsretailers.com.au/docs/HIA%20Presentation%20to%20BGRA%20Forum%20on%2020%2011%2008.pdf.

Hudnut, W. (2003). *Halfway to everywhere*. Washington, DC: Urban Land Institute.

IGA-Buro. (2005). *Die Andere Stadte: IBA Stadtumbau 2010*. Berlin: IGA-Buro.

Jager, M. (1986). Class definition and the esthetics of gentrification: Victoriana in Melbourne. In: N. Smith & P. Williams (Eds), *Gentrification of the city* (pp. 78–91). Boston: Allen & Unwin.

Jakubowicz, A. (1984). The green ban movement: Urban struggle and class politics. In: J. Halligan & C. Paris (Eds), *Australian urban politics*. Melbourne: Longman Cheshire.

Jones, C., Leishman, C., & Watkins, C. (2004). Intra-urban migration and housing submarkets: Theory and evidence. *Housing Studies, 19*, 269–283.

Kelly, P. (1992). *The end of certainty.* Sydney: Allen & Unwin.

Kendig, H. (1979). *New life for old suburbs: Postwar land use and housing in the Australian inner city.* Sydney: Allen & Unwin.

Kendig, H. (1984). Gentrification in Australia. In: B. London & J. Palen (Eds), *Gentrification, displacement and neighborhood revitalization* (pp. 235–253). Albany, NY: State University of York Press.

Knox, P. (1993). *The restless urban landscape.* Englewood Cliffs, NJ: Prentice Hall.

Lee, S., & Leigh, N. (2007). Intrametropolitan spatial differentiation and decline of inner-ring suburbs: A comparison of four metropolitan areas. *Journal of Planning Education and Research, 27*(2), 146–164.

Lees, L. (2000). A reappraisal of gentrification: Towards a 'geography of gentrification'. *Progress in Human Geography, 24*, 389–408.

Lees, L., Slater, T., & Wyly, E. (2008). *Gentrification.* London: Routledge.

Lewis, M. (1999). *Suburban backlash: The battle for the world's most liveable city.* Hawthorn: Bloomings Books.

Lucy, W., & Phillips, D. (2000). *Confronting suburban decline: Strategic planning for metropolitan renewal.* Washington, DC: Island Press.

Maclennan, D., & Bannister, J. (1995). Housing research: Making the connections. *Urban Studies, 32*, 1581–1585.

Maher, C. (1994). Residential mobility, locational disadvantage and spatial inequality in Australian cities. *Urban Policy and Research, 12*(3), 185–191.

Massey, D. (1995). The conceptualisation of place. In: D. Massey & P. Jess (Eds), *A place in the world: Places, culture and globalization.* Oxford: Oxford University Press.

Montgomery, C. (1992). Explaining home improvement in the context of household investment in residential housing. *Journal of Urban Economics, 32*, 326–350.

Munro, M., & Leather, P. (2000). Nest-building or investing in the future? Owner-occupiers' home improvement behaviour. *Policy & Politics, 28*(4), 511–526.

Newton, P. (Ed.) (2008). *Transitions: Pathways towards sustainable urban development in Australia.* Dordrecht: Springer.

Newton, P. (2010). Beyond greenfield and brownfield: The challenge of regenerating Australia's greyfield suburbs. *Built Environment, 36*(1), 81–104.

Nicolaides, B., & Wiese, A. (Eds). (2006). *The suburb reader.* New York: Routledge.

NSW Department of Planning. (2005). *City of cities: A plan for Sydney's future.* Sydney: NSW Department of Planning.

NSW Department of Planning. (2006a). BASIX fact sheet. Available at http://www.basix.nsw.gov.au/information/common/pdf/basix_fact_sheet.pdf

NSW Department of Planning. (2006b). BASIX alterations and additions discussion paper. Available at http://www.basix.nsw.gov.au/information/common/pdf/basix_alts_adds_req/alts_adds_req_sheet.pdf

NSW Department of Planning. (2010a). *Metropolitan development program MDP 2008/2009 report.* Sydney: NSW Department of Planning.

NSW Department of Planning. (2010b). *Metropolitan strategy review: Sydney towards 2036.* Sydney: NSW Department of Planning.

Orfield, M. (2003). *American metropolitics: The new suburban reality.* Washington, DC: Brookings Institution.

Pickett, C. (1997). *The fibro frontier: A different history of Australian architecture.* Sydney: Powerhouse Museum.

Pinnegar, S. (2007). *Dragging our heels: Progress towards subregional housing market strategies and assessment.* State of Australian Cities National Conference Published Papers, Adelaide, 2009.

Pinnegar, S. (2009). The question of scale in housing-led regeneration: Tied to the neighbourhood? *Environment and Planning A, 41*(12), 2911–2928.

Pinnegar, S., Marceau, J., & Randolph, B. (2008). Innovation for the carbon constrained city: Challenges for the built environment industry. *Innovation Management, Policy and Practice, 10*(2–3), 303–313.

Puentes, R., & Warren, D. (2006). *One fifth American: Comprehensive guide to America's first suburbs.* Washington, DC: Brookings.

Randolph, B. (2006). *Delivering the compact city in Australia: Current trends and future implications.* Research Paper no. 6. City Futures Research Centre, UNSW, Sydney.

Randolph, B., & Freestone, R. (2008). *Problems and prospects for suburban renewal: An Australian perspective.* Research Paper no. 11. City Futures Research Centre, UNSW, Sydney.

Randolph, B., Pinnegar, S., Easthope, H. & Tice, A. (2010). A submission to the metropolitan strategy review. Available at http://www.fbe.unsw.edu.au/cf/MetroStrategy.pdf

Roddewig, R. (1978). *Green bans: The birth of Australian environmental politics.* Sydney: Hale & Iremonger.

Rofe, M. (2009). Globalization, gentrification and spatial hierarchies in and beyond New South Wales: The local/global nexus. *Geographical Research, 47*, 292–305.

Sandercock, L. (1975). *Cities for sale: Property, politics and urban planning in Australia.* Melbourne: Melbourne University Press.

Searle, G. (2007). *Sydney's urban consolidation experience: Power, politics and community.* Urban Research Program Research Paper, 12 March 2007. Available at http://www.griffith.edu.au/_data/assets/pdf_file/0018/48600/urp-rp12-searle-2007.pdf

Seek, N. (1983). Adjusting housing consumption: Improve or move. *Urban Studies, 20*, 455–469.

Short, R., Hanlon, B., & Vicino, T. (2007). The decline of the inner suburbs: The new suburban gothic in the United States. *Geography Compass, 1*, 641–656.

Slater, T. (2006). The eviction of critical perspectives from gentrification research. *International Journal of Urban and Regional Research, 30*(4), 737–757.

Smith, N. (1979). Toward a theory of gentrification: A back to the city movement by people not capital. *Journal of the American Planning Association, 45*(4), 538–548.

Smith, N. (1996). *The new urban frontier: Gentrification and the revanchist city.* London: Routledge.

Smith, N., & Williams, P. (1986). Alternatives to orthodoxy: Invitation to a debate. In: N. Smith & P. Williams (Eds), *Gentrification of the city* (pp. 1–14). Boston: Allen & Unwin.

Spearritt, P. (2000). *Sydney's century.* Sydney: UNSW Press.

Spearritt, P., & DeMarco, C. (1988). *Planning Sydney's future.* Sydney: Allen & Unwin.

Stilwell, F. (2005). The changing city: An Australian political economic perspective. *Opolis, 1*(2), 1–16.

The Sunday Telegraph. (2010). Starting all over again: More than 60 years after the post-war building boom, Sydney suburbs are getting a facelift, *The Sunday Telegraph*, 6 April 2010. Available at http://www.dailytelegraph.com.au/property/starting-all-over-again/story-e6freztr-1225851317940

Troy, P. (1978). *Federal power in Australia's cities.* Sydney: Hale and Ironmonger.

Vandermark, E., & Harrison, P. (1972). *Development activities in four Sydney suburban areas.* Canberra: Urban Research Unit, Research School of Social Sciences, Australian National University.

Whitehand, J., & Carr, C. (2001). *Twentieth century suburbs: A morphological approach.* New York: Routledge.

Williams, P. (1986). Class constitution through spatial reconstruction? A re-evaluation of gentrification in Australia, Britain and the United States. In: N. Smith & P. Williams (Eds), *Gentrification of the city* (pp. 56–77). Boston: Allen & Unwin.

Wulff, M. (1993). An overview of Australian housing and locational preference studies: Choices and constraints on the housing market. *Urban Policy and Research, 11*(4), 230–237.

CHANGING URBANIZATION PATTERNS IN THE BRAZILIAN METROPOLIS

Suzana Pasternak and Lucia Maria Machado Bógus

INTRODUCTION

In the second half of the 20th century, cities in South America underwent an intense growth process. Vast metropolitan areas were formed, characterized by the dispersion of dwellings to the suburbs. Throughout the 1970s, and mainly following the restructuring that affected these countries in the 1980s, the process of suburbanization underwent some changes, which reflect the nature and the extent of the integration of the cities to the new international division of labor (Sassen, 1991; Friedmann, 2006; Friedmann & Wolff, 2006). The main characteristics of these changes, according to Cardoso and Queiros Ribeiro (1996), were the following:

- Destabilization of the older industrial areas, substituted by new industrial facilities in the outlying regions, creating new centralities and transforming the metropolises into urban multimodal complexes;
- Changes in the central areas and their specialization in financial and management services;
- Residential renewal in the central areas resulting in the rise of luxury homes, targeting the new emerging socio-professional classes;

Suburbanization in Global Society
Research in Urban Sociology, Volume 10, 231–251
ISSN: 1047-0042/doi:10.1108/S1047-0042(2010)0000010012

231

• Extreme social polarization in the urban areas, between the rising elites
  and the impoverished groups that comprise the unskilled and undocu-
  mented labor market.

The international literature on the impacts of globalization on large cities
has insistently pointed to the increase in residential segregation. Three
mechanisms have been identified as the causes of this phenomenon:
globalization, which by disseminating neoliberal ideas throughout the
world, generated changes in the regulatory models and paradigms that guide
urban policy; institutional reforms toward market liberalization and the
property and housing market were undertaken in various countries; real
estate prices became the central mechanism for distributing the population
throughout the city, reinforcing income inequality as the determinant of
urban spatial organization. At the same time, privatization exacerbated the
growing inequality of access to the services and infrastructure that ensure
urban well-being, especially with regard to quality. The wealthier areas,
where those with greater purchasing power concentrate, have at their
disposal an abundant supply of goods and services, whereas the areas
populated by the poor are supplied with inferior goods and services.
Further, globalization caused structural changes originating in the
transformation of the productive base of the cities, creating trends toward
social polarization. The social structure of the great metropolises is no
longer represented by a pyramid, and is expressed instead by an hourglass
where the middle positions narrow while the extremities widen. Simultaneously, there has been an increase in the distance between the average
incomes of the higher and lower strata.

These phenomena lead to an increase in residential segregation as
exclusive neighborhoods are formed for those in the higher strata, while the
medium and the lower strata are subject to a process of downward social
mobility and displaced to other neighborhoods, thus diminishing the degree
of social mixture in the cities. This trend is reinforced by the emergence of
new social groups with high incomes and, inspired by new cultural models,
leads to the search for exclusive locales within the city in which to construct
their social identity. These processes increase residential segregation,
increasing lack-of-safety perception in the cities, thus driving social groups,
especially those of greater means, to seek protection in territorial isolation.

Globalization and outsourcing increased social polarization as the
extremes on the social hierarchy distance themselves and become more
accentuated in global cities, as has been argued by authors such as
Preteceille (1995) and Hamnett (1994). They point out that in Paris and

London, this process took different forms. In Madrid, the result of generalized social changes was the elevated professionalization of the social categories. According to Maldonado (2000), the decline in income distribution in the period 1981–1991 and growth of the middle classes led to differences experienced by the groups.

Cities are in constant internal flux. Downtown areas decline or change in terms of form and function. In the Brazilian metropolis, new poverty pockets are formed, serving as home for the impoverished population segments, while others gain ground and move into exclusive residential neighborhoods. Spatial divisions are nothing new, but the ways in which they have taken hold in recent decades lead to important questions about the causes, scale, form, and location of the residential spaces. There is consensus in the literature that significant changes in intraurban space have been occurring since the 1970s. The globalization process, which alters production modes and erodes state intervention, produces new technologies and new power relationships that influence urbanization patterns and the structure of metropolitan regions.

In contrast to what occurred in the developed countries, Brazilian cities reflect in their dynamics the results of a severe economic crisis and high inflation (in the 1990s, annual inflation topped 1,000 percent). In this decade, referred to as "the lost decade," the increase in poverty and unemployment and the rise in violence and crime left their mark on Brazilian cities, including an increase in shanty towns and unregulated development. In the last half of the century, the economy began to adjust and some restructuring effects started being felt. Perhaps it is too early to refer to Brazilian cities as global, but they have already experienced the consequences of the country's insertion into the globalization process. The privatization of services in the 1990s altered access to income, housing, and public services, thus changing the pattern of socio-spatial inequality.

This chapter sets out to analyze the social-organization general tendencies in three Brazilian metropolises and their consequences on socio-spatial organization. São Paulo, the industrial and financial capital of the country; Rio de Janeiro, former capital of the country; and Salvador, which was the seat of the Brazilian government until 1763, have been selected to examine the consequences of these changes. Among the questions to be examined are as follows:

- What has changed in the social structure throughout the last decade? What are their similarities and differences across the three metropolitan regions?

- What is the relationship between the transformations in the social structure and the changes in the pattern of spatial segmentation in the three metropolises? Did the socio-spatial transformations follow the same trend in all three?
- Have the phenomena observed in the developed countries – renewal of the downtown areas, the transformation of the metropolitan nuclei into centers of financial and service industries, changes in the older industrial zones, and social and spatial dualism – also occurred in the metropolises of the Southern Hemisphere?

A BRIEF HISTORY OF THE CITIES

São Paulo, Rio de Janeiro, and Salvador all are highly populated metropolises. In the southeast, the metropolitan region of São Paulo, with its 39 municipalities, had a population of almost 18 million people in the year 2000, Rio de Janeiro, with its 17 municipalities, had almost 11 million inhabitants. The metropolitan region of Salvador, in the northeast, had 10 municipalities and a little over 3 million inhabitants.

Salvador served as the seat of government in Brazil until 1763 and was the most important city in the country. The transfer of the capital to Rio de Janeiro, decline of the main local export (sugar cane), and industrial concentration in the south-central region affected the metropolis, which underwent a long period of economic and population stagnation. This continued up into the mid-20th century, when the discovery of oil stimulated demographic growth both in the capital and in some of the municipalities in the metropolitan area. In the 1970s and 1980s, the federal government financed the installation of a copper processing industry and of a large petrochemical center in one of the municipalities. As a result, the city of Salvador and some of the metropolitan municipalities experienced an enormous rise in population and underwent a drastic change in their social structure, with a broadening and diversification of the middle classes and the emergence of a modern (though more modest) industrial proletariat.

Rio de Janeiro was the capital from 1763 to 1960, when the government was transferred to Brasília. It is currently the second largest city in the country after São Paulo. Urban development in Rio de Janeiro has always been marked by the existence of vast, poor outlying areas and "invasions" of the hillsides by the lower-income populace who took up residence there. The city housed an important banking sector and headquarters offices of numerous private and state-run companies, had an expansive transport system, while the competitive axis of industry shifted to São Paulo along with much of the banking and corporate headquarters, and the federal public administration apparatus moved to Brasília. Rio de Janeiro still maintained its status as the center for advanced services. By the end of the 20th century, however, its growth dropped dramatically to just 1.1 percent per year between 1980 and 1991 and 1.2 percent between 1991 and 2000.

With more than 10.9 million inhabitants, São Paulo is the largest metropolis in the country. Almost half of the state residents are concentrated in there. Greater São Paulo is one of the five largest megacities in the world, the others being Tokyo, Seoul, Mexico City, and Mumbai.

At the turn of the 20th century, São Paulo offered favorable conditions for the accumulation of capital and attracted a steady flow of European migrants who came to work on the coffee plantations. It is estimated that between 1888 and 1900, nearly 900,000 immigrants transited São Paulo, 70 percent of them from Italy. During this time of intense immigration, the city experienced its first industrial surge, based mainly on the textile and food industries whose factories occupied the floodplains adjacent to the railway lines, forming São Paulo's first working-class neighborhoods. As a consequence, there was an intense demographic burst that increased the demand for housing and land and also the rise of an urban proletariat and a new elite, no longer linked to coffee, commerce, or banking.

The expansion of the mass transport network and the introduction of bus services around 1924 gave way to the development of new areas, expanding urban perimeter limits. So while suburban trains led at first to expansion to more remote areas, in the 1930s city buses had their routes expanded. The city already had well-defined areas: bourgeois and middle-class homes at the higher elevations and working-class neighborhoods in the lowlands along the rivers and railroad lines. In 1950, the city of São Paulo had over two million inhabitants and grew by 5 percent in the 1950s and 1960s, reaching nearly six million inhabitants by 1970. In 2000, the city of São Paulo alone had over 10 million residents. Its urbanized area, which occupied $874 \, km^2$ in 1962, climbed to $2,139 \, km^2$ in 2002.

The municipality of São Paulo is the site of headquarters offices, including those of banks and large domestic and international companies, as well as of specialized service providers. It is also home to the wealthy (estimated 60 percent of Brazilian millionaires reside here). Beyond the city, the metropolis of São Paulo contains within it myriad municipalities with distinct industrial profiles, which house the headquarters of automobile manufacturers, pharmaceutical companies, and logistics centers.

THE SOCIO-OCCUPATIONAL STRUCTURE OF THE THREE METROPOLITAN AREAS

As noted above, the three metropolitan regions present very different population sizes: São Paulo with 17.8 million inhabitants in 2000, Rio de Janeiro with 10.9 million, and Salvador with three million. Despite these differences in scale, it is evident that the three metropolises experienced peripheral growth in the 1990s, with Salvador's 3.59 percent rate of peripheral growth outstripping that of São Paulo (2.55 percent) and Rio de Janeiro (1.71 percent). The two southeastern metropolises experienced population loss and functional decline in their downtown areas. This peripheral urbanization frequently results in environmental destruction. All three areas moved toward more extensive urbanization, with larger urban population, fewer agricultural workers, and a socio-occupational structure that reflects the loss of industrial workers and the gain in service workers and college-educated professionals.

Employment rates vary from 37 percent in Salvador to 40 percent in São Paulo. Local unemployment is significantly higher in Salvador, where unemployment reached 21.7 percent of the total economically active population in 2007.

Both São Paulo and Rio de Janeiro saw a net loss of employment in the formal economy during the decade (119,000 and 238,000 jobs, respectively); Salvador had an increase of 113,000 jobs in the formal sector, likely the result of government investment in the region.

Employment in the informal sector is estimated by comparing formal jobs with the total employed population. In both São Paulo and Rio de Janeiro, the increase in informal employment was higher than that in Salvador: in Rio de Janeiro, employment in the informal sector increased from 35.5 percent in 1991 to 47.2 percent in 2000; in São Paulo, where informal employment is historically lower, the number increased from 20.0 to 34.9 percent (a remarkable 81 percent increase). During the same period in Salvador, informal employment climbed from 29.8 to 37.1 percent, a 10-year increase of 25 percent. The increase in informal employment in all three metropolises accompanied a sharp decline in industrial jobs and a large increase in service jobs during the last decade of the 20th century. The most industrialized metropolis – São Paulo – experienced the greatest loss in formal employment. All metropolises posted an increase in service sector jobs – a 20 percent increase in Rio de Janeiro, a 30 percent increase in São Paulo, and a 60 percent increase in Salvador, where more than 80 percent of formal employment is found in the service sector.

Regarding demographic growth and formal employment, we can conclude that

- All three metropolitan regions present peripheral growth. Historically, the periphery has been the focal point of poverty in Brazilian cities. The question is: "Is this growth due only to where the poor reside or can those at higher income levels also be found at the city borders?" The remaining sections in this chapter aim at answering this question.
- All three metropolitan regions had different levels of growth in informal work: the city with the smallest share of informal work (São Paulo) was also the city with the highest growth in this category. The impact of the new production forms was probably the greatest where there used to be a more assembly-line organization style as it was in São Paulo.

SOCIO-OCCUPATIONAL STRUCTURE IN THE THREE METROPOLISES

We examined the socio-occupational structure of the three metropolitan regions by looking at 24 socio-occupational categories, organized within eight larger groups (including large and small employers, college-educated professionals, mid-level occupations, specialized and nonspecialized tertiary workers, secondary workers, and farm workers). The result of this analysis, developed by the national research network of the Observatório das Metrópoles, is shown in the appendix. (See Table A1).

The first striking point is the similarity among the social structures of the metropolitan regions: the higher-rank categories (large employers, college graduates, and small employers) ranged from 12.4 percent of the total number of the employed in Rio de Janeiro to 10.18 percent in Salvador; the mid-level categories, between 27 and 28 percent; and the urban lower-income workers, between 59 and 61 percent. The most significant differences are found within the manual laborers, particularly between the industrial workers and the nonspecialized service workers.

Analyzing the *higher-level categories* in the socio-occupational hierarchy, we note that the large employers are the least represented group in the three metropolises, followed by the small employers and the college-educated professionals. The reduction in large employers in São Paulo was about 36,000 out of a total of 90,000 jobs, or nearly 40 percent. Some hypotheses to explain this include the shift of these employers away from the metropolis, the reduction in their numbers due to bankruptcy (in the 1990s, many companies closed, especially mid-sized companies), and the decline in the number of companies due to mergers and acquisitions (which started by the 1990s). In Rio de Janeiro, the proportion of college-educated professionals is considerably higher than that in São Paulo and Salvador. This is mainly due to the proportion of those employed in the public sector. Although it has been 50 years since Rio de Janeiro was the federal capital, it still carries within its socio-occupational structure a large share of federal employees as it is still the home of many state-run companies. The high concentration of large industrial and financial companies headquarters in São Paulo did not give rise to an increase in the proportional weight of large employers or college-educated professionals, although it should be noted that the weight of private large employers and large employers in São Paulo surpasses those in the other two metropolitan regions.

The largest percentage of employment in the *mid-level categories* was found in São Paulo (28.2 percent), followed closely by Rio de Janeiro. In São Paulo, the office workers, supervisors, and technicians accounted for this higher percentage, whereas in Rio de Janeiro, this group comprised health, education, and public safety professionals. The mid-level profiles in Salvador and Rio de Janeiro include more occupations linked to the public sector than in São Paulo.

Within *urban manual categories*, the number of secondary workers ranged from 24 percent in São Paulo to 19 percent in Salvador. Even with the recent loss of industrial workers in São Paulo, this sector is greater than Rio de Janeiro and Salvador. The percentage of those working in civil construction in São Paulo is surpassed both in Salvador (with 8.0 percent) and in Rio de Janeiro (7.3 percent). This is a sector characterized by unskilled manual laborers earning lower salaries and poorer work conditions than those in other industrial sectors.

The highest proportion of specialized and nonspecialized tertiary workers is found in Salvador, due mostly to the high percentage of street vendors (10 percent of the employed workforce). This is typical of Salvador as employment problems led the poor to this type of precarious activity that offers no social protection. In the 1990s, structural reforms included an inflation stabilization program (*Plano Real*), intense and rapid economic liberalization, a far-reaching privatization process, greater emphasis on the market role, and restructuring of the federal apparatus. The adjustment and the restructuring that accompanied these measures were marked by a reduction in job vacancies, which led to massive increase of street vendors.

In Rio de Janeiro, street vendors also comprise nearly 10 percent of the workforce. São Paulo was also hit hard, but those at higher income levels were able to absorb part of this unskilled labor, hiring them as domestic servants (7.2 percent of the workforce).

The social structures described above are the consequence of economic transformation on the metropolitan labor market in the 1990s. The crisis of the 1980s and the adjustments of the 1990s affected all the metropolises. The decline of industrial workers during the "lost decade" occurred in all of them being more accentuated in São Paulo, where this proportion was the highest. Between 1991 and 2000, São Paulo and Salvador continued losing industrial workers. In Rio de Janeiro, where industry never had the same importance, the loss was somewhat less.

In contrast to the decline in industrial laborers and mid-level occupations in Rio de Janeiro and São Paulo, there was an increase in specialized service providers and college-educated professionals, a pattern that was already underway in the 1980s. Some of the industrial laborers may have been absorbed by the specialized tertiary sector, especially the service sector that in all three grew more than commerce workers. It seems that following the dual city theory, the base of the pyramid is widening. In Rio de Janeiro, the relative percentage remained unchanged in the 1990s, declining by two percentage points in Salvador, which holds the largest proportion of nonspecialized tertiary workers.

This analysis suggests that the largest and richest Brazilian metropolis (São Paulo) was the most strongly affected by the economic transformations during the second half of the 20th century, as its labor market was better structured and its industries were particularly impacted by the productive restructuring. In fact, the occupational structure of all three metropolises maintained certain stability, albeit in combination with some new trends:

- A significant rise in college-educated professionals, explained by both social mobility and the proliferation of public and private universities that occurred during the last decade of the 20th century.
- Outsourcing, with a sharp increase in specialized tertiary workers in the three metropolises.
- A relative deproletarization, with a decline in traditional and modern manual laborers in the metropolises but with a rise in auxiliary service manual laborers in São Paulo and Rio de Janeiro and a rise in civil construction manual laborers in Salvador and Rio de Janeiro.
- An increase in nonspecialized tertiary workers, which occurred only in São Paulo.

• A relevant decline in large employers in São Paulo and Rio de Janeiro. In São Paulo, the large employers experienced a strong relative decline in excess of 20 percent. Another process in evidence was the departure of large employers from the private sector of the municipal nucleus, where a relative 20 percent decline occurred, with a slight rise in this category in the other municipalities. Thus, the elite leadership class, in addition to being in decline, also shifts its place of residence within the metropolitan region of São Paulo. Gated condominiums throughout the metropolis, in less populous municipalities and with remaining traces of rural life, become the new residential choice for the most affluent social classes, in their escape from the pollution, noise, and violence of the large city.

CHANGE IN RESIDENTIAL LOCATION

Based on the initial questions posed and the classification of the social categories described above, we introduce an analysis of the pattern of spatial distribution within each of the three metropolises under study. For each metropolis, a socio-spatial typology was constructed, based on the 2000 census and, for São Paulo and Rio de Janeiro, another one based on the 1991 census. The socio-spatial typology included five major types of areas: "high-end," "mid-range," "manual laborer," "lower-income," and "agricultural," determined by the relation of the average profile of each area to the average profile of the metropolises as a whole. For Salvador, the census data did not permit the construction of a typology for 1991, hindering the evolutionary analysis of this metropolis. The minimal spatial unit utilized for the construction of the typology was the AED (area of geographic expansion, which brings together census sectors and is based on the unit that the IBGE (Brazilian Institute of Geography and Statistics) provides to researchers). In São Paulo, there are 812 areas; in Rio de Janeiro, 443; and in Salvador, 108. A factorial analysis was conducted through binary correspondence, followed by the hierarchical classification of the resulting conglomerates. Each type expresses a determined degree of social homogeneity and concentration of socio-occupational categories in a group of areas (Figs. 1–3).

The areas corresponding to the "*high-end*" type are defined by a higher concentration and greater relative number of large employers and college-educated professionals. In the case of São Paulo, the number of large employers in the high-end areas is three times greater than their relative weight in the average of the employed populations in all areas in the year

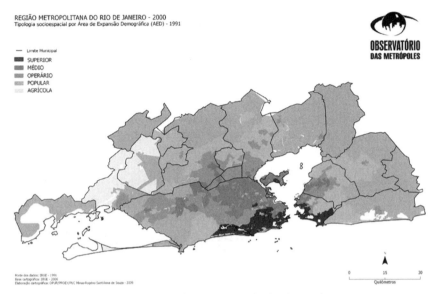

REGIÃO METROPOLITANA DO RIO DE JANEIRO - 2000
Tipologia socioespacial por Área de Expansão Demográfica (AED) - 1991

OBSERVATÓRIO
DAS METRÓPOLES

— Limite Municipal
■ SUPERIOR
■ MÉDIO
▥ OPERÁRIO
▨ POPULAR
▦ AGRÍCOLA

Fig. 1. Metropolitan Area of Rio de Janeiro.

2000. For college-educated professionals and small business owners, the proportion is 2.6 times greater and for small employers 2.5 times greater. In Salvador, large employers in the high-end areas are 4.7 times the average of other areas. The concentration of these categories is also a marked feature of the high-end areas: in São Paulo, nearly two-thirds (63.5 percent) of large employers live in the high-end areas. In Rio de Janeiro and in Salvador, the concentration is somewhat less, with around just over half (55.2 percent in Rio de Janeiro and 52.73 percent in Salvador) residing in the high-end areas.

The "*mid-level*" areas are marked by the strong presence of commercial workers and generalized service providers, although these groups are not as concentrated in a given type of area as are the other categories. In São Paulo, more than one-third (37.8 percent) of the mid-level occupations reside in mid-level areas, which are also home to a large percentage of college-educated professionals and tertiary workers. A similar mix can be found in the mid-level areas of Rio de Janeiro and Salvador, where nearly half (45.71 percent) of those in the mid-level occupations reside in 2000. But these areas are also home to approximately 40 percent of college-educated professionals and tertiary workers. The areas classified as "mid-level" are characterized by a very diverse mix, not only with the hierarchically higher categories, but also with some of the lower ones, especially the tertiary workers.

Município de Salvador
Tipologia socioespacial por Área de Expansão Demográfica (AED) - 2000

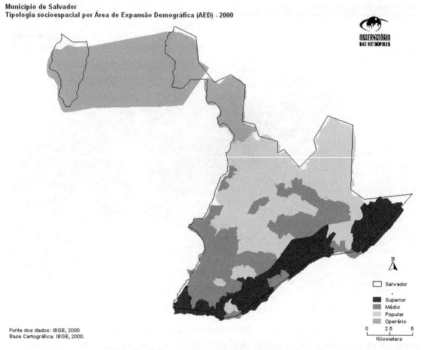

Fonte dos dados: IBGE, 2000
Base Cartográfica: IBGE, 2000.

Fig. 2. Metropolitan Area of Salvador.

The "*manual laborer*" areas are those in which industrial manual laborers are concentrated. In São Paulo, 40 percent of the industrial manual laborers reside in these areas. In Salvador and in Rio de Janeiro, where the industrial manual laborers represent a smaller proportion of the workforce, these areas are not so clearly defined, and many industrial manual laborers will be present in the "lower-income" areas.

The "*lower-income*" areas are the more common residence for the unskilled manual laborers who work in civil construction and the unskilled tertiary workers. In Salvador, 45 percent and in Rio de Janeiro, 52 percent of the unskilled tertiary workers reside in lower-income areas. The lower-income areas of Salvador and Rio de Janeiro present a greater mixture than those of São Paulo, with a strong residential presence of secondary and tertiary workers.

The "*agricultural*" type of areas are now few in number and serve as the residence of a very small portion of the population of São Paulo and Salvador; in Rio de Janeiro, no area was classified as agricultural. In São Paulo, however, there is a strong presence of agricultural workers in this

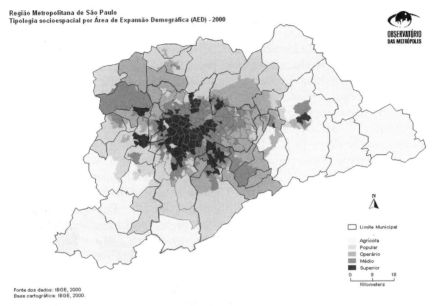

Região Metropolitana de São Paulo
Tipologia socioespacial por Área de Expansão Demográfica (AED) - 2000

OBSERVATÓRIO
DAS METRÓPOLES

N

☐ Limite Municipal

Agrícola
Popular
Operário
Médio
Superior

0   9   18
Kilometers

Fonte dos dados: IBGE, 2000
Base cartográfica: IBGE, 2000.

Fig. 3.   Metropolitan Area of São Paulo.

type of area, and in Salvador the agricultural area is heavily populated by the lower-income class (civil construction manual laborers and nonspecialized tertiary workers).

The first great distinction to be noted is that São Paulo was home to the most balanced distribution of the working population throughout the various types of urban areas (high-income, mid-level, manual laborer, and lower-income): nearly 30 percent of its employed population lived in mid-level areas, another 30 percent in manual laborer areas, and the remaining 40 percent divided between the high-income and lower-income areas. In Rio de Janeiro, one third of the employed lived in lower-income areas and another third in mid-level areas of the metropolis. In Salvador, nearly 60 percent of those employed lived in lower-income areas and another 40 percent in mid-level areas. These two metropolises present a territorialization that can be termed "lower-income/mid-level," and a social structure that is "mid-level/ tertiary." São Paulo is the only city to have manual laborer areas in significant numbers, although these areas have diminished both in number and in proportion to the resident population in the decade of the 1990s.

The second great distinction between the metropolitan regions is the greater presence of high-income areas in São Paulo, both in relation to territorial size (number of areas) and in the proportion of the population in these areas (22.5 percent of the areas and 28 percent of the employed population). In Rio de Janeiro and in Salvador, the number was half that of São Paulo. In São Paulo, a significant part of the high-income areas is of low density, with individual houses set apart with yards. In Rio de Janeiro, the high-income classes reside in apartments concentrated in high-density areas, as a high premium is placed on ocean views, a fact which makes the attractive beachside area and its immediate surroundings the preferred residential location of the elites. In São Paulo, only 34 percent of the housing stock in the high-income areas consisted of apartments in 2000, while in Rio de Janeiro, this figure was 81 percent. Salvador, as a coastal metropolis, follows the same pattern as Rio de Janeiro. The low density of the high-income areas in São Paulo explains the wide distribution of the elites throughout a larger territorial space and, therefore, with a less precise social demarcation.

There are differences in the profile of the high-income areas of São Paulo in comparison with the other two metropolises: among São Paulo residents, only 24.4 percent of the employed were large employers or college-educated professionals, while in Salvador this figure was 29.2 percent, and in Rio de Janeiro 35 percent. Another unique feature of São Paulo is that its high-income areas extend beyond the city limits, into eight municipalities in the metropolitan region, including Santo André, São Caetano, São Bernardo, Guarulhos, Santana do Parnaíba, Mogi das Cruzes, Barueri, and Cotia. In Rio de Janeiro, only the municipalities of Niterói and Nova Iguaçu included high-income areas. In Salvador, the presence of high-income areas along the Atlantic coast is plainly evident, both in Salvador proper and in Lauro de Freitas, along a nearly continuous line, interrupted only by one high-density lower-income area (Amaralina). We can further observe that in São Paulo and Rio de Janeiro, for which 1991 data are available, the high-income areas show a trend toward increased concentration of the elites throughout the decade.

The mid-level areas make up the majority of the spatial segments in all three metropolises, ranging from 30.9 percent in São Paulo to 35.2 percent in Salvador. The profile is quite mixed: aside from the mid-level occupations, their residents also include high percentages of tertiary and secondary, and even nonspecialized tertiary, workers, in addition to a not insignificant percentage of college-educated professionals.

The territories we refer to as "mid-level" are those with a greater social mix, or, in other words, they are less segregated. This stands in contrast to the self-segregation of the elites and the involuntary isolation of the lower-income classes. In São Paulo, which had a strong manual laborer presence in 1991, the concentration of secondary workers in this type of area is evident: 40.5 percent of the manual laborers reside there. In Rio de Janeiro and in Salvador, the situation is totally different: in Rio de Janeiro, there were more manual laborers living in "lower-income" type areas (51.8 percent) than in the manual laborer territories. In Salvador, most manual laborers reside in "lower-income" and "mid-level" areas. The manual laborer areas of the three metropolises under study are not homogenous. The literature on the manual laborer neighborhoods emphasizes the diversity of these territories. Even in São Paulo, the most manual laborer-intensive metropolis of the three under study, in this type of area there is a high percentage of mid-level categories and nonspecialized tertiary workers.

Throughout the 1990s, the "lower-income" areas gained large numbers of nonspecialized tertiary workers. The lower-income areas in São Paulo have become more widespread, and now include mid-level and college-educated professionals. The territorial breadth of lower-income type areas in Rio de Janeiro and in Salvador is noteworthy; in Salvador, the majority of the population (57.8 percent) lived in areas of this type, while in the metropolis of Rio de Janeiro, the proportion living in lower-income areas reached 38.9 percent. The data for Salvador reflect a territory with many poor areas, although mid-level, tertiary, and secondary workers also reside in them.

Agricultural areas are now rare in the metropolises. Rio de Janeiro had none in 2000, and in São Paulo and Salvador they accounted for less than a percent of the population. These two metropolises include large proportions of nonspecialized tertiary and secondary workers, and it is believed that the expansion of these two metropolises is inducing lower-income classes to reside in territories once dedicated to agriculture, thus transforming the green belt into ever more populous territories.

CONCLUSIONS

Based on the theoretical statements regarding the trend toward social and urban polarization in the large metropolises accompanying globalization, various authors have debated the impacts of these transformations on the pattern of the appropriation and use of the urban environment. In the case of the Brazilian metropolises, the "rich downtown/poor periphery" model still prevails. The basic questions, according to Marcuse and Van Kempen (2000) are, first, whether there is something different about cities of today that distinguishes them from the cities of the past; second, what accounts for differences among the cities under study; and third, what would be the consequences of the possible increase in socio-spatial inequality. Although they recognize that globalization does not automatically produce a determined spatial pattern, Marcuse and Van Kempen raise the hypothesis that the transformations associated with it are leading the way toward a new urban order, with a spatial concentration of a new kind of poverty, on the one hand, and highly sophisticated and well-paying urban activities, on the other. This would lead to an increase in spatial divisions, of boundaries and walls between classes, and to an ever more fragmented and segregated city and metropolitan region.

The analysis of the typographies of areas in São Paulo, Rio de Janeiro, and Salvador points up the following:

- With regard to the high-income areas, opposing trends are in evidence: if, on the one hand, they have become more exclusive, with a greater proportion of the hierarchically superior categories residing in high-income areas, the proportion of large employers and especially college-educated professionals living in other areas has also increased (at least in São Paulo and Rio de Janeiro, where one can compare 1991 and 2000). Large employers and higher-income professionals remain in the most affluent areas, or they move out toward real estate at the cities' periphery. These expanded boundaries are present in all three metropolises: in São Paulo, in the southwest of the state and northwest of the metropolis (Alphaville and adjacent areas in Barueri); in Rio de Janeiro, toward Barra da Tijuca; and in Salvador, along the beachfront, in the municipality of Lauro de Freitas. Thus, there is a common trend in the three metropolises, and that is the expansion of high-income earners toward areas with higher real estate values, often residing in gated condominiums.

- The mid-level areas are extremely diversified in all three metropolises. The majority of the spatial segments in all three metropolises fall into this category. Their existence contradicts the hypothesis of increased segregation, as they are inhabited by a social mix, in contrast to the high-income areas, where there exists a strong concentration of the high-income categories. Even in Salvador, the relatively poorest metropolis, 38 percent of the employed population in 2000 resided in this type of area. Furthermore, the mid-level categories spread throughout the urban landscape. In São Paulo, spatial evidence of this dispersion can be found in verticalization, with two- and three-bedroom apartments built at mid-level standards being unveiled along what was once the periphery. Condominiums and closed communities with mid-level houses are also part of the strategy of developers, who perceive the demand for this type of product on the part of the middle class.

- The manual laborer areas are little in evidence in Rio de Janeiro or Salvador, although secondary workers make up nearly 20 percent of their population. The only metropolis with an extensive manual laborer area is São Paulo, where nearly half of the secondary workers are manual laborers in modern and traditional industry. But even in São Paulo, social diversity increased between 1991 and 2000, with a greater presence of specialized tertiary workers and nonspecialized workers. The question that arises is whether this greater social diversity of manual laborer neighborhoods will mean an end to long-standing class solidarity, and/or whether it would tend to strengthen new forms of interaction among the classes (Lago & Mammarella, 2000).

- The lower-income areas are less homogenous, and include the presence of secondary and tertiary workers, and even that of mid-level workers and college-educated professionals. The spatial deconcentration of these levels results in a more diverse metropolis and a persistent expansion at the periphery. One hypothesis is that the deconcentration of the hierarchically high-income levels and the occupation of territory brought about by this expansion resulted in rising land and real estate prices, thus leading to the expulsion of the lower-income levels toward ever more distant points, and the creation of bedroom communities in peripheral municipalities. This phenomenon is present in all three metropolises.

- The few remaining agricultural areas of São Paulo and Salvador are located at the extremes of the two metropolises. Although less inhabited, these areas are the residential hub of population segments associated with the secondary, tertiary, and particularly the nonskilled tertiary groups, all poorly remunerated. The agricultural areas are at the boundary line of the expanding areas of lower-income housing.

Despite the concentration of elite groups in the high-income areas, the diffusion of the middle- and high-income levels throughout the metropolitan region has created more diverse areas. Although it cannot be said that the center–periphery pattern has now been transcended, metropolises such as São Paulo, Rio de Janeiro, and Salvador have become more segmented and in some ways less segregated in spatial terms, although the physical proximity between the various classes is at time accompanied by a greater social distance between them, as is made patently clear by the presence of gated condominiums. Studies of other Latin American metropolises (Ribeiro & Lago, 2000; De Mattos, 2004; Duhau, 2005; Carvalho, Pasternak, & Bogus, 2010) highlight additional changes in the structuring of urban space:

- The decline and emptying of older downtown areas, such as the historic centers of Salvador, Rio de Janeiro, and São Paulo.

- The creation of new centralities, such as business centers, large commercial and service centers, and convention centers, as witnessed in Faria Lima Avenue and Berrini Avenue in São Paulo, Barra da Tijuca in Rio de Janeiro, and Tancredo Neves Avenue and adjacent areas in Salvador.
- The dissemination of new residential patterns and real estate investments aimed at the upper and middle-income classes, with emphasis on horizontal closed condominiums in areas such as Barueri, Santana do Parnaíba, and Cotia, in metropolitan São Paulo, along the beach of Lauro de Freitas, in Salvador, and in the expansion of Rio de Janeiro toward Barra da Tijuca, the only region of the city in which the higher-income population is larger than the lower-income population (Cardoso & Queiros Ribeiro, 1996). Condominium developments have generally been built in areas that were previously more remote and occupied by lower-income groups; the increased segmentation is expressed by explicit physical and symbolic separation, such as fences, walls, and sophisticated security systems.
- The continued expansion of the metropolitan area, with the spread of lower-income housing toward the most distant areas, associated not only with population growth, but also with the transformations in the labor market, which have led many households to seek less expensive housing.

The analysis presented here does not point to a reduction in the middle-income segments, as the literature on globalization has affirmed. And despite the fact that São Paulo is the location of the headquarters offices of 42 of the 100 largest companies in Brazil and 61 of the 100 largest banks, there has been no increase at the top of the social pyramid. With respect to the socio-spatial structure, the following transformation points are common to Rio de Janeiro, Salvador, and São Paulo:

- The emptying out of the historic downtown areas, in spite of public policies aimed at urban renewal.
- The increased isolation of the elites, despite their diffusion throughout the metropolitan area. This is evidenced by the phenomenon of condominiums and gated communities along the southwest axis of São Paulo and along the Atlantic beaches of Rio de Janeiro, as well as in Salvador over the past 30 years.
- The maintenance of a pattern of peripheral growth, with lower-income layers living at ever greater distances from the center; at the same time, we see greater social mixing throughout the other areas.

These results suggest that there is not a singular or uniform pattern of suburbanization across metropolitan regions in Brazil. Future research must examine the degree to which the patterns observed here are similar to those found in other South American metropolitan areas, and the degree to which these changes are found in metropolitan regions in others areas of the world, as suggested by recent literature on globalization and neoliberal restructuring.

REFERENCES

Cardoso, A., & Queiros Ribeiro, L. C. (1996). *Dualização e reestruturação urbana. O caso do Rio de Janeiro*. Rio de Janeiro: Observatório de Políticas Urbanas. IPPUR-FASE.

Carvalho, I., Pasternak, S., & Bogus, L. M. M. (2010). Transformações metropolitanas: São Paulo e Salvador. Cadernos CRH. Revista do Centro de Recursos Humanos da Universidade Federal da Bahia, no. 1 (1987). Salvador, UFBA, pp. 302–321.

De Mattos, Carlos, C. A. (2004). Redes, nodos e cidades: Transformação da metrópole latino americana. In: L. C. Q. Ribeiro (Org.), *Metrópoles. Entre a coesão e a fragmentação, a cooperação e o conflito*. São Paulo: Editora Perseu Abramo; Rio de Janeiro: FASE/ Observatório das Metrópoles, pp. 157–196.

Duhau, E. (2005). As novas formas de divisão social do espaço nas metrópoles latino americanas: uma visão a partir da cidade do México. *Caderno CRH: revista do Centro de Recursos Humanos da UFBA*, Salvador, 18(45), set./dez., pp. 25–34.

Friedmann, J. (2006). The world city hypothesis. In: N. Brenner & R. Kell (Eds), *The global city reader* (pp. 67–71). New York: Routledge (first published in Development and Change, 1986).

Friedmann, J., & Wolff, G. (2006). World city formation: An agenda for research and action. In: N. Brenner & R. Kell (Eds), *The global city reader* (pp. 57–71). New York: Routledge (first published in International Journal of Urban and Regional Research, 1982).

Hamnett, C. (1994). Social polarization in global cities: Theory and evidence. *Urban Studies, 31*, 410–424.

Lago, C. L., & Mammarella, R. (2009). Da hierarquia de classes à organização do espaço intra-urbano: um olhar comparativo sobre as grandes metrópoles brasileiras. Caxambu, 33° Encontro Anual da ANPOCS, 22 p.

Maldonado, J. L. (2000). *Economia, emprego e desigualdade social em Madri*. In: L. C. Q. Ribeiro (Org.), *O futuro das metrópoles: desigualdade e governabilidade* (pp. 177–204). Rio de Janeiro, Revan/FASE.

Marcuse, P., & Kempen, R. (2000). *Globalizing cities: A new spatial order?* London: Blackwell Publishing Ltd.

Preteceille, E. (1995). Division sociale de l'espace et globalization: les cas de La metrópole parisienne. *Societés Contemporaines, 22*, 33–68.

Ribeiro, L. C. Q., & Lago, L. (2000). O espaço social nas grandes metrópoles brasileiras: São Paulo, Rio de Janeiro e Belo Horizonte. *Cadernos Metrópole, 4*, 9–32.

Sassen, S. (1991). *The global city*. New York: Princeton University Press.

APPENDIX

Table A1. Socio-occupational structure of the three metropolises in 2000.

Socio-occupational Categories	São Paulo (%)	Rio de Janeiro (%)	Salvador (%)
Large employers	0.77	0.6	0.65
Public sector leaders	0.17	0.2	0.25
Private sector leaders	0.43	0.3	0.30
Leaders	1.37	1.2	1.20
Self-employed, college-educated professionals	1.96	2.0	1.19
Employed, college-educated professionals	3.66	3.6	3.06
Statutory, college-educated professionals	0.44	1.1	0.65
College-educated professors	1.77	2.0	1.65
College-educated professionals	7.83	8.8	6.55
Small employers	2.65	2.4	2.43
Office occupations	10.58	9.2	10.25
Supervisory occupations	5.33	4.3	4.16
Technical occupations	6.35	5.7	5.36
Mid-level health and educational occupations	3.26	4.2	4.88
Public safety, judicial, and postal occupations	1.53	2.9	2.16
Artistic and similar occupations	1.10	1.4	1.09
Mid-level occupations	28.15	27.8	27.90
Commerce workers	9.72	9.7	9.97
Specialized service providers	9.62	11.0	11.46
Tertiary workers	19.34	20.7	21.43
Modern industry workers	7.10	3.9	4.08
Traditional industry workers	4.59	3.9	3.17
Auxiliary service manual laborers	5.99	5.1	4.16
Construction manual laborers	6.32	7.3	7.98
Secondary workers	24.01	20.2	19.38
Domestic workers	7.22	5.3	5.32
Street vendors and odd-jobbers	3.72	8.8	9.82
Nonspecialized service providers	5.22	4.3	4.83

Table A1. (*Continued*)

Socio-occupational Categories	São Paulo (%)	Rio de Janeiro (%)	Salvador (%)
Nonspecialized tertiary workers	16.16	18.4	19.96
Farm workers	0.50	0.6	1.15
Total	100.00	100.0	100.00

This structure was developed by the national research network Observatório das Metrópoles, headquartered at IPPUR/UFRJ (Federal University of Rio de Janeiro) (http://www. observatoriodasmetropoles.net). In its construction, we group the occupations enumerated in the demographic censuses of 1991 and 2000, in 24 categories, seeking to follow the following principles of division: capital (employers) and labor (not employers), large (more than 11 employees) and small capital, salaried labor, self-employed labor, manual labor, nonmanual labor, and activities of control and of execution. Also taken into consideration was the differentiation between sectors of production, such as secondary and tertiary. Finally, among those employed in the secondary sector, a distinction was drawn between the modern and traditional sectors of the industry. See Ribeiro, L. C. Q., & Lago, L. C. (2000). O espaço social das grandes metrópoles brasileiras: *Rio de Janeiro, São Paulo e Belo Horizonte* [*The social space of the large Brazilian metropolises: Rio de Janeiro, São Paulo and Belo Horizonte*]. *Cadernos Metrópole*, (4), 9–32.

Source: Demographic Census of 2000; tabulations by Observatório das Metrópoles.

GOVERNING HETEROGENEITY IN THE CONTEXT OF 'COMPULSORY CLOSENESS': THE 'PACIFICATION' OF *FAVELAS* IN RIO DE JANEIRO

Leticia Veloso

INTRODUCTION

In Brazil, to speak of the 'suburb' is to evoke a rhetoric of need and subordination, and in Rio de Janeiro this is even more the case because, there, 'suburb' tends to connote something very different from the usually upper- or middle-class neighbourhoods the same term brings to mind, say, in the United States. This is because, in general, in wealthier countries the term mostly connotes affluence and 'white flights', while in the Global South it can include *both* such wealthier areas *and* the largely impoverished peripheries. This is very much the case in Rio: to live in a 'suburb', there, tends to mean that one comes from a poorer background and needs to content oneself with living far removed from the cultural, social and economic centre of the city inhabited by elites – often, suburbanites spend up to three hours only to get to their jobs, and then the same amount of time to get back home again at the end of a tiresome day.

On the one hand, this is because Rio has not followed the – elsewhere prevalent – pattern whereby affluent residents increasingly exit the city

Suburbanization in Global Society
Research in Urban Sociology, Volume 10, 253–272
Copyright © 2010 by Emerald Group Publishing Limited
ISSN: 1047-0042/doi:10.1108/S1047-0042(2010)0000010013

centre and move towards outlying areas that are considered more privileged. In Rio, it is the very heart of the city that remains the most favoured: adjacent to the city centre lies the Southern Zone (*Zona Sul*), by far the wealthiest area.[1] On the other hand, this is because Rio has not experienced the phenomenon of outlying gated communities in the same way as São Paulo, where entire 'edge cities' have been built, far away from the centre and based on the premise of gated security. While there are of course gated communities all around the city, they are not concentrated in specific (outlying) areas as is the case of São Paulo.[2]

A third important point is that, historically, the very poorest have been excluded from *both* the centralised formal neighbourhoods *and* the outer suburbs, equally 'formal' in the sense that they are actually part of the city, paying their taxes and participating in the formal economy, which is not the case with *favelas*. From the late nineteenth century onwards, they have begun occupying Rio's many hills, both around the city centre and in the peripheries, originating the so-called *favelas*, which are informal neighbourhoods based on squatting and auto-construction. Some *favelas* are quite close to elite neighbourhoods such as *Ipanema* and *Copacabana*, yet most are located in the very heart of Rio's suburbia; the relationship is always uneasy. It is thus that a most peculiar urban pattern has been created, whereby formal and informal, upper, middle and lower classes, *and* the very poor may literally share the same geographic space.[3]

Further, over the past 20 or 30 years, conflict between 'formal' areas and *favelas* has been mounting, mostly due to the flourishing drug traffic and the violence it gives rise to. Hence, none of this can be understood without mention to urban violence, which is key to both shaping and understanding these developments: reaching all-time highs over the 1980s and 1990s, the ever-present menace of urban crime has made its way into both the cityscape and people's subjectivities in profound ways. The problem of urban violence will be central to the analysis offered here, simply because the presence and fear of violence are so determinant in shaping the very nature of urban (and especially, suburban) living in Rio.

To better understand these intricate relationships between urban and suburban, *favela* and non-favela, and the underlying question of violence, I offer the concept of 'compulsory closeness'. By this term, I seek to make sense of how life in Rio is defined by a series of parameters of distance and proximity that are relative rather than absolute, and are produced by ambiguous strategies of separation and proximity different from those documented in other metropolises. 'Compulsory closeness', I suggest, is integral to understanding urbanisation, suburbanisation and the *favela* in

Rio, a city where 'urban' and 'suburban', and 'centre' and 'periphery', are so entangled that the very adequacy of such concepts needs to be rethought.

Besides developing the concept of 'compulsory closeness', this chapter briefly describes a recent social intervention project: the attempted 'occupation' and 'pacification' of various *favelas* by the state government. Starting in late 2008, such 'occupation' (or 'pacification') is an urban planning strategy that (1) explicitly seeks to erradicate violence in such areas by (re)taking control of the territory through the expulsion, by police, of once-dominant drug trafficking gangs and (2) thereby allows *favela* inhabitants more immediate access to citizenship rights and public services. In the process, however, and as an urban planning strategy, its ultimate purpose, or its logical consequence, could be to facilitate the integration between *favela* and 'formal' city.[4] As such, this 'pacification' can be seen as one strategy for addressing broader issues of urban heterogeneity and differentiation in the space of Rio. While it is still too early to assess its actual effects on both *favelas* and city, a few commentaries can already be sketched.

RIO DE JANEIRO: A CITY OF SPECIFICITIES

There are a few aspects characteristic of Rio that must be mentioned when investigating phenomena related to suburbanisation, or peripheralisation. First are Rio's abysmal crime rates. One of the most violent cities in the world, Rio has seen both actual crime rates and its own dubious reputation as a site of remarkable violence grow steadily over the past 20 years. And, though statistics on violent crime are difficult to pin down, a few figures may illustrate this point. Current average yearly homicide rates in Rio are around 43 per 100,000 inhabitants, roughly 10 times higher than Mumbai, for example, a city with a similar population and similar poverty rates (Misse, 2006). By contrast, Paris, where violence has also been making media headlines quite often, though obviously for very different reasons, has a homicide rate of 1 per 100,000 (CESEC, 2006).

Yet this average rate in Rio does not even begin to scratch the surface of how extremely routinised violence has become in certain areas: in times of exacerbated conflict between drug gangs and police (or between rival gangs) in *favelas*, for example, and particularly in those *favelas* located in the suburbs, this rate has, on some occasions, reached 250 per 100,000 inhabitants, as high as Colombia at the height of civil war (CESEC, 2006). There are more than 4,000 people killed in the city per year, 1,000 of them by police (NUPESP/ISP, 2006).[5]

Second, that Rio has been the setting of such violence is particularly disturbing to *cariocas*, because of the time-honoured imagery of a 'wonderful city', a tropical paradise blissfully resting between lush mountains and stunning beaches, 'one of the most beautiful cities in the world', praised for both its beauty and its ideals of urban conviviality.[6] In fact, the epithet 'the wonderful city' was coined in the early twentieth century by a French writer who wanted to convey her admiration for the city's beautiful scenery (Carvalho, 1987). Yet, this idyllic imagery has been continuously challenged over the past 20 years, especially for those living in the peripheries, because of the escalation of crime. This is made clear by the following interview with a 23-year-old man who lives in an impoverished suburb in the Northern part of Rio:

> A.: Shooting here, shooting there. You go through the Red Line, man, there's a shooting there, it goes by *Pavuna*, there's the *Pedreira* hill there.[7] I was there on a bus one time, the driver [took a wrong turn and] passed by that part [of the road] that goes directly into the *favela*, then a police officer [in the middle of the road] said: "Are you crazy?" (...) Because the guys were up there [the drug traffickers were up on the hill], and the police down here. From there they see everything, but down here [at the foot of the hill] the police can't see them. There're a lot of houses here. It reaches the people. (...) A rifle bullet can go through brick, and into a house.

Finally, in Rio, contact between the different is much more immediate than in most other cities, largely because of how the crime-ridden *favelas* have become key features of the lived environment. This peculiarity, far from creating a haven of peaceful conviviality, is what ultimately reinforces much of the conflict that seems so prevalent in the city. As opposed to Caldeira's (2000) description of São Paulo, the gap between haves and have-nots and the fear of crime in Rio have not produced exactly the same kind of exacerbated segregation as in São Paulo.

This is largely because of Rio's peculiar geography, for its many hills and long waterfront have favoured a form of unplanned urban occupation whereby houses and roads have historically been built, literally, wherever nature would permit. It was this unplanned pattern that ultimately led to the peculiar (and enduring) forms of squatter settlements – on hills and other uncharted areas – that eventually became today's *favelas* (Carvalho, 1987; Valladares, 2005). As a result, they are now closely woven into the cityscape: some in the very midst of elite neighbourhoods, but most others inside the working-class suburbs of the Northern part of the city. In the case of the proximity between *favelas* and working-class suburbs, an especially tricky relationship developed because of the combination of physical proximity, similarity in social standing, since residents of both *favelas* and working-class suburbs are poor and marginalised, and symbolic distance. And, while all are poor and violence takes its toll on both spaces, it is *favelas* that bear the stigma of marginalisation.

Of course, spatial proximity does not necessarily breed familiarity or a sense of equality, neither on the part of those living in the *favelas*, nor of those fortunate enough to live outside them. And sharing a space does not mean that symbolic boundaries are not drawn, or even reinforced. As Bourdieu has put it (2003, p. 165), the belief that spatial proximity between persons who are distant in social space might bridge such distance is but a chimera, for 'nothing is more intolerable than the physical proximity (experienced as promiscuity) between socially distant persons'. Rather, what this constant proximity has created is a somewhat morbid symbiosis: even though *favelas* have come to symbolise all that is unruly, inhospitable and dangerous in the city, everyone, from the very wealthy to the suburban working classes, depend on the services and labour provided by those who live in them (Burgos, 2005; Carvalho, 1987).

Thus, unlike most other metropolises, differentiation in Rio neither breeds nor results from spatial segregation in any straightforward manner, simply because regular daily contact is a fact of life for almost everyone. A *favela* in Rio is not the same, in terms of spatial, cultural and socio-economic segregation, as a ghetto in Chicago (Venkatesh, 2000, 2006, 2008; Wacquant, 2007, 2008) or in Philadelphia (Anderson, 1999), for example: though neither is entirely severed from the wider society, the degrees of interaction and visibility are very different. Not the least because the ghetto is not visible from the 'outside' (Venkatesh, 2000; Wacquant, 2007, 2008), while in a typical Rio *favela*, visibility is a given (Alvito & Zaluar, 2005; Valladares, 2005).

And, though it is true, just as with the American ghetto, that other *cariocas* may never visit a *favela*, the opposite does not hold: *favela* residents do interact with their 'formal' counterparts, be it because they are employed by them or because, on occasion, they simply use the same space. Of course, this interaction is limited at best, and at its worst marked by stigmatisation and prejudice. But I suggest that it is still accurate to say that both worlds are not as physically isolated as is the case, for example, of American ghettos, though perhaps it is precisely this predicament that leads to de facto distance being produced (and reproduced) through other, more symbolic means. That there are no rigid physical boundaries is the very reason why distance and proximity are so ambiguous in Rio: being physically close means that differences are thrown right at one's face all the time, which is what eventually produces the need for symbolic distance-making.

'DUALISATION' AND SYMBOLIC DISTANCE-MAKING

Even though people of all classes still presume Rio to be a beautiful, 'wonderful' city, in recent times this image seems to have been over-shadowed by that of a 'partitioned city'. This term was coined by Ventura (1994), an outspoken newspaper commentator who has specialised in writing about Rio's urban problems, and who wrote a widely read book under this title. By this term, Ventura tries to make sense of the presumed dichotomy, also analysed by sociologist Maria Alice Carvalho, between the 'asphalt world' and its many surrounding *favelas* (Carvalho, 1987). For Carvalho (*ibid.*), life in Rio is determined by the insurmountable segregation between two entirely different worlds, governed by different rules and inhabited by people condemned to never become integrated into one common polis.

After several years of research in various *favelas*, I have found similar views expressed by people of all classes and backgrounds. Those living in *favelas* will often refer to themselves as *o pessoal do morro* ('the people from the hill'), and will point out their difference from *o pessoal lá de baixo* ('the people from down there'). The same term *o pessoal do morro* is used by non-*favela* residents, but those residents do not employ a specific term to refer to themselves. Not living in a *favela* is already the unmarked category, and people may not find it necessary to label themselves in any manner other than saying that they are *cariocas*.

As sociologist Leite (2000, p. 74) points out, it is precisely this image of *favela* residents as entirely 'different' from other people that allows them to be readily equated, in popular imaginations, with 'criminals.' Starting in the late 1970s, Leite shows, when the government discontinued its former policies for removing *favelas* by relocating their inhabitants, the number of *favelas* in Rio de Janeiro has risen markedly: from 376 in 1980 to 603 in 1996 (Leite, 2000, p. 85), to over 1,000 as of 2010. Through this process, argues Leite, one effect has been that poverty has increasingly been imagined as something characteristic of *favelas* (though this is not true at all). Another has been the assumption, by many *cariocas* who live outside *favelas*, of an inherent 'relationship between poverty and the *favela* with criminality, through the association of poor labourers and *favelados* (*favela* residents) with criminals' (*ibid.*). Further, it is important to understand that most crime in Rio is related to the increasing power of the drug gangs, and that the bulk of drug trafficking is located in the city's *favelas*, which is what eventually helps explain this perceived metonymic equivalence between *favela* residents and criminality (cf. Veloso, 1998, n.d.). One immediate effect of such processes is that, though *favelas* remain geographically close to the formal neighbourhoods, not only has this physical proximity not led to any real approximation, but it can also be said to have increased the stigmatisation and scapegoating of *favela* residents. A peculiar pattern is thereby created, one in which city and *favela*, though physically close, nonetheless coexist as if they were miles apart.

'COMPULSORY CLOSENESS' OR THE VIOLENCE OF PROXIMITY

There is, then, an imagined division at play here, between those living outside *favelas*, especially in the more violent suburban areas, and those living in the *favelas*, who are stigmatised just by living there. Such perceptions become, in the eyes of those who hold them, almost a self-fulfilling prophecy when they note that most drug trafficking is indeed carried out in the city's *favelas*, and that it is the drug gangs that most commonly stage the most severe manifestations of violence. And they further mention that the daily terror the gangs impinge upon residents also spills outside *favela* borders, sometimes leaving everyone under siege, as is the case with the recurring 'sweeps', shutdowns (Penglase, 2005), buses set on fire, enormous rocks thrown on passing cars and so on.

Most of these episodes – and, in fact, most of the violence in Rio – tend to concentrate in and around the working-class suburban areas of the Northern part of the city, precisely where Rio's most violent *favelas* are located, and it is their 'compulsory closeness' to the *favela* that suburbanites tend to blame for the daily violence they experience. Hence, for anyone living in such working-class suburbs nowadays, everyday life is indeed strongly determined by this unwanted proximity. It is in reality, however, the proximity to the drug-related criminal groups who hide in the *favelas* that so deeply affects their lives. But, symbolically, and though most *favela* residents are *not* involved in crime, it is the whole *favela* that gets blamed. In this manner, a deep segregation is (re)produced between *favela* and working-class suburb, even though residents of both areas may be remarkably similar to one another as far as class or socio-economic standing are concerned.

What is at play here is a process we may call 'compulsory closeness', for it imposes contiguity but ends up reinforcing difference, rather than bridging it. The relationship between *favelas* and working-class suburbs is exemplary in this respect: most poor neighbourhoods in the peripheries are home to at least one or two *favelas*, and especially in the Northern portion of the city, those are often among the most violent of Rio – meaning that some of the most violent drug gangs have their headquarters there; as such, they terrorise both *favela* residents and others on a daily basis. It is this proximity that makes the experience of differentiation and separation so specific in Rio, and so different from many other places: as shown by the fear of crime that is so constitutive of life in this city, its experience is at the same time more random and more generalised, for everyone, for the sheer reason that the different are so geographically close to each other.

I find the concept of 'compulsory closeness' useful in explaining such processes. By this term, I wish to highlight how, in Rio, proximity is imposed by geography, which imposes the presence of difference on everyone: not only rich and poor, and not only the very poor in and outside *favelas*, but also victims and criminals are permanently in contact, so that crime finds virtually no boundaries. Hence, in this context of rampant violence that leaves everyone more or less scared, afraid and prone to being victimised, proximity is imposed by geography, and difference is forced upon those who feel vulnerable.

As Bourdieu has argued in his discussion on social space and poverty, since social space is inscribed at the same time in spatial structures and in the mental structures that are embodiments of those structures, space is a key site where power asserts itself and is exercised (2003, p. 163). And, of course, it is therefore also a site where power's more subtle, though by no means less violent, form manifests itself – that of symbolic violence (*ibid.*). In the case of 'compulsory closeness', symbolic violence works in the following manner. The stigmatisation inscribed in their place of living symbolically degrades *favela* residents simply for living there. Yet, *favelas* and other areas are inextricably linked by geography. But this spatial proximity of socially different persons does not lead to social approximation. Rather, due to symbolic violence, it can only breed more stigmatisation, which is a symbolic mode of distance-making.

In this world of blurred boundaries, anyone conceptualised as an 'other' can become even more rigidly marked as 'suspicious' or 'dangerous'. Therefore, 'compulsory closeness' does not produce 'unification'. In turn, this is also what helps validate reproduce the ongoing demonisation and scapegoating of certain categories of people. Because it reinforces stigma and the ongoing marginalisation of those thus stigmatised, it leads to more partition and separation. Only, it does so in symbolic terms rather than through actual spatial segregation. In other words, this 'compulsory closeness' reinforces symbolic separation *precisely because* physical separation is neither significant nor possible. It is the physical closeness that is, as I have called it, 'compulsory', and this is precisely what augments the symbolic distance between those lying at each pole of the social spectrum and everyone else along the spectrum.

A LIGHT AT THE END OF THE TUNNEL: THE OCCUPATION AND 'PACIFICATION' OF *FAVELAS*

As a result of what I have called 'compulsory closeness', Rio's residents live both physically close to each other and symbolically segregated. At the centre of this differentiation is the divide (symbolic, more so than geographic) between the 'formal' city and the *favelas* or, in Rio parlance, between the 'asphalt' and the 'hill'. This, in turn, is especially acute in the relationship between poor *favela* residents and the (often equally poor) residents of working-class suburbs surrounded by *favelas*: because of the proximity of violence and due to their less-than-comfortable proximity in class and social standing, symbolic distance-making and the stigmatisation of *favelas* become ever more strongly reinforced.

In this section, I expand on this argument by describing, briefly, a recent urban planning strategy that has attempted to address both sides of this equation that makes up life in Rio – violence and 'compulsory closeness'. Historically, most urban planning projects have focused on the many problems faced by *favelas*, such as poverty, exclusion, violence, discrimination and so on, rather than think in terms of strategies that might benefit the entire city. While there have been *favelas* in Rio de Janeiro since the final decades of the nineteenth century (Alvito & Zaluar, 2005), and while the escalation of crime has been going on since at least the late 1970s (Misse, 2006), urban policies targeted at both phenomena have, for reasons that go far beyond the purposes of this chapter, until very recently been scarce and pulverised. In relation to drug-based urban violence, comprehensive strategies have been virtually non-existent, and for the most part, localised police raids in specific *favelas* were staged in place of more consistent policies. With dismal results, one may add, for often it is the innocent who get killed when isolated police groups enter the *favelas* in search of criminals.

And, as for the *favela* itself as a problem for urban planning, planners, academics and the general population have struggled with a rather thorny dilemma: is the best strategy to 'urbanise' the *favela* and thus make it truly part of the 'formal' city, or should the city come to terms with the fact that *favelas* have become nearly independent from the city, with their own rules, their culture, their specificities and, most importantly, their informal nature, as shown by the fact that virtually all housing is auto-constructed on squatted land (Alvito & Zaluar, 2005; Valladares, 2005)? In other words, should the city force itself on the *favelas*, for example, by granting residents ownership of their land and, in turn, demanding that they begin paying taxes like all 'formal' citizens do, or through thorough urbanisation projects to make them look more like 'formal' neighbourhoods? Or, alternatively, should the *favela* be allowed to continue existing as an 'internal fringe', a token, not only of its embedded marginality, but also of its specificity as a world in itself? In Rio, such controversies have, historically, abounded, and these two seemingly irreconcilable positions had, until now, remained just that – incompatible (Valladares, 2005).

Until 2008, one of the most ambitious projects attempted had been the *Favela-Bairro* (*Favela*-Neighbourhood) programme, whose name is almost self-explanatory: initiated in 1993 by Rio's City Hall, its goal was to integrate, in urban as well as in social terms, the *favelas* into the formal network of neighbourhoods. To do so, it was assumed that the *favela* was so intrinsically different from a 'proper' neighbourhood mainly because it lacked certain basic *urban* features, such as streets and driveways, parks and other public spaces, and a functional transportation system. As such, the notion was that providing the *favelas* with such spaces would transform them into 'proper' neighbourhoods (*bairros*). It was thus hoped that not only would the space of the *favela* no longer *look* irredeemably different from that of regular neighbourhoods, but also, in a significant leap of faith, stigmatisation and prejudice would no longer reproduce themselves as easily if both sides of the divide (city and *favela*) were sharing the very same urban spatial model.[8] Results, alas, were mixed, for while the *Favela-Bairro* programme was able to introduce some important improvements in a few *favelas*, it has succeeded neither in completely transforming even one *favela* into a 'real' neighbourhood nor in bridging the long-standing gap within the 'divided city'.

Since late 2008, however, a more ambitious programme has been designed by the government of the State of Rio de Janeiro: the so-called 'occupation' and 'pacification' of Rio's *favelas*, one at a time, slowly and consistently, with the explicit goal of driving out drug traffickers so as to end internal violence and, as an expected result, foster integration between 'hill' (*morro*) and 'asphalt' (*asfalto*). Tellingly, it is not a strategy initiated by urban planners, it is a public security policy designed to (1) occupy *favelas* formerly dominated by the drug trafficking gangs, (2) thereby drive out the gangs,

(3) so as to free residents from the appalling levels of everyday violence they need to endure and (4) thus create a more positive atmosphere all around that can pave the way for more encompassing social services for residents. Ideally, these measures together would also foster the potential integration between *favela* and 'formal' city.[9]

The project's underlying assumption is threefold: one, that the main problem victimising both *favelas* and their neighbouring areas is the drug-related violence; two, that this is a key source of the imposed segregation between *favelas* and the 'asphalt'; and three, as a logical consequence of one and two, that once the problem of violence is successfully addressed and peace restored (hence the label, 'pacification'), more integration between both sides of the divide would follow.

In terms of its implementation, this 'pacification' strategy is supposed to work as follows: first, a group of elite police officers breaks into one *favela* and expels any resident drug gang members, ideally confiscating their weapons and breaking down their hideouts. Then, a special police unit is implanted inside that *favela*, called *Unidade de Polícia Pacificadora* (Pacifying Police Unit), formed by newly admitted elite members of the police force especially trained for that purpose, and each unit comprised of a couple hundred officers, permanently stationed inside each particular *favela*. Finally, after such unit has been consolidated, it is expected that a new experience of the urban may be constructed, one freed from routinised violence, segregation and discrimination. This is because, it is assumed, once the main reason for the symbolic distance between *favelas* and their bordering neighbourhoods (that is, drug-related crime), is no longer as prevalent, this new urban experience will be able to bridge between 'hill' (*morro*) and 'asphalt'.

Such 'UPPs' (from the acronym) are supposed to work via community policing, inspired in US and Canadian models: 'a concept and a strategy based on the partnership between populations and the institutions from the public security area. The Rio de Janeiro government is investing 15 million *reais* in the qualification of the Police Academy so that, until 2016, around sixty-thousand new police officers can be trained. Until the end of 2010, it is expected that 3.5 thousand new cops will have been allocated to the new Pacifying Units'.[10] This presumed 'new police', ideally set against the 'old' one, notoriously violent and abusive against the poor, is termed the 'peace police' (*polícia da paz*) and, according to the commanding officer in charge of the project, this intended new model of policing 'promotes the approximation between population and police, joint with the strengthening of social policies inside the communities. In regaining territories occupied for decades by traffickers (...), UPPs bring peace to the communities'.[11]

One obvious logical contradiction embedded here is easy enough to see: a 'peaceful' police, one whose presumed *raison d'être* is not to exercise social control, or even to *keep* the peace, but to actually *bring* peace; a notion completely at odds with long-standing meanings ascribed to police in Brazil (cf. Holston, 2008; Holston & Caldeira, 1998; Mitchell & Wood, 1999). Especially in *favelas*, the police have notoriously been feared nearly as much as the drug gangs, for the sheer violence they are known to exercise against all residents. In this light, attempting to improve living conditions inside and outside of the *favelas* through *more* policing seems an incongruity at best; a point not lost on residents of both *favelas* and working-class suburbs when they first came into contact with such 'pacification'.

But, even with its internal contradictions and the uneasy implications of implementing a social engineering project based on policing and control, I would like to suggest that there are other issues at stake in this project that may have profound (and, potentially, even positive) implications for how the entire city is governed. After all, even though, explicitly, the 'pacification' is being phrased in terms of the interests of the *favelas* being thus occupied and 'pacified', the 'pacification' plan is also intended as a project *for the city*, rather than one targeted solely at *favela* needs. As José Mário Beltrame, the Secretary of Public Security for the State of Rio de Janeiro who is in charge of implementing the project, has put it:

> Inaugurated on December 23rd, 2009, the Pacifying Police Unit of *Pavão-Pavãozinho/ Cantagalo* is the fifth UPP and the third implemented in the Southern Zone of Rio (...). Together, these three have been forming a new *security corridor* by the seaside, from *Leme* to the *Ipanema* beach. The two communities are located in the noblest area of Rio de Janeiro, between the neighbourhoods of *Ipanema* e *Copacabana* and have *one of the most privileged views of the city.*[12]

Again, the irony is quite explicit here: while on one level the 'pacification' plan presents itself as a strategy *for the communities*, premised on expelling crime and producing a more intimate relationship with the 'communitarian police', on another level it is concern over the *city's* security that shapes the Secretary's words. The pacified 'corridor' reaching from *Leme* to *Ipanema*, from this point of view, is not understood in reference to the inhabitants of these *favelas* but to those living in the 'noblest area' of the city. The *favelas*, in turn, appear in this discursive construction only as sites for catching some of the 'best views' of Rio.

A few paragraphs later in his text, the Secretary is even more explicit in this respect: when commenting on the permanent state of violence endured by both *favela* residents and the wider Rio population on account of the fighting drug gangs, he offers that 'regardless of the complicated routine, the city attracts more and more tourists every year. Rio is indeed a unique and privileged place. Therefore, we have decided to put into practice a new tool for ending confrontations'.[13] Again, the benefits of the 'pacification' plan for Rio as a whole and as a tourist site are, in this particularly statement, prioritised.

It would, however, be easy to treat this new project as yet another urban planning strategy that, in being a priori discriminatory against *favelas* and their residents, is bound to fail for the sheer prejudice and discrimination it supposedly embodies, as had been the case with other urban planning strategies before (Valladares, 2005). In any case, it is still, of course, too early to assess the true impact and legacy of the 'pacification' project for Rio as a city. But it seems fair to say that there is also something else, and more important, at stake here, something with the potential to truly make an impact on the *city* as a whole, rather than be but another strategy for fostering and protecting middle-class sensibilities through the reproduction of the unequal power dynamics between the 'asphalt' and the *favelas*.[14]

A caveat is in order, though, before proceeding with the argument. The view of the *favela* as a *problem*, not in itself but *for the city*, is a recurrent trope in Brazil, as France-based Brazilian sociologist Valladares has convincingly shown (2005): she argues that, historically, academic and policy-oriented analyses of Rio's *favelas* have been strongly shaped by middle-class fears and anxieties about the poverty, misery and violence that all *favelas* are thought to embody. In general, she says, both academic works and public policies have tended to construct the *favela* as, first and foremost, *the* site of violence, illegality and exclusion; a presupposition that, she offers, lies behind even the most widely accepted academic analyses, such as that proposed by the concept of the 'divided city' (cf. Valladares, 2005, p. 20). One important implication of this manner of thinking is that, when both academics and planners think about the *favela*, what tend to get emphasised are the problems the *favela* presumably raises *for the city*, rather than the interests of its own residents.

The very emphasis placed on conducting the process through a newly trained police force, rather than merely employing the services of 'old timers' used to abusing the poor (cf. Mitchell & Wood, 1999), already is at least one small step towards considering *favela* residents' needs. As is the broader logic of 'pacification', which is designed to function in two stages: in its first stage it is supposed to be truly a policing project, with the implementation of the new units and communitarian policing, but its intended second stage is predicated on the implementation of a string of social services for the local population, such as health and education services, or programmes for children, women and senior citizens. At the time of this writing, all 10 occupied areas are already well under way in setting up the 'communitarian police' units, and they are now getting ready to implement a vast array of planned social services. It is, then, the junction of both aspects, policing and services, that is the key to the 'pacification' project.

On the other hand, it is not because it started out as a public security strategy designed to fight crime in the *favelas* that the 'pacification' cannot have important effects on the city as whole. I suggest, in fact, that those may very well go beyond either the more immediate concerns with tourism and 'beautiful views' expressed in the above-reproduced statements by Secretary Beltrame or Valladares' powerful sociological critique of the *'favela* as problem' (2005). For, while the 'pacification' remains rife with contra-diction, mostly due to difficulties in overcoming both the ongoing record of police brutality and the long-standing stigmatisation of *favelas*, my preliminary research has been showing that many residents in both 'occupied' *favelas* and the surrounding areas have been pleasantly surprised by the immediate effects they are experiencing in their daily lives.[15]

From the point of view of *favela* residents, the main benefit that immediately comes to their minds when they are considering their own perceptions of the 'pacification' is, of course, the marked decrease in all-around violence. They are deeply satisfied with the fact that their daily routine is no longer marred by the presence of heavily armed drug traffickers a few feet away from their homes, and even happier about the absence of shootings between gangs and police in their backyards, even though some point out that 'there are still criminals going around, but at least they are not armed like they were before'.[16] When asked to elaborate on this, many will be glad to explain how different it feels to no longer need to be afraid of regular shootings right by their windows, and to not be threatened by the gangs on a daily basis.

As for their relations with the police, while most residents still feel suspicious and rather unwilling to trust them, and while especially youth may resent the increased control they are now under, in some of the 'pacified' *favelas*, it is beginning to become common for people to start building at least some moderate forms of relationship with the officers. In some cases, they may even invite officers to share a meal with them in their homes; something entirely unthinkable in earlier days. Most importantly, however, is that (even though the research is still in progress and these data are necessarily preliminary) virtually everyone seems to assess the new situation and their relationship with the police, in very positive terms.

Further, some also point out that, as they say, their 'right to come and go has been greatly improved'.[17] As they explain it, before the 'occupation', they were often afraid to walk around and tended to avoid, for example, staying out outside the *favela* until very late, lest they would meet with a police raid or the local gang on their way home at night. Now, however, they may feel like taking a stroll outside the *favela* more often, knowing that the risk of being hurt by a stray bullet or of being searched (and, possibly, hurt, by police) on their way back home is minimal. As one youngster put it, 'we now feel more like the city belongs to us, because we can use it more often. We can go to different places, move around more. We are free to walk around, go down the hill and enjoy the city just like everybody else, and we don't need to stay locked up on this hill all the time'.[18]

From the point of view of residents of two adjacent neighbourhoods adjacent to this *favela*, perceptions seem more varied, and they mostly focus on two viewpoints. One is a more 'moderate' one: people will generally say they tend to agree with the overall project, but are still suspicious that either 'the criminals will return' or 'nothing will change much because the *favela* will continue to be the *favela*'. Or, even, that while 'the pacification may be good for people living in the *favela*, for us it can make life worse, because now the criminals will come down the hill'.[19] What this position implies, of course, is an unwillingness to even conceive of the *favela* as part of the city.

Alternatively, other residents espouse a different point of view, one that might be termed 'optimistic'. It is rather different from the first one, and has been increasingly voiced by mostly younger informants from the two neighbourhoods. They, differently from their elders, seem more willing to embrace the very idea of the 'pacified *favela*' as part of the city. And not only do they express this in rather explicit terms, as when they say that they think the UPPs 'will be great because they are trying to unify the city,' but they also enact it in practice: it is becoming more common, in these two neighbourhoods, for youth from 'the asphalt' to visit the *favela*, some perhaps to do some sightseeing, others to go to parties and others still (as was the case of one middle-class college student) even to attend percussion lessons with a samba musician 'from the hill', as she explained. As such, these youth are, unknowingly, answering a recent request made by Secretary Beltrame: the police will continue to occupy more and more *favelas* all through 2010, he said, but 'either society embraces and accepts these areas, or nothing will change at all. Hence, the police are issuing a plea: go up the hill, it belongs to the city'.[20]

Most important for the purposes of this chapter, however, are the implications of the 'pacification' for these three areas. This particular *favela* is located in the midst of two suburban, working-class neighbourhoods. Residents in and outside the *favela* tended to function precisely along the logic of 'compulsory closeness' that I have portrayed above: a negative logic based on stereotypes and stigma, even though they all shared very similar working-class, impoverished backgrounds. Living in a poor suburb on the fringes of the city and living in a *favela* near that same suburb, after all, are not intrinsically different experiences. But, due to the relative position occupied by 'suburb' and 'favela' in the Rio cityscape, they operated as if they were worlds apart.

In this sense, suburbanites, well aware of their own marginalisation (and of the quotidian violence they experienced), were all too ready to blame *favelas* and their residents for their own sorry predicament, by the same token also distancing themselves, symbolically, from that unwanted way of life. They were very keen, for example, to blame their close neighbours for all the violence, and to carefully avoid any 'polluting' contact with anything or anyone coming from the *favela*.

Now, however, though some are still slow to acknowledge that something may be changing in the *favela*, most others seem increasingly willing to adopt a more positive perception: when the extreme degree of violence they were used to begins to fade, and when they therefore no longer feel that they need to be afraid all the time, they may finally be willing to acknowledge that, deep down, *favela* residents are not as different from their own working-class subjectivities as they had imagined. 'Compulsory closeness', in this sense, may perhaps no longer merely reproduce, but actually begin to contribute to bridging the ingrained (and symbolic) distance that used to be the rule between poor *favela* residents and poor suburbanites.

Perhaps, it may even help them acknowledge one important point: that both suburban *favelas* and suburban working-class neighbourhoods share something more profound than merely the same geographic space: in their common physical distance from the city centre, and in their difficulties in bridging this distance, they are both situated in a position of marginality and subordination vis-à-vis the central middle- and upper-class neighbourhoods. Perhaps, also, one unintended consequence of the 'pacification', at least in the case of suburban neighbourhoods and *favelas*, may be that 'compulsory closeness' may begin to work in their favour: rather than augment the symbolic distance between both spaces, once the main source of their ongoing distance-making (that is, violence and the fear thereof) begins to diminish, maybe residents can begin to focus on their, on one level, very similar relationship to the city centre. In so doing, maybe they can begin to realise that, rather than two worlds apart, they are both marginalised and discriminated against by the city centre, and maybe they can even begin to demand public policies that might address this predicament.

At this point, it is only possible to point out such preliminary perceptions and understandings. After all, it is too early to assess any enduring results, especially since one must remain attentive to the many contradictions inscribed in this project: it is a 'pacification' brought about by police, and an urban planning strategy that seeks to reconstitute the city solely from within the *favelas* rather than through a more comprehensive project that would simultaneously target both *favela* and the 'formal city'. Still, I would like to conclude by suggesting that this self-stated 'occupation' and 'pacification' may go to some length in at least attempting to produce a new experience of the urban. If, that is, it manages to continuingly bridge differences and bring together populations and experiences that were once physically close, yet symbolically segregated. As such, it may signify a process that would be almost the opposite of that documented for other cities. Most notably, the walled São Paulo so aptly described by Caldeira (2000).

What this may mean for the city, again, is that, if carried out well, that is, in ways that are attentive to the needs of *both favela* residents and this broader need for overcoming stigmatisation and symbolic distance, it could add a new, positive meaning to what I have termed 'compulsory closeness'. That is, the 'asphalt' and the 'hill' would continue to be living under a closeness that is 'compulsory', for it is bred by the very geography of the city. But, they would now be truly living together, not merely sharing the same space without ever meeting for real. They would, in short, be part of one and the same city, thereby (potentially) contributing to the reconstruction of the very meanings of concepts such as 'urban', 'suburban' and *'favela'*.

NOTES

1. The exception being the rapidly growing neighbourhoods to the West: *Barra* and *Recreio*, for example, are two middle- to upper-class outlying neighbourhoods that could be said to bear resemblances to the suburbanisation experienced by US cities throughout the twentieth century: they are located several miles away from the centre and mostly inhabited by those who wish to flee the confusion of the city. Even so, these neighbourhoods are not labelled 'suburbs' – 'suburbs', in Rio, are virtually

always poorer or lower-middle class neighbourhoods far away from both city and jobs.

2. Again, exceptions are *Barra* and *Recreio*, two Miami-inspired neighbourhoods, where highways, car-based lifestyles and large distances between buildings prevail. To most *cariocas*, however, both are still seen as intrinsically different from 'true' Rio de Janeiro, with its close-by buildings and bustling pedestrian presence and the close encounters both bring about (Dos Santos & Veloso, 2009).

3. There are today over 1,000 *favelas* in the metropolitan area of Rio de Janeiro, and over 80% of them are located in suburbia. They are home to over 1,200,000 people.

4. As of now, there have been 'pacified' *favelas* in both central and suburban areas.

5. Crime rates are notoriously difficult to gather, mostly because of variations in methodology and difficulties in recording the data. I choose to use the data produced by two of Brazil's most reliable research institutes specialising in crime: the *Centro de Estudos de Segurança e Cidadania* ('Center for the Study of Security and Citizenship', CESEC), affiliated with Cândido Mendes University, and the *Instituto de Segurança Pública* ('Office for Public Security') affiliated with the Rio de Janeiro government.

6. *Cariocas* used to imagine their city as a haven of harmony, where (presumably) rich and poor could interact in peace through a very particular form of sociability, epitomised by outdoor living, informal clothing and laid-back sexuality (Dos Santos & Veloso, 2009).

7. The 'Red Line' he is referring to is an expressway built to help ease traffic from Downtown Rio to the Northern Zone. Originally treated as an urban planning 'solution', it is now widely considered one of the most dangerous routes in Rio, for it crosses several *favelas* ruled by different drug trafficking gangs that engage in shootings either between themselves or with the police, so that stray bullets and *sweeps* are common occurrences. *Pavuna* is a lower-middle-class suburb, and *Pedreira* is a *favela* nearby.

8. Available at http://www.prourb.fau.ufrj.br/cidades/favela, retrieved on 18 August 2010.

9. At the time of this writing, 10 *favelas* have already been occupied, comprising around 20% of Rio's entire *favela* population – no small feat indeed. And, while it is not known which *favelas* will be occupied next, several others may follow over the course of 2010 and beyond.

10. Available at http://upprj.com.br, retrieved on 1 September 2010.

11. *Ibid.*

12. Available at http://upprj.com.br, retrieved on 18 August; text written by Secretary Beltrame himself. *Leme* borders and lies to the north of *Copacabana*, which in turn borders and lies to the north of *Ipanema*. The three neighbourhoods are located by the famous Rio beachside and, together, they do indeed form the 'noblest' area of Rio – jointly with *Leblon*, to the south of *Ipanema* but which is not referred to here because it does not house any *favela* in the strict sense of term; it houses one public housing project that has not been included in the 'pacification' plan. *Pavão-Pavãozinho* is the large *favela* complex in *Copacabana*, while *Cantagalo* lies in the midst of *Ipanema*.

13. *Ibid.*

14. See Veloso and Ferreira (2008).

15. Not to mention two other, even more concrete, effects that are being documented: one, the decrease in crime rates both in and outside the *favelas*, and two, the escalation of housing prices, again, both in and out of *favelas*, in a development that can be positive for everyone involved.

16. Interview with a 30-year-old mother of two who lives in a *favela* in the Northern Zone of Rio.

17. Interview with a 52-year-old woman who lives in the *favela* and works as a cleaning woman.

18. Interview with a 17-year-old student, unemployed but looking for work outside the *favela*.

19. Those excerpts are all from interviews conducted with middle-class informants from two working-class neighbourhoods. I have, as of now, conducted 20 interviews in those neighbourhoods, and about half of them express similar views.

20. Available at http://upprj.com.br.

REFERENCES

Alvito, M., & Zaluar, A. (2005). *Um Século de Favela*. Rio de Janeiro, Brazil: FGV.

Anderson, E. (1999). *Code of the street. Decency, violence, and the moral life of the inner city.* New York: Norton & Company.

Bourdieu, P. (Ed.) (2003). *A Miséria do Mundo*. Rio de Janeiro, Brazil: Vozes.

Burgos, M. B. (2005). Cidade, Territórios e Cidadania. *Dados – Revista de Ciências Socias, 48*(1), 189–222.

Caldeira, T. (2000). *Cidade de Muros. Crime, Segregação e Cidadania em São Paulo*. São Paulo, Brazil: Edusp.

Carvalho, M. A. R. (1987). *Quatro Vezes Cidade*. Rio de Janeiro, Brazil: Sette Letras.

Centro de Estudos de Segurança e Cidadania (CESEC). (2006). *Annual Report 2006*. Rio de Janeiro, Brazil: Universidade Cândido Mendes.

Dos Santos, E., & Veloso, L. (2009). Consumo e Sociabilidade na Construção do Imaginário Carioca. In: L. Barbosa, F. Portilho & L. Veloso (Eds), *Consumo: Cosmologias e Sociabilidades*. Rio de Janeiro, Brazil: Mauad.

Holston, J. (2008). *Insurgent citizenship: Disjunctions of democracy and modernity in Brazil.* Princeton, NJ: Princeton University Press.

Holston, J., & Caldeira, T. (1998). Democracy, law, and violence: Disjunctions of Brazilian citizenship. In: F. Agüero & J. Stark (Eds), *Fault lines of democracy in post-transition Latin America*. Miami, FL: University of Miami North–South Center Press.

Leite, M. P. (2000). Entre o Individualismo e a Solidariedade: Dilemas da Política e da Cidadania no Rio de Janeiro. *Revista Brasileira de Ciências Sociais, 15*(44), 73–90.

Misse, M. (2006). *Crime e Violência no Brasil Contemporâneo: Estudos de Sociologia do Crime.* Rio de Janeiro, Brazil: Lumen Juris.

Mitchell, M. J., & Wood, C. H. (1999). Ironies of citizenship: Skin color, police brutality, and the challenge to democracy in Brazil. *Social Forces, 77*(3), 1001–1020.

NUPESP/ISP: Núcleo de Pesquisas do Instituto de Segurança Pública. (2006). *Annual Report.* Rio de Janeiro, Brazil: Secretaria de Estado de Segurança Pública.

Penglase, R. B. (2005). The shutdown of Rio: The poetics of drug trafficker violence. *Anthropology Today*, *21*(5), 3–6.

Valladares, L. (2005). *A Invenção da Favela: Do Mito de Origem à Favela.Com*. Rio de Janeiro, Brazil: Editora Fundação Getúlio Vargas.

Veloso, F., & Ferreira, S. G. (Eds). (2008). *É Possível. Gestão da Segurança Pública e Redução da Violência*. Rio de Janeiro, Brazil: Contracapa.

Veloso, L. (1998). We don't kill citizens: Police violence and the double discourse on citizenship in Brazil. *Análisis Politico*, *34*(May/August), 47–63.

Veloso, L. (n.d.). *Outcasts, outlaws, citizens: Children, violence, and rights, in Brazil*. Book manuscript.

Venkatesh, S. (2000). *An American project*. Chicago: Chicago University Press.

Venkatesh, S. (2006). *Off the books. The underground economy of the urban poor*. Cambridge, MA: Harvard University Press.

Venkatesh, S. (2008). *Gang leader for a day. A rogue sociologist takes to the streets*. London: Penguin Books.

Ventura, Z. (1994). *Cidade partida*. São Paulo, Brazil: Companhia das Letras.

Wacquant, L. (2007). *Urban outcasts. A comparative sociology of advanced urban marginality*. London: Polity.

Wacquant, L. (2008). *As Duas Faces do Gueto*. São Paulo, Brazil: Boitempo.

THE CHANGING IMAGE OF SUBURBAN AREAS IN LATIN AMERICA AND THE ROLE OF LOCAL GOVERNMENT

Sonia Roitman

INTRODUCTION

The image of Latin American suburbs has changed in the last two decades as they have become more heterogeneous with the development of gated communities that coexist with poor-household settlements. Developers, local government staff and gated community residents are the main actors involved in the process of urban development of the periphery.

This chapter analyses the development of gated communities on the periphery from the perspective of local governments in Argentina and Mexico: it looks at how politicians and officers justify gated communities, what the opinions about these residential developments are, and how the relationships with developers and gated community residents are established.

The main argument of the chapter is that there seems to be a contradictory situation regarding gated communities as local government staff usually see them as 'anti-urban' and they do not agree with the values behind them, but at the same time, they accept (and sometimes also encourage) their development arguing that it is what a particular social

Suburbanization in Global Society
Research in Urban Sociology, Volume 10, 273–292
Copyright © 2010 by Emerald Group Publishing Limited
All rights of reproduction in any form reserved
ISSN: 1047-0042/doi:10.1108/S1047-0042(2010)0000010014

group asks for and might be a solution to individual security. Hence, this chapter is divided into four sections. The first section explains the dynamics of growth and social differentiation in the Latin American periphery and the development of gated communities. The second section examines the main actors involved in urban development, considering their features and duties. The third section presents an analysis of the local government and their position in relation to the growth of gated communities, based on empirical information obtained through semi-structured interviews with local government staff over the last years. Finally, the conclusion goes back to the initial argument of the chapter emphasising the contradictory relationship between gated communities and local governments.

LATIN AMERICAN SUBURBS AND THE SPREAD OF GATED COMMUNITIES

Some years ago, when discussing suburbs in the United States, there was a dominant image of homogeneous spaces, single-family housing, non-Hispanic white families with children and mostly professional and car-dependent households. However, this homogeneity has been largely contested and several authors have opened up the diversity of US suburbs (see Nicolaides & Weise, 2006). The latter appeared as a solution to urban problems, especially noise, pollution and other activities different than the residential use. They were an escape from the city, although suburban residents worked in the city centres. There was a strong relationship between suburbs and city centres, which led to interpretation of suburbanisation as 'a concept that suggests both escape from and dependence on the city' (Sassen, 1994/2001, p. 210).

In the case of Latin American cities, suburban growth was more segregated. Many areas were specifically built for affluent residential use and other areas were informal settlements, concentrations of social housing developments for the lower income groups. Social differentiation in the periphery was established according to geographical locations, such as the north-south or the east-west divides. This has nowadays changed with the development of gated communities, which are sometimes located next to informal settlements and social housing developments. This changes the image of suburbs into more heterogeneous spaces, although it seems to be a more complex process than in the United States.

Historically, the Latin American city has been a segregated city (Roitman & Giglio, 2010; Sheinbaum, 2010). Spanish conquerors and their descendants built urban settlements around the main city square. The closer to the square, the more affluent families were. It was a 'compact city model' (Borsdorf, 2003). Later on, at the beginning of the 20th century, affluent families moved closer to the new-built avenues or closer to new urban parks designed as an image of the French parks and poor European migrants established in the large abandoned houses in the centre converted into multi-family houses known as *conventillos* or *vecindades*. Since the 1930s, with the improvement of motorways and the use of the automobile, affluent groups started going to the suburbs or the countryside over the weekends to practise elitist sports and relax from city life. Thus, *Tortugas Country Club*, the first gated community in Argentina, was built in the outskirts of Buenos Aires for the members of *Tortugas Rugby Club* to stay over during the weekend. However, as explained by Ballent (1999), living outside the city was considered as the necessary opposition to urban living and the city-suburbia relationship was perhaps more complementary rather than opposi-tional. Few other gated communities appeared in Buenos Aires between the 1930s and the 1950s. Houses were small and rustic as weekend use did not demand large areas or upscale housing designs. In the case of Mexico City, *Lomas de Chapultepec*, the first Mexican garden city, was also built around the 1930s and *Jardines del Pedregal* in the 1950s (Sheinbaum, 2010).

Since the 1950s, cities grew with the industrialisation processes and the consequent move of people from rural areas. Those who could not longer settle in the city centre established themselves in the periphery of the city, in newly built working-class neighbourhoods or deficient housing areas with no good services and infrastructure. The periphery was clearly divided with some areas for affluent families and other areas for working-class families. In Buenos Aires, the affluent suburbs (*Belgrano* and *San Isidro*) were located in the north of the city, while in Santiago de Chile they were located in the north-east (*Providencia* and *Vitacura*). In Mexico, *Colonia Roma* and *Colonia Juárez* were situated in the western side of the city, close to the new avenue *Paseo de la Reforma*, a model copied from the French *Champs-Elysées* (Sheinbaum, 2010). Affluent residential areas located in the periphery were a minority in contrast to large housing developments for lower middle class and poor residents.

In the following years, with the improvement of motorways that reduced commuting times from the periphery to the city centre, affluent families increasingly moved to the periphery. Suburbia turned into the opposite – and not complementary as before – to living in the centre as families were looking for larger areas and more comfort, being closer to nature (i.e. more green areas and less polluted and noisy environments) and sport amenities. In the mid-1990s and beginning of the 2000s, when urban insecurity and fear of crime increased, having security was also a major factor in moving to the periphery and, in particular, moving to the growing number of newly built gated communities. Developers and the media also encouraged families to move to gated communities where they could develop a sense of community and be in contact with families with similar lifestyles, interests and values. These developing companies were transnational companies or national ones but heavily influenced by foreign ideas that spread the model of gated communities as a residential option worldwide.

Gated communities can be defined as 'closed urban residential settlements voluntarily occupied by a homogeneous social group, where public space has been privatised by restricting access through the implementation of security devices. Gated communities are conceived as closed settlements from their inception and are designed with the intention of providing security to their residents and prevent penetration by non-residents; their houses are of high quality and have services and amenities that can be used only by their residents, who pay regular compulsory maintenance fees. They have a private governing body that enforces internal rules concerning behaviour and construction' (Roitman, 2008b, p. 8).

The literature on gated communities has widely discussed for their social, economic, political and urban impacts (see Roitman, 2010). Some authors consider that the expansion of gated communities in the periphery contributes to the fragmentation of the city. Janoschka (2002) talks about a 'city of islands' – *ciudad de islas* – as gated communities are closed and isolated objects that do not want to integrate to already built nearby areas. Duhau and Giglia (2008) also refer to gated communities as 'space of islands' – *espacio insular*; however, they emphasise that their development does not contribute to a 'dispersed city', but on the contrary, they serve to 'fill in' vacant areas in the periphery. The latter might be the case of Mexico City, which is the object of study of Duhau and Giglia; however, it is difficult to generalise this for all Latin American cities. On the contrary, recent urban development seems to have encouraged more to what Graham and Marvin (2001) call 'splintering urbanism' as the development of infrastructure networks and technological mobilities contribute to the fragmentation of the social and material fabrics of cities.

The arrival of gated communities on the urban periphery usually brought a general improvement to the area as there were more services and infrastructure available. Developers (or other private sector companies) built retail facilities next to gated communities to be used mainly by their residents. Other services like banks, medical centres, entertainment venues, and even office spaces and schools and universities were also located in the periphery. The growth of Pilar, a city in the outskirts of Buenos Aires, is one of the best examples of this (Roitman & Phelps, 2009). In addition, motorways accesses were usually improved, as well as street lighting, outside gated communities. These areas also benefited from other infrastructure improvements like sewage and sanitation or other services like rubbish collection and telephone/Internet networks.

The expansion of this type of residential development is accompanied by a further process of privatisation of the city. Public space and free access tend to diminish while there is an increasing negotiation for the use of the space. Barriers, controlled access and private parking areas turn into urban obstacles in a context of an intensive use of private automobile.

With the development and spread of gated communities over the last two decades, there are more affluent families living in the periphery of Latin American cities (Fig. 1). This has changed the character of suburbia becoming more heterogeneous and more important, creating areas where poor and affluent residents coexist in close proximity (Fig. 2). However, this does not necessarily mean integration between different social groups

Fig. 1. Houses in a Gated Community in the Periphery of Buenos Aires (Argentina). Picture by Sonia Roitman.

Fig. 2.   A Poor Neighbourhood on the Left and the Wall of a Gated Community on
the Right, Querétaro, Mexico. Picture by Sonia Roitman.

(Roitman, 2008b). On the contrary, the walls and fences of gated communities might increase social distancing. This means that while in the earlier time social segregation in Latin American cities was at a large scale, now it is in a reduced scale (Sabatini & Cáceres, 2004). In some cases like in the metropolitan area of Buenos Aires, 'the higher the percentage of poor households, the higher the concentration of gated communities' (Libertun de Duren, 2007, p. 608). Libertun de Duren found in her study that '70 percent of those [suburban gated communities] were located in the three municipalities with the highest proportion of poor households over the past three decades' (*ibid.*, p. 609). This was particularly a result of planning decisions made by local governments, which along developers and gated community residents are currently the main actors encouraging suburban development.

(SUB)URBAN DEVELOPMENT ACTORS

Cities are the space for the interconnection of different social actors who mainly represent three spheres: public (national, regional and local governmental tiers), private (developers, land owners, real estate agents and residents) and the civil society (groups and different types of associations like resident associations and professional associations) (Roitman, 2008a). Some of these actors are global (or transnational) actors, like international investments or construction companies, while others are local, such as the local government or resident associations. Both global and local actors are influenced by global and local processes and phenomena, such as financial and construction trends.

Gated communities are an urban phenomenon that responds to globalisation trends, but they also get local features. Additionally, their residents are local actors who are highly integrated into globalisation processes: they might work for global companies, travel abroad, consume articles and develop habits from other countries, and share similar lifestyles with citizens from different countries creating 'globalised' or 'transnational' lifestyles.

Global tendencies have encouraged the development of these residential areas. There is an 'imitation process' based on the United States suburban model (Thuillier, 2005) of social homogeneity and family life. Wu (2005) comments that in the case of China, gated communities adopt Western designs and foreign names like 'Orange County Beijing'. Some developers have exported their 'models' to other countries, while some architectural offices from the United States have designed the master plans of gated communities located in Latin America. For instance, the master plan of the largest and one of the most prestigious gated communities in Mendoza, Argentina, was designed by EDSA, an architecture office based in Florida, following landscape and architecture designs used in the United States. Additionally, many investment companies are transnational companies. However, developers need to consider local influences and the particular needs and interests of local residents. In this sense, while most gated communities in Latin America are targeted at families, there are gated communities for elderly people in the United States and gated communities mainly for young couples or single residents, like Bow Quarter, in London. Additionally, although developers and investors involved in gated community development mainly follow a global or an international logic of operation, they need to interact with local operational factors, such as planning regulations, which are context specific. This produces a 'clash' of logics, as later explained. Most of these projects have precarious legal arrangements or do not comply with planning regulations (Thuillier, 2005; Roitman, 2008b).

Within the public sphere, local governments have gradually acquired more responsibilities in urban planning processes. They have a closer and more direct contact with local residents and their interests and needs, and thus they usually have more legitimacy and representation than regional or national governments. Also, because they have a smaller structure and are less complex, local governments are able to adapt faster to global influences (Pírez, 2002). However, political will and leadership are needed to achieve this. One of the main problems of local governments is their lack of trained staff as well as financial resources to provide rapid responses to the demands of the citizens and the private sector (Thuillier, 2005). This creates a 'clash' between the operational logic of the private sector, which is usually fast in response to the current needs and demands of the market, and the logic of the public sector, which is slower and depends on political decision-making. The local government is in many cases unable to control development and redevelopment (UN-Habitat, 2009) and turns from 'controller' to 'enabler' of the private sector (Pírez, 2002).

Informality is not only a feature of poor-household settlements but also refers to housing projects that might have a formal appearance, but in reality do not comply with planning regulations. In this sense, UN-Habitat argues:

> In addition to the processes of informal settlement (…), in many cities there is much informality in the development of middle- and upper-income residential neighbour-hoods. Landowners often manage to obtain detailed layout and building permission for developments in areas not zoned for immediate development, either because the development permission process is ineffective or through the influence or corruption. Such areas are often gated communities, built to high standards and self-sufficient in terms of services, but may not comply with broad strategic planning or environmental policies. Alternatively, development may occur in designated areas, but at a higher density or lower building standard than specified because development and building-control officers are powerless to enforce regulations or can be prevailed upon through influence or under-the-counter payments. Reports of buildings constructed in this way are all too frequent. Formal service provision sometimes lags behind the development of such areas. (UN-Habitat, 2009, p. 133)

Using their faculties to decide on urban planning regulations, local governments take different attitudes regarding the development of gated communities: while some favour them, others are against their development, although the first situation is more common as they represent a source of income and a way of rapid improvement for their local territories, as already explained. According to some authors, 'Urban planning proposals and development schemes for transforming urban landscapes typically serve the interests of political elites and monied interests – indeed, the city is often envisioned as a site for the production of value – symbolic and monetary …' (Low & Lawrence-Zuñiga, 2003, p. 20).

Libertun de Duren (2007) has analysed the changes in the planning regulations for gated communities in the metropolitan area of Buenos Aires (Argentina) over the last four decades. According to her, there was a series of changes that progressively encouraged the construction of gated communities in some municipalities: first in 1977 gated communities were allowed by municipal approval to privatise public streets, then in 1986 the requirements for any minimum area for development were dropped, and later in 1999 municipalities were given full discretionary power to grant planning permits for gated communities.

The development of gated communities involves the actions of developers and local governments, which usually have different working logics, as explained in this section. In addition, the demands of gated community residents need to be considered by both developers and local governments, as illustrated in the next section. Local governments have a key role in allowing or limiting the development of gated community projects as they have the legal rights to define their own planning regulations. The next section explores the opinions of some local government staff on the development of gated communities.

GATED COMMUNITIES THROUGH THE LENS OF THE LOCAL GOVERNMENT

This section analyses the image that gated communities in Latin America have for local government staff, which refers here to political positions as well as to managers and officers. Several themes, such as the reasons for their development, the benefits they have for the local government and the relationship between gated communities and local government, are explained through the opinions given by people working for local governments in different Latin American cities. Data was collected through semi-structured interviews conducted between 2003 and 2010 with eight staff members who held different positions in local governments of Buenos Aires and Mendoza (Argentina) and Querétaro (Mexico).[1]

As the opinions given by interviewees will show here, there seems to be a contradictory situation regarding gated communities as local government staff usually see them as 'anti-urban' and they do not agree with the values behind them, but at the same time, they accept (and sometimes also encourage) their development arguing that it is what a particular social group desires, and might be a solution to personal security.

Starting with the reasons explaining the fast development of gated communities over the last two decades, the change of land use and planning regulations (or the lack of planning regulations) have been important factors encouraging their expansion. However, it is important to consider that although there are similar trends regarding the development of gated communities in Latin American cities, some municipalities have favoured them more than others. The difference is not between countries, but between cities and sometimes even between municipalities that are part of the same metropolitan area. Differences are based on four elements: planning regulations, sufficient municipal staff, land availability and municipal poverty conditions. In the first case, the deputy director of urban development of the municipality of Querétaro (Mexico) explains that while some other municipalities in Querétaro[2] encourage the development of gated communities '*because of a total lack of regulations*', his municipality does not because '*we [in this municipality] have urban plans that have been approved by law and we have a code of construction ... however, this doesn't mean that we have all sorted out, there are still legal voids that allow for all these things to happen ...*'.

Additionally, some local governments developed a policy of tax exemptions and change of land use to attract new developments in their territory, as a local councillor from the suburbs of Buenos Aires comments:

> ... *there was an initial policy to encourage the construction of gated communities. Some times taxes were exempted over a period of time to encourage the location of gated communities. This is not happening any more. Many rural lands were urbanised and gated communities were built there. ...*

The second aspect that influences the development of gated communities is the technical capacity and sufficient number of municipal staff, as in some cases local government staff are not able to cope with the high demand of projects submitted for planning approval, and therefore controls are less rigid. An interviewee comments: '*the organisational structure here is larger* [than in other municipalities]... *we are at least five people to think about urban planning issues, while in Corregidora* [another municipality] *they are only two* [people]' (deputy director of urban development, Querétaro, Mexico). In the case of Argentina, one interviewee explains: '*The local government doesn't have the capacity in terms of number of people and skilled people to do this* [control urban growth]. *Now the municipality is improving and getting skilled people in all the managerial positions, who are able to take decisions*' (director of planning, local municipality in Buenos Aires, Argentina).

In relation to land availability, there are some municipalities that do not have empty urban land, and therefore it is not possible to build new developments. For instance, in the case of the metropolitan area of Mendoza in Argentina,[3] which is made up of six municipalities, while Capital (Mendoza City) has only one gated community and Godoy Cruz has seven, Luján de Cuyo has 28 developments which have been built in the last 15 years and still a lot of land available for residential use (Roitman, 2008b).

Finally, those municipalities that have higher levels of poverty within their population seem to have favoured more the development of gated communities. As explained by Libertun de Duren (2007, p. 607) for the situation in Buenos Aires Metropolitan Area: 'municipalities with a high percentage of poor households have facilitated the development of gated communities as a way to increase local employment and real estate investment'. Gated community residents contribute to the local economy as taxpayers and as consumers of goods and services (*ibid.*).

Urban insecurity and increasing fear of crime are the most common justifications for the existence of gated communities in most cities around the world, but particularly in Latin America. This is usually mentioned by all actors involved in the development of gated communities: '*Because of insecurity, affluent groups have been obliged to move to gated communities to preserve their material goods … but other social groups are also demanding us to allow them to close off their neighbourhoods*' (director of urban planning, local government in Mendoza Province, Argentina).

However, as explained in the first section of this chapter, it is not only because of insecurity but also because some families seek a better quality of life: '*people move there because there is a claim for security … and* [also] *people who want to live with particular living conditions*' (mayor, local government in Mendoza Province, Argentina). As explained in previous sections of this chapter, the initial development of gated communities away from the city centre was related to better living conditions:

> … *the first gated communities that appeared in the 1990s are related to the expansion of the vehicle stock that increased a lot and then traffic increased … and some people started looking for another type of life, a better quality of life … this was before security was a problem … and people started moving to the periphery and to particular residential suburbs … the problem was that there were no schools there, no public transport, no supermarket(s)* … (local councillor, municipality in Mendoza Province, Argentina)

In the case of the city of Querétaro (located two hours away by car from Mexico City), its deputy director of urban development provides further reasons for the development of these projects: '*After the 1985 earthquake, many people migrated from Mexico City ... there is a huge growth* [in Querétaro]... *people* [still] *come looking for exactly the opposite as* [what] *Mexico city* [is]. *If Mexico city is a dense city, with many high-rise buildings and a lot of urban concentration, they want to find a rustic and open-air life style ... Also people want to have their own territory and the supply of residences in high-rise buildings hasn't been attractive because people want to be the owners of a piece of land'.* The latter explains the increase of single-family housing in suburban areas, although over the last years there is increasingly more supply of apartment ownership in suburbia.

Processes promoting social polarisation and the worsening living conditions of some social groups are also considered as processes encouraging the development of gated communities:

> ... *[the future of gated communities] will be related to the solution of security conditions ... the demand will increase or decrease in relation to whether society maintains the current levels of dismantling or this improves ... If we have 50 percent of poverty and 25 percent of marginality, the demand for gated communities will increase exponentially. ...*
> (director of urban planning, local government, Mendoza Province, Argentina)

However, it is important to consider here that some actors believe there is an oversupply of this type of housing option: '*There is currently a huge number of new gated communities on offer, but they don't respond to the real demand ... because the demand is within the group with minimum wages'* (deputy director of urban development, Querétaro, Mexico).

As noted, globalisation trends, the opening of the market economy to foreign investments and the improvement of road infrastructure also contributed to the development of gated communities. In relation to what happened in Buenos Aires, the director of planning of Pilar, a suburban municipality with the highest number of gated communities in Argentina, mentions: '*The "boom" happened in the 1990s with the de-regulation of the state, the administrative decentralisation and globalisation. There was a large amount of foreign direct investment in real estate businesses in Pilar'.*

In relation to foreign investments, there was also investment by national companies in suburban areas. In the case of Querétaro in Mexico:

> ... *national developers came in the 2000s and bought rural land, and later asked for a land use change from rural to urban, increasing a lot the land plus-value and therefore making business ... this change of land use was easy to make ... now it is not so easy. ...* (deputy director of urban development, Querétaro, Mexico)

This process of land use change shows the strong influence developers have over planning processes, as commented in the previous section. According to the same interviewee, '*... developers have gained from us in*

Querétaro … to the extent that they are practically those who command. The ones who command and do what they want'. However, this same person expresses that there is *'a very good relationship'* with developers because

> *… we want a growing and blossoming municipality, so we have given developers a lot of facilities to make the city grow. In addition, many of them have also been part of the local government and then moved to the private sector or they own land; their families are the landowners of the city so they've managed the growth of the city for their benefit. …*

The idea of developers who modify urban planning and the lack of political power and also lack of knowledge by local governments is illustrated by what happened in the province of Buenos Aires when gated community development was in its best moment:

> *… After the boom, speculation came. Some important [commercial] groups took some fiscal land because there was no control from the municipality, like saying: 'I am buying 100 hectares and will take 50 hectares more that are next to it and are owned by the municipality to build the golf course'. The municipality couldn't do anything or didn't want to do anything. There are three reasons for not doing anything: they don't want to do anything, they don't know what to do, or they can't do anything. The municipality could have done something if it had had the strength and political will to do this. There is always a problem between money and politics. Money will always go first. The event is always before the norm. …* (director of planning, local municipality, Buenos Aires, Argentina)

This also shows the difficult situation behind the role of the government being either an 'enabler' of the private sector initiatives or a 'controller'. However, some governments have been able to reinforce their control power:

> *… [the relationship] with the developers is very good. The government always sees someone who is coming to invest here very well. There are situations in which they want to pass over the government and we suffer that a lot. The first problems appear in the planning department: we give them a permit to do A and they do B, they take public streets, etc. … In theory we can demolish something, but this has never happened [before]. Once you demolish one square metre, people become more careful … We can stop construction work. We've now stopped several construction works. So they will have to pay a fine …* (director of planning, local municipality, Buenos Aires, Argentina)

There are some cities that do not have planning guidelines for the development of gated communities, and planning permits are given according to discretion-based decisions. The local councillor of a municipality in the province of Mendoza, Argentina, explains the local situation: *'there is not a general norm for gated communities, so there are exception ordinances to build this type of neighbourhood … each situation is analysed and gets a planning permit'*. In the case of Querétaro, some gated communities do not have a municipal permit to be closed off, but there does not seem to be opposition about this because their residents are part of the political or economic elite of the city. As the local deputy planning director explains: '*People who live there* [referring to EC[4]] *are politicians and government people who have managed to keep the development as private, even when we all know that it should work as an open neighbourhood*'.

In relation to gated community residents, they are not only seen as '*politicians*' as stated in the previous quotation, but also as '*people with money ... with large houses of 300 square metres or even 500 square metres and they usually have people who help them with the house cleaning*' (deputy director of urban development, Querétaro, Mexico). Through the lens of the local government, residents are also considered as '*people with very high purchasing power*' (planning director, local municipality, Mendoza, Argentina) as well as '[people with] *another quality of life*' (local councillor, Mendoza, Argentina). The last two comments show how local government staff do not usually consider themselves as belonging to this social group, which sometimes brings up some prejudices or negative attitudes towards gated community residents. Talking about gated community residents and their lifestyles, a local councillor says: '*there is a very distant relationship among neighbours ... everybody minds their own business ... there is competence for how you are dressed or what you bought ... and people have an elitist group of friends ... but I'd move there to give security to my children*' (local councillor, Mendoza, Argentina). The last part of the comment shows how despite the negative aspects they might have, residents and non-residents would prefer to live in gated communities because of personal security.

Gated community residents are a homogeneous group in relation to the society as a whole; however, there are important differences within the group. A non-resident explains: '*... it is a homogenous group because they have a house, a car,* [attend] *private schools, and so on ... but then there are differences, there are guys with a lot of money and others with less money*' (local councillor, Mendoza, Argentina).

With regards to the relationship between local government staff and gated communities, especially with their residents and their homeowners associations, there is usually a good relationship. However, it is not a very frequent one as there are no many issues to be discussed. The mayor of one municipality in Mendoza explains:

> *... we don't have a constant relationship with the residents of P. [a gated community] because we usually have a constant relationship with those neighbourhoods that have problems ... but we have had some dialogue with them for particular issues and it's always been a good dialogue. ...*

He further comments on the situation with one gated community:

> ... *There were some problems and complaints from the people living [outside] close to the gated community ... and our role was always to be an intermediary between the two groups to avoid conflicts and try to solve the problems of the non-gated neighbourhoods that were weaker in relation to that gated community. ...*

The relationship between local government and gated community residents is sometimes difficult as there are prejudices and negative attitudes involved, as expressed by a local councillor in Mendoza, Argentina:

> ... *the relationship between the local government and gated communities should be very good, but the high hypocrisy and resentment by some government staff who take the gated communities concept for political speculation makes it difficult ... It should not be like this because in the case of P. [one gated community], we asked them [the Homeowners Association] to do some infrastructure works and they did it. They pay taxes and they collaborate with some [state] schools of the area ... [and] they create job opportunities for gardeners, maids, [and] security staff ...*

This shows that as much as gated communities are a contested subject within the academic community, they are also a contested subject at the local government level, and probably for society as a whole.

The latter quotation also illustrates the main contradiction that exists in relation to gated communities. Although they might be considered as a negative element for the city dynamics, they are allowed and encouraged based on the economic benefits they bring. Gated communities '*can give us jobs so we have tried that those in need* [unemployed] *have access to them*' (local councillor, municipality in Buenos Aires, Argentina). Another local government staff adds: '*It's good for the local government because you don't need to give them* [gated community residents] *the service of security nor public health ... they have private security and private health insurance*' (local councillor, Mendoza, Argentina). Another councillor further elaborates on the benefits for the local government: '*the taxes they pay for are for rubbish collection, street cleaning and maintenance of the green areas ... but we only do the rubbish collection so it's cheaper for us* [the local government] *and therefore more convenient*' (local councillor, Mendoza, Argentina).

Gated community residents provide also economic benefits for governments as they are good taxpayers:

> ... *Our municipality is not an industrial or agricultural municipality so we live out of services ... our revenues come from the national or provincial governments and from our taxes and fees for inspections, permits, and licenses. So everything that means a harmonic development benefits us ... and of course if the residents contribute with the tax payment and they are good taxpayers who pay high taxes, it is even better for us ... and they allow us*

> *to pay for services for those who can't pay … but this doesn't mean that I'd like all developments to be like that … I want a city where residents are compromised with the city. …* (mayor of local municipality in Mendoza, Argentina)

Gated communities are also believed to benefit local areas as they bring new services and infrastructure. A local councillor from a municipality in Buenos Aires Metropolitan Area comments on this topic:

> *… I don't say they [gated communities] are privileged [neighbourhoods] but they have got the solutions to their problems very fast and this has not happened in more deprived localities or neighbourhoods. Many of these still have deficits in relation to services and infrastructure. So we have to give them services and we will have to create [more] services and infrastructure … . It's easier with gated communities because they have prepared their space and they have provided the services they need by themselves. …*

The latter would argue against the idea that one of the benefits of gated communities is the extension of infrastructure in their local areas, and emphasises that progress and area upgrading is done mainly for the benefit of gated communities and not for non-gated areas, but there might be some particular benefits for the surrounding area in the provision of services and infrastructure.

Despite all these benefits, local government staff are also aware of the problems gated communities bring to the city, like closure of streets and worsening of traffic as they encourage the use of private transport. The director of planning of a municipality in Mendoza says: '*gated communities represent a challenge for us* [the local government] *because they create urban problems … they interrupt road infrastructure and the vehicular circulation is interrupted, in addition to the great expansion of the number of vehicles in the city … if you have obstacles in the city, this is an additional cost for everybody*' and he adds: '*gated communities create more problems than solutions because even if they mean more security for the group that lives inside, they mean lots of problems for the society as a whole*'.

Interviewees also mention the social consequences of gated communities:

> *… I think they [gated communities] don't benefit us because they only create ghettoes. On the one hand, it benefits the municipality because street cleaning and maintenance is done by the gated community. And the municipality doesn't have that duty anymore and it is great! But I think that at the social level we create ghettoes … society is differentiated according to the cultural and economic level you have. …* (deputy director of urban development, Querétaro, Mexico)

These opinions illustrate the difficult and unstable balance regarding positive and negative aspects of gated communities through the lens of the local government. One of the negative points is based on the privatisation of public space as expressed by this interviewee:

> ... *although the model of the gated community has a great demand today, I think that looking at it in a longer period of time, it can't be a solution because the concept of public space as a common place has to prevail in the end ... public space is the one that allows us to share things with others in the urban space, if we compromise public space, we will have to face the consequences of this. ...* (director of planning, local municipality in Mendoza, Argentina)

In relation to the idea of gated communities representing the 'anti-urban', the mayor of a local municipality in Mendoza, Argentina, says:

> ... *If you think how we live and how we would like to live, and the ideal society, then gated communities are against that ... I've thought about this a lot, for my private life, but I also understand that some people would like to live like that ... I always say that I would like a social and geographically integrated society and I think gated communities don't contribute to this concept, but I also know there are situations that override me and we need to consider what people want. ...*

Trying to manage this contradiction between the 'anti-urban' feeling and the demands for gated communities on the other hand, this interviewee adds:

> ... *I would allow the development of gated communities with two conditions: First, they are allowed by the legislation. Second, they are not in the centre of the urban fabric because when there are large developments in central areas, these are obstacles for the police, firemen and ambulance services. ...*

Although local governments might not always agree with the development of gated communities, they see them as suburban entities that will continue to expand regardless of the local government's position, which seems to undermine the role of local government on urban dynamics and growth. Interestingly, local governments have more powers in relation to urban development but, at the same time, seem to be more vulnerable to the demands of affluent residents and developers.

CONCLUSIONS

This chapter has illustrated the change of image that suburban areas in Latin American cities have had over the last two decades as a consequence of the development of gated communities based on the opinions expressed by local government staff from three cities. The new reality in the periphery is that the construction of this type of affluent residential option means that poor and affluent areas are located in close spatial proximity, although this does not mean social interaction between different social groups.

Gated communities have been encouraged by residents, developers and also local governments. Residents who can afford this lifestyle look for better life quality, greener and larger areas, sports infrastructure and especially a protected residential environment with efficient security devices. Developers reinforce the need for a secure architecture and encourage ostensibly 'foreign' lifestyles. These projects are now part of the landscape of most cities. However, some local governments, which usually have the responsibility to allow or not the construction of gated communities in their territory, seem to have favoured them more than others. There are four elements that have influenced their decisions: planning regulations, sufficient municipal staff, land availability and municipal poverty condition.

Although it is difficult to generalise the situation for all Latin American cities, it is possible to highlight some trends related to the development of gated communities. One of this refers to the attitude of local governments to the gated communities' expansion. Despite the number of gated communities located in their territories, local governments seem to move within a precarious situation. On one hand, local government staff believes that gated communities oppose to the idea of a city as they privatise public space and fragment the urban fabric encouraging social differences. On the other hand, they accept them as a residential option for some social groups and focus on their accompanying benefits. Gated communities benefit the local economy increasing consumption, bring revenues for local governments and also diminish the burden on local governments' responsibilities through the supply of private services. Local governments try to act as 'controller' of the private activities of developers and protect the interests of all citizens; however, in many cases they are closer to the role of 'enabler' as they try to keep good relationship with powerful developers and elite gated community residents.

NOTES

1. Interviews were conducted in Spanish. Quotes have been translated by this author. The research done in Buenos Aires in 2009 was funded by the UCL-Abbey Research Award.

2. The metropolitan area of Querétaro is made up of four municipalities: Querétaro, Corregidora, Huimilpan and El Marqués.

3. The metropolitan area of Mendoza is made up of six municipalities: Capital, Godoy Cruz, Guaymallén, Maipú, Las Heras and Luján de Cuyo.

4. Full names of the gated communities mentioned by the interviewees are not given here to protect their anonymity.

ACKNOWLEDGEMENT

The author is grateful to the interviewees who generously shared their opinions and experiences.

REFERENCES

Ballent, A. (1999). La 'casa para todos': grandeza y miseria de la vivienda masiva. In: F. Devoto & M. Madero (Eds), *Historia de la vida privada en Argentina. Tomo III: La Argentina entre multitudes y soledades. De los años treinta a la actualidad* (pp. 19–45). Buenos Aires: Taurus.

Borsdorf, A. (2003). Cómo modelar el desarrollo y la dinámica de la ciudad latinoamericana. *EURE, XXIX*(86), 37–49.

Duhau, E., & Giglia, A. (2008). *Las reglas del desorden: habitar la metrópoli*. Mexico: Siglo XXI and UNAM Azcapotzalco.

Graham, S., & Marvin, S. (2001). *Splintering urbanism. Networked infrastructures, technological mobilities and the urban condition*. London and New York: Routledge.

Janoschka, M. (2002). Urbanizaciones privadas en Buenos Aires: ¿hacia un nuevo modelo de ciudad latinoamericana? In: L. F. Cabrales Barajas (Ed.), *Latinoamérica: países abiertos, ciudades cerradas* (pp. 287–318). Guadalajara, Mexico: Universidad de Guadalajara – UNESCO.

Libertun de Duren, N. R. (2007). Gated communities as a municipal development strategy. *Housing Policy Debate, 18*, 607–626.

Low, S., & Lawrence-Zuñiga, D. (2003). Locating culture. In: S. Low & D. Lawrence-Zuñiga (Eds), *The anthropology of space and place: Locating culture* (pp. 1–47). Malden, MA: Blackwell.

Nicolaides, M., & Weise, A. (Eds). (2006). *The suburb reader*. New York: Routledge.

Pírez, P. (2002). Buenos Aires: Fragmentation and privatization of the metropolitan city. *Environment and Urbanization, 14*, 145–158.

Roitman, S. (2008a). Planificación urbana y actores sociales intervinientes: el desarrollo de urbanizaciones cerradas. *Scripta Nova. Revista Electrónica de Geografía y Ciencias Sociales, XII* 270(54).

Roitman, S. (2008b). *Urban social group segregation: A gated community in Mendoza, Argentina*. PhD thesis, Unpublished. University College London, London.

Roitman, S. (2010). Gated communities: Definitions, causes and consequences. *Urban Design and Planning (ICE), 163*(DP1), 31–38.

Roitman, S., & Giglio, M. (2010). Latin American gated communities: The latest symbol of historic segregation. In: S. Bagaeen. & O. Uduku (Eds), *Gated communities: Social sustainability in contemporary and historical gated developments* (pp. 63–78). London: Earthscan.

Roitman, S., & Phelps, N. A. (2009). Does the 'closed' city contribute to the 'open city'? The recent growth of Pilar, Argentina'. *Proceedings of 10th N-AERUS conference,* Institute for Housing and Urban Development Studies, Rotterdam, The Netherlands, October 1–3, 2009.

Sabatini, F., & Cáceres, G. (2004). Los barrios cerrados y la ruptura del patrón tradicional de segregación en las ciudades latinoamericanas: el caso de Santiago de Chile. In: G. Cáceres & F. Sabatini (Eds), *Barrios Cerrados en Santiago de Chile: entre la exclusión y la integración residencial* (pp. 9–43). Santiago de Chile: Pontificia Universidad Católica de Chile – Instituto de Geografía & Lincoln Institute of Land Policy.

Sassen, S. (1994/2001). A new geography of centers and margins: Summary and implications. In: R. Le Gates & F. Stout (Eds) (2001), *Cities in a world economy* (1994); *The city reader* (2nd ed.), reimpression. London: Routledge.

Sheinbaum, D. (2010). Gated communities in Mexico City: A historical perspective. In: S. Bagaeen & O. Uduku (Eds), *Gated communities: Social sustainability in contemporary and historical gated developments* (pp. 79–91). London: Earthscan.

Thuillier, G. (2005). Gated communities in the metropolitan area of Buenos Aires, Argentina: A challenge for town planning. *Housing Studies, 20*(2), 255–271.

UN-Habitat. (2009). *Planning sustainable cities: Global report on human settlements 2009.* London: Earthscan.

Wu, F. (2005). Rediscovering the 'Gate' under market transition: From work-unit compounds to commodity housing enclaves. *Housing Studies, 20*(2), 235–254.

THE PLANNED SUBURBANIZATION OF A CITY-STATE: SINGAPORE'S NEW TOWNS

Rita Padawangi

INTRODUCTION: POWER RELATIONS AND NEW TOWNS

Discussions on the implications of power relations among the state, market, and society in urban plans and planning processes are usually centered on urban issues. Studies on suburbanization generally look at suburbs and satellite towns as "spillovers" of high density in the cities, deteriorating conditions of the innercity – particularly in the case of the United States – as well as the longing for living closer to nature. During the twentieth century, both the garden suburb and garden city movements in Britain influenced the planning of new communities overseas. The garden city movement of Ebenezer Howard, emphasizing new and attractive planned towns with their own socialisitic administration, employment, and local facilities, has strong echoes in Singapore's new towns, although the adaptation

Suburbanization in Global Society
Research in Urban Sociology, Volume 10, 293–317
Copyright © 2010 by Emerald Group Publishing Limited
All rights of reproduction in any form reserved
ISSN: 1047-0042/doi:10.1108/S1047-0042(2010)0000010015

of the concept in Singapore is more towards the physical landscapes and built greeneries rather than embracing the whole idea of the garden city.

This chapter looks at the relationship between the state, the market, and the society to analyze the formation of new towns, using Singapore as the case study. Combining archival research and field observation, this chapter looks into the lives of the communities in these new towns and sees the relevance of the experience on the ground with the relationship between the state, the market, and the society in the planning process. To do so, the chapter starts by introducing the background of the public housing program, the new town model in Singapore, and the integration between housing with other urban plans (Fig. 1). This study will review existing studies about Singapore's new towns and provide details through field observation of everyday life in selected towns and community activities within the neighborhood, and place them in the framework of power relations in society.

Fig. 1. A Typical Scene of Housing Blocks in Singapore's New Towns. Photograph taken by author.

PUBLIC HOUSING AS EMERGENCY HOUSING

Massive Renewal: The Role of the State

According to the World Urbanization Prospects by the United Nations,[1] Singapore is 100% urban. With the absence of agriculture in the country, except for a few limited farms that are far from fulfilling domestic demands, the image of Singapore as an industrialized and "modern" city has been perpetuated by various policies and tourist materials. While this is not necessarily wrong, it is not quite accurate either. Just like cities being composed of various urban neighborhoods, Singapore consists of various localities. The localities in Singapore, however, are largely controlled through a centralized planning process, which includes the creation of the new towns as part of the public housing program.

The modern Singapore started through the history of colonization, and the new towns emerged as a solution to overcrowding. Under the British rule, the island was not yet known as a city-state. Rather, the colony differentiated the "municipal area" that had clear boundaries within the Settlement of Singapore. In the first half of the twentieth century, this municipal area, which later became the city center of Singapore, was relatively overcrowded when compared with European standards. A report by the Housing Committee in 1947 shows that the average density of the municipal area of Singapore was approximately 300 persons per acre "with numbers of large blocks of houses, often back-to-back, with densities rising to 1,000 or more to the acre" (Housing Committee, 1947). The report also pointed out the dilapidated conditions of century-old shop-houses that hosted approximately 18 persons per building.

The Singapore Improvement Trust (SIT) was established through the Singapore Improvement Ordinance Bill in 1927 to provide housing for the poor (Wong & Guillot, 2005, p. 45). The focus of SIT's objectives was on quantity of housing, speed of development, cheap price, and hygiene standards. After the country obtained self-government, the Housing and Development Board (HDB) was formed in 1960, which saw the development of over 50,000 housing units in its first five years. Schools, markets, shops, clinics, and playgrounds were standard facilities for housing estates that offered low-cost flats to move people from dilapidated slum areas (Housing & Development Board, 1970). The HDB also implemented the " 'self-contained' satellite town" concept, one for each five-year phase since 1960. These new towns were relatively large-scale developments that consist of several neighborhoods.

The first satellite town was Queenstown, approximately five miles southwest of the city center. Containing mostly two-room and three-room flats, the 19,372 flats in the seven neighborhoods of this satellite town were expected to house between 150,000 and 160,000 people (Housing & Development Board, 1970). The second satellite town, Toa Payoh, was built in the second five-year program and was located five miles north of the city center. Described as "will be much more self-contained than Queenstown," Toa Payoh was to house 150,000–200,000 people in 30,000–35,000 units. Forty percent of the flats were built as one-room rental flats, and 45% were built as three-room flats for sale. The satellite town had a 40-acres town center, "aimed at providing a focal point containing all the facilities the residents needed, a place for social gathering and a point of orientation to the satellite of Toa Payoh" (Housing & Development Board, 1970, p. 35). In the design, this goal was translated into a continuous 45-foot pedestrian mall that formed a "shopping parade" to connect residents with entertainment facilities, the market, the library, and the post office. While Queenstown was connected to other parts of the island through public bus transportation services, Toa Payoh Town Center was the location of the largest bus interchange in Singapore.

Public housing development in Singapore was often termed as a nation-building project. In the early stages, the HDB had stated that the success measure of the public housing program was not only increasing home-ownership rate and the drop in crime rate but also the warding off of communist ideology from the residents of public housing estates. Clancey (2003) noted the political nature of the relocation by breaking out the social networks of the communist wing, which is also acknowledged by the HDB in their first decade report. "The final measure of Singapore's low-cost housing success is the total failure of Communist and communalist appeals to people in the Board's estates and the drop in crime" (Housing & Development Board, 1970, p. 9). This anticommunist approach, while contextual to the Cold War period, is a clear indication that there was an ideological objective in rehousing of the population, rather than just building flats.

Slum Clearance and Economic Growth

The state and the market often go hand in hand in urban development and redevelopment: while the state holds the power and authority, the market holds the capital (Lim & Padawangi, 2008, p. 308). However, the development of Singapore's new towns showed blurring boundaries between the state and the market. Since its early establishment, the HDB functioned like a "normal property company, maintaining properties and paying taxes for housing estates under its management" (Housing & Development Board, 1970). Between 1960 and 1970, there were more developments for rental flats, but homeownership flats by the HDB rapidly increased since then, because of the introduction of the CPF Public Housing Scheme, in which CPF savings[2] can be used to finance flat purchase. In addition, the housing development was also in tandem with urban renewal, which was defined as not only to improve living conditions but also to provide better employment opportunities. Once people from the cramped and dilapidated slums were moved to the new estates and satellite towns, slum clearance projects were undertaken. Thus, satellite towns were not only to form self-contained communities but also to reserve strategic central areas for economic and commercial development.

A place can only be defined by the people by attaching meanings to space. Friedmann (2008) put an emphasis on the role of the civil society in defining city spaces as places. The HDB clearly stated that the urban renewal in Singapore, namely slum clearance, was not only for "social betterment" but "also to ensure to ensure proper and speedy development of the country. Strategic and valuable slum-ridden areas in the central area must be cleared for economic development and to make possible bold planning, transportation and traffic schemes to ensure that the country can progress and expand according to plan" (Housing & Development Board, 1970).

In contrast with development of residential properties as purely profit-making endeavor by offering the homes to the open market, the establishment of the new towns in Singapore was a catalyst that was provided by the state to secure strategic spots for private sector investments. This shows a tandem between the state and the market interests as was commonly found around cities in Pacific Asia in the 1960s (Douglass, 2007), but the planned new towns of Singapore were materializations of a visibly strong role of the state. Like many urban redevelopment projects, the shifting of population to the new towns involved detaching local inhabitants from their original communities, associations, and informal networks in the city center. While this fits in the definition of "place-breaking" (Friedmann, 2008) as top-down intervention that separates urban space and society, the resettled population got housing with infrastructure services that were unavailable in the slums that were plagued by tuberculosis problems due to poor living conditions. Missing in this equation, however, was the voices of the people from the ground about their previously established communities.

As of 2010, Singapore has built in total 23 new towns. With the operation of continuously expanding mass rapid transit (MRT) system in 1987, the more recent new towns get farther away from the old city center. Tampines New Town, which won the World Habitat Awards from the Building and Social Housing Foundation of the United Nations, finished construction in 1990 and was approximately seven miles away from the city center. In more recent new towns, private sector investment becomes more obvious with the inclusion of shopping malls in the town center. Tampines currently has three malls around the MRT station; new towns Sengkang and Punggol also have one shopping mall each at the town center, and so were Bukit Batok and Yishun. Undoubtedly, these malls become spaces where residents go and shop, but the types of shops and dining places in these malls resemble more of chain brands and restaurants in the city center; they can be copied from one town to another. To use Lefebvre's framework of production of space in mapping the state–market–society relationships in the new towns, the increasingly visible commodification of space in the town centers is indication of the emerging abstract space – which prioritizes the accumulation of wealth and capital (Lefebvre, 1991 [1974]) – in the towns that were government-driven. While older town centers in Toa Payoh and Bedok feature pedestrian-friendly outdoor spaces with row of small shops on the first floor that resembles shop-house arrangement with their 6-foot walkways, currently these shops also feature chain brands, interweaving in-between local shops. More recently, shopping centers grew at the town centers, marking the visibility of private sector investments in the new towns that are known as government-initiated projects.

SOCIAL LIFE IN SINGAPORE'S NEW TOWNS

With the early flats built in one- to three-room configurations, there was drastic change to the living arrangement of the population. The "Simpson Report," written by W.J. Simpson in 1907, mentioned the shop-house as the most common type of dwelling in Singapore. The Report of the Housing Committee in 1947 stated that Singapore has been "a city of shop-houses" for "the last 100 years" (Housing Committee, 1947). The average 18 persons per building were transformed into high-rise living. Percentage households living in shop-houses had been steadily declining from 31.1% in 1966 to 12.6% in 1970 and 5.5% in 1980. Meanwhile, those living in public housing flats saw dramatic increase, from 25.4% in 1966 to 30.9% in 1970, 67.4% in 1980, and up to 86% in 2004 (Tai, 1988; Lu, 2003). A typical three-room flat consisted of two bedrooms, one bathroom, one toilet, one kitchen, and one living room, which add to a total of approximately 60 square meters. In 1984 – 20 years after the development of the first new town – the average household size was 4.4 (Tan & Phang, 1991). The estimation of resident population living in public housing flats for 2009 is 82%.[3]

In line with the role of public housing in the nation-building project, housing estates were coupled with community development programs. Liu Thai Ker, former Chief Executive Officer (CEO) of the HDB, stated in 1985 that the HDB's role in community development is inseparable from the estate management functions (Liu, 1985, p. 15). Critiques continuously came from various scholars: the loss of community occurred by relocating the residents from kampongs (urban villages and slums) into cookie-cutter high-rise buildings. Tai (1977) noted that the relocation provided better housing for the people, but the new high-rise estates could not reconstruct the community ties and human relationships in the kampongs. Through intergenerational change, however, the population may not retain the memory of dehousing and rehousing. Rather, more residents experience public housing flats as their first homes, and hence their first neighborhoods.

Using field observation and qualitative interviews with residents in public housing estates, Lu (2003) argued that residents do play a part in community life. Some of the interviewees still had nostalgia over living in a kampong as associated with togetherness, but currently residents also established informal networks and knew their neighbors; they are familiar with their surroundings and utilize common spaces such as the void decks on the first floor of the building. Nevertheless, Lu (2003) also acknowledged that the current meaning of community is different from that in the kampongs because people have wider nonlocal networks through schools, workplace, clubs, or other associations.

Social characteristics of the population in the new towns are inseparable from government policies. In March 1989, the HDB introduced the Ethnic Integration Policy, which regulates proportions of ethnic groups in a housing estate. The legislation was a response to the trend in rising proportion of similar ethnic groups in some new towns. For example, the HDB projected that in Bukit Merah Estate, without policy intervention, the proportion of the Chinese would be up from 88.4% in 1988 to 93.1% in 2000. Similarly, in Bedok New Town, the Malays would be 43% of the population in 2000, up from 24.5%, if there was no intervention. The Ethnic Integration Policy would impose quota for each ethnic group in purchasing flats, either applying for new flats to the HDB or buying resale flats from the market, so that the ethnic composition would resemble the national proportions (Ooi, Siddique & Soh, 1993), which was approximately 14.7% Malays, 77.7% Chinese, 6.3% Indians, and 1.3% other ethnicities. Ethnic groups live side by side in harmony, but preference to be closer to neighbors of similar ethnicities persists (Tai, 1988).

As transportation infrastructures developed, newer towns could be located farther away from the city center and still be connected. The developments of these new towns are results of collaborations among different government agencies. The Urban Redevelopment Authority prepares the Concept Plan, which lays out the strategic land use and transportation plan for the next 40 to 50 years and is revisited every 10 years. Besides the Concept Plan, there is also the Master Plan, which is a more detailed plan that maps the permissible land use and allowable density of developments. Inside the Master Plan, there are land use plan, landed housing areas plan, building height plan, parks and waterbodies plan, activity generating uses plan, and conservation plan. These plans are also in line with transportation plans by the Land Transport Authority and the Water Master Plan of 1972.

The new towns in Singapore, therefore, are manifestations of a slew of plans that are laid out along with national strategies. The first estates and new towns were built focusing on quantity and speed, which the HDB argued to catch up with what SIT could not fulfill. Achievements during the first decade of public housing were measured based on how many flats were built every five years. "In the first two years of this program [sic], plus 1,682 units completed in 1960, the Board had just about matched the 23,019 units completed by the SIT in 32 years" (Housing & Development Board, 1970, p. 8). Toa Payoh was the first new town that places the issue of character and image, by emphasizing the amenities provided in the town center (Teo, 1996; Housing & Development Board, 1970). After the 1980s, new towns offered more options in housing types, including five-room flats and executive apartments. Upgrading of public housing estates in after 2000 resulted in the makeover of public housing blocks – not just facades but may also involve having an additional room for each flat and balconies, depending on whether the residents concur with the proposed designs.

In newer towns, especially the "second," "third" generations onwards, which were built after 1965, a wider range of public facilities were made available, from community centers to sports halls. Besides the amenities that are provided in the town centers, neighborhood markets, shops and parks, and shared spaces on the first floors of the buildings that open chances for informal encounters, there are also formal organizations in the form of community centers and resident committees as a conscious effort to promote "neighborly interaction" (Tai, 1988, p. 129).

Informal Encounters: From Void Decks to Kopitiams

On the notice board on the first floor of Block 30, there was a colorful A4-size poster. It said "Be Responsible. Do not litter!" The poster featured a caricature of an elderly woman, patting the head of a cat that was eating a bunch of food: fish and dry food. The second frame showed a sitting area in a void deck which had empty drink bottles on its concrete table and some trash on the ground. This frame had a red X mark on it, signaling that this was not a favorable situation. The third frame showed various trashes thrown into a bin, followed by a sentence "Dispose your litter into the bins" (Padawangi, 2010a) (Fig. 2).

Except for older flats that have residents on the first floor, public housing building blocks generally keep the first floor open or reserved for public services. An open first floor is usually known as void decks, which residents

Fig. 2. Notice Board of the Town Council in One of the Building Blocks in a New Town at the East Side. Photograph taken by author.

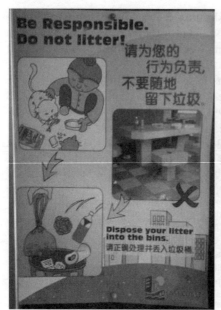

Fig. 3. Instructions on "How to be Responsible in Feeding [Stray] Cats."
Photograph taken by author.

can use for informal gatherings, or, in the case of larger void decks, for functions such as weddings and funerals. The lift lobby on the first floor has a couple of notice boards to post announcements and posters from the town council, and many posters, in fact, indicate familiar issues in the everyday life in the communities, such as littering issues, bicycle riding in corridors, fighting dengue, and energy conservation (Fig. 3).

From one of the posters on the notice board in the field note, which was a general poster produced by the East Coast Town Council, it is clear that feeding stray cats is a common phenomenon in the neighborhoods. The cats can become proxies for informal gatherings, and even shared interests with other localities through the media. Stray cats are part and parcel of life in the new towns, and the existence of stray cats becomes one of the hooks for informal encounters. It is a common sight to find one or more cats loitering around the first floor of a public housing building. The HDB prohibits residents to keep cats in the flats, although it is obvious that many do keep them as pets. For certain, not all residents like the sight of cats loitering around their neighborhoods,[4] and there were also violent acts against cats that a few of them were found dead in an estate for being thrown from above, which was condemned by the Society for the Prevention of Cruelty to Animals (SPCA). So far, there is no regulation against stray cats, but residents can file complaints to have them taken.

The stray cats are not the only reason to have informal encounters. The first floors of public housing flats are usually provided with fixed seats and tables, and these spaces are often used for informal chats. From a regular observation at a neighborhood in Bedok New Town, these spaces are used almost every day. Interestingly, observations in various estates show that most of the residents who utilize these spaces are considerably senior. This is also the case at a neighborhood in Toa Payoh New Town:

> It was about 2.30 pm on a Sunday afternoon. The same group of women, most of them seem to be above 50 years, were sitting on the first floor of Block 53. There were eight of them altogether. They were chatting in a Chinese dialect, which I could not understand. However, they were very animated in their conversation and their voices could be heard from at least 10 meters before. They did not only utilize the benches provided on the first floor, but they also use chairs. I was sure that they brought their own chairs, or at least some of them who reside on the first floor could provide those chairs. (Padawangi, 2008)

However, it may be too early and skewed to assume that the youths are not as involved in the community compared with the previous generations. The older generation may have spent more time in the neighborhood, thus become more attached and familiar with fellow residents. Ooi (2004) cited a survey of the use of public spaces that found void decks as the most popular gathering space in more established precincts, but not so much in newer estates, because the older ones were designed more to serve multiple purposes such as weddings, funerals, and activities by the grassroots organizations.

The new towns are also designed following the "precinct" concept, in which a few blocks are designed as a neighborhood with shared facilities such as children's playground. Although a survey of residents in the 1990s found that residents did not identify the identity and character of the new town based on precincts (Teo, 1996), these shared facilities do become places of informal encounters. Playgrounds are facilities for children in the neighborhood; typically, they are equipped with playground slide and jungle gym. Especially on weekends, the playground becomes a place to meet with others. The playground increases opportunities for children to meet with neighbors as well as for their parents or grandparents who were waiting for them to meet with other custodians. The caregivers, however, are not only immediate family members but may well be domestic helpers, who are often part of the households in Singapore, especially those with both parents working full time.

Informal community life in Singapore is inseparable from the *kopitiams*. Historically, *kopitiams* had been part of the everyday lives of migrant workers in colonial Singapore. "*Kopitiam* culture is part of an everyday lifestyle that cuts across all class and ethnic backgrounds and in outlets that range from upmarket chains in the city center to the quiet neighborhood *kopitiam* in the heartland" (Lai, 2010, p. 22). The word *kopitiam* itself means "coffee shop" in *Hokkien*,[5] respectively. Historically, these were informal food stalls with strong ethnic dimension in terms of the food and the patronage. It was a place to go not only to eat and drink but also to meet and chat with friends and build fraternities.

In the past, *kopitiams* also became places to get information. Lai (2010) noted the subscription of *kopitiams* to the *Rediffusion* channel, the first commercial and cable-transmitted radio station in the island, to attract customers. *Kopitiams* also installed televisions when they became affordable in the 1960s and 1970s.

Along with the resettlement of people from the central area to the new towns – known to locals as heartlands – the centrality of *kopitiams* in the everyday life is also transferred. *Kopitiams* are available at town centers and street corners. They are no longer informal street stalls but have been incorporated into formal establishments, in which stallholders would pay rent to the HDB or the management. Current *kopitiams* in the new towns now tend to feature foods from mixed ethnicities; much of this is attributed to the government's emphasis on "racial harmony" in promoting community life.

Town centers can also feature large-scale food centers. Bedok New Town, for example, has a large "cooked food center" with at least a hundred different food stalls, ranging from drink stalls, Chinese food, Indian food, and snacks. However, smaller coffee shops at the ground level and corner of housing blocks feature a different atmosphere. While the large-scale centers are located near big crowds at the center, the corner coffee shops usually feature more or less 10 stalls. These places feature smoking and nonsmoking areas; the smoking area being underneath an extension tent beyond the building. Patrons of *kopitiams* vary – they can be the whole family, a group of friends, or neighborhood residents who just order take-away food. The sports game playing on the television screen – usually football matches – shows that *kopitiams* are also places for people to hang out with friends and watch the games. This was obvious during the World Cup 2010 season, when two cable television providers were criticized for setting high price for the World Cup packages. Comments from "heartlanders" published in a local newspaper show that many prefer to skip the subscription, because

Fig. 4. A Busy *kopitiam* During the World Cup 2010 Season, which Shows Men as the Majority Patrons. Photograph taken by author.

they could easily go downstairs and watch the World Cup matches at the *kopitiam*[6] (Fig. 4).

The *kopitiam* model in the new towns indicates the adoption of historically familiar settings into the planned communities. The building blocks are massive and standardized, and there are specific guidelines on the facilities to be provided in the precincts. However, residents interpret and redefine spaces to become their own places. They utilize common spaces for informal gatherings. For example, a group of senior men gather every late afternoon at the side of the *kopitiam* at Block 26 in one of the precincts in Bedok New Town, chatting in Chinese dialect while smoking and drinking beer. The gatherings become more intense during special seasons such as the football World Cup that occurs only once in four years. These informal gatherings are common and homogeneous throughout various new towns. Yet, they also make each precinct special, particularly for the residents.

CENTRALIZED PLANNING AND FORMAL ENCOUNTERS

Architectural Designs and Social Interactions

Community life in Singapore is more than just a set of informal interactions. As pointed out by a 87-year-old male resident at Bedok New Town: "This is a great neighborhood. You have a market nearby ... not just one, but a few. You need food, you can just go down. Most important, if you have children, there are a lot of schools around." The conscious efforts to form communities in these *tabula rasa* developments are institutional as much as communal.

As stated in the *Public Housing Design Handbook*: "HDB is not building housing estates but towns and 'cities' because of the high densities involved and the comprehensive nature of the development" (Housing & Development Board, Architectural Department, 1995, p. 1). Buildings and towns are designed to be "a place that is pleasant and people-oriented"; and the HDB stated that designing public housing "is synonymous with creating communities" (Housing & Development Board, Architectural Department, 1995, p. 11). The design of new towns is comprised of precincts that cover 400–600 dwelling units each. Each precinct has common facilities that include car park, playground, void deck, and covered communal spaces.

On July 12, 1989, the then National Development Minister S. Dhanabalan announced a massive plan to renovate public housing blocks. Known as the "upgrading program," the renovation aimed to "add quality and distinctiveness to estates which are now uniform."[7] Spanning over 15 years, the program covers improvements inside flats, within each building block, and on the precinct level. These upgrading programs, especially the move to restrict access by nonresidents to public areas in the blocks, aim "to create small communities with a distinct sense of identity, ownership and belonging, so community ties in each neighborhood will be stronger and residents will not feel compelled to move out in order to upgrade."[8] The upgrading program, therefore, officially marks the shift from housing for emergency needs to increasing satisfaction.

Narratives on the upgrading program mostly linked the quality of apartments, buildings, and spaces between buildings to community involvement. Minister Dhanabalan also stated "The upgrading program will do more than give a facelift to old blocks. It should bring about a complete change in the perception of public housing."[9] Mr. Tan Soo Khoon, a member of parliament (MP) for Brickworks GRC[10] in 1989, expressed that senior citizens were left behind after the next generation moved out from the estates. "We find it hard to recruit young blood to run the grassroots organizations here."[11] A commentary on *The Straits Times* on July 14, 1989 pointed the weakness of the old estates as "large faceless estate" and monotonous, and it was important that the upgrading program give some "measure of distinctiveness."[12]

In these upgrading programs, the HDB consulted the residents on whether or not they would agree to the renovation, especially when it includes alterations to the interior of the apartment. The residents would be presented with the design and had to cast votes whether they agreed. The renovation would only take place when the majority voted for it because the upgrading program would also require residents to pay. The then Prime Minister Lee Kuan Yew said that the town councils should provide "community leadership" to help residents choose the models and designs in the upgrading program.[13] The upgrading program shows that there was room for the civil society to convey their preferences, and the objective of the renovations was related with community development. Yet, the forms of participation in this program had been structured by the state, and the call for town councils to become community leaders was an indication on how the state places itself vis-à-vis the society.

The physical looks of the buildings, however, are not the most effective elements to strengthen the character and the identity of new towns. A survey in two new towns in 1996 showed that residents did not perceive precinct design and flat design as rendering uniqueness (Teo, 1996). They are more likely to identify their towns from the town centers and the parks. In 1983, Singapore's well-known architect William Lim wrote:

> I have mixed feelings about the Bedok New Town Center. The intimate scale of low-rise buildings, the introduction of pedestrian shopping, the plants and landscape, the informal atmosphere, the roofed wet-market, the food centre, the restaurants and traditional coffee shops and the spaces allocated for informal activities contribute towards a busy and responsive centre for the community. A park is located immediately adjoining the shopping centre. So is the Area Office for residents and the large bus interchange. Like many places of this nature, it lacks focal points and the buildings are not great works of architecture. (Lim, 1983, p. 7)

The hustle and bustle of Bedok New Town Center still goes on until today, almost 30 years after Lim's comment, although there is not much change to the architecture except for a new entry sign and accessible landscaping. While architecture design is important to enhance quality of life, the heart of the community life in the new towns lies within the allocation of spaces for informal gatherings. As also reiterated by observations in this study, Ooi (2004, p. 109) noted that the most frequently used spaces are nearby shops, fresh food market, coffee shops, and hawker centers, which are not consciously planned to encourage social interaction. Design plays a role in social interaction, which is most obvious in the provision of void decks that can cater for informal chats. In a way, standardized designs help in promoting these interactions by ensuring the availability of spaces. Nevertheless, the impact of design on social interaction is limited into encouraging people to use the space. In regard to whether they use the space and how they use the space is left to the people on how they would define and redefine the common spaces.

The homogeneity of Singapore's new towns is obvious from the looks of the built environments. Chua (1996) stated that homogeneity reduces inequality as a desirable outcome. However, these standardized precincts and towns impose limits to interpretations of space and how people could redefine them. As previously discussed, the role of Singapore government in the creation of new towns was considerably strong, and there was very little space for the public to convey their interests and opinions about public spaces they would like to see. These planned precincts and blocks were facilitating spaces for informal encounters of the residents, but the informal encounters were framed by the availability of spaces.

People's Association and Community Life

The formal community life in Singapore is inseparable from the establishment of community centers and the political party. Immediately after World War II, community centers were developed purely for recreational purposes. The People's Association (PA) was set up on July 1, 1960 to draw the different communal groups to meet and unite the diverse population. Participation in recreational, social, and educational activities was viewed as potential means to unite different racial, language, religious, and cultural groups and to promote community leadership, which were the main objectives of the PA. No less than 115 community clubs, water venture, or People's Association Organization spread throughout the island. These centers often offer facilities such as badminton and tennis courts in multipurpose halls, basketball courts, and table tennis rooms. Some centers even have health and fitness rooms, music rooms, and computer rooms.

> I agree with your Chairman [of the Home Owners' Association] that a Residents' Association like yours is "an essential pillar of social life." Undoubtedly, the principle of co-operation must be applied to any group of men living together, however small the group may be. But what we should aim at is more than just co-operation and mutual tolerance; we need to develop a sense of community even within a housing estate. You need to make people feel a sense of belonging and a sense of commitment to the welfare of all while living closely together. It must, in the course of time, develop this community spirit among the residents, and once this spirit becomes a reality, then you can have a rich and meaningful community life. Without this spirit, living together in a housing estate can be **a sterile, tedious and sometimes even unpleasant experience**. (Mr. Chan Chee

Seng, Senior Parliamentary Secretary to the Ministry of Social Affairs, 30 October 1972, emphasis added)[14]

The formal community activities are arranged more by the PA and not the HDB. Besides the "hardware" facilities that are regulated through the design handbook of public housing buildings and blocks, the "software" of formal community life consists of government-based community organizations (Tai, 1988, p. 138). The PA, also a statutory board on the same level as the HDB, was established on July 1, 1960, with the aim to "promote racial harmony and social cohesion."[15] Currently, the HDB website calls for volunteering for the community to be a "good neighbor," and provides a link to the PA website for more information on how to be a grassroots volunteer.[16] The PA defines the vision for the community as "a great home and a caring community, where we share our values, pursue our passions, fulfill our hopes, and treasure our memories" through building and bridging communities "in achieving One People, One Singapore."[17] The community centers still offer recreation facilities, and the grassroots organizations that conduct activities in the centers function as a link between the government and the people.[18]

Interestingly, the story about new towns in Singapore is dominated by the narratives about public housing and the role of the central government, although there are also private housing options in Singapore. For public housing residents, there are Residents' Committees (RCs) under the PA as organizers of community activities and as means of communication to and from the government, namely the People's Action Party.[19] The RCs started in 1978 "to promote neighborliness, racial harmony and community cohesiveness amongst residents within their respective RC zones in HDB estates."[20] In 1988 there are 249 RCs, and in 2010 the number has grown to 556.[21] The RC offices are usually located in the first floor of a public housing building in the zone. Later, in June 1998, the PA formed Neighborhood Committees (NCs) to cover residents in private housing estates, and in 2010 there are already 106 NCs.[22]

The strong role of the government in the PA, which is a formal institution meant to foster community building in Singapore, has resulted in the withering of traditional clans and associations in the former settlements. "The disruption of the old type of institutions has caused some strain and problems of adjustment to the public housing residents in Singapore" (Tai, 1988, p. 141), especially in its early establishment. Some of the functions of the traditional organizations have been replaced by government-based community organizations (Tai, 1988, p. 141), which indicate a strong role of the state, even in the establishment of civil society groups. From this perspective, even the grassroots organizations in the new town communities are pseudostate due to their closeness to the state actors. By constitution, the chairman of the PA Board is always the Prime Minister. Although the Prime Minister only attends the board meeting once every year, the Deputy Chairman, who is more involved in the activities and attends meetings at least once a month, is also a minister. The rest of the board members consist of eight appointees by the Prime Minister, and four elected members from the 83 corporate members of the PA.[23]

Through an interview with a representative of the PA, the institution is aware of some skepticism about its community-building mission due to its closeness to the government.[24] Nevertheless, as the representative reiterates, the PA takes pride in its function as a bridge between the people and the government, including facilitating events in which new public policies are explained by government people who are involved in the making. RC meetings also often involve representatives from the government or state apparatuses such as the police to hear about safety concerns from the residents.

The formal and informal divide of social encounters in the new towns becomes increasingly obscure when it comes to the interest groups under the PA. The PA mobilizes volunteers, which reach over 30,000 grassroots leaders in mid-2010, to form informal interest groups within their communities. The fluidity of these interest groups makes them similar to the purely informal encounters, for they could become anything from organized sports games to afternoon chats in the void decks or *kopitiams*. The difference is on the presence of one or more grassroots leaders as the catalyst of these informal groups. The structure of the PA goes all the way from the 84 Citizens' Consultative Commitees (CCCs) as an "apex body" that coordinates all the activities under each constituency to the RCs and the Community Center Management Committees that manages community centers and their activities.

Although it is challenging to count all the volunteers in grassroots activities, the PA still has an organized flow of communication channel to the grassroots. A reflection of this organization is in holding community events. Among various community events, usually the grassroots would be involved to celebrate the anniversary of the constituency. The scale of the event can range widely from a local dinner to a large-scale show.

After showing my ticket, my hosts and I were given program sheets and we entered the field. There were structures covering the whole field with theatre-style seats on each side

of the stage. We took seats at a row that directly faced the stage. On the left, I saw
swarms of people in red shirts taking their seats. It turned out that our seating area was
for the "white shirt" group – but none of us wore white. There were center seats reserved
for "VIP"; these were those that directly in front of the stage – seats with the best view.
I started wondering who the VIPs were. I looked at my ticket and found out that the
Guest of Honor for that night was the Prime Minister himself. (Padawangi, 2010b)

In the above event, before the arrival of the Prime Minister the shows
were not exactly like what was stated in the program. Most of the shows
were sing-along with various community groups that went together on the
stage. Each group consisted of at least 30 people on the stage and the songs
they sang were printed in the program sheets. The groups keep changing
every 10 minutes or so, but many of the songs were similar – each group
performed songs from each ethnic group – approximately one English song,
two to three Chinese songs, one Tamil song, and one Malay song.
Interestingly, the Tamil and Malay songs were the same whichever group
performed, although the Chinese songs were different. After the Prime
Minister arrived at 8 pm, the show went exactly as stated in the program
sheets, and the sing-alongs repeated the songs that were sung before the
Prime Minister arrived. The sing-alongs before became preparations for
the audience to get themselves familiar with the songs when they sang with
the Prime Minister.

The idea for the June event came out in February of the year and the
preparation activities started in March 2010. The formal sense of
community life was obvious in the event, as the song and the shows were
selected to represent a lively community and racial harmony. The example
of the constituency anniversary above shows that a community event could
become quite formal, especially when there were national-level guests with
many protocols to follow.

Despite the conscious effort to encourage volunteering and participation
in various activities, the rate of community participation in organized
activities in the new towns is generally low. The sample household survey
in 1998 shows that the only 13.2% of respondents participated in
institutionalized community activities in the past 12 months (Housing &
Development Board, Research and Planning Department, 2000, p. 72) This
was a decrease from five years before when the rate was 17.8%.[25] In 1998,
the most activities participated are those organized by committees and
associated activities, followed by festivals/holidays and residents' committee
activities. The sample household survey indicates that activities such as
tours and excursions were also well received (11%) and was popular among
the elderly and housewives. Older residents tend to participate more in

community activities, but the reason is mostly because of time availability. Moreover, the younger people who participate in the workforce are usually part of multiple social groups, more than just based on their localities.

CONCLUSION: NEW TOWNS AS MANIFESTATIONS OF POWER RELATIONS

Contrary to the general trend in developing countries where suburban areas are results of urban sprawl, Singapore's "suburbs" or "new towns" are parts of a centralized plan. In the Southeast Asian region, many capital cities became mega-urban regions that are composed of several municipalities. Metro Manila in the Philippines consists of 17 municipalities.[26] Jakarta in Indonesia also experienced urban sprawl. New towns in Jakarta, such as the Bumi Serpong Damai and Lippo Karawaci, were built by private developers as a tool to make profit out of the property boom. Because of the strong hold of the market in the creation of these towns as well as the development of the suburbs, these new towns were built to capitalize on the housing demand.

In the Singapore case, there was housing demand in the beginning of the new town developments, and the demands continued to rise along with the growth of the economy and the population. Nevertheless, the new town development is not only about housing the population, but, as had been noted by various scholars such as Wong and Yeh (1985), Chua (1996, 1998), and Ooi (2004), is part of a larger nation-building project. As opposed to new towns as private, market-driven communities, the narrative of new towns in Singapore is about public housing. The experience in Singapore shows that, instead of being a container for spillover effect of economic growth in the city, new towns are strategies to direct the growth and hence are materialization of the strong role of the state in the production of urban space. Despite Singapore's centralized planning, new towns are places to decentralize the population. However, the role of the market is still visible in many aspects, from rising property prices to the malling of town centers.

New towns in Singapore are highly planned, not only in terms of the location, size, density, and building types but also about the ethnic characteristics and organized social activities. The state also regulates the ethnic composition of residents in public housing, and more recently, the composition of citizen and noncitizen owners of the flats. Although private housing is available in Singapore and is also an option for the people to reside in, the affordability of public housing and the sense of belonging to the neighborhood make the public housing estates continuously an attractive choice for a first home. Despite the lack of participation in community activities, residents still develop a sense of belonging in their estates. This is partly because informal encounters are still strong in these standardized precincts.

At the same time, although the narratives about new towns in Singapore are dominated by public housing, the concept of new town development itself was pushed by the view of clearing strategic sites for commercial development. Chua (1998) noted that the public housing system in Singapore is a "mixed decommodification with market": decommodification in terms of the monopoly of the HDB and the removal of land from the market. New towns that are located farther and farther from the city center also serve for the commodification of the area in the central city for commercial use.[27] Urban renewal was idealized as a "joint partnership between private entrepreneurs and the Government" (Housing & Development Board, 1970, p. 59). Hence, the private sector is a key player during the development of the new towns. The position that the state put them in development plan had contributed to the strategy of decentralization of population.

The Singapore case also shows that new towns may not necessarily be considerably far from the central city. New towns in Singapore are cities within a city. This may be comparable to ethnic enclaves or community areas in a city, but when centrally planned as new towns, there are standardized amenities and facilities. Moreover, the town centers can develop as pedestrian-friendly areas without being disrupted by vehicular movements. They facilitate people to congregate, walk about, as well as to have temporary markets and festivals.

Because of the standardization of the amenities, there had been "homogenization of lifestyle" as was identified by Chua (1996) as reducing inequality. Despite the homogenized social and design characteristics, these are still neighborhoods that residents can identify with and develop a sense of belonging. Although they are results of government-driven plans, these towns show the existence of informal networks and encounters that can potentially support a lively community. The layout of the precincts may be similar because it follows the same design template, but the residents articulate the spaces to make it their own, albeit limited by standardized physical features. The physical qualities of the buildings contribute to the level of satisfaction about the living condition, as was seen in the upgrading program, but the sense of belonging is mostly contributed by the liveliness of the neighborhood.

This shows the resilience of the communities in forming networks, but the continuously strong presence of the state in the development of the new towns as well as the community organizations makes the institutionalized social activities relatively standardized and yet again leads to the homogeneity of the new towns.

As the Singapore case has demonstrated, analyzing the suburbanization phenomenon is inseparable from examining the state–market–society power relationships. The nature of the power relations would determine the nature of the new towns. When suburbanization and new town developments are driven by the private sector as the developers of the properties, they are often results of lack of planning control by the local government or the state. In Singapore, the new towns are the results of highly planned development. It does not mean that the private sector is diminished in the property market, but the allocation of land is regulated by the government. The central role of the state also paves the way for a formal and centralized community organization to go hand in hand with these new towns, which was rooted in the concern of centralizing political participation and channeling residents' concerns. As seen in the process, the private housing was not as central in this formal community involvement. Comparably, new towns that are developed by the private sector would not have such priorities as the main goal of the development would be to make profit out of the property market. Nevertheless, the triangle of state–market–society is still the prevalent discourse of new towns in Singapore, and, despite the distinct model that Singapore's new towns show against market-driven towns in the region, it is still the state–market tandem that dominates the developments.

NOTES

1. World Urbanization Prospects: The 2007 Revision Population Database, http://esa.un.org/unup/, accessed June 15, 2010.

2. CPF stands for Central Provident Fund. The CPF Board collects a fraction of citizens' and residents' incomes to be put in the each individual CPF savings account, which can be used as retirement funds.

3. Housing Development Board (2009).

4. *The New Paper* on June 9, 2010 featured a letter from a reader, which stated he was disturbed by the mess that cat feeders make on the void decks. Two letters from readers were published on June 15, 2010 on the same paper as responses, in which they appreciate the existence of the cats as means to make people appreciate animals.

5. *Hokkien* is a Chinese dialect.

6. *The New Paper*, June 10, 2010.

7. *The Straits Times.* (1989). Housing Board to transform its estates. *The Straits Times*, July 12.

8. Minister S. Dhanabalan, as quoted by *The Straits Times.*

9. *The Straits Times.* (1989). Upgrading of old HDB estates can make the young stay. *The Straits Times*, July 24.

10. GRC is "Group Representation Constituency."

11. *The Straits Times.* (1989). Upgrading of old HDB estates can make the young stay. *The Straits Times*, July 24.

12. *The Straits Times.* (1989). People make communities. *The Straits Times*, July 14.

13. *The Straits Times.* (1989). PM outlines two major tasks for councilors. *The Straits Times*, July 2.

14. Speech by Mr. Chan Chee Seng, Senior Parliamentary Secretary to the Ministry of Social Affairs, at the Inaugural Meeting and Dinner of the Syed Alwi Road HDB Home Owners' Association, Monday, October 30, 1972.

15. http://www.pa.gov.sg/about-us.html, accessed June 14, 2010.

16. HDB InfoWeb. How Can We Be Good Neighbours. Heartland Beat: Be A Good Neighbour (http://www.hdb.gov.sg/fi10/fi10333p.nsf/w/GNBeGdNeighbour? OpenDocument, accessed June 14, 2010)

17. http://www.pa.gov.sg/about-us.html, accessed June 14, 2010.

18. The board of the People's Association is chaired by the Prime Minister.

19. The functions of RCs are to

- promote neighbourliness, harmony, and cohesiveness amongst residents;
- liaise with and make recommendations to government authorities on the needs and aspirations of residents;
- disseminate information and gather feedback on government policies and actions from residents; and
- promote good citizenship amongst residents. (onePA website, http://www. pa.gov.sg/our-network/grassroots-organisations/residents-committees.html, accessed June 11 2010)

20. http://www.pa.gov.sg/our-network/grassroots-organisations/residents-committees.html, accessed June 14, 2010.

21. Figure obtained from People's Association, as of June 15, 2010.

22. Figure obtained from People's Association, as of June 15 2010.

23. Corporate members consist of various institutions in the country, which include, among all, academic guilds, cultural and educational organizations, and sports associations.

24. In Seah's writing in 1973, *Community Centres in Singapore: Their Political Involvement*, it was argued that after the first election in 1959 when the People's Action Party (PAP) won convincingly, the party viewed these centers as "potential institutions of political support" when there were more centers constructed throughout the island (Seah, 1973, p. 16). The PA, however, does not allow party political activities in its events or on its premises. The facilities and grassroots network are used to explain and gain feedback on government programs.

25. Housing & Development Board, Research and Planning Department (1995).

26. With the differentiation between terms "city" and "municipality" in the Philippines, Metro Manila is often referred as consisting of 16 cities and 1 municipality.

27. "Hence, slum clearance and Urban Renewal in Singapore must be undertaken not only for social betterment, but also to ensure proper and speedy development of the country. Strategic and valuable slum-ridden areas in the Central Area must be cleared for economic development and to make possible bold planning, transportation and traffic schemes to ensure that the country can progress and expand according to plan" (Housing & Development Board, 1970, p. 59).

ACKNOWLEDGMENT

The author wishes to thank the People's Association, Ms. Liew Yihui Andrea, Mr. Lim Weida, Ms. Yanchun Ong, Ms. Divya Sunder Ramchand, Ms. Liyana Suradi, and Ms. Chong Su Li for their support in providing information to affirm findings from field observation.

REFERENCES

Chua B. H. (1996). *Private ownership of public housing in Singapore*. Working Paper No. 63. Asia Research Centre, Murdoch University, Perth, Australia.

Clancey, G. (2003). *Toward a spatial history of emergency: Notes from Singapore*. Asia Research Institute Working Paper Series No. 8, August 2003. Available at http://www.ari.nus.edu.sg/pub/wps.htm

Douglass, M. (2007). The globalization of capital cities: Civil society, The neoliberal state and the re-construction of urban space in Pacific Asia. In: M. Hsiao & K. C. Ho (Eds), *Capital cities in Asia Pacific: Primacy and diversity*. Taipei: Academia Sinica, Monograph series.

Friedmann, J. (2008). Reflections on place and place-making in the cities of China. *International Journal of Urban and Regional Research, 32*(1), 257–279.

Housing Committee. (1947). *Report of the housing committee*. Singapore: Government Printing Office.

Housing & Development Board. (1970). *First decade in public housing: 1960–1969*. Singapore: Housing & Development Board.

Housing & Development Board. (2009). *Because We Care ...: HDB Annual Report 2008/2009*. Singapore: Housing & Development Board. Available at http://www.hdb.gov.sg/fi10/fi10221p.nsf/0/d4a0f107613b79944825766200236310/$file/index.html. Accessed on June 15, 2010.

Housing & Development Board, Architectural Department. (1995). *Public housing design handbook*. Singapore: Housing & Development Board.

Housing & Development Board, Research and Planning Department. (1995). *Social aspects of public housing in Singapore: Kinship ties and neighbourly relations*. Singapore: Housing & Development Board.

Housing & Development Board, Research and Planning Department. (2000). *Social aspects of public housing in Singapore: Kinship ties and neighbourly relations*. Singapore: Housing & Development Board.

Lai, A. E. (2010). *The Kopitiam in Singapore: An evolving story about migration and cultural diversity*. Asia Research Institute Working Paper Series No. 132, January 2010. Available at www.ari.nus.edu.sg/pub/wps.htm

Lefebvre, H. (1991 [1974]). *The production of space*. Oxford: Blackwell.

Lim, W. S. W. (1983). *Public housing and community development: The Singapore experience*. Singapore: Mimar, Architecture in Development.

Lim, M., & Padawangi, R. (2008). Contesting Alun-alun: Power relations, identities and the production of urban space in Bandung, Indonesia. *International Development Planning Review, 30*(3).

Liu, T. K. (1985). Overview. In: A. K. Wong & S. H. K. Yeh (Eds), *Housing a nation: 25 years of public housing in Singapore*. Singapore: Housing & Development Board.

Lu, Y. T. (2003). *Everyday living in pigeon holes: An investigation of community in public housing, academic exercise*. Singapore: Department of Geography, Faculty of Arts and Sciences, National University of Singapore.

Ooi, G. L. (2004). *Future of space: Planning, space and the city*. Singapore: Institute of Policy Studies, Eastern Universities Press.

Ooi, G. L., Siddique, S., & Soh, K. C. (1993). *The management of ethnic relations in public housing estates*. Singapore: The Institute of Policy Studies, Times Academic Press.

Padawangi, R. (2008). Field Notes from observation in Toa Payoh New Town, April 13.

Padawangi, R. (2010a). Field Notes from observation in Bedok New Town, June 1.

Padawangi, R. (2010b). Field Notes from Bukit Timah 55th Anniversary Celebration: Hand in Hand, June 19.

Seah, C. M. (1973). *Community centres in Singapore: Their political involvement*. Singapore: Singapore University Press.

Tai, C. L. (1977). *Life and living environment in kampongs and HDB public housing estates in Singapore*. Singapore: Institute of Humanities and Social Sciences, College of Graduate Studies, Nanyang University.

Tai, C. L. (1988). *Housing policy and high-rise living*. Singapore: Chopmen.

Tan, A. H. H., & Phang, S. Y. (1991). *The Singapore experience in public housing*. Singapore: Centre for Advance Studies, National University of Singapore, Times Academic Press.

Teo, S. E. (1996). Character and identity in Singapore new towns: Planner and resident perspectives. *Habitat International, 20*(2), 279–294.

Wong, A. K., & Yeh, S. H. K. (Eds). (1985). *Housing a nation: 25 years of public housing in Singapore*. Singapore: Housing & Development Board.

Wong, T. C., & Guillot, X. (2005). *A roof over every head: Singapore's housing policy between state monopoly and privatisation*. Bangkok, Thailand: Sampark.

WEBSITES

http://www.pa.gov.sg
http://www.hdb.gov.sg

BUILDING FOR WHAT AND WHOM? NEW TOWN DEVELOPMENT AS PLANNED SUBURBANIZATION IN CHINA AND INDIA[☆]

Lan Wang, Ratoola Kundu and Xiangming Chen

ABSTRACT

The new town concept originated from the ideal city model of Ebenezer Howard and expanded from Europe to America in the 1900s. It has reemerged as a site for accommodating population from highly dense urban centers of China and India since the early twenty-first century. The massive infusion of public and private investments has enabled the emergence of new towns in China and India as planned centers of world-class residential, commercial, and work spaces. The rational goal of de-densifying the crowded central cities can lead to a more balanced distribution and use of resources across the metropolitan regions with more spacious housing for the growing middle class in China and India. Yet it is a relatively small number of the wealthy and mobile people who

[☆] Lan Wang's research for this paper was supported by the Program for Young Excellent Talents in Tongji University.

Suburbanization in Global Society
Research in Urban Sociology, Volume 10, 319–345
ISSN: 1047-0042/doi:10.1108/S1047-0042(2010)0000010016

have turned out to be beneficiaries of the mostly high-end housing and well-developed transport infrastructure that evokes social and economic polarizations and political contestations. In this chapter, we will examine: (1) how these top-down planned and developed new towns have reshaped the urbanization process of the megacities in India and China, (2) the socio-spatial influence of these settlements on the central city as well as the surrounding rural areas, and (3) the expected and actual spatial users (both old and new residents) of the new towns? We address these questions by organizing two pairs of cases in a systematic framework: Anting New Town and Thames Town in Shanghai, China and Rajarhat New Town and the Kolkata West International City (KWIC) near Kolkata, India.

INTRODUCTION

New town development is often, but not exclusively, associated with the general and broad process of suburbanization. A new town is a planned community typically constructed in a previously undeveloped area. Conceived as a necessary instrument of planned and balanced urbanization in the metropolitan area, a new town can function as a new economic growth pole and a magnet or destination for investments and population that may spill from a nearby metropolitan center. In the long wake of new town development in Western industrialized countries, new town development has been catching up with a vengeance in rapidly urbanizing and industrializing countries like China and India in recent years. In fact, new town development in China and India has taken on even more striking dimensions and consequences given the scale of their large cities, the latter's accelerated suburban spread, and the strong local penetration of global capital. It is therefore timely and instructive to offer a comparative study of new town development, and its intended and unintended outcomes, as they are being shaped by the historical conjuncture of contexts and conditions just mentioned.

New town development in China and India is not omnipresent and uniform across all cities and regions. Instead it has been happening most prominently and intensively around the dominant megacities like Shanghai and Kolkata. Within the different regulatory frameworks, land ownership and planning regimes in China versus India, both Shanghai and Kolkata governments have initiated similar new town programs at their fringes to accelerate suburbanization – promoting urban development in suburban areas. This chapter investigates decision making in the planning process, the purposed and targeted population, the actual spatial users and the socio-spatial influence of new urban townships in Shanghai and Kolkata. The globally oriented new towns in Shanghai, for instance, Thames Town in Songjiang New City and Anting New Town in the Shanghai International Automobile City, exacerbate social segregation in a form of gated community and generate inequity between spatial users of new towns and the surrounding residents. As one of the largest state-regulated planned township project, Rajarhat New Town outside Kolkata provides world-class amenities and high-end commercial housing to the professionals working in the IT sectors with global connection contrasts sharply against the local poor, while the KWIC completely funded by foreign companies is planned as a large-scale gated community with global standards of comfort and quality of life. This type of planned suburbanization changes the urban landscape, redistributes the regional resource, and extends globalization's impact to new and larger local territories.

Large population and high population density in megacities are two unavoidable realities of urbanization in China and India. The permanent population of Shanghai reached 19.2 million at the end of 2009, while it also attracted more than 6 million floating workers from rural areas all around China. The urbanization rate of Shanghai reached 86.8 percent in 2006, ranking No. 1 in China (China International Urbanization Strategy Research Committee, 2007). Urbanization in the suburban area of Shanghai has contributed to this high rate. The so-called "One City, Nine Towns" plan initiated by the local state in 2000 has dramatically reshaped the landscape of the suburban area of Shanghai after 10 years since its launch. Ten small townships were identified for each suburban districts of Shanghai metropolis among the proposed 140 towns at the inception of the twenty-first century (see Fig. 1). The 10 new towns serve as pilot projects to execute a top-down suburbanization model. Initiated by the former Mayor Liangyu Chen, the development of new towns in Shanghai has financially and administratively supported by the metropolitan government. The state has dominated in the process of urban design, land acquisition, and infrastructure construction in a mechanism of semipublic new town development corporations. These large-scale human settlements plug in the original landscape, relocate local residents, and reconfigure the spatial relationship between the central city and the suburbs.

In India, a national policy has been announced to promote the growth of 100 new towns of one-million target population by the year 2020. As the oldest and the third largest metropolis in India after Mumbai and Delhi, Kolkata started its large-scale new town program in the early 1990s to

Fig. 1. Locations of the Ten New Towns of Shanghai. *Source:* Chen, Wang, and Kundu (2009).

decentralize the crowded core municipal area with dilapidated infrastructure. Rajarhat New Town and the KWIC are two of the new towns located at the fringe of Kolkata (see Fig. 2). The new towns are conceived either as a new residential enclave with job opportunities to create an economic growth pole of IT industry and to ease the increasing pressure of urbanization in megacities or planned as a large-scale gated community with global standard housing and amenities to attract high-income and upwardly mobile population. The fringes of Kolkata have informal settlements to accommodate floating population working in informal economic sectors. The planned new towns, providing modern infrastructure and Western-style high rise apartment housing, contrast sharply against these urban informal settlements as well as the rural settlements in the fringes. These new towns are planned on greenfields, thus impacting farmers and their agriculture-based lifestyle adversely. Often, the boundaries of planned new town developments infringe upon the existing formal and informal settlements that have been built over time in the peripheral areas (see Fig. 3). It can be said that the current rapid urbanization of the peripheral reaches of Kolkata paves its way through numerous social and spatial conflicts with the formation of planned new towns.

The original new town model, known as the Garden City created by Sir Ebenezer Howard in the United Kingdom in 1898, has influenced urban development in Europe and America since the early 1900s. The Garden City was planned to be self-contained community surrounded by greenbelts and composed of residential, industrial, and agricultural sections. Howard idealized this type of new towns had capacities to decrease downtown population, to capture both the advantages of artificial and natural environments, and to promote equity between urban and rural areas as well as among the ones living in new towns. The townships called Letchworth and Welwyn at the periphery of London were developed under the guidance of the Garden City model. Even though these townships have faced decline and have failed in attracting the downtown population in its long history, the idea of the new town has been disseminated to other regions of the world. Asian planners, for instance, are struggling with problems associated with high-density populations and crowded downtowns, and searching for solutions. Historically, new towns have served as the ideal and pragmatic model to de-densify the congested central cities in history. New town development today, however, has more functions and different purposes than those of its originator and antecedents.

In this chapter, we examine the development of new towns in Shanghai and Kolkata to illustrate how this model shapes the suburbanization process

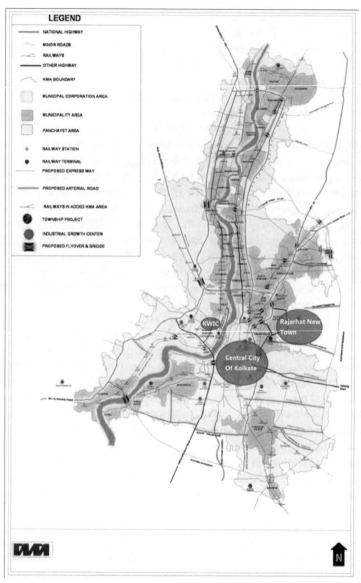

Fig. 2. Locations of the Two New Towns of Kolkata. *Source:* Kolkata Metropolitan Development Authority and Authors' rendition.

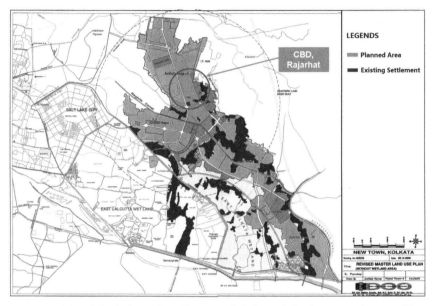

Fig. 3. Planned Rajarhat New Town and Informal Settlements. *Source:* West
Bengal Housing and Infrastructure Development Company.

in these two cities and its socio-spatial influence on local residents. The two
pairs of cases are organized in a systematic framework: Anting New Town
and Thames Town in Shanghai, China and Rajarhat New Town and the
KWIC near Kolkata, India. The critical questions we address include what
is the real purpose for local government to plan and build these new towns
within the different political institution of Shanghai and Kolkata? What is
the target population of housing in the new towns? Who are the actual
spatial users and what causes the outcomes? How does planned
suburbanization in China and India for government-perceived public
interests end up having very uneven and unintended and widely varied
individual consequences for local residents?

To address these questions, we begin with an exploration of the processes
of suburbanization in Shanghai and Kolkata with a focus on stages,
drivers, and outcomes of megacities' suburbanization within globalization.
We then reexamine the assumptions of global city model and extract hidden
insights from the global city-region perspective to theorize planned
suburbanization. This is followed by a comparison of new towns in
these two cities in terms of their development purpose, target market, and

institutional arrangement in order to illustrate the planned suburbanization in Asian cities. We focus on the socio-spatial impacts of new towns on their actual and intended users. We conclude on the theoretical and practical implications from this special paradigm of planned suburbanization and their meaning for local residents and long-term urban development. We call for a more comprehensive, comparative, and analytical approach in understanding the socio-spatial consequence of planned suburbanization in global city-regions.

(SUB)URBANIZATION IN CHINA AND INDIA: WITH A FOCUS ON SHANGHAI AND KOLKATA

A Pair of Urban Giants

China and India face similar challenges in their urbanization process, rooted in a huge population base, high population density, and rapid growth. The estimated population of China in 2010 is 1.34 billion in a geographic area of 9.6 million square kilometers, while that of India is 1.18 billion in a geographic area of 3.3 million square kilometers. The urbanization rate of China in 2010 is about 47 percent today, while approximately one-third of India's population live in urban areas. As Woetzel et al. (2009) estimated, about 350 million rural people would flow into Chinese cities by 2025, which would push China's urban population to the one billion mark by 2030, with 221 cities each accommodating over one million people. For India, Sankhe et al. (2010) projected that about 590 million people would live in cities by 2030, and 68 cities would have over one million people. This combined urban growth of China and India would account for more than 62 percent of Asian urban population growth and 40 percent of global urban population growth from 2005 to 2025, during which nearly 2.5 billion Asians will live in cities, accounting for almost 54 percent of the world's urban population (Dobbs & Sankhe, 2010).

A striking outcome of the rapidly moving frontier of China and India's urbanization will be a significant space (re)making for their massive, continuously expanding urban populations, especially in their megacities. These cities in both China and India are confronted with same challenge to promote people-oriented, environmental-friendly and sustainable urban development. How could city government solve social and ecological problems associated with the expansion of urban areas? How to plan and guide the development at urban peripheries to achieve a sustainable development? What type of urbanization or suburbanization would decrease population density in the central city without damages to the ecosystem of rural areas?

China and Shanghai

New town development at the fringes of megacities has been practiced as a special model of suburbanization in history and reconfigured in China and India in the new century. The process of Shanghai suburbanization has been associated with new town development and industrial expansion. As early as 1946, the Great Shanghai Plan, the first master plan for Shanghai, followed the idea of "organic decentralization" and proposed a series of townships, each of which would target to have 160,000–180,000 people in the suburban area of Shanghai. Each new town was planned under the guidance of the Garden City model developed by Howard. The master plan of Shanghai was revised in 1959, in which 12 satellite towns were identified, and the construction of five of them was started to support industry development. In the Shanghai Master Plan (the 1986 version), two industrial clusters were designated as new satellite cities. These townships serve as focal points to accelerate industrialization and accommodate workers in the factories. Industrial sectors to support the townships have been either based on local resources or transferred from Shanghai's central city in economic restructuring.

In the twenty-first century, Shanghai began to experience a new stage of suburbanization featuring a new type of townships mainly focusing on real estate development instead of industrialization. Since about 2000, the suburbs of Shanghai have been brought into the development agenda of metropolitan government due to the pressure of increasing urban population, the requirement of real estate development, and the demand of new economic growth poles. The so-called "Double Increase and Double Decrease" policy for the 600-square-kilometer central city was announced around 2000 to increase green and open spaces and to decrease building height and site density, which pushed real estate developers' constant search for vacant land into the much more expansive 6,000-square-kilometer municipal territory. Private developers in China, however, usually invest in mature urban areas instead of suburbs that lack amenities and facilities. The state's involvement in suburbanization process, such as providing starting funds for transportation infrastructure construction, therefore becomes necessary. To beautify the suburbs of Shanghai, former Mayor Liangyu Chen initiated the "One City, Nine Towns" program to accelerate urbanization in the suburban area. In the Shanghai Master Plan (the 2001 version), the 10 new towns program was included and interpreted to guarantee its implementation. Furthermore, a regional urban system plan called "1966" was unveiled in 2006 as a core element of the 11th Five-Year Plan of Shanghai Economic and Social Development. It involved planning not only one central city and 9 new towns but also 60 new townships and 600 central villages in the entire municipal region. These top-down plans and programs started to change the suburban landscape.

In the process of implementing the new town program, the Shanghai municipal government, cooperating with the 10 suburban district governments, identified the location of a new town for each suburban district, organized planning and design competition for the 10 new towns, provided starting fund to relocate local residents, and acquired farmland. A typical semipublic developer, New Town Development Corporation, was established for each new town. New town development, as a mechanism of urbanizing Shanghai's suburbs, has happened in a way that the state, instead of market, basically dominates resources relocation, chooses housing types, and handles infrastructure construction. The planned duplication of landscape, building style, and amenities of Western European cities in the 10 new towns produced exotic landscape and space in suburban areas (Chen et al., 2009). The suburbanization within the rapidly globalizing process demonstrates a strong orientation for agents and professionals connecting with global economy. High-end housing and a global lifestyle in the new towns contrast sharply with that of the original local sites (Table 1).

India and Kolkata

In India, as in China, the process of rapid urbanization had its most pronounced effect on the existing urban centers, leading to the production of megacities that spill over the existing spatially and politically constructed city limits. In India too the process of urbanization has been largely city oriented (Shaw, 2007), with a high percentage of urban population concentrated in Class I[1] cities, particularly those which are located within states that have been performing well economically (Kundu, 2007). In the 1970s and 1980s, the peripheral fringes had been viewed as the dumping grounds for urban problems – squatter settlements, polluting industries, and waste. Thus, these areas were considered marginal to the core urban areas and became increasingly degenerate with dwindling investments and neglect. However, with deindustrialization and the movement of multinational

Table 1. A Comparative Profile of Four New Towns.

Names of New Towns	Shanghai International Automobile City	Songjiang New City	Rajarhat New Town	Kolkata West International City (KWIC)
Location to downtown	Northwest	Southwest	Northeast	Northwest
Distance to downtown	32 km	40 km	10 km	9 km
Planned area	68 km²	36 km²	30.75 km²	1.579 km²
Planned population	80,000 for Anting New Town	500,000	750,000	36,000 residential
Local administration	Jiading District	Songjiang District	Rajarhat and Bhangor, North and South 24 Paraganas districts of West Bengal	Howrah District
City-regional administration	Shanghai municipal government		Government of West Bengal	Kolkata Metropolitan Development Authority
Metropolitan area	6,340 km²		1,854 km²	
Metropolitan population	18.58 million (2007) (permanent population)		15 million (2005)	
Downtown area	620 km²		187.33 km²	
Downtown population	9.15 million (2000 Census) 8 million (planned in 2020)		4.85 million (2001 census) and 6 million floating population daily	

Source: Adapted from Chen et al. (2009).

corporations based around information technology and allied services into the Indian economy, the demand for large and contiguous tracts of land for new real estate development projects as well for commercial development has increased manifold. Since planned suburbanization involves the provision of infrastructure and services along with land development prior to the housing development and occupation by residents, new townships are only possible in the peripheral areas of existing cities, where land costs are cheaper and the regulatory context less stringent in matters of land conversion to urban use as well as in matters of residential densities and other relevant urban planning and development norms. Moreover, retrofitting the existing urban centers into cities with global living and working standards would be extremely expensive and impossible given the high densities, aging infrastructure and services, and narrow roads. Therefore, the spatial expansion of urban areas in India is taking place in the peripheries of the existing large cities, extending to the adjacent rural and semiurban areas, reducing the physical differences and distances between the city and its rural hinterland.

Planners in India have over time addressed the changing core–periphery relationships in a variety of ways – from concentrating upon city-specific issues through master plans to more comprehensive regional development plans. In the 1970s and 1980s, the central government of India funded several developments that aimed at decongesting core cities by developing satellite cities or counter-magnets while simultaneously limiting densities in the cities through the Urban Land Ceiling Act of 1976. However, with reforms being initiated in the economic sector, cities in India came to be regarded as the engines of growth, and thus large-scale reinvestments were initiated to rejuvenate and improve infrastructure networks in existing metropolitan areas. Since 1990s, privatization of urban services and infrastructure provision and strengthening of urban local bodies to compete for private investments, often international, have led to the creation of exclusive, large-scale urban developments that include residential, commercial, industrial, and other land uses in a well laid out planned format, outside the city boundaries.

By the 1970s and 1980s, the core city of Kolkata within the larger metropolitan area was extremely densely populated and congested. As a result, much of the urban growth occurred to the southern and eastern peripheries of the core city in an unplanned manner through squatting or illegal subdivision of agricultural land. Historically and politically, these new population outgrowths were a result of Hindu refugee influxes from neighboring Bangladesh as well as migrants from the neighboring economically backward states of Orissa and Bihar in eastern India. With the threat of massive cholera outbreaks in the overcrowded city of Kolkata in the late 1960s, the Basic Development Plan was prepared to concentrate upon providing solutions for the rapidly degenerating urban environment within the core city area. During the same time, plans were laid by the state government for the development of two satellite townships – Kalyani and Salt Lake – to decongest the core by offering planned and affordable living spaces in the outlying areas. Although Salt Lake city became a successful satellite township because of its proximity to the core (8.5 km from CBD), Kalyani failed to materialize as a fully functional satellite township as even many of the administrative offices and businesses refused to locate to a township that was far from the busy core (88 km from CBD). Both, however, were built with the intention to increase buildable land primarily for housing purposes across a broad spectrum of income groups.

Since the 1960s, there has been a strong faction within the planning community in Kolkata that recognized the need for a more regional focus to urban development plans. Although the Basic Development Plan of 1966 recommended a two-centered strategy of urban decentralization by focusing on Kolkata and Howrah as core areas, a new proposal was floated in 1970–1971 for a multinucleated metropolitan structure that drew an analogy between the urban structure and a living organism redefining the core–periphery relationship. This proposal became the basis for the "Area Development Strategy" in 1974, the Development Perspective Plan prepared in 1976, and subsequently the Perspective Plan and Action Program for the Calcutta Metropolitan Area (CMA) in 1981 to recast the idea of multinucleated metropolitan organism into a hierarchy of urban centers, existing and new. Thus, the characteristics of an extended metropolitan region were beginning to emerge, and planners as well as administrators were trying to grasp it in all its complexity.

In the 1990s, at least half a dozen townships as well as many large housing enclave projects were built or initiated in the outlying areas (Sengupta, 2006). However, most did not follow the recommended locations and were concentrated in the eastern fringes of the core city, thereby defeating the city-region–based plans for future urban expansions. Compared to the earlier planned developments, these new developments are much larger in size, are financed by national and international investors, are equipped with world-class amenities, and are mostly high-rise developments with planned common spaces in between. Most of the developments are clustered around the emerging IT industry located in the electronic complex in Sector 5 of Salt Lake, designated as a special economic zone for IT and ITES (IT-enabled services). These new self-sufficient and large-scale developments, spear-headed by quasi-government institutions as well as large private developers, signal a change from the satellite townships of before in that they are now central to the process of urbanization rather than the fringes of the city, changing the dynamics of core–periphery relationships in the urban area.

A Theoretical Interlude

The preceding overview of suburban and new development around Chinese and Indian megacities triggers a critical question of where to turn theoretically to guide the focused comparison of the four new towns in the next section. The literature on global cities teaches us a lot about their functional influence as control and command centers, relative positions in worldwide hierarchies and networks, and local social and spatial inequalities. But it shows us relatively little about the global cities' relations with their immediate and broader regional hinterlands, even though there was clear evidence that globalization via foreign investment and transnational migration had long spread beyond the central city and penetrated the suburban areas of American metropolises such as New York and Chicago (Greene, 1997; Muller, 1997). This insufficient attention to the city-region nexus could be attributed to dual strong emphases of the global city literature on (1) the external positions and functions of global cities in the world economy and (2) the structure and consequences of their globalized local economy and society. Compared to mature global city-regions with dominant international service functions such as finance, globalizing cities have very different mixes of economic sectors and functions that foster the growth of their own distinctive regional spaces and activities (Chen & Orum, 2009).

The investment-driven economic boom of Shanghai since the early 1990s has driven up land and labor costs in its densely populated central city where land has become more scarce, and thus more difficult and expensive for investors to lease. The average wages both of factory workers and technicians in Shanghai are now more than double those of their counterparts in interior cities, while the average pay for managers and senior managers in Shanghai is three times higher. In 2005, the annual pay of manual labor in Shanghai averaged US$2,979 compared to the large interior cities of Chongqing and Chengdu at US$1,787 and US$1,489, respectively. Land cost in Shanghai approximately doubled that in some secondary cities in the Yangtze River Delta (YRD). So, development began to spill into the surrounding YRD region, especially to booming secondary cities such as Suzhou and Kunsan, and even smaller cities like Wujiang. Since 1999, Suzhou has attracted over 1,000 industrial enterprises set up by Shanghai-based companies with a total capitalization of over US$5 billion. Shanghai became the largest investor in Suzhou, accounting for over 35 percent of the total capital investment by 2004. In 2005, Suzhou's GDP ranked fifth in the country at US$50.8 billion, and its industrial output totaled US$150 billion, good enough for second place behind Shanghai (Chen, 2007).

The loss of capital and companies was seen by Shanghai as a threat to its broad manufacturing base, prompting the Shanghai government to launch an initiative of keeping old manufacturing jobs and growing new ones in Jiading (where Anting New Town is located) and Qingpu districts bordering Jiangsu Province. The new towns could be seen as an important effort of the Shanghai municipal government to use real estate to offset the city's slipping manufacturing advantage relative to lower-cost nearby cities as well as its proactive role in creating a form of integrated metropolitan development. It also illustrates the spatially expanded role of real estate, as part of a global city's finance, insurance, and real estate (FIRE) cluster, in producing global city-regions. This process appears to be accelerating and more intensive in globalizing megacities like Shanghai and Kolkata than established and mature global cities such as New York and London. The spatial differentiation between the central core and new towns at Shanghai helps further a healthy deconstruction of the global city model and a (re)construction of a global city-region perspective that is more pertinent to the cases in this study.

NEW TOWN DEVELOPMENT IN THE SUBURBAN AREAS OF SHANGHAI AND KOLKATA

New town development in Shanghai's suburbs initiated by the government in 2000 differs in function and meaning from the historical satellite towns developed for industries. Shanghai planners pursue an organic decentralization of the crowded central city, using new towns as focal points. Moreover, new towns became a significant economic development strategy, especially to exploit new land for promoting real estate. The purpose also includes improving urbanization quality of the outskirt of Shanghai, breaking the dual structure of urban and rural area and mitigating their divide and disparity.

In the "One City, Nine Towns" program, Songjiang New City in Songjiang District and the Shanghai International Automobile City in Jiading District were designated as pilot projects among the planned townships. These two new towns, as a planned suburbanization mechanism, exhibit particular features of design idea, planning process, and development outcome. The design idea including land use structure, landscape style, and housing type is basically predefined by planning authorities and state-owned developers. The planning process has not involved local stakeholders' voice, but relied on foreign design firms and local planning officials. As a consequence, the development outcome changes the original landscape and breaks the social balance in the region. These development features define and determine the actual spatial user of new towns.

Targeting at downtown decentralization, new towns in Shanghai's suburbs were planned as an integrated township with exotic features to attract the kind of new residents who cherish Western architecture and landscape. Thames Town, as the first residential development project in Songjiang New City, follows the designated England style. The floor area ratio (FAR) of this $1 km^2$ residential enclave is only 0.29 with all single-family houses surrounded by a lot of green space. The central government policy, which restricts this type of housing due to limited land resource in China, costs Thames Town dearly in either market price or living quality. Different from England villas in Thames Town, Anting New Town, the major residential section of the Shanghai International Automobile City, is duplicated from Weimar, a Germany township. This design orientation is determined by the basic economic sector of old Anting Town – automobile industry – with Shanghai Volkswagen Co. Ltd as the anchor. Spread across $3.9 km^2$ of land, the township is designed as a residential area with mixed housing types and an expected population of 80,000. The total FAR of Anting New Town is about 0.46 with a water area of 200,000 square meters (Huang, Liu, & Xu, 2005). Four-to-six-floor condominiums are planned in the central section, surrounded with multifamily houses and single-family houses. The expected housing buyers include wealthy households from downtown, and middle-to-senior-level employees in the Volkswagen joint venture company. These designs determine the cost of housing construction and housing prices.

The relationship of new towns with the central city is crucial to achieve the plan objective of attracting downtown population. The distances of these two new towns to the central city of Shanghai are 32 km for Anting and 40 km for Songjiang, respectively. Metro lines go from downtown to these two outskirt townships, though the operation of metros has lagged behind the new town construction. The distance between the Anting Metro Station of No. 11 line and Anting New Town, however, is about 2 km, 25 minutes by feet, and 10 minutes by bus. The new town is located next to the Hu-Ning (A11, Shanghai to Nanjing) Expressway, which brings convenience to automobile users. A station of No. 9 Metro Line going from downtown to Songjiang New City is about 4 km away from Thames Town, while the Hu-Hang (A8, Shanghai to Hangzhou) Expressway passes through the south of the new town. Three bus lines link the Songjiang New City Metro Station to Thames Town. Automobile is the most convenient commuting tool for residents in these new settlements because of the allocation of transportation facilities. Transportation infrastructure connecting the new towns to the central city severely limits the choices of low-income households.

The decisions about new towns had been made among the municipal and district planning authorities together with state-owned developers. The exclusive planning process without local residents has created totally new human settlements on farmland without any consideration of local living demand. Affordable housing, one of the important responsibilities of the local government, has not been put into the plans and development agenda of new towns. This top-down planning and development approach pursues the imagined space that wealthy consumers see as link to the global economy and society. Decision makers assume that the potential buyer of the housing in new towns would cherish a Western lifestyle and be attracted by exotic architecture and landscape features. The combined involvement of mayors, municipal planning officials, and semipublic corporation CEOs leads to exceptions in planning administration, such as shortened review and approval.

In Kolkata, new town development has diverse approaches that lead to different spatial and social outcomes. Rajarhat New Town, one of the largest state-regulated planned township projects in India, is planned as a self-contained growth center with mixed housing types, while the KWIC, funded by a hundred percent foreign direct investment, focuses primarily on high-end real estate development. The state-level government institution of West Bengal dominated decision makings in the planning process of Rajarhat New Town in terms of location selection, land acquisition and housing style, and therefore guaranteed the provision of affordable housing. A multinational firm called Beyond Limit International Ltd, united by the Slim Group of Indonesia and Universal Success Group in Singapore, made a deal with the government of West Bengal and the Kolkata Metropolitan Development Authority to fully control the development of the KWIC. They pursued property-led development strategy in this new town, aiming at capturing exchange value of farmland through attracting highly mobile population from the congested and polluted downtown area. The institutional structure in the new town development process, whether state-led or market driven or combination of both, has led to unplanned sprawl in the fringes of the Kolkata city, leading to the rapid urbanization and speculative property development in erstwhile villages and small towns.

Different from the Shanghai new towns located more than 30 km away from the central city, Kolkata new urban townships are planned at the northeastern and northwestern fringes of the city with a distance of 9–10 km. Expressways have been built to connect the new towns with the urban core. Residents in Rajarhat rely on automobile traveling to the downtown or commuting within the new city. With a total planned area of 30.8 km^2 and an expected population of one million, Rajarhat New Town was planned as a job-housing balanced city to attract IT industries and associated service industries. Young professionals working in IT sectors with global connections purchased housing units in Rajarhat for job opportunities in the city. The KWIC with an expected residential population of 36,000 on the land of 4 km^2, however, presents to be a large-scale residential development project. It is marked as a property providing quality of life at global standards. Foreign investment pursues short-term benefit from the sale of 6,100 bungalows and four high-rise residential towers. The construction of the KWIC is undergoing with a presale of housing. The units have been all sold out. It illustrates property-led development targeting the high-income consumers as a profit-promising investment for foreign investors in developing countries.

The state-dominated Rajarhat New Town was planned and constructed in a more balanced way in terms of housing, land use, and job opportunity than that of the KWIC controlled by private investors. Both of these two new towns have confronted with protests from original farmers and urban poor in and around the site, though the new town plans have still been implemented. As described in the global city model, an inequity has been created between professionals with global economic connections and workers in service industries (Sassen, 1991). The maids, gardeners, and drivers provide supports to the professionals working in IT sectors with a large gap of income between these two groups of people. The downtown inequity in global cities extends its pattern to the suburban areas of megacities in developing countries. Use of property-led development to capture short-term return of investment in new town development in India exhibits globalization impact that reshapes the landscape, social relationship, and resource allocation of megacities' suburbs.

In the planning and construction process of the new towns in both Shanghai and Kolkata, the state plays the key role in initiating new town programs to promote suburbanization. Private developers have worked together with or taken the lead in real estate development to capture exchange value of greenfield in suburbs. Original local residents in each case are excluded from the decision-making process. The Garden City model of equity between residents of urban and rural areas has been reapplied to Asian megacities to ironically create diverse inequities in new towns. This type of top-down planned suburbanization becomes an instrument to generate revenues and job opportunities that is similar to global cities' downtowns. International and domestic investments flow into the new growth poles of Chinese and Indian megacities to generate globalized local space in a planning process.

SPATIAL USERS AND SOCIO-SPATIAL INFLUENCE OF THE NEW TOWNS

When you visit Thames Town of Songjiang New City, you are likely to see few people on the streets. The first thing you will notice upon entering are the lovely guards in redcoats. It feels like a ghost city, but functions as a weekend resort or a popular scene for wedding photos, especially in front of the town's central church towering over the Tudor-style single-family houses and the British-style pubs nearby. The vacancy in Thames Town, however, does not mean a low purchase rate of its expensive houses, which have been largely sold out. The scarcity of low-density single-family houses with plenty of green space brings value and investment potential to Thames Town. The average housing price rose from 10,000 yuan per square meter in March 2009 to 17,000 yuan per square meter in May 2010 (see Fig. 4). The buyers of the mansions costing over five million yuan (close to one million US$) usually purchase them as a speculative investment, instead for local living and commuting to work in downtown Shanghai. The limited investment mechanism in China pushes wealthy people to invest in properties. The so-called "hot money (*re qian*)" chases high-profit housing in and around large Shanghai and other large Chinese cities.

The distance from metro stations and existing facilities leads to inconvenience for inhabitants living in the new township. A lady we interviewed in Thames Town was a housewife going out for grocery shopping by car. She told us that she enjoys the quiet living environment in this exotically featured township. Some families come to Thames Town for

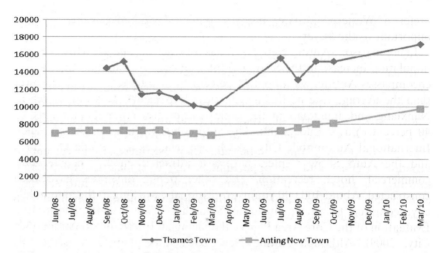

Fig. 4. The Average Housing Prices of Thames Town and Anting New Town, Shanghai (in Chinese Yuan Per Square Meter). *Note:* 6.7 Chinese yuan equal one US dollar. *Source:* Graphed from www.sskk.com – One of the portals to a lot of information on the Shanghai real estate market.

weekends as they usually have the primary residence in central Shanghai. The original official idea about de-densifying the downtown through new towns has not materialized. Moreover, the large amount of floor area and expensive rent make it difficult to lease the villas. This luxury residential environment in terms of low-density of land use, buildings, and population is underused and exemplifies a tremendous waste of land and high opportunity cost for the original farmland.

The lack of industrial plan in the entire Songjiang New City has contributed to the low occupancy of Thames Town. Although the new University District in Songjiang brings a large number of students and faculty into this region, most of them are not users of these expensive villas. The unclear client base has caused uncertainty in housing design and sale. The designer for the Thames Town project was Atkins – a British design firm – which was also the winner of Songjiang New City Master Planning International Competition. During interview, a staff of the company revealed that they were not clear about the targeted market. They just duplicated the landscape of England townships on the empty farmland. The facade of the buildings in Thames Town is also a hundred percent duplication, while the layout of housing units is slightly adjusted to meet the domestic market demand. The underlying rationale is to attract people who prefer a Western lifestyle, but the potential exchange value is more important to the buyers.

In comparison, Anting New Town has a higher occupancy. However, the population increase in the Shanghai International Automobile City, which encompasses Anting, was about 11 percent from 2000 to 2005, much lower than the average rate of Jiading District (25 percent). Townships such as Nanxiang and Jiangqiao in the same district grew their populations by 40 percent (Yu & Luo, 2009). The automobile facilities in the Shanghai International Automobile City, which also includes a Formula One track and the Auto Show Center, have not attracted enough people. Few commercial, hotel, recreation, and other public amenities have been constructed. About 100,000 young professionals, working in the automobile city, continue to prefer living in Shanghai (The Post-Implementation Evaluation of the Core Area Plan of the Shanghai International Automobile City, 2009). Although Anting New Town was planned to serve this population locally, it has failed in providing attractive commercial, medical, and educational facilities to achieve this goal. After five years, there is only one restaurant in the New Town today. For services in daily life, current residents have to go to the old Anting Township, which is about 4 km away from the new town, or the central city of Shanghai.

From field interviews, we found out that the housing price of Anting New Town started at 4,000–5,000 yuan (US$600–700) per square meter and reached over 10,000 yuan (more than US$1,500) in 2010 (see Fig. 4). The rent for a two-bedroom apartment is advertised as 2,300–2,500 yuan (US$300–400). Most owners of the housing units still live in the central city, while rent out their second houses in this new town as a source of additional income. During a recent visit to Anting, a realtor told us that about one-third of the houses are occupied and half of the residents, mostly rented, are German professionals working for the Volkswagen plant in the nearby auto city. The cultural center of Anting New Town has become a magnet for German expatriates We also learned that while Chinese young professionals and workers in the Shanghai International Automobile City prefer small apartments at low prices and sufficient local commercial amenities to live locally, new construction in Anting New Town tends to focus on single-family houses and larger townhouses.

Both Thames Town and Anting New Town were designed and built as a sort of gated community bounded by man-made river and/or a highway, but their residents have had difficulty accessing such amenities as restaurants and grocery stores, partly due to the physical distance and separation of the new communities from the existing townships. Uniformed security guards check visitors carefully at the entrance of Anting New Town and Thames Town. Gardeners, maids, guards live in the surrounding rural area, and some of them are the original residents of the sites who had been displaced. The building style and the new housing prices made it impossible for the original farmers to afford living there. This new town development has taken place on greenfield and displaced the original residents to the surrounding area of or at poor locations within the new towns. The original farmers would be urbanized in a simplistic administrative approach. For instance, in a section with a geographic area of $19\,km^2$ in Songjiang New City, 15,000 farmers were allowed to change their rural *hukou* (household registration) into the urban *hukou* of Songjiang township as a compensation of land acquisition (Wang, 2001). The new town developments in Shanghai reflect the changing focus of urban development and the state-driven approach to suburbanization.

As to new towns being developed in the periphery of Kolkata, the current process of land assembly in Rajarhat has squeezed out the rural and the urban poor from access to land and decision-making structures, and led to the eruption of more sporadic forms of organized political resistance to the profit-driven expropriations of peripheral land among the rural poor. At the same time, some of the spatial outcomes such as the mini-gated communities and the mixed income housing developments have paradoxically become the grounds for a new politics of dis-engagement, new forms of alliance (and exclusion) that is engaged by the new urban middle-class inhabitants in protection of place and private property. This highlights the need to view the process of producing the periphery as political, deeply embedded in the spatial and social arrangements and partially understood as a generative process that simultaneously opens up and closes off new spaces for urban political participation.

Benjamin, Bhuvaneswari, Rajan, and Manjunath (2008) have argued that while the new exclusive enclaves in India are created by private capital (large developers both foreign and domestic), they are underwritten by the actions of the state – through land acquisition (eminent domain, land acquisition, etc.) large-scale improvement projects, and dedicated civic amenities. Regarding both the Rajarhat New Town and the KWIC, wherein the state has acted as an active facilitator of real estate developments through the creation of special purpose planning and development vehicles, the land acquisition process has led to the violent dispossession and displacement of the existing peasants and urban poor who had been living in these outlying areas. The rapid social, physical, and economic transformations of the fringe areas with the sudden emergence of an urban lifestyle, amidst greenfields, have disrupted agriculture-based livelihoods, have led to unemployment among the erstwhile farm laborers, and subsequently have led to their absorption into the low-grade, low-paying job market. The rapid transformation of their living and work arrangements is particularly brutal upon the women in lower income group who suddenly find themselves having to step outside the confines of their villages to work as maids in the nearby high-rises. With the social and physical distance between the existing and the new dwellers increasing, in recent years, developments in Rajarhat have encountered stiff resistance from farmers, urban squatters, and farm- and fishery-based occupants who have refused to part with their lands at the low compensation.

With the defeat of the longest running Communist-led government in West Bengal over its sudden turn toward rapid industrialization and urbanization, these resistances have received political support from the emerging Opposition party. A case in point is the inability of Housing and Infrastructure Development Corporation (HIDCO) to provide electricity to Action Areas II and III as farmers in a village called Chhapna, Patharghata *Panchayat*, have refused to part with their land for setting up an electric substation for the Rajarhat New Town. Moreover, many of the local leadership in the surrounding villages as well as within the planned area of Rajarhat have refused to sign any of the building sanction plans for the new town area. This has prompted HIDCO and the newly formed New Town Kolkata Development Authority to design an online system for submitting and approving building plan sanctions that will effectively bypass the local leadership, creating new grounds for political and administrative conflicts.

For the new urban middle class, however, such developments offer the opportunity to live away from the congestion and pollution of the city since they are ensconced within the protective walls of their gated communities. These private gated islands not only have their own dedicated electricity supply, water supply, but are also governed privately and internally by powerful resident welfare associations. Although in Rajarhat New Town many of the residential areas have mixed income developments, the KWIC is exclusively designed for the relatively rich and well-connected nonresident Indian population. Moreover, the mixed income developments have become the grounds for new urban conflicts as socially and economically diverse groups are expected to mingle and do away with the social barriers that restricted their socializing to a great extent. To illustrate, in one of the Public Private Partnership (PPP) led housing developments called Alaktika Housing, the association formed by the higher income group residents went to court against the cooperative society formed by the lower and middle income group residents over the use of a common facility.

The new township developments in Kolkata reflect the changing political and economic conditions in the state as well as in the country. For example, in keeping with the thrust on the IT sector, the high-end retail sector and real estate geared for the emerging new middle classes and rising disposable incomes; the plan for Rajarhat New Town had a special land use category for use related to IT/ITES industries, a new commercial business district. The planning norms were drawn (and redrawn) flexibly to allow high-rise developments. Confronted with the multiplicity of land use claims in the periphery, the state agencies joined forces with the local politicians and developers, across the political divide, to persuade, coerce, negotiate with, and sort through existing settlements selectively to distribute different packages and gradations of compensation, thus fragmenting any unified form of resistance from the existing population in the periphery.

Politically, the rural and urban poor in the periphery are increasingly losing traction in matters of local development. The rural poor are now at the mercy of either the big private developers or the politics of the opposition party that has questioned and resisted development at the cost of displacement of. If, in the past, the rural poor had some say in the local governance through the *panchayat* systems or village-level institutionalized community meetings, they are being increasingly bereft of this space of political participation as the local *panchayat* heads are aligning themselves with the big developers or else with the local opposition party instead of representing the interests of the village inhabitants. Nonelected, parastatal organizations such as the HIDCO have become significantly powerful in determining the development of the peripheries, thereby doing away with the space for active citizen's involvement in the development process.

To summarize the key comparative point, the expected spatial users of new towns of both Shanghai and Kolkata include urban middle class and wealthy people with high mobility. The gated communities with Western-style architecture and modern infrastructure attract speculators, foreign managers in multinational firms, and Chinese young professionals. Original farmers and urban poor are excluded from the decision-making processes of planning and construction, the new town facilities, and the high-standard urban life. The socio-spatial structure of suburban areas of the megacities in both China and India has been reshaped into a more segregated and unequal pattern. Although the local state of Shanghai urbanizes suburban farmers via an administrative fiat as changing their *hukou*, in Kolkata the protests by local farmers and others who lose their livelihoods due to suburbanization goes largely unheard. In both contexts, however, the newly developed suburban towns have become a new territory for a nexus of public officials, semipublic and private developers, and international investors to exploit the exchange value of land with limited consideration of the vested interests and rights of the original spatial users.

CONCLUSION: BUILDING FOR WHAT AND WHOM?

At the theoretical level, we have bypassed the global city model, both conceptually and analytically, and invoked the broader perspective on global city-regions, which points us outward to look at the new suburban dynamics around the rapidly globalizing Chinese and Indian megacities like Shanghai and Kolkata. What we have actually found and examined is the development of new towns as a form of suburbanization planned and driven by the state, primarily the local one. However, the Shanghai new towns are much more (local) state-led than their Kolkata counterparts where the state has been more of a facilitator, especially in the KWIC. Although the officially pronounced goal of this model of new town development is to de-densify the crowded central cores, it has functioned as a powerful instrument for capturing the exchange value of farmland through attracting wealthy and mobile investors from downtown and overseas. The high real estate prices in the new towns reflect their development priority as opposed to the value of planned demographic deconcentration and broader regional balance. The dominance of global (European) influence on the design of the Shanghai new towns, coupled with involvement of global capital in the Kolkata new towns, only serves to reinforce and complement the leading role of the state in planning and directing suburbanization.

We would not have chosen to study new town development as planned suburbanization if it has been a smooth process and achieved most, if not all, of its intended goals and outcomes. In fact, it has been somewhat imbalanced and variedly contentious. Regarding the Shanghai new towns, they have not become full-fledged residential communities due to the lack of living amenities, the lagged construction of mass transit, and the distance to the metro stations. Again, the high housing prices have allowed only wealthy speculators with an exotic taste to buy into the new towns without a commitment to living there. The Kolkata cases have fared better in this regard because of the distance of new towns to and the dilapidation of the city core. The disparities between the ideal and rational planning of the new towns and the realities of development reveal the inherent limitations of this approach to large-scale suburbanization around the Chinese and Indian megacities.

Most removed and detached from the rational goals of this model of new town development is a set of real and mostly undesirable circumstances and consequences for the original local residents. In developing the new towns, the Shanghai municipal and local governments relocated the farmers to the outside of or at the marginal locations within the new towns without providing them with sufficient and affordable amenities and job opportunities. In Kolkata, these developments have triggered both speculative unplanned real estate development as well as protests against the forced acquisition of fertile lands for the construction of both the Rajarhat New Town and the KWIC, which contrasts with the absence of voice and resistance in the Chinese context. More than anything else, these different responses in China and India expose the same exclusive and elitist nature of building new towns that end up benefiting the state and wealthy private investors at the expense of the poor and powerless. Although many such big and small planned new townships are being planned and executed around the core area of Shanghai and Kolkata, with the emergence of a new upper and middle class with high disposable incomes – it remains to be seen if such inequitable spatial and social outcomes are politically and socially sustainable in the near future.

NOTE

1. Class I city – City with a population of more than a hundred thousand persons as defined in the Census of 1991.

REFERENCES

Benjamin, S., Bhuvaneswari, R., Rajan, P., & Manjunath, R. (2008). 'Fractured' terrain, spaces left over, or contested? A closer look at the IT-dominated territories in east and south Bangalore. In: D. Mahadevia (Ed.), *Inside the transforming urban Asia – Policies, processes and public action.* New Delhi: Concept.

Chen, X. (2007). A tale of two regions in China: Rapid economic development and slow industrial upgrading in the Pearl River and the Yangtze River Deltas. *International Journal of Comparative Sociology, 48*(2), 79–113.

Chen, X., & Orum, A. (2009). Shanghai as a new global(izing) city: Lessons for and from Shanghai. In: X. Chen (Ed.), *Shanghai rising: State power and local transformations in a global megacity.* Minneapolis, MN: University of Minnesota Press.

Chen, X., Wang, L., & Kundu, R. (2009). Localizing the production of global cities: A comparison of new town developments around Shanghai and Kolkata. *City & Community, 8*(4), 433–465.

China International Urbanization Strategy Research Committee. (2007). Chinese urbanization rate investigation report. Presented at the Third International Summit on China's Urbanization, Beijing, November 22, 2009.

Dobbs, R., & Sankhe, S. (2010). Comparing urbanization in China and India. *McKinsey Quarterly* (July), 1–3.

Greene, R. P. (1997). Chicago's new immigrants, indigenous poor, and edge cities. *The ANNALS of the American Academy of Political and Social Science, 551*, 178–190.

Huang, J., Liu, Y., & Xu, F. (2005). Research on the planning for Anting new town of the Shanghai international automobile city. *Ideal Space, 6*, 84–92.

Kundu, A. (2007). Urbanization and urban governance: Search for a perspective beyond neoliberalism. In: A. Shaw (Ed.), *Indian cities in transition* (p. 29). Hyderabad, India: Orient Longman.

Muller, P. O. (1997). The suburban transformation of the globalizing American city. *The ANNALS of the American Academy of Political and Social Science, 551*, 44–58.

Sankhe, S., Vittal, I., Dobbs, R., Mohan, A., Gulati, A., Ablett, J., Gupta, S., Kim, A., Paul, S., Sanghvi, A., & Sethy, G. (2010). *India's urban awakening: Building inclusive cities and sustaining economic growth* (April). McKinsey Global Institute. McKinsey & Company.

Sassen, S. (1991). *The global city: New York, London, Tokyo.* Princeton, NJ: Princeton University Press.

Sengupta, U. (2006). Government intervention in public private partnership in housing in Kolkata. *Habitat International, 30*, 448–461.

Shaw, A. (Ed.) (2007). *Indian cities in transition.* New Delhi: Orient Longman.

The Post-Implementation Evaluation of the Core Area Plan of the Shanghai International Automobile City. (2009). Internal evaluation report. Prepared by China academy of urban planning and design.

Wang, Z. (2001). The typical meaning of the leapfrog development model of Shanghai Songjiang new city. *Urban Planning Forum, 6*, 12–15.

Woetzel, J., Mendonca, L., Devan, J., Negri, S., Hu, Y., Jordan, L., Li, X., Maasry, A., Tsen, G., & Yu, F. (2009). *Preparing for China's urban billion* (March). McKinsey Global Institute. McKinsey & Company.

Yu, S., & Luo, Z. (2009). Planning and thinking about Shanghai's suburban new towns. *Urban Planning Forum, 3*, 13–38.

TERRITORIAL EXPANSION AND STATE RESCALING: A CRITIQUE OF SUBURBANIZATION STUDIES IN CHINA

Xuefei Ren

WHAT'S IN CHINESE SUBURBS?

Wangjing is a large residential cluster located at the intersection of the Fourth Ring Road and the airport expressway in the northeast part of Beijing. The area is a "suburb" according to official statistics and academic accounts, which often classify urban areas beyond the historical old city as suburbs. Due to its proximity to the airport and major expressways, Wangjing has developed quickly since the late 1990s. As more high-rise luxury apartment buildings get built, the area's population has reached 150,000 as of 2010, including more than 30,000 foreign expatriates living here amid Chinese urban professionals. Across the airport expressway from Wangjing is the 798 Factory, a hip arts quarter developed within a former electronics factory built in the 1950s. Looking for large studio space, a few artists moved into the Bauhaus-style workshops here in the late 1990s, and quickly bookstores, coffee shops, and galleries followed suit. By 2005, the 798 Factory had become the center of the contemporary Chinese art scene and home to many prestigious international galleries. Outside the factory

Suburbanization in Global Society
Research in Urban Sociology, Volume 10, 347–366
Copyright © 2010 by Emerald Group Publishing Limited
All rights of reproduction in any form reserved
ISSN: 1047-0042/doi:10.1108/S1047-0042(2010)0000010017

compound is a working-class neighborhood developed in the 1950s to house workers at the nearby factories and their families. The living conditions here have not changed much for decades, with some families still sharing common kitchens and bathrooms with their neighbors in dilapidated apartment buildings. To the west side of Wangjing, after about a 15-minute drive along the Fourth Ring Road, one reaches the Olympic Park, a brand-new area of parks, stadiums, five-star hotels, golf courses, and exclusive gated communities of villas – all developed in the short period before the 2008 Beijing Olympics. Beyond the Fifth Ring Road, one can see many "urban villages," former agricultural villages that have become populated by migrant workers with low-paid jobs – taxi drivers, construction workers, waiters, nannies, security guards, and street vendors. Unable to afford to live in the central city, migrant workers rent rooms from local peasants at the city's edge. Many of these villages are to be demolished soon to make space for commercial property development, and the migrant worker tenants will have to move to another village farther away from the city.

Suburbanization – a concept with strong North American connotations evoking images of lower density, automobile-based residential settlements – is often used to describe urban developments and expansions on the periphery in Chinese cities. In spite of the recent transformations of suburbs in the United States, such as the increasing density, demographic diversity, and the flattening population growth, the literature of suburbanization is still very much dominated by studies of low-density, demographically homogenous, and relatively affluent middle-class suburbs. Many stereotypes of suburbia of the 1950–1970s are still reproduced today by media and academic publications. The US model of suburbanization of the postwar period, which is an exception rather than the rule and occurred under a unique set of historical conditions, has been overgeneralized in the studies on suburbanization, while other types of suburbanization processes, such as those taking place in Europe, are largely overlooked. The American model of suburbanization generates confusion when used to describe the urban reality of territorial expansions on the edge of Chinese cities.

Urban peripheries of Chinese cities are mosaics of different social worlds coexisting in geographic proximity. In a Chinese suburb, one can find high-rise apartment buildings, gated communities of low-density villas, socialist workers' villages, artist quarters, migrant ghettos, and many other different types of settlements such as new central business districts (CBDs), university parks, and satellite new towns. In addition to the heterogeneity of socioeconomic composition, the high density of population and dependency on public mass transit in such areas further make the US model of suburbanization ill-equipped to capture the nature and process of urban territorial expansion in China. In spite of this misfit, there has been a rise in urban studies attempting to understand the sociospatial restructuring of Chinese cities through the lens of North American suburbanization. By assembling various statistics to show the decline of population in inner cities, urban territorial expansion, and the growth of population and economic activities on the periphery, some argue that Chinese cities have entered the age of suburbia (Feng & Zhou, 2003; Zhou, 2004; Li & Tang, 2005). Noticing that the Chinese case does not neatly conform the US model, others argue that China might have reached the stage of "post-suburbia" (Wu & Phelps, 2008). The evidence used here includes mixed land developments, the proximity between work and residence, the even lower density developments in exurbs and rural areas, and the greater role of local governments in determining the trajectories of suburban developments – all of which diverge from the classical model of American suburbanization, characterized by homogenous land uses, long commutes, population growth in the areas outside the inner city, and the limited role of local governments. A detailed literature review is provided in the next section, and here it suffices to say that the US model of suburbanization dominates the current field of studies on suburbanization, and most scholarship on Chinese suburbanization takes the US model as the ultimate reference framework in their investigation.

This chapter first critiques the current field of suburbanization studies on Chinese cities, which is dominated by demographic analyses of spatial distributions of population. By reviewing the most recent publications I will show how the category of suburbs (as opposed to inner cities) is artificially created for the sake of international comparisons. I will then review urban territorial expansions in the post-1990s period in China and examine the underlying dynamics of state power rescaling and capital accumulation. The centrifugal movement of population and industries could not have taken place without state power restructuring at the metropolitan scale or, specifically, without the devolution of power to urban governments to enable cities to expand their jurisdictional areas and annex surrounding rural counties. Based on empirical evidence from Beijing and Shanghai, I will then focus on some of the new urban spaces emerging on the periphery of China's megacities. The chapter concludes with a critique of the categorical approach of understanding cities through territorial concepts (such as inner cities versus suburbs) and urges instead for a processual approach to studying the context-specific urban expansions worldwide.

FROM SUBURBIA TO POST-SUBURBIA
IN CHINA: A CRITIQUE

Suburbanization is a major research topic in urban China studies, as urban territorial expansions have been taking place at an unprecedented pace and the compact urban form of traditional Chinese cities has become scattered and discontinuous due to economic growth and migration. Major geography departments at universities in China have undertaken large projects to study the trends of urban expansions in major metropolitan areas such as Beijing, Shanghai, Nanjing, Hangzhou, and Guangzhou. In general, suburbanization research in China is characterized by its reliance on census data and the imperative to conduct international comparisons. The field of study has advanced with the availability of data from the 1982 and 2000 censuses. Scholars have conducted demographic analyses tracing the changes in the spatial distribution of population from 1980 to 2000 across urban districts in major metropolitan areas. For example, in their pioneering and widely cited study, Zhou and Ma (2000) identify the driving forces of suburbanization such as the marketization of land, the relocation of manufacturing from inner cities to suburbs, the rise of service industries, the improvement of transportation links connecting cities and suburbs, and the availability of capital – both foreign and domestic – for housing and other infrastructure developments in suburbs. However, due to the time of writing – the late 1990s when many of the trends of urban territorial expansions were just emerging and were not easily identifiable, Zhou and Ma (2000) were inconclusive about the spatial structure of suburbs and urged more fieldwork to be done to examine the key features of China's suburban landscape and the haphazard land use patterns in the suburbs.

With the release of the fifth population census of 2000, a large number of studies appeared analyzing population change at the level of urban districts. In their study on demographic spatial distribution in Beijing, Feng and Zhou (2003) use the 2000 census to trace population growth and decline across urban districts in Beijing, and they find that the population has declined slightly in the inner city and increased sharply in inner suburbs and moderately in outer suburbs. They further examine the population change across different residential groups, such as residents with urban *hukou* (i.e., official household registration), permanent (i.e., more than six months of residency) and temporary migrants (i.e., less than six months), and find that inner suburbs have attracted the largest number of permanent and temporary migrants. Similar trends are confirmed in another study on

Shanghai by Li and Tang (2005), which finds that most population increase has occurred in inner suburbs – areas within 20 kilometers from the city center. As will be discussed later, the categorization of inner city, inner suburbs, and outer suburbs is rather arbitrary in most of these studies. The so-called inner and outer suburbs are de facto urban districts under the direct control of city governments, rather than semi- or fully independent suburbs as in the Unites States. In another study, Feng and Zhou (2005) analyze the spatial variation of population in Hangzhou – a major metropolitan area city near Shanghai on China's east coast, based on data from several national censuses. They find centripetal movements of population during the 1960–1970s, centrifugal movements of population in the 1980s, and the further acceleration of suburbanization of population after the 1990s. The study has also examined urban industrial land use data and finds the quickening pace of industrial suburbanization between 1996 and 2000.

In a more recent article, Feng, Zhou, and Wu (2008b) analyze the different stages of suburbanization in Beijing since 1990 and compare suburbanization in China and the West. Using the 2000 population census, they argue that the startling differences identified in earlier research (e.g., Zhou & Ma, 2000) have begun to fade off. The new round of suburbanization since 1990 has seen more market-driven rather than government-led processes. For example, they account, "residential suburbanization is driven by rising car ownership and preference for suburban villas and quality housing; industrial relocation is facilitated by the development of suburban industries; and retail suburbanization began to appear in the form of large shopping malls and retail parks" (Feng et al., 2008b, p. 84). They caution that this is not to suggest that Chinese suburbanization takes an identical form as in the West. But they attribute the differences to the stages of suburbanization, which implies that as suburbanization in China progresses, it might acquire more features resembling American suburbanization. This explicit approach of modeling on the US suburbanization and trying to identify converging trends is prevalent in most suburbanization studies on China (Feng, Wu, & Logan, 2008a; Feng, Wang, & Zhou, 2009; Wang & Yang, 2010; Song, Wang, Zhang, & Peng, 2007). For example, Feng et al. (2009) examine the population density pattern in Beijing since the 1980s based on census data, and they find a monocentric model in 1982, a dual-centered model in 1990, and a seven-centered model in 2000. They conclude that "this transition ;in Beijing's urban form toward poly-centrality is similar to trends in most Western cities" (p. 779). The domination of the US model of suburbanization might be attributed to the growing number of Chinese urban scholars educated in the United States, as well as the increasing research collaborations between American and Chinese universities.

Yixing Zhou, senior geographer at Peking University and one of the leading researchers on suburbanization, summarizes below the agenda of suburbanization research:

> studying the timing, conditions, scale, magnitude, mechanisms, development, and consequences of suburbanization in China, and by comparing it to the West, similarities and differences should be sought in order to enrich theories on suburbanization. (Zhou, 2004, p. 8)

The reliance on census data and the imperative to compare with the US model of suburbanization have led to the approach of arbitrarily creating the categories of inner cities and suburbs. Administratively speaking, suburbs do not exist in China. Owing to the structure of the national urban system – divided between the urban and the rural – the in-between category of "suburban" needs to be invented for the sake of comparability. Unlike the United States, in China it is not possible for suburbs with independent revenue and taxation structures to develop outside city limits, owing to the highly centralized governance structure and the nonelectoral political system. Therefore, in order to create the Chinese equivalents of inner cities and suburbs for comparison, urban geographers have adopted the approach of classifying historical old cities built before 1949 as inner cities, and all other urban districts beyond the old cities as suburbs. Thus, what are classified as suburbs here are de facto urban districts under the direct control of municipal governments, and they differ greatly from politically semi-independent suburban settlements in the United States. The artificial demarcation of inner cities and suburbs by district boundaries also contradicts the mental map of city residents, who often use ring roads (i.e., expressways) instead for spatial reference. However, for the sake of compatibility with census data, administrative boundaries are preferred over other geographic units. To quote from Zhou (2004):

> Research on suburbanization in China must adopt the approach of dividing the cities being studied into inner city, inner suburbs, and outer suburbs ... once we determine the boundaries of the inner city, inner suburbs, and outer suburbs, we should not easily alter it, because suburbanization is a process of centrifugal movement of urban processes and only with fixed boundaries can we track the changes in this process. (pp. 9, 10)

This artificial classification of suburbs has led to inflated estimations of the degree of suburbanization, and some scholars conclude that China has entered the age of suburbia – referring to the rapid growth of population, industries, and retail developments outside the historical city (Feng & Zhou, 2003, 2005). The statement is largely exaggerated because the historical old city is geographically confined and has strict regulations for new construction, and most new developments after the 1990s have taken place outside the historical city and, therefore, are counted as evidence of suburban growth. In other words, by classifying a large percentage of the urban territory as suburban, current studies conflate metropolitan-wide urban developments and population growth as suburbanization.

Noting the striking socioeconomic heterogeneity on the urban periphery of Chinese cities that do not conform the classical US model of suburbanization, Wu and Phelps (2008) suggest that Chinese cities might have arrived at the stage of post-suburbanization. Wu and Phelps (2008) propose a composite definition of the term "post-suburbanization" – including criteria such as population decline in suburbs, mixed land use patterns, and a greater balance between work and residence – and they argue that Chinese cities fit most of these criteria (except population decline) and, therefore, "while China has yet to enter a post-suburban era, some individual new settlements can be considered as Chinese variants on some elements of post-suburbanization" (p. 464). Albeit putting a greater emphasis on the differences between suburbanization in China and that in the United States, ultimately Wu and Phelps (2008) share the same comparative framework (i.e., the West) as in other studies reviewed, and the same linear assumption that Chinese and Western cities differ only in the stages of development, and eventually there will be more converging trends than what we observe today.

Overall, in suburbanization studies on China, the category of suburbs is artificially created to make the Chinese case comparable to that of the United States. By dividing cities into inner cities, inner suburbs, and outer suburbs along district boundaries, most studies have reached the conclusion that suburbanization is happening rapidly in Chinese cities, as evidenced by the slight decline of population in inner city districts, the sharp increase in inner suburbs, and the moderate increase in outer suburbs since the 1990s. Both the "suburbia" and "post-suburbia" arguments take the United States as the reference framework, and they share the same assumption that urbanization in China is still in its early stage and will eventually exhibit similar patterns to those observed in the West. This imperative to compare to the West has prevented a processual approach to study territorial expansion and to understand China's urban growth in its own right by focusing on the context-specific urban spatial restructuring.

TERRITORIAL EXPANSION, STATE RESCALING,
AND CAPITAL ACCUMULATION

One of the most consistent trends identified in the suburbanization studies on China is the sharp population increase in "inner suburbs" – the districts immediately surrounding the historical urban center. The population growth in these urban districts is often attributed to the relocation of residents from the urban center during urban renewal and the arrival of migrants. Urban renewal in Chinese cities has accelerated since the mid-1990s, and monetary compensation has replaced onsite rehousing of displaced residents. Because of the inadequacy of this compensation, the displaced residents often have to relocate farther away from the center, where housing costs are lower. The urban districts spreading beyond the historical center are often endowed with more available land for development. Owing to their cheaper property prices and relatively good transportation infrastructure, these districts have attracted both the relocated locals and new migrants – with the latter increasingly exceeding the former in numbers.

The current scholarship typically attributes the sharp population increase in "inner suburbs" to two groups of factors – "government-dominated" and "market-oriented" forces. For example, Feng et al. (2008b) examine residential, industrial, and retail suburbanization in Beijing and conclude that prior to 1990 suburbanization was mostly government-led – caused by the relocation of people and industries by order of city governments – but since 1990 market mechanisms have dominated, such as commercial land and housing development, industrialization of villages, and market investment in enterprises on the periphery. In the post-1990s period, relocation of people and enterprises by administrative order has been happening less frequently – except in the case of megaevents such as the Beijing Olympics and the Shanghai World Expo. Feng et al. (2008a, 2008b) label these two forms of suburbanization as "passive" and "active" – based on whether the decision-making is top-down, from the government, or bottom-up, from land users.

What is overlooked in this dichotomous account of government versus market forces, or passive versus active suburbanization, is the enabling role of the state in facilitating market forces in the sociospatial restructuring on the urban periphery. The most crucial factor that drives the metropolitan-wide redistribution of people and industries, I argue, is state power rescaling – the reshuffling of state power at different geopolitical scales. In the Chinese case, this is seen in the devolution of decision-making authority from the national government to municipal governments, and the scaling up of power, authority, and resources from rural counties, townships, and villages to municipal governments. Greatly empowered as the result of state rescaling, municipal governments are now able to undertake various strategies for capital accumulation, such as expanding their jurisdictional areas by annexing surrounding counties and townships as urban districts.

The territorial expansion of Chinese cities, enabled by state rescaling and geared toward capital accumulation, has been the driving force for many of the suburbanization trends identified by the current scholarship. The widely documented population growth in "inner suburbs" propelled by "market-oriented" factors could not have taken place without territorial expansions by city governments through annexation and mergers. Since the 1990s, most major metropolitan areas, including Shanghai, Beijing, Wuhan, Guangzhou, and Shenzhen, have expanded their jurisdictional territories by abolishing surrounding counties and turning them into urban districts, and in the process, they have opened up more land for development. Having replaced village collectives and township governments with limited authority, city and district governments now oversee large-scale land transactions and directly interact with private investors through land leasing.

The most prominent example of this type of territorial expansion is the founding of Pudong New District in Shanghai in the early 1990s. The name "Pudong" refers to the area on the east side of the Huangpu River that runs across Shanghai. Most of the built-up area of Shanghai is on the west side of the river. Before the 1990s, Pudong was mostly farmland, sparsely populated, and it was jointly administered by Huangpu, Yangpu, and Nanshi districts and Chuansha County. In 1993, the Shanghai city government was given authority by the central government to establish the Pudong New District, which consists of four economic districts: Lujiazui Trade and Finance Zone on the western tip of Pudong, which has now become the financial hub of China; Waigaoqiao Free Trade Zone in the northeast, which is the largest free trade zone in mainland China; Jinqiao Export Processing Zone, which has a concentration of many joint-venture factories and has recently become the main residential area for foreign expatriates working in Shanghai; and Zhangjiang High-Tech Park. In May 2009, the central and city governments allowed Pudong New District to merge with Nanhui district, and after the merger Pudong now has an area of 522 square kilometers and a population of over 1.5 millions. In most suburbanization studies, Pudong is counted as an "inner suburb" and its spectacular development serves as evidence for suburbanization by "market forces." However, the transformation from farmland to China's top financial hub with a resident population of 1.5 millions could not have been possible without the rearrangement of administrative hierarchies through merging, annexing, and newly creating urban districts and expanding the jurisdictional territories of existing ones. It is state power rescaling that has paved the way for territorial expansion, capital accumulation, and the geographic redistribution of population and industries.

SOCIAL MOSAICS ON THE PERIPHERY

Many new types of urban spaces have emerged in Chinese cities, most of which have been brought under the label of "suburbanization." These include, for example, state-planned new towns, migrant enclaves, artist villages, gated communities, exclusive villas, middle-class high-rise islands, resettlement housing projects, new CBDs, and ecological cities. This section reviews each type of these new urban spaces and examines the heterogeneous social worlds on the periphery. This can supplement the current suburbanization literature that is divided between quantitative demographic analyses and qualitative case studies that focus on a particular type of development, such as urban villages (Liu, He, Wu, & Webster, 2010), newtowns (Chen, Wang, & Kundu, 2009), or industrial parks (Zheng & Zhou, 2005). This section provides a taxonomy of settlement types emerging on the urban–rural fringes in Chinese cities in the post-1990s period and highlights the underlying logics of state-led capital accumulation that produce these new spaces.

State-Planned Satellite Newtowns

To alleviate the population pressure in central city districts, governments of large cities such as Beijing and Shanghai have been developing satellite newtowns at their peripheries. The largest such exercise is the *One City-Nine Town* program adopted by the Shanghai city government in 2001. Nine towns in the larger Shanghai metropolitan area were chosen as sites to develop suburban residential, manufacturing, and commercial centers. European planning firms were invited to draft urban master plans for these newtowns so that each one would adopt the built-environment features of a European country – such as the German town Anting and the British town Songjiang (Fig. 1). However, eight years after the start of the program, these state-planned newtowns have attracted very little residential population. The newly

Fig. 1. The German-Themed Anting Newtown in Shanghai, Master Planned by Albert Speer Associates.

built residential neighborhoods are beyond the financial reach of local residents and displaced peasants, and they are not attractive to middle-class Shanghai residents either, owing to their lack of public transportation. Developers, many of whom have strong connections with the government, have dropped out of the program for lack of promise of profitability, and the deficit from land acquisition, relocation of peasants, and new construction has skyrocketed for many of the local governments. In 2010, a few of the original nine towns with weaker economies dropped out of the program. The planned satellite newtown program in Shanghai shows the mixed results of state-led suburbanization efforts (see Wang, Kundu, & Chen, this volume).

University Towns

Since 2000 there has been a wave of construction of new university campuses on urban peripheries across the country. Some universities have sold their downtown campuses and transferred land use rights to private developers to gather funds for constructing new campuses far away from city centers. Cities such as Shenzhen, Guangzhou, and Shanghai have encircled large plots of agricultural land at the urban fringe for the construction of university towns. The largest such development is Songjiang University Town in Shanghai (built between 2000 and 2005), located about 30 kilometers from the center of Shanghai and occupying an area of 500 acres of former agricultural land (Fig. 2). Land was acquired from farmers and the project was commissioned to a development company with strong connections to the Songjiang district government.

The university town is poorly served by public transportation. Prior to the opening of subway line no. 9 in 2007, there were only four bus routes connecting the university town to the central city. Even with the opening of the new subway, students and professors still need to take a bus to reach the subway station and the average commute to the city is more than an hour. University towns across the country follow similar patterns of

Fig. 2. Neoclassical University Campuses, Songjiang, Shanghai.

Fig. 3. Commercial Housing Projects in Agricultural Fields, Songjiang, Shanghai.

development – land acquisition by the state and public–private partnerships for development – and they exhibit similar problems too: poor public transportation and a lack of cultural amenities. University towns are often used as a strategy to boost commercial real estate developments on the periphery by attracting a population of students and faculty first (Fig. 3).

Migrant Villages, College Graduate Ghettos, Artist Villages

Many villages on the periphery of large cities have been populated by various newcomers seeking cheaper housing. Migrant workers typically rent rooms from local peasants in the peripheral villages and commute to cities to work. Drawn to the profit from rent, many peasants have undertaken major construction and renovations of their farmhouses – by adding more floors and more rooms – and have become landlords making a living solely from collecting rent. Recently, artists and new college graduates have also joined the army of migrant workers and temporarily settled in many villages at the urban–rural fringe. In northeast Beijing, large artist villages such as Caochangdi and Songzhuang have become home to thousands of artists. In the northwest, near the software parks in Haidian district, Tangjialing village has attracted more than 50,000 college graduates, many of whom are unemployed or have low-paid jobs and are unable to afford to live in more central locations. These various types of urban villages are mostly transitional in nature; as commercial property developments expand outward, most urban villages will soon be demolished, with both peasants and tenants displaced.

Gated Communities, Exclusive Villas, Expat Colonies

Exclusive gated communities have also appeared on the landscape of Chinese cities. Most residential neighborhoods in China are literally "gated" – with fences and security guards hired by property management companies. But some gated communities of exclusive villas on the periphery distinguish themselves by their low-density layout, family orientation, abundant public green space, and higher percentage of foreign residents. Shunyi district in Beijing and Pudong in Shanghai are well known for large, exclusive communities of expatriates. With some developed by private developers and some by state companies, these communities exclusively target and serve the expatriates working for multinational corporations (and their families), offering various amenities such as elite international schools, state-of-the-art gyms, and shopping facilities specializing in products from the home countries of the expats (Fig. 4). These gated communities often have convenient access to expressways and can be easily reached by car, but most of them resist extensions of public transportation to their territories. The exclusive expat colonies operate like extraterritorial spaces serving members of the transnational capitalist class.

Middle-Class High-Rise Islands, Retail Chains, Resettlement Housing

As inner city neighborhoods have been increasingly gentrified by more affluent newcomers, the majority of middle-class residents have become unable to afford to live in city centers and often settle in neighborhoods of high-rise apartments on the periphery. Most of the displaced former residents of inner cities have also been relocating to these communities. Different from the state-planned newtowns on the far edge of cities, the

Fig. 4. Campuses of International Schools in Green Villas, Pudong, Shanghai.

middle-class communities are much more densely populated, closer to city centers, and better served by public transit. Drawn by the large population, international retail chains such as IKEA, Carrefour, and Walmart are ubiquitous in these neighborhoods. These communities have also become entry points for migrant workers, who often open up small neighborhood shops filling the gaps left by international chains. By the early 2000s, several extra-large middle-class communities had appeared – such as Huilongguan and Tiantongyuan in Beijing and Xinzhuang in Shanghai. Some of these neighborhoods have a population of over 200,000, and have become cities within cities.

Socialist Workers' Villages

Workers' villages were mostly constructed in the 1950s and 1960s close to industrial plants outside the city limits. These are often large working-class neighborhoods offering low-rent public housing for workers and their families. Inside these neighborhoods one can find restaurants, hospitals, schools, cinemas, and other amenities catering to the needs of residents. Some workers' villages disappeared during the urban renewal in the 1990s. The commercial pressure to "redevelop" the remaining workers' villages has been high in recent years, but many large workers' villages are still untouched, because of the difficulty and the cost of relocating and resettling the residents, and also because of the complex property ownership. Some workers have bought their rental housing but others continue renting, and the mixed ownership leads to disagreements about demolition and redevelopment decisions. In recent years, as the facilities and living conditions worsen in these neighborhoods, some families have also rented out their apartments to migrant workers and relocated to newer middle-class neighborhoods elsewhere. Like urban villages, the former socialist workers' villages are another place where one can find large number of migrant workers.

New CBDs

The new CBDs developed since the 1990s are mostly located outside of historical old cities. In the early 1990s, Shanghai started to develop its new financial district in Pudong, inviting four prestigious international planning firms to draft master plans in order to gain publicity (Olds, 1997; Ren, 2008). A few years later, Beijing followed suit by building a CBD in the Chaoyang district, which is often classified as "inner suburb." By now, Pudong and Chaoyang CBDs have become the financial hubs of China, home to hundreds of regional headquarters of multinational firms. The former factories, enterprises, and residents in these districts were all relocated. In addition to creating favorable policies to attract firms, city governments and private developers have also aggressively pursued international architects to promote the brand-new CBDs, commissioning them to design many high-profile office skyscrapers. The new CBDs are strategic spaces for capital accumulation in the making of China's global cities.

Model Eco-Cities

China has seen a wave of eco-city developments on the periphery of megacities – starting with Dongtan in Chongming County in Shanghai. In

2005, the British firm Arup was commissioned to plan and design Dongtan as an ecologically friendly city with green buildings, zero greenhouse-gas emissions, and energy self-sufficiency. No vehicles are allowed in the city and public transportation is powered by electricity or hydrogen. Dongtan was scheduled to be finished before the Shanghai Expo in 2010, but so far the project has fallen behind the schedule and no construction has taken place. Middle-class Shanghai families go visit Dongtan as a weekend vacation destination, and local authorities are allowing vehicles there to attract tourists. Eco-cities such as Dongtan have become a new promotional strategy in real estate developments across the country, and international planning firms are often invited to execute the design. But in many places, due to the lack of commitment and funding, many of the green design principles remain only on the drawing board, and the new eco-cities are no different from conventional office and residential blocks in energy use.

Economic and Technological Development Zones, Free Trade Zones, Export Processing Zones, Industrial Parks, Logistic Hubs

The globalizing Chinese cities differ largely from other global cities in their reliance on manufacturing. In addition to the aforementioned new types of spaces, the Chinese urban periphery is also a production space with various industrial parks, export processing zones, free trade zones, and logistic hubs. Most industries have relocated from the center to the periphery of cities, and city governments have also been providing various incentives to attract foreign direct investment to these industrial zones. Megastructures of modern factories and barracks-style workers' dorms dot the landscape of the industrial periphery, where the majority of the world's consumer products are manufactured and shipped with "Made in China" labels. Recently, there have been frequent incidents of walkouts and strikes by factory workers demanding higher wages, indicating the contentious labor relations on the periphery. In this sense, the Chinese urban periphery is also a strategic site for large-scale mobilization and social movements by the disfranchised industrial working class.

From newtowns to eco-cities to factory complexes, the urban fringes in China's megacities are patchworks of heterogeneous land uses. These new settlements, exhibiting different landscape features, are produced by similar underlying logics of state-led capital accumulation. In almost every type of new development, the forces of decentralized state power in city and district governments – manifest in the acquisition of land, relocation of residents, commissioning of international architects, policing of marginalized populations, and implementation of favorable policies to lure foreign investment – can be easily identified. As cities encircle more land under their jurisdiction, local governments continue to pave the way for urban expansion by authorizing new developments on the periphery.

DISCUSSION

The field of suburbanization research is dominated by studies on middle-class suburbia, and the US model of suburbanization is overly generalized. In the recently emerging field of suburbanization research on Chinese cities, the US model of suburbanization has become the ultimate framework for comparison, and by assembling statistics from censuses and other surveys, most studies aim to identify either divergent or convergent trends between Chinese and American suburbanization. To make the data comparable to international cases, previous studies have often taken a static approach of classifying districts of Chinese cities into the dichotomous categories of inner cities and suburbs – defining the historical old cities as inner cities and all the rest as suburbs. Owing to the fact that most developments after the 1990s have taken place outside of the historical old cities, this artificial classification has led to an exaggerated estimation of suburbanization, so that some have concluded that China has entered the age of suburbia or even post-suburbia.

This chapter questions the approach of classifying suburbs by district boundaries for the sake of international comparisons, and provides an up-to-date assessment of the heterogeneous urban spaces and complex socio-economic compositions on the periphery of China's megacities. I have shown that the urban periphery in China is a mosaic of different social worlds sharing a common underlying logic of spatial production, that is, state-led capital accumulation. I have argued that the key to understanding urban territorial expansions in China is state power rescaling – the devolution of political power from the central government to city governments (i.e., scaling down) and the merging of townships, counties, and villages by city governments (i.e., scaling up). Power, authority, and resources have been converging at the level of city governments, which enables cities to authorize newer development projects on the periphery in order to promote urban growth. In the process, the already marginalized population – migrants, peasants, and the urban poor – is further pushed away from the center.

While adopting a comparative perspective can help illuminate the similarities and differences of Chinese and Western suburbanization, trying to fit the Chinese case into the US model of suburbanization will certainly limit further investigations into the context-specific processes of urban expansions in China's megacities. The socioeconomic conditions of postwar America are radically different from what are facing Chinese cities today, and searching for converging trends of suburbanization in the two contexts will remain an exercise of futility. As Kenneth T. Jackson writes in the conclusion of his book *Crabgrass Frontier*:

> No other nation, however, is likely ever to be as suburban as the United States is now, if only because their economic resource and prospects are even more limited than those of the American republic. Thus the United States is not only the world's first suburban nation, but it will also be its last ... The extensive deconcentration of the American people was the result of a set of circumstances that will not be duplicated elsewhere. (1985, p. 304)

Instead of the static approach of studying cities by geographic categories such as inner cities and suburbs, and the typical practice of transplanting such categories from one context to another for comparison, a processual approach is far better to understanding the globalized and capitalist urbanization worldwide. In the Chinese case, this would lead to a critical examination of state-led strategies of capital accumulation and their manifestations in urban landscapes. Only by adopting a processual approach can we go beyond understanding the growth of Chinese cities in terms of "suburbia" or "post-suburbia," and can we study the underlying dynamics that produce China's megacities in their own right.

REFERENCES

Chen, X., Wang, L., & Kundu, R. (2009). Localizing the production of global cities: A comparison of new town developments around Shanghai and Kolkata. *City and Community*, *8*(4), 433–465.

Feng, J., Wang, F., & Zhou, Y. (2009). The spatial restructuring of population in metropolitan Beijing: Toward polycentricity in the post-reform era. *Urban Geography*, *30*, 779–802.

Feng, J., Wu, F., & Logan, J. (2008a). From homogenous to heterogeneous: The transformation of Beijing's socio-spatial structure. *Built Environment*, *34*, 482–498.

Feng, J., & Zhou, Y. (2003). 1990 niandai Beijing shi renkou kongjian fenbu de zuixin bianhua [*The latest development in demographic spatial distribution in Beijing in the 1990s*]. *City Planning Review (chengshi guihua)*, *27*, 55–63.

Feng, J., & Zhou, Y. (2005). Suburbanization and the changes of urban internal spatial structure in Hangzhou, China. *Urban Geography*, *26*, 107–136.

Feng, J., Zhou, Y., & Wu, F. (2008b). New trends of suburbanization in Beijing since 1990: From government-led to market-oriented. *Regional Studies, 42*, 83–99.

Jackson, K. (1985). *Crabgrass frontier: The suburbanization of the United States.* Oxford: Oxford University Press.

Li, Y., & Tang, Z. (2005). 1982–2000 nian shanghai shi jiaoqu shehui kongjian jiegou jiqi yanhua *[Transformation of social space structure in the suburban areas of Shanghai from 1980 to 2000].* *Urban Planning Forum (chengshi guihua xuekan)* (6), 27–36.

Liu, Y., He, S., Wu, F., & Webster, C. (2010). Urban villages under China's rapid urbanization: Unregulated assets and transitional neighborhoods. *Habitat International, 34*, 135–144.

Olds, K. (1997). Globalizing Shanghai: The 'Global Intelligence Corps' and the building of Pudong. *Cities, 14*, 109–123.

Ren, X. (2008). Architecture as branding: Mega project developments in Beijing. *Built Environment, 34*, 517–531.

Song, J., Wang, E., Zhang, W., & Peng, P. (2007). Housing suburbanization and employment spatial mismatch in Beijing. *ACTA Geographica Sinica, 62*, 387–396.

Wang, C., & Yang, S. (2010). A comparative study on the changing population spatial pattern and the resultant inner-city and suburb conflicts between American metropolises and China's metropolises: The case of Shanghai. *Urban Planning International, 25*, 74–79.

Wang, L., Kundu, R., & Chen, X. (2010). Building for what and whom? New town development as planned suburbanization in China and India. In: M. Clapson & R. Hutchison (Eds), *Research in urban sociology: Suburbanization in global society*, Bingley, UK: Emerald.

Wu, F., & Phelps, N. A. (2008). From suburbia to post-suburbia in China? Aspects of the transformation of the Beijing and Shanghai global city regions. *Built Environment, 34*, 464–481.

Zheng, G., & Zhou, Y. (2005). Research on the effect of Beijing economic and technological development area on Beijing's suburbanization. *Urban Planning Forum*, 23–47.

Zhou, Y. (2004). Jiu chengshi jiaoquhua de jige wenti yu Zhang Xiaoming taolun *[Discussion with Zhang Xiaoming on suburbanization].* *Xiandai Chengshi Yanjiu*, 8–12.

Zhou, Y., & Ma, L. J. C. (2000). Economic restructuring and suburbanization in China. *Urban Geography, 21*, 205–236.